Kubernetes and Docker –
An Enterprise Guide

Effectively containerize applications, integrate
enterprise systems, and scale applications in
your enterprise

Scott Surovich

Marc Boorshtein

BIRMINGHAM—MUMBAI

Kubernetes and Docker – An Enterprise Guide

Commissioning Editor: Vijin Boricha

Acquisition Editor: Savia Lobo

Senior Editor: Rahul Dsouza

Content Development Editor: Carlton Borges/Alokita Amanna

Technical Editor: Soham Amburle

Copy Editor: Safis Editing

Project Coordinator: Neil Dmello

Proofreader: Safis Editing

Indexer: Priyanka Dhadke

Production Designer: Aparna Bhagat

First published: November 2020

Production reference: 2061120

Published by Packt Publishing Ltd.

Livery Place

35 Livery Street

Birmingham

B3 2PB, UK.

ISBN 978-1-83921-340-3

www.packt.com

To my wife, Kim, for always being supportive and understanding of my technology addiction – I couldn't have finished this book without your support. To my mother, Adele, and in loving memory of my father, Gene (Gene-O!), for everything they taught me – to never give up, and that I can do anything that I set my mind to.

- Scott Surovich

To my wife, for supporting me in the establishment of Tremolo Security and my giving up a full-time salary to build this company; to my sons for keeping me on my toes; to my mom for raising me and giving me my persistence, and in memory of my dad, who pushed me to be my own boss.

- Marc Boorshtein

Packt.com

Subscribe to our online digital library for full access to over 7,000 books and videos, as well as industry leading tools to help you plan your personal development and advance your career. For more information, please visit our website.

Why subscribe?

- Spend less time learning and more time coding with practical eBooks and videos from over 4,000 industry professionals

- Improve your learning with Skill Plans built especially for you

- Get a free eBook or video every month

- Fully searchable for easy access to vital information

- Copy and paste, print, and bookmark content

Did you know that Packt offers eBook versions of every book published, with PDF and ePub files available? You can upgrade to the eBook version at packt.com and, as a print book customer, you are entitled to a discount on the eBook copy. Get in touch with us at customercare@packtpub.com for more details.

At www.packt.com, you can also read a collection of free technical articles, sign up for a range of free newsletters, and receive exclusive discounts and offers on Packt books and eBooks.

Foreword

The pace of innovation in our industry never seems to slow down. The container and Kubernetes communities exemplify this concept. From its initial release in mid-2014, Kubernetes has not only grown exponentially as a project, but it's also revolutionized industries around software development, infrastructure, security, and continuous delivery. In a few short years, Kubernetes and the concepts that power it have changed how we'll deliver technology for the next 10 years or more.

When talking with customers, I find the struggle with staying up to date can be one of the biggest challenges when taking advantage of containers and Kubernetes. The most useful tool to keep up with this constant change is a strong understanding of the fundamental concepts and tools that make them possible. If you understand how Kubernetes essentially works, the frequent growth and changes in the Kubernetes ecosystem become tools to be leveraged instead of changes to be fretted over. Unfortunately, the only way to have that level of understanding with a complex system such as Kubernetes is to have experience using it in multiple situations.

Marc and Scott bring a mountain of experience to *Kubernetes and Docker: the Complete Guide.* The practical examples built from their experience help you separate the signal from the noise to master that fundamental knowledge. When you understand the relationships between the components that make up Kubernetes, container runtimes such as Docker, and the host operating systems, you begin to grow the skills that make containers the revolutionary technology they've become.

As you read the chapters and work through this book's examples in your own environment, please take the occasional minute to step back and think through how what you're doing can bring you practical value and help solve the challenges you face. Kubernetes and containers have changed the landscape of our industry because they provide a more effective way to bring value to our end users. Focusing on that value will help you incorporate it into your own solutions and make that promise real for your own end users.

All the best.

Jamie Duncan

Author, OpenShift in Action

Contributors

About the authors

Scott Surovich has been involved in the industry for over 20 years and is currently the Global Container Engineering Lead at a global Tier 1 bank, working on global Kubernetes design and delivery standards, including the surrounding ecosystem. His previous roles include working on other global engineering teams, including Windows, Linux, and virtualization. His enterprise experience has allowed him to work with multiple companies on their early Kubernetes offerings, including Kasten, Reduxio, VMware, and Google.

Scott also holds the CKA, CKAD, and Mirantis Kubernetes certifications. As part of the pilot group, he was one of the first people to receive Google's premier certification as a Google Certified Hybrid Multi-Cloud Fellow.

I would like to thank all those people who have supported me in my life and career. I have been lucky in terms of the support and encouragement that I have received from my family, friends, employer, teammates, and managers. Thank you all for the support!

Marc Boorshtein has been a software engineer and consultant for nearly 20 years and is currently the CTO of Tremolo Security, Inc. Marc has spent most of his career building identity management solutions for large enterprises, U.S. Government civilian agencies, and local government public safety systems. In recent years, he has focused on applying identity to DevOps and Kubernetes, building open source tools to automate infrastructure security. Marc is a CKAD, and can often be found in the Kubernetes Slack channels answering questions about authentication and authorization.

In addition to my family, I wish to thank my customers, both commercial and open source, who have seen the potential our software provides and taken a chance on a smaller player with different ideas, and, of course, to those of you reading this book!

About the reviewer

Peter Benjamin is a software engineer with experience in operations and information security, as a Red Team, Blue Team, and application security engineer. He is currently employed as an infrastructure engineer, enabling and empowering product developers to build and deploy secure, scalable, and cloud-native applications running on modern, distributed systems and infrastructure. Peter has a deep technical background in the Go programming language and Kubernetes. He is an active member of the open source community and a contributor to Kubernetes and other CNCF projects and initiatives.

I would like to thank my wife, Megan, and our two children, Madison and Daniel, for their support and patience, and I would also like to thank the authors, Scott and Marc, and Packt Publishing for the opportunity to review this great book. Even I walked away having learned a thing or two.

Packt is searching for authors like you

If you're interested in becoming an author for Packt, please visit `authors.packtpub.com` and apply today. We have worked with thousands of developers and tech professionals, just like you, to help them share their insight with the global tech community. You can make a general application, apply for a specific hot topic that we are recruiting an author for, or submit your own idea.

Table of Contents

3
Understanding Docker Networking

Section 2:
Creating Kubernetes Development Clusters, Understanding objects, and Exposing Services

4
Deploying Kubernetes Using KinD

5

Kubernetes Bootcamp

6
Services, Load Balancing, and External DNS

Section 3:
Running Kubernetes in the Enterprise

7
Integrating Authentication into Your Cluster

8
RBAC Policies and Auditing

9
Deploying a Secured Kubernetes Dashboard

10
Creating PodSecurityPolicies

11
Extending Security Using Open Policy Agent

12
Auditing using Falco and EFK

13
Backing Up Workloads

14
Provisioning a Platform

Assessments

Other Books You May Enjoy

Index

Preface

Kubernetes has taken the world by storm, becoming the standard infrastructure for DevOps teams to develop, test, and run applications. Most enterprises are either running it already, or are planning to run it in the next year. A look at job postings on any of the major job sites shows that just about every big-name company has Kubernetes positions open. The fast rate of adoption has led to Kubernetes-related positions growing by over 2,000% in the last 4 years.

One common problem that companies are struggling to address is the lack of enterprise Kubernetes knowledge. Since the technology is relatively new, and even newer for production workloads, companies have had issues trying to build teams to run clusters reliably. Finding people with basic Kubernetes skills is becoming easier, but finding people with knowledge on topics that are required for enterprise clusters is still a challenge.

Who this book is for

We created this book to help DevOps teams to expand their skills beyond the basics of Kubernetes. It was created from the years of experience we have working with clusters in multiple enterprise environments.

There are many books available that introduce Kubernetes and the basics of installing clusters, creating deployments, and using Kubernetes objects. Our plan was to create a book that would go beyond a basic cluster, and in order to keep the book a reasonable length, we will not re-hash the basics of Kubernetes. You should have some experience with Kubernetes before reading this book.

While the primary focus of the book is to extend clusters with enterprise features, the first section of the book will provide a refresher of key Docker topics, and Kubernetes objects. It is important that you have a solid understanding of Kubernetes objects in order to get the most out of the more advanced chapters.

What this book covers

Chapter 1, Understanding Docker and Containers Essentials, helps you learn what problems Docker and Kubernetes address for developers. You will be introduced to different aspects of Docker including the Docker daemon, data, installation, and using the Docker CLI.

Chapter 2, Working with Docker Data, discusses how containers need to store data, with some use cases only requiring ephemeral disks, while others require persistent disks. In this chapter, you will learn about persistent data and how Docker can be used with volumes, bind mounts, and tmpfs to store data.

Chapter 3, Understanding Docker Networking, introduces you to networking in Docker. It will cover creating different network types, adding and removing container networks, and exposing container services.

Chapter 4, Deploying Kubernetes Using KinD, shows how KinD is a powerful tool that allows you to create a Kubernetes cluster ranging from a single node cluster to a full multi-node cluster. The chapter goes beyond a basic KinD cluster explaining how to use a load balancer running HAproxy to load-balance worker nodes. By the end of this chapter, you will understand how KinD works and how to create a custom multi-node cluster, which will be used for the exercises in the following chapters.

Chapter 5, Kubernetes Bootcamp, covers most of the objects that a cluster includes, whether you need a refresher on Kubernetes, or are if you are newer to the platform. It explains the objects with a description of what each object does and its function in a cluster. This chapter is meant to be a refresher, or a "pocket guide" to objects – it does not contain exhaustive details for each object, as that would require a second book.

Chapter 6, Services, Load Balancing, and External-DNS, teaches you how to expose a Kubernetes deployment using services. Each service type is explained with examples, and you will learn how to expose them using both a Layer-7 and a Layer-4 load balancer. In this chapter, you will go beyond the basics of a simple Ingress controller, installing MetalLB, to provide Layer-4 access to services. You will also install an incubator project called external-dns to provide dynamic name resolution for the services exposed by MetalLB.

Chapter 7, Integrating Authentication into Your Cluster, considers the question of how users will access your cluster once it is built. In this chapter, we'll detail how OpenID Connect works and why you should use it for accessing your cluster. We'll also cover several anti-patterns that should be avoided and why they should be avoided.

Chapter 8, RBAC Policies and Auditing, demonstrates how, once users have access to a cluster, you need to be able to limit their access. Whether you are providing an entire cluster to your users or just a namespace, you'll need to know how Kubernetes authorizes access via its **role-based access control** system, or **RBAC**. In this chapter, we'll detail how to design RBAC policies, how to debug them, and different strategies for multi-tenancy.

Chapter 9, Securing the Kubernetes Dashboard, looks at the Kubernetes Dashboard, which is often the first thing users try to launch once a cluster is up and running. There's quite a bit of mythology around the security (or lack thereof). Your cluster will be made of other web applications too, such as network dashboards, logging systems, and monitoring dashboards too. This chapter looks at how the dashboard is architected, how to properly secure it, and examples of how not to deploy it with details as to why.

Chapter 10, Creating *Pod Security Policies,* deals with the security of the nodes that run your `Pod` instances. We will discuss how to securely design your containers so they are harder to abuse and how to build policies to constrain your containers from accessing resources they don't need. We'll also cover the deprecation of the `PodSecurityPolicy` API and how to handle it.

Chapter 11, Extending Security using Open Policy Agent, provides you with the guidance you need to deploy OpenPolicyAgent and GateKeeper to enable policies that can't be implemented using RBAC or PodSecurityPolicies. We'll cover how to deploy GateKeeper, how to write policies in Rego, and how to test your policies using OPA's built-in testing framework.

Chapter 12, Auditing Using Falco and EFK, discusses how Kubernetes includes event logging for API access, but it doesn't have the ability to log events that may be executed inside a Pod. To address this limitation, we will install a project that was donated to the CNCF called Falco. You will also learn how to present the data that is captured by Falco using FalcoSideKick and the **EFK** stack (**ElasticSearch, FluentD, and Kibana**). You will get hands-on experience by looking for events in Kibana and creating a custom dashboard that contains important events.

Chapter 13, Backing Up Workloads, teaches you how to create a backup of your cluster workloads for disaster recovery, or cluster migrations, using Velero. You will go hands-on and create a backup of example workloads and restore the backup to a brand-new cluster to simulate a cluster migration.

Chapter 14, Provisioning a Platform, has you building a platform for automating a multi-tenant cluster with GitLab, Tekton, ArgoCD, and OpenUnison. We'll explore how to build pipelines and how to automate their creation. We'll explore how the objects that are used to drive pipelines are related to each other, how to build relationships between systems, and finally, how to create a self-service workflow for automating the deployment of pipelines.

To get the most out of this book

You should have a basic understanding of the Linux, basic commands, and tools such as Git and a text editor such as vi.

The chapters contain both theory and hands-on exercises. We feel that the exercises help to reinforce the theory, but they are not required to understand each topic. If you want to do the exercises in the book, you will need to meet the requirement in the following table:

Requirements for the chapter exercises	
Ubuntu Server	18.04 or higher

All exercises were using Ubuntu, but most of them will work on other Linux installations. The Falco chapter has steps that are specific to Ubuntu and the exercise will likely fail to deploy correctly on other Linux installations.

If you are using the digital version of this book, we advise you to type the code yourself or access the code via the GitHub repository (link available in the next section). Doing so will help you avoid any potential errors related to the copying and pasting of code.

Download the example code files

You can download the example code files for this book from your account at www.packt.com. If you purchased this book elsewhere, you can visit www.packtpub.com/support and register to have the files emailed directly to you.

You can download the code files by following these steps:

1. Log in or register at www.packt.com.
2. Select the **Support** tab.
3. Click on **Code Downloads**.
4. Enter the name of the book in the **Search** box and follow the onscreen instructions.

Once the file is downloaded, please make sure that you unzip or extract the folder using the latest version of the following:

- WinRAR/7-Zip for Windows
- Zipeg/iZip/UnRarX for Mac
- 7-Zip/PeaZip for Linux

The code bundle for the book is also hosted on GitHub at `https://github.com/ PacktPublishing/Kubernetes-and-Docker-The-Complete-Guide`. In case there's an update to the code, it will be updated on the existing GitHub repository.

We also have other code bundles from our rich catalog of books and videos available at `https://github.com/PacktPublishing/`. Check them out!

Code in Action

Code in Action videos for this book can be viewed at `http://bit.ly/2OQfDum`.

Download the color images

We also provide a PDF file that has color images of the screenshots/diagrams used in this book. You can download it here: `https://static.packt-cdn.com/ downloads/9781839213403_ColorImages.pdf`.

Conventions used

There are a number of text conventions used throughout this book.

`Code in text`: Indicates code words in text, database table names, folder names, filenames, file extensions, pathnames, dummy URLs, user input, and Twitter handles. Here is an example: "The final component to identify is `apiGroups`. This is an additional area of inconsistency from the URL model."

A block of code is set as follows:

```
apiVersion: rbac.authorization.k8s.io/v1
kind: ClusterRole
metadata:
  name: cluster-pod-and-pod-logs-reader
rules:
- apiGroups: [""]
  resources: ["pods", "pods/log"]
  verbs: ["get", "list"]
```

When we wish to draw your attention to a particular part of a code block, the relevant lines or items are set in bold:

```
- hostPath:
    path: /usr/share/ca-certificates
    type: DirectoryOrCreate
  name: usr-share-ca-certificates
- hostPath:
    path: /var/log/k8s
    type: DirectoryOrCreate
  name: var-log-k8s
- hostPath:
    path: /etc/kubernetes/audit
    type: DirectoryOrCreate
  name: etc-kubernetes-audit
```

Any command-line input or output is written as follows:

```
PS C:\Users\mlb> kubectl create ns not-going-to-work
namespace/not-going-to-work created
```

Bold: Indicates a new term, an important word, or words that you see onscreen. For example, words in menus or dialog boxes appear in the text like this. Here is an example: "Hit the **Finish Login** button at the bottom of the screen."

Tips or important notes
Appear like this.

Get in touch

Feedback from our readers is always welcome.

General feedback: If you have questions about any aspect of this book, mention the book title in the subject of your message and email us at customercare@packtpub.com.

Errata: Although we have taken every care to ensure the accuracy of our content, mistakes do happen. If you have found a mistake in this book, we would be grateful if you would report this to us. Please visit www.packtpub.com/support/errata, selecting your book, clicking on the Errata Submission Form link, and entering the details.

Piracy: If you come across any illegal copies of our works in any form on the Internet, we would be grateful if you would provide us with the location address or website name. Please contact us at copyright@packt.com with a link to the material.

If you are interested in becoming an author: If there is a topic that you have expertise in and you are interested in either writing or contributing to a book, please visit authors.packtpub.com.

Reviews

Please leave a review. Once you have read and used this book, why not leave a review on the site that you purchased it from? Potential readers can then see and use your unbiased opinion to make purchase decisions, we at Packt can understand what you think about our products, and our authors can see your feedback on their book. Thank you!

For more information about Packt, please visit packt.com.

Section 1: Docker and Container Fundamentals

In this first section, we will review important Docker and container concepts, and the benefits that Docker provides to developers. After a quick review of Docker, we will move on to how we can add persistent data to a container and how to work with Docker networking to expose containers to the outside world. These basic concepts are essential to fully understanding Kubernetes and understanding how containers run a cluster.

This part of the book comprises the following chapters:

1
Docker and Container Essentials

Containers are one of the most transformational technologies that we have seen in years. Technology companies, corporations, and end users have all adopted it to handle everyday workloads. Increasingly, **common off-the-shelf** (**COTS**) applications are transforming from traditional installations into fully containerized deployments. With such a large technology shift, it is essential for anyone in the Information Technology realm to learn about containers.

In this chapter, we will introduce the problems that containers address. After an introduction to why containers are important, we will introduce the runtime that launched the modern container frenzy, Docker. By the end of this chapter, you will understand how to install Docker and how to use the most common Docker CLI commands.

In this chapter, we will cover the following topics:

- Understanding the need for containerization
- Understanding Docker
- Installing Docker
- Using the Docker CLI

Let's get started!

Technical requirements

This chapter has the following technical requirements:

- An Ubuntu 18.04 server with a minimum of 4 GB of RAM, though 8 GB is suggested

You can access the code for this chapter by going to the following GitHub repository: `https://github.com/PacktPublishing/Kubernetes-and-Docker-The-Complete-Guide`.

Understanding the need for containerization

You may have experienced a conversation like this at your office or school:

Developer: *"Here's the new application. It went through weeks of testing and you are the first to get the new release."*

….. A little while later ….

User: *"It's not working. When I click the submit button, it shows an error about a missing dependency."*

Developer: *"That's weird; it's working fine on my machine."*

This is one of the most frustrating things a developer can encounter when delivering an application. Often, the issues that creep up are related to a library that the developer had on their machine, but it wasn't included in the distribution of the package. It may seem like an easy fix for this would be to include all the libraries alongside the release, but what if this release contains a newer library that overwrites the older version, which may be required for a different application?

Developers need to consider their new releases, as well as any potential conflicts with any existing software on the user's workstations. This often becomes a careful balancing act that requires larger deployment teams to test the application on different system configurations. It can also lead to additional rework for the developer or, in some extreme cases, full incompatibility with an existing application.

There have been various attempts to make application delivery easier over the years. First, there are solutions such as **VMware**'s **Thinapp**, which virtualize san application (not to be confused with virtualizing an operating system). It allows you to package the application and its dependencies into a single executable package. This packaging eliminates the issues of an application's dependencies conflicting with another application's dependencies since the application is in a self-contained package. This provided application isolation not only eliminates dependency issues but also provides an enhanced level of security and eases the burden of operating system migrations.

You may or may not have heard of application streaming before reading this book. It sounds like a great solution to the "it worked on my machine" issue. There are many reasons it hasn't taken off as expected, though. For starters, most offerings are paid solutions that require a substantial investment. Besides licensing, they require a "clean PC," which means that for every application you want to virtualize, you need to start with a base system. The package you want to create uses the differences between the base installation and anything that was added after the initial system snapshot. The differences are then packaged into your distribution file, which can be executed on any workstation.

We've mentioned application virtualization to highlight that application issues such as "It works on my machine" have had different solutions over the years. Products such as **Thinapp** are just one attempt at solving the problem. Other attempts include running the application on a server running **Citrix** or **Remote Desktop**, **Linux containers**, and even **virtual machines**.

Introducing Docker

The industry and even end users needed something that was easier and cheaper – enter Docker containers. Containers are not a new technology; they have been used in various forms for years. What Docker did was make them accessible to the average developer.

Docker brought an abstraction layer to the masses. It was easy to use and didn't require a clean PC for every application before creating a package, thus offering a solution for dependency issues, but most attractive of all, it was *free*. Docker became a standard for many projects on GitHub, where teams would often create a Docker container and distribute the Docker image or **Dockerfile** to team members, providing a standard testing or development environment. This adoption by end users is what eventually brought Docker to the enterprise and, ultimately, what made it the standard it has become today.

While there are many books on Docker, this book focuses on the base topics of Docker that are used to interact with containers. This book will be focusing on what you will need to know when trying to use a local Kubernetes environment. There is a long and interesting history of Docker and how it evolved into the standard container image format that we use today. We encourage you to read about the company and how they ushered in the container world we know today.

While our focus is not to teach Docker inside-out, we felt that those of you who are new to Docker would benefit from a quick primer on general container concepts. If you have some Docker experience and understand terminology such as ephemeral and stateless, feel free to continue to the *Installing Docker* section.

Understanding Docker

This book was created with the assumption that you have some basic knowledge of Docker and container concepts. We realize that not everyone may have played with Docker or containers in the past, so we wanted to present a crash course on container concepts and using Docker.

> **Important Note**
>
> If you are new to containers, we suggest reading the documentation that can be found on Docker's website for additional information: `https://docs.docker.com/`.

Containers are ephemeral

The first topic to understand is that container images are ephemeral.

For those of you who are new to Docker, the term ephemeral means short-lived. By design, a container can be destroyed at any time and brought back up with no interaction from a user. In the preceding example, someone interactively added files to a web server. These added files are only temporary since the base image does not have these files included in it.

This means that once a container is created and running, any changes that are made to the image *will not* be saved once the container is removed, or destroyed, from the Docker host. Let's look at an example:

1. You start a container running a web server using **NGINX** on your host without any base **HTML** pages.

2. Using a Docker command, you execute a `copy` command to copy some web files into the container's filesystem.

3. To test that the copy was successful, you browse to the website and confirm that it is serving the correct web pages.

4. Happy with the results, you stop the container and remove it from the host. Later that day, you want to show a co-worker the website and you start your NGINX container. You browse to the website again, but when the site opens, you receive a 404 error (page not found error).

What happened to the files you uploaded before you stopped and removed the container from the host?

The reason your web pages cannot be found after the container was restarted is because all containers are **ephemeral**.

Whatever is in the base container image is all that will be included each time the container is initially started. Any changes that you make inside a container are short-lived.

If you needed to add permanent files to the existing image, you would need to rebuild the image with the files included or, as we will explain in the *Persistent data* section later in this chapter, you could mount a Docker volume in your container. At this point, the main concept to understand is that containers are ephemeral.

But wait! You may be wondering, *"If containers are ephemeral, how did I add web pages to the server?"*. Ephemeral just means that changes will not be saved; it doesn't stop you from making changes to a running container.

Any changes made to a running container will be written to a temporary layer, called the **container layer**, which is a directory on the local host filesystem. The Docker storage driver is in charge of handling requests that use the container layer. This location will store any changes in the container's filesystem so that when you added the HTML pages to the container, they will be stored on the local host. The container layer is tied to the container ID of the running image and it will remain on the host system until the container is removed from Docker, either by using the CLI or by running a Docker prune job.

If a container is ephemeral and the image cannot be written to, how can you modify data in the container? Docker uses image layering to create multiple linked layers that appear as a single filesystem.

Docker images

At a high level, a Docker image is a collection of image layers, each with a JSON file that contains metadata for the layer. These are all combined to create the running application that you interact with when a container image is started.

You can read more about the contents of an image on Docker's GitHub at `https://github.com/moby/moby/blob/master/image/spec/v1.md`.

Image layers

As we mentioned in the previous section, a running container uses a container layer that is "on top" of the base image layer, as shown in the following diagram:

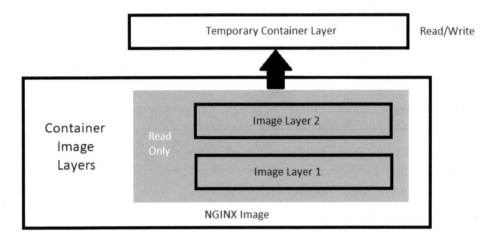

Figure 1.1 – Docker image layers

The image layers cannot be written to since they are in a read-only state, but the temporary container layer is in a writeable state. Any data that you add to the container is stored in this layer and will be retained as long as the container is running.

To deal with multiple layers efficiently, Docker implements copy-on-write, which means that if a file already exists, it will not be created. However, if a file is required that does not exist in the current image, it will be written. In the container world, if a file exists in a lower layer, the layers above it do not need to include it. For example, if layer 1 had a file called /opt/nginx/index.html in it, layer 2 does not need the same file in its layer.

This explains how the system handles files that either exist or do not exist, but what about a file that has been modified? There will be times where you'll need to "replace" a file that is in a lower layer. You may need to do this when you are building an image or as a temporary fix to a running container issue. The copy-on-write system knows how to deal with these issues. Since images read from the top down, the container uses only the highest layer file. If your system had a /opt/nginx/index.html file in layer 1 and you modified and saved the file, the running container would store the new file in the container layer. Since the container layer is the topmost layer, the new copy of index.html would always be read before the older version in the image layer.

Persistent data

We will talk about how to use persistent disks in *Chapter 2, Working with Docker Data*. For now, we will just provide a brief introduction.

Being limited to ephemeral-only containers would severely limit the use cases for Docker. It is very likely that you will have some use cases that will require persistent storage, or data that will remain if you stop a container.

This may seem like we are contradicting our earlier statement that containers are ephemeral, but that is still true. When you store data in the container image layer, the base image does not change. When the container is removed from the host, the container layer is also removed. If the same image is used to start a new container, a new container image layer is also created. So, the container is ephemeral, but by adding a Docker volume to the container, you can store data outside of the container, thus gaining data persistency.

Docker provides persistency through a few methods, which we will discuss in more detail in *Chapter 2, Working with Docker Data*, but for now, know that Docker does provide a method to persist your data.

Accessing services running in containers

We will talk about how to expose containers in *Chapter 3, Understanding Docker Networking*. For now, we will just provide a brief introduction.

Unlike a physical machine or a virtual machine, containers do not connect to a network directly. When a container needs to send or receive traffic, it goes through the Docker host system using a bridged **NAT network** connection. This means that when you run a container and you want to receive incoming traffic requests, you need to expose the ports for each of the containers that you wish to receive traffic on. On a Linux-based system, `iptables` has rules to forward traffic to the Docker daemon, which will service the assigned ports for each container.

That completes the introduction to base containers and Docker. In the next section, we will explain how to install Docker on a host.

Installing Docker

The hands-on exercises in this book will require that you have a working Docker host. You can follow the steps in this book, or you can execute the script located in this book's GitHub repository, in the `chapter1` directory, called `install-docker.sh`.

Today, you can install Docker on just about every hardware platform out there. Each version of Docker acts and looks the same on each platform, making development and using Docker easy for people who need to develop cross-platform applications. By making the functions and commands the same between different platforms, developers do not need to learn a different container runtime to run images.

The following is a table of Docker's available platforms. As you can see, there are installations for multiple operating systems, as well as multiple CPU architectures:

Platform	X86_64	ARM	ARM64/AARCH64
Docker Desktop Windows	✓		
Docker Desktop MacOS	✓		
CentOS	✓		✓
Debian	✓	✓	✓
Fedora	✓		✓
Ubuntu	✓	✓	✓

Figure 1.2 – Available Docker platforms

> **Important Note**
>
> Images that are created using one architecture cannot run on a different architecture. This means that you cannot create an image based on x86 hardware and expect that same image to run on your Raspberry Pi running an ARM processor. It's also important to note that while you can run a Linux container on a Windows machine, you cannot run a Windows container on a Linux machine.

The installation procedures that are used to install Docker vary between platforms. Luckily, Docker has documented many of the installation procedures on their website: https://docs.docker.com/install/.

In this chapter, we will install Docker on an Ubuntu 18.04 system. If you do not have an Ubuntu machine to install on, you can still read about the installation steps, as each step will be explained and does not require that you have a running system to understand the process. If you have a different Linux installation, you can use the installation procedures outlined on Docker's site at https://docs.docker.com/. Steps are provided for CentOS, Debian, Fedora, Ubuntu, and there are generic steps for other Linux distributions.

Preparing to install Docker

Before we start the installation, we need to consider what storage driver to use. The storage driver is what provides the union filesystem, which manage the layers of the container and how the writeable layer of the container is accessed.

In most installations, you won't need to change the default storage driver since a default option will be selected. If you are running a Linux kernel that is at least version 4.0 or above, your Docker installation will use the `overlay2` storage driver; earlier kernels will install the `AUFS` storage driver.

For reference, along with the `overlay2` and `AUFS` drivers, Docker supports the `devicemapper`, `btrfs`, `zfs`, and `vfs` storage drivers. However, these are rarely used in new systems and are only mentioned here as a reference.

If you would like to learn about each storage driver, take a look at the following Docker web page, which details each driver and their use cases: `https://docs.docker.com/storage/storagedriver/select-storage-driver/`.

Now that you understand the storage driver requirements, the next step is to select an installation method. You can install Docker using one of three methods:

- Add the Docker repositories to your host system.

- Install the package manually.

- Use a supplied installation script from Docker.

The first option is considered the best option since it allows for easy installation and making updates to the Docker engine. The second option is useful for enterprises that do not have internet access to servers, also known as "air-gapped" servers. The third option is used to install edge and testing versions of Docker and is not suggested for production use.

Since the preferred method is to add Docker's repository to our host, we will use that option and explain the process we should use to add the repository and install Docker.

Installing Docker on Ubuntu

Now that we have finished preparing everything, let's install Docker:

1. The first step is to update the package index by executing `apt-get update`:

    ```
    sudo apt-get update
    ```

2. Next, we need to add any packages that may be missing on the host system to allow HTTPS apt access:

    ```
    sudo apt-get install apt-transport-https ca-certificates
    curl gnupg-agent software-properties-common
    ```

3. To pull packages from Docker's repository, we need to add their keys. You can add keys by using the following command, which will download the gpg key and add it to your system:

    ```
    curl -fsSL https://download.docker.com/linux/ubuntu/gpg |
    sudo apt-key add -
    ```

4. Now, add Docker's repository to your host system:

    ```
    sudo add-apt-repository "deb [arch=amd64] https://
    download.docker.com/linux/ubuntu $(lsb_release -cs)
    stable"
    ```

5. With all the prerequisites completed, you can install Docker on your server:

    ```
    sudo apt-get update
    sudo apt-get install docker-ce docker-ce-cli containerd.
    io
    ```

6. Docker is now installed on your host, but like most new services, Docker is not currently running and has not been configured to start with the system. To start Docker and enable it on startup, use the following command:

    ```
    sudo systemctl enable docker && systemctl start docker
    ```

Now that we have Docker installed, let's get some configuration out of the way. First, we'll grant permissions to Docker.

Granting Docker permissions

In a default installation, Docker requires root access, so you will need to run all Docker commands as root. Rather than using `sudo` with every Docker command, you can add your user account to a new group on the server that provides Docker access without requiring `sudo` for every command.

If you are logged on as a standard user and try to run a Docker command, you will receive an error:

```
Got permission denied while trying to connect to the
Docker daemon socket at unix:///var/run/docker.sock: Get
http://%2Fvar%2Frun%2Fdocker.sock/v1.40/images/json: dial unix
/var/run/docker.sock: connect: permission denied
```

To allow your user, or any other user you may want to add to execute Docker commands, you need to create a new group and add the users to that group. The following is an example command you can use to add the currently logged on user:

```
sudo groupadd docker
sudo usermod -aG docker $USER
```

The first command creates the `docker` group, while the second command adds the user account that you are currently logged in with to the `docker` group.

To add the new membership to your account, you need to log off from the system and log back on, which will update your groups.

Finally, you can test that it works by running the standard hello world image (note that we do not require `sudo` to run the Docker command):

```
docker run hello-world
```

If you see the following output, then you have successfully installed Docker and granted your non-root account access to Docker:

```
Unable to find image 'hello-world:latest' locally
latest: Pulling from library/hello-world
1b930d010525: Pull complete
Digest: sha256:fc6a51919cfeb2e6763f62b6d9e8815acbf7cd2e476ea353743570610737b752
Status: Downloaded newer image for hello-world:latest

Hello from Docker!
This message shows that your installation appears to be working correctly.

To generate this message, Docker took the following steps:
 1. The Docker client contacted the Docker daemon.
 2. The Docker daemon pulled the "hello-world" image from the Docker Hub.
    (amd64)
 3. The Docker daemon created a new container from that image which runs the
    executable that produces the output you are currently reading.
 4. The Docker daemon streamed that output to the Docker client, which sent it
    to your terminal.

To try something more ambitious, you can run an Ubuntu container with:
 $ docker run -it ubuntu bash

Share images, automate workflows, and more with a free Docker ID:
 https://hub.docker.com/

For more examples and ideas, visit:
 https://docs.docker.com/get-started/
```

Figure 1.3 – Output for hello-world

Now that we've granted Docker permission to run without sudo, we can start unlocking the commands at our disposal by learning how to use the Docker CLI.

Using the Docker CLI

You used the Docker CLI when you ran the hello-world container to test your installation. The Docker command is what you will use to interact with the Docker daemon. Using this single executable, you can do the following, and more:

- Start and stop containers
- Pull and push images
- Run a shell in an active container
- Look at container logs
- Create Docker volumes
- Create Docker networks
- Prune old images and volumes

This chapter is not meant to include an exhaustive explanation of every Docker command; instead, we will explain some of the common commands that you will need to use to interact with the Docker daemon and containers. Since we consider volumes and networking to be very important to understand for this book, we will go into additional details on those topics.

You can break down Docker commands into two categories: general Docker commands and Docker management commands. The standard Docker commands allow you to manage containers, while management commands allow you to manage Docker options such as managing volumes and networking.

docker help

It's common to forget an option or the syntax for a command, and Docker realizes this. Whenever you get stuck trying to remember a command, you can always use the `docker help` command to refresh your memory.

docker run

To run a container, use the `docker run` command with the provided image name. Before executing a `docker run` command, you should understand the options you can supply when starting a container.

In its simplest form, an example command you can use to run a NGINX web server would be `docker run bitnami/nginx:latest`. While this will start a container running NGINX, it will run in the foreground:

```
23:58:39.23
23:58:39.23 Welcome to the Bitnami nginx container
23:58:39.23 Subscribe to project updates by watching https://github.com/bitnami/bitnami-docker-nginx
23:58:39.23 Submit issues and feature requests at https://github.com/bitnami/bitnami-docker-nginx/issues
23:58:39.23 Send us your feedback at containers@bitnami.com
23:58:39.24
23:58:39.24 INFO  ==> ** Starting NGINX setup **
23:58:39.25 INFO  ==> Validating settings in NGINX_* env vars...
23:58:39.25 INFO  ==> Initializing NGINX...

23:58:39.26 INFO  ==> ** NGINX setup finished! **
23:58:39.27 INFO  ==> ** Starting NGINX **
```

Figure 1.4 – NGINX container startup

To run a container as a background process, you need to add the `-d` option to your Docker command, which will run your container in detached mode. Now, when you run a detached container, you will only see the container ID, instead of the interactive, or attached, screen:

```
[root@localhost ~]# docker run -d bitnami/nginx:latest
5283811f91f02ecc2d0adf5ed74ea001b5136b6991e4ff815ee03a0691a05735
```

Figure 1.5 – Docker run output

By default, containers will be given a random name once they are started. In our previous detached example, the container has been given the name silly_keldysh:

Figure 1.6 – Docker naming example

If you do not assign a name to your container, it can quickly get confusing as you start to run multiple containers on a single host. To make management easier, you should always start your container with a name that will make it easier to manage. Docker provides another option with the run command: the --name option. Building on our previous example, we will name our container nginx-test. Our new docker run command will be as follows:

```
docker run --name nginx-test -d bitnami/nginx:latest
```

Just like running any detached image, this will return the containers ID, but not the name you provided. In order to verify the container ran with the name nginx-test, we can list the containers using the docker ps command.

docker ps

Every day, you will need to retrieve a list of running containers or a list of containers that have been stopped. The Docker CLI has an option called ps that will list all running containers, or if you add an extra option to the ps command, all containers that are running and have been stopped. The output will list the containers, including their container ID, image tag, entry command, the creation date, status, ports, and the container name. The following is an example of containers that are currently running:

CONTAINER ID	IMAGE	COMMAND	CREATED
72212346d765	nginx	"nginx -g 'daemon of…"	6 seconds ago
7967c50b260f	rancher/rancher:latest	"entrypoint.sh"	3 days ago

Figure 1.7 – Currently running containers

This is helpful if the container you are looking for is currently running. What if the container was stopped, or even worse, what if you started the container and it failed to start and then stopped? You can view the status of all containers, including previously run containers, by adding the -a option to the docker ps command. When you execute docker ps -a, you will see the same output from a standard ps command, but you will notice that the list may include additional containers.

How can you tell what containers are running versus which ones have stopped? If you look at the STATUS field of the list, the running containers will show a running time; for example, Up xx hours, or Up xx days. However, if the container has been stopped for any reason, the status will show when it stopped; for example, Exited (1) 3 days ago.

```
IMAGE          COMMAND                 CREATED          STATUS
nginx          "nginx -g 'daemon of…"  10 minutes ago   Up 10 minutes
nginx          "nginx -g 'daemon of…"  12 minutes ago   Exited (0) 10 minutes ago
```

Figure 1.8 – Docker PS output

A stopped container does not mean there was an issue running the image. There are containers that may execute a single task and, once completed, the container may stop gracefully. One way to determine whether an exit was graceful or if it was due to a failed startup is to check the logs of the container.

docker start and stop

To stop a running container, use the docker stop option with the name of the container you want to stop. You may wish to stop a container due to the resources on the host since you may have limited resources and can only run a few containers simultaneously.

If you need to start that container at a future time for additional testing or development, execute docker start container name, which will start the container with all of the options that it was originally started with, including any networks or volumes that were assigned.

docker attach

You may need to access a container interactively to troubleshoot an issue or to look at a log file. One method to connect to a running container is to use the docker attach container name command. When you attach to a running container, you will connect to the running containers process, so if you attach to a container running a process, you are not likely to just see a command prompt of any kind. In fact, you may see nothing but a blank screen for some time until the container outputs some data to the screen.

You must be careful once you attach to the container – you may accidentally stop the running process and, in turn, stop the container. Let's use an example of attaching to a web server running NGINX. First, we need to verify that the container is running using docker ps:

```
CONTAINER ID     IMAGE                  COMMAND                CREATED          STATUS
bbadb2bddaab     bitnami/nginx:latest   "/entrypoint.sh /run…" 9 seconds ago    Up 7 seconds
```

Figure 1.9 – docker ps output

Using the attach command, we execute docker attach bbadb2bddaab:

```
root@Blade:~# docker attach bbadb2bddaab
```

Figure 1.10 – docker attach output

As shown in the preceding screenshot, once you attach to the running container process, it appears that nothing is happening. When you attach to a process, you will only be able to interact with the process, and the only output you will see is data being sent to standard output. In the case of the NGINX container, the attach command has attached to the NGINX process. To show this, we will leave the attachment and curl to the web server from another session. Once we curl to the container port, you will see logs outputted to the attached console:

```
root@Blade:~# docker attach bbadb2bddaab
172.18.0.1 - - [04/Mar/2020:18:50:42 +0000] "GET / HTTP/1.1" 200 612 "-" "curl/7.58.0"
172.18.0.1 - - [04/Mar/2020:18:50:43 +0000] "GET / HTTP/1.1" 200 612 "-" "curl/7.58.0"
172.18.0.1 - - [04/Mar/2020:18:50:44 +0000] "GET / HTTP/1.1" 200 612 "-" "curl/7.58.0"
172.18.0.1 - - [04/Mar/2020:18:50:45 +0000] "GET / HTTP/1.1" 200 612 "-" "curl/7.58.0"
```

Figure 1.11 – STDOUT output from the container

Attaching to a running container has varying benefits, depending on what is running in the container.

We mentioned that you need to be careful once you attach to the container. Those who are new to Docker may attach to the NGINX image and assume that nothing is happening on the server or the attach failed. Since they think that there may be an issue, since it's just sitting there, they may decide to break out of the container using the standard *Ctrl + C* keyboard command. This will send them back to a bash prompt, where they may run docker ps to look at the running containers:

```
root@Blade:~# docker ps
CONTAINER ID        IMAGE        COMMAND        CREATED        STATUS        PORTS        NAMES
root@Blade:~#
```

Figure 1.12 – docker ps output

Where is the NGINX container? We didn't execute a docker stop command, and the container was running until we attached to the container. Why did the container stop after the attachment?

When an attachment is made to a container, you are attached to the running process. All keyboard commands will act in the same way as if you were at a physical server that was running NGINX in an interactive shell. This means that when the user used *Ctrl + C* to return to a prompt, they stopped the running NGINX process. If a container's running process stops, the container will also stop, and that's why the `docker ps` command does not show a running container.

Rather than use *ctrl-c* to return to a prompt, the user should have used *Ctrl + P*, followed by *Ctrl + Q*.

There is an alternative to the `attach` command: the `docker exec` command. The `exec` command differs from an `attach` command since you supply the process to execute on the container.

docker exec

A better option when it comes to interacting with a running container is the `exec` command. Rather than attach to the container, you can use the `docker exec` command to execute a process in the container. You need to supply the container name and the process you want to execute in the image. Of course, the process must be included in the running image – if you do not have the bash executable in the image, you will receive an error when trying to execute bash in the container.

We will use a NGINX container as an example again. We will verify that NGINX is running using `docker ps` and then using the container ID or the name, we execute into the container. The command syntax is `docker exec <options> <container name> <process>`:

```
root@Blade:~# docker exec -it nginx-test bash
I have no name!@0a7c916e7411:/app$
```

Figure 1.13 – docker exec example

The option we included is `-it`, which tells `exec` to run in an interactive TTY session. Here, the process we want to execute is bash. Notice how the name changed from the original user and hostname. The host name is `Blade`, while the container name is `0a7c916e7411`. You may also have noticed that the current working directory changed from ~ to `/app` and that the prompt is not running as a root user, as shown by the $ prompt.

You can use this session the same way you would a standard **SSH** connection; you are running bash in the container.

Since we are not attached to the container, *ctrl-c* will not stop any process from running. To exit an interactive session, you only need to type in exit, followed by *Enter*, to exit the container. If you then run docker ps, you will notice that the container is still in a running state:

```
root@Blade:~# docker exec -it nginx-test bash
I have no name!@0a7c916e7411:/app$ exit
exit
root@Blade:~# docker ps
CONTAINER ID        IMAGE                 COMMAND               CREATED           STATUS
0a7c916e7411        bitnami/nginx:latest  "/entrypoint.sh /run…"  12 minutes ago    Up 12 minutes
root@Blade:~#
```

Figure 1.14 – docker ps output

Next, let's see what we can learn about Docker log files.

docker logs

The docker logs command allows you to retrieve logs from a container using the container name or container ID that you retrieved using the docker ps command. You can view the logs from any container that was listed in your ps command; it doesn't matter if it's currently running or stopped.

Log files are often the only way to troubleshoot why a container may not be starting up, or why a container is in an exited state. For example, if you attempted to run an image and the image starts and suddenly stops, you may find the answer by looking at the logs for that container.

To look at the logs for a container, you can use the docker logs <container ID or name> command.

To view the logs for a container with a container ID of 7967c50b260f, you would use the following command:

```
docker logs 7967c50b260f
```

This will output the logs from the container to your screen, which may be very long and verbose. Since many logs may contain a lot of information, you can limit the output by supplying the `logs` command with additional options. The following table lists the options available for viewing logs:

Logs Options	Description
-f	Follow the log output (can also use --follow).
--tail xx	Show log output starting from the end of the file and retrieve xx lines.
--until xxx	Show log output before the xxx timestamp. xxx can be a timestamp; for example, 2020-02-23T18:35:13. xxx can be a relative time; for example, 60m.
--since xxx	Show log output after the xxx timestamp. xxx can be a timestamp; for example, 2020-02-23T18:35:13. xxx can be a relative time; for example, 60m.

docker rm

Once you name a container, the assigned name cannot be used to start a different container unless you remove it using the `docker rm` command. If you had a container running called `nginx-test` that was stopped and you attempted to start another container with the name `nginx-test`, the Docker daemon would return an error, stating that the name is in use:

```
Conflict. The container name "/nginx-test" is already in use
```

Figure 1.15 – Docker naming conflict error

This container is not running, but the daemon knows that the container name was used previously and that it's still in the list of previously run containers.

If you want to reuse the same name, you need to remove the container before starting another container with that name. This is a common scenario when you are testing container images. You may start a container only to discover an issue with the application or image. You stop the container, fix the image/application issue, and want to redeploy using the same name. Since the name was in use previously and is still part of the Docker history, you will need to remove the image before reusing the name.

We haven't discussed volumes yet, but when removing a container that has a volume, or volumes, attached, it's a good practice to add the -v option to your remove command. Adding the -v option to the `docker rm` command will remove any volumes that were attached to the container.

Summary

In this chapter, you learned how Docker can be used to solve common development issues, including the dreaded "It works on my machine" problem. We also presented an introduction to the most commonly used Docker CLI commands that you will use on a daily basis. We closed out this chapter by looking and how to handle persistent data for a container and customizing container networking.

In the next chapter, we will cover why, and how, containers use persistent data. We will explain each data type that can be attached to a container, including volumes, bind mounts, and tmpfs.

Questions

1. A single Docker image can be used on any Docker host, regardless of the architecture used.

    A. True

    B. False

2. What does Docker use to merge multiple image layers into a single filesystem?

    A. Merged filesystem

    B. NTFS filesystem

    C. EXT4 filesystem

    D. Union filesystem

3. What is the most commonly used Docker storage driver when using a Kernel that is above version 4.0?

    A. AUFS

    B. ZFS

    C. VFS

    D. Overlay2

4. When you edit a container's filesystem interactively, what layer are the changes written to?

    A. Operating system layer

    B. Bottom-most layer

    C. Container layer

    D. Ephemeral layer

5. Assuming the image contains the required binaries, what Docker command allows you to gain access to a container's bash prompt?

    A. `docker shell -it <container> /bin/bash`

    B. `docker run -it <container> /bin/bash`

    C. `docker exec -it <container> /bin/bash`

    D. `docker spawn -it <container> /bin/bash`

6. When a container is stopped, the Docker daemon will delete all traces of the container.

    A. True

    B. False

7. What command will show you a list of all containers, including any stopped containers?

    A. `docker ps -all`

    B. `docker ps -a`

    C. `docker ps -list`

    D. `docker list all`

2
Working with Docker Data

At one time, containers were used for stateless workloads that could scale up, scale quickly, and move from one location to another without impacting the workload. Stateless workloads limit the type of containers you can run, prohibiting you from running anything beyond items that are stored in the base image.

In this chapter, we will cover the following topics:

- Why you need persistent data
- Docker volumes
- Docker bind mounts
- Docker tmpfs mounts

Let's get started!

Technical requirements

This chapter does not have any technical requirements.

If you want to create volumes using the examples in this chapter, you can use the Docker host that we created in *Chapter 1, Docker and Container Essentials*. The volumes that we'll be using for examples in this chapter are not required for future chapters.

You can access the code to create a Docker host from *Chapter 1, Docker and Containers Essentials* by going to the following GitHub repository: `https://github.com/PacktPublishing/Kubernetes-and-Docker-The-Complete-Guide`.

Why you need persistent data

Let's consider an example use case where you may want to write data to a persistent location from a container.

Let's say you have a system that requires you to deploy a **MySQL** database fronted by a web-based application running on **NGINX**. You start both containers for the application using standard `docker run` commands. You do some initial testing with the users and they confirm that everything is working as expected. The users were successful when it came to adding records, querying for records, editing, and deletions – this all worked correctly. After a few days of the container running, you receive an email from security telling all users that all MySQL servers need to have a new patch deployed as soon as possible to address a security vulnerability.

You quickly work on a new MySQL image that includes the newest patch and push it to your container registry. Working with the users, you decide a time to deploy the new container and start the process by doing the following:

- Stopping the running container.
- Running the new image using the same container name that the previous image used. To do this, you need to remove the current container using the `docker rm` command.
- Starting the new MySQL container.

After the container starts up, you log in to verify that MySQL is running and to confirm that the patch has been applied. Next, you log into the application and search for a record in the database and receive a record not found error. You find this to be odd since the system has been running for a few days. To troubleshoot further, you log into the database directly to check the health of the database and discover that there are no databases on the server.

What happened to your database? Why does it appear that the database server has been wiped out and reinitialized? You know the system was working over the last few days and everything was running as expected, that is, right up to the point that you downloaded a new MySQL image and started it in place of the original container.

Recall from our ephemeral discussion in *Chapter 1, Docker and Container Essentials,* that the writeable layer for the container is ephemeral and that all the data that's written to it will be lost when the container is removed, even if you start a container with the same name. When you removed the container to reuse the name, the container layer that contained the database was deleted. When the new container was started, it created a new container layer and when MySQL started up, it didn't see any of its base files and created a new, fully initialized, MySQL instance.

Of course, you don't want to lose your database every time you need to deploy a new version of the database server. Since the container layer is ephemeral, you need to store your database outside the base layer on something that will persist between image upgrades. So far, we have been telling you that containers are ephemeral, so how can you configure your container to save data?

Luckily, Docker includes the ability to add persistent data to a container using two methods:

- Docker volumes
- Docker bind mounts

There is also a third option that offers storage using the host's RAM, called **tmpfs**. This type of mount is not persistent through container restarts, Docker restarts, or host reboots. It is only used as a location to temporarily store data in high-speed RAM and is truly ephemeral. While it does not offer persistency, there are specific use cases where selecting tmpfs can be beneficial.

Which option should you select when you need to run containers that require persistent data? Both volumes and bind mounts function similarly, storing files on the local host filesystem to provide persistency to your container. The final decision comes down to understanding how each option is managed, and what data it may expose if used improperly.

Docker volumes

Docker volumes are the preferred option to add persistent data to a container. A volume is nothing more than a directory on the local host that is mapped to the container using a volume mount. When you create a volume, a new directory is created on the host filesystem, commonly under /var/lib/docker/volumes/<volume ID>/. If you have root access to the host, you can look at the file structure as you would any other directory. The following screenshot shows the directories under the volumes directory from a Docker host running containers using volumes:

```
01a33357ddacce87762e4e84bafac11240b3c1ea9280e308891d059c65fa2c0c
59cad006b82cf2d51e8313bff7b0cb971d098b71eb32ca47360bcdbb76268b79
8e8c2cd1771d6299d90ed666bb781ed01403e11a1d3972482178a11089a0ada6
a3d8b42a5bdb615b81aef2cc294c88bfa46d737139a475a5acbd32f66d8ab67a
c14c408cdae19757e985c6a4e0d6f6cbaf212e281891209c136cbd845867df79
da5eab82d7d424f2a3af1fdd43d9f6edea3ff5b3f690f5c748f7eeccd67650a7
e0f5c8cb418296b820de1594a2bee3fcdbe2aa36c4dc0d201133337b45650b2f
```

Figure 2.1 – Docker folder directories

To maintain information between restarts, Docker stores key metadata in various databases on the host using Boltdb, which is a fast database written in Go that's used to store persistent key values. There are two Boltdb databases that you may come across when browsing the /var/lib/docker folder:

- /var/lib/docker/volumes/metadata.db: Maintains metadata for Docker volumes, such as the name, driver, labels, and options

- /var/lib/docker/network/files/local-kv.db: Maintains metadata for Docker networks

Since we are focusing on data in this chapter, we will use the metadata.db database. As you will see later in this chapter, when you create a Docker volume, you can provide options such as a name or label. This information is stored in the database to maintain volume persistence.

Here is an example from metadata.db in JSON format for a Docker volume called webdata:

```
webdata{"Name":"webdata","Driver":"local","Labels":null,
"Options":null}
```

Every Docker volume has a directory in the /var/lib/docker/volumes directory. In each volume folder, there is a directory called _data that contains the actual data for the container.

Before using a volume with a container, it must be created. Creating a Docker volume can be done manually using the Docker CLI or automatically by the Docker daemon when a container is started. Since both methods are created by Docker, they are owned and managed by Docker itself, making it is easy to manage and track them using the Docker CLI.

Creating a volume using the CLI

To create a Docker volume, we can use the volume management options:

```
docker volume <option>
```

The available options are as follows:

Docker Volume Options	
Option	**Description**
create	Creates a new volume that can be mounted in a container.
inspect	Lists details of the volume, including the creation date, driver, labels, host mountpoint, name, options, and scope.
ls	Lists all Docker volumes.
prune	Deletes all unused Docker volumes.
rm	Deletes a volume, or multiple volumes, by name.

Table 2.1 – Volume management options

To create a new volume, use the create option:

```
docker volume create <optional volume name>
```

After executing create, you will see the volume name that was created. If you did not provide the optional volume name, Docker will assign a volume ID as the name. Creating a volume without providing a volume name is known as an anonymous volume:

```
[root@localhost docker]# docker volume create
bcbec7f0a0c6390a149f49dfae610cabdd2e8e670f9f6ba221fc6910865ee150
```

Figure 2.2 – Anonymous volume output

An anonymous volume can be difficult to keep track of as you add additional containers to your host that use volumes. Therefore, it is considered a best practice to name your volume at creation time, rather than allowing Docker to generate a long anonymous volume name.

Any volume that you provide a volume name for at creation is called a named volume. To create a named volume, you need to supply the volume name to the `docker volume create` command:

```
[root@localhost docker]# docker volume create pv-mysql-data
pv-mysql-data
```

Figure 2.3 – Named volume output

Once a volume is created using either method, you can verify that the directory was created for your volume by looking in `/var/lib/docker/volumes`. You will find a directory with the name of the volume that was returned by the `create` command.

Now that you know how to create a volume, the next step is to use it with a container.

Mounting a volume in a container

The process to mount a volume in a container is the same as the one that's followed for a named or anonymous volume. We already went over the process of creating a volume using the Docker CLI, but we didn't explain how to let Docker automatically create a volume.

In this section, we will explain how to have Docker automatically create a volume and mount it. We will also explain how to mount a previously created named volume to a container.

When mounting a volume in a container, you need to provide one of two options to the `docker start` command. The two options you can use to mount volumes are `--mount` or `-v`. If you are running a standard container, you can use either option, but `-v` is the most commonly used option.

Earlier in this chapter, we created a volume called `pv-mysql-data`. We now want to start our MySQL container with the named volume so that we will have a persistent database. To mount a volume in your container, you need to pass the `-v` option when starting the container. The `-v` option requires two arguments: the volume name and the container mountpoint. In the following example command, you can see the command to start MySQL with a named volume mount. We also added some additional options that are being passed to the container, specifically the `-e` option, which is used to set an environment variable:

```
docker run --name mysql-01 -v pv-mysql-data:/var/lib/mysql -e
MYSQL_ROOT_PASSWORD=my-password -d mysql
```

This will start a container running MySQL, with a name of `mysql-01`, that mounts a volume called `pv-mysql-data` in a mount point called `/var/lib/mysql` in the container. The last option, which is using `-e`, creates an environment variable that is called `MYSQL_ROOT_PASSWORD`, which is set to `my-password`.

Once the container is up and running, you can look at the volume directory to verify that MySQL mounted the volume correctly by checking the data in the directory:

```
[root@localhost docker]# ls volumes/pv-mysql-data/_data/
 auto.cnf        binlog.000002   ca-key.pem    client-cert.pem   ib_buffer_pool   ib_logfile0
 binlog.000001   binlog.index    ca.pem        client-key.pem    ibdata1          ib_logfile1
```

Figure 2.4 – MySQL persistent volume

As you can see, the new volume contains all the standard files that are created when a new MySQL server is started for the first time.

We also mentioned that you can let Docker create the volume automatically, instead of creating the volume yourself. To have Docker create the volume upon container startup, run the same command that you would if you were using a pre-created volume. For example, using the previous MySQL example, let's assume *we did not* pre-create the volume using the `docker volume create` command.

Let's execute the same command:

```
docker run --name mysql-01 -v pv-mysql-data:/var/lib/mysql -e
MYSQL_ROOT_PASSWORD=my-password -d mysql
```

When we do this, the Docker daemon will recognize that there is no existing volume named `pv-mysql-data` and one will be created before it's mounted in the container.

Mounting an existing volume

Unlike the container layers, which are also stored on the local host, volumes are not lost if a container is removed from Docker. In our MySQL upgrade example from earlier, we upgraded our database server to a newer version. Since we wanted to keep the container name the same as the previously deployed container, we removed the old container and started the new container with the same name. By removing the container, we removed the container layer that was stored on the local filesystem.

To avoid losing our database after an upgrade, or after a container has been removed from our host, we can mount the existing volume in our new running container. Since volumes are not deleted by default, the data is still on the local filesystem and ready to be used by any other container.

When we stop and remove our MySQL server, the volume remains intact. When we start the new MySQL container, we only need to supply the -v option using the same volume name that was used in the original container. This is why creating a named volume is preferred over an anonymous volume. In our example, we created a named volume called pv-mysql-data. To run the new container, using the same volume, we can use the docker run command with the -v option, as shown here:

```
docker run --name mysql-01 -v pv-mysql-data:/var/lib/mysql -e
MYSQL_ROOT_PASSWORD=my-password -d mysql:v2
```

This will launch our new mysql:v2 container with the same volume as the previous container, with the existing database completely intact.

Mounting a volume in multiple containers

What if you had an application that requires multiple containers, and each of them requires the exact same data? While you could create a volume for each container and copy the data into each, a more efficient method would be to share a single volume between multiple containers.

One unique characteristic of Docker volumes is that multiple containers can access the same volume. While this sounds like an easy solution to provide a single location to shared data, you need to keep in mind that not every application plays nicely when multiple processes access the same data. Using our database example, starting up a second container using the same volume would cause the second container's MySQL server to fail at startup. Since the files are locked by the first container's database, the second container cannot gain exclusive access to the database to mount it. If you look at the logs for the second instance, you will see the error shown here:

```
[System] [MY-010116] [Server] /usr/sbin/mysqld (mysqld 8.0.19) starting as process 1
[ERROR] [MY-012574] [InnoDB] Unable to lock ./ibdata1 error: 11
[ERROR] [MY-012574] [InnoDB] Unable to lock ./ibdata1 error: 11
[ERROR] [MY-012574] [InnoDB] Unable to lock ./ibdata1 error: 11
[ERROR] [MY-012574] [InnoDB] Unable to lock ./ibdata1 error: 11
```

Figure 2.5 – Locking error output

There are use cases where a shared volume will offer benefits to your application. Imagine that you were running a few instances of a web server on your host that only presented data that was retrieved from a folder that changed nightly. One option would be to create a new container each night using a pipeline, but for this example, we will assume that you do not have a CI/CD system in place.

Instead, you may have a process on the host that pulls the data into the directory where the Docker volume has been created. Each web server will use a volume mount, using the same Docker volume. This allows each container to access the data from a single shared location, without any changes needing to be made to the base image.

To accomplish this, you simply need to supply the same mount option to each container when the container starts. For example, we have created a volume called `webdata` on our host, and we want to launch four NGINX servers that will use the data in the Docker volume. When you start each instance, you just use the same `webdata` named volume:

```
docker run --name webserver01 -v webdata:/opt/web/data -d
bitnami/nginx:latest
docker run --name webserver02 -v webdata:/opt/web/data -d
bitnami/nginx:latest
docker run --name webserver03 -v webdata:/opt/web/data -d
bitnami/nginx:latest
docker run --name webserver04 -v webdata:/opt/web/data -d
bitnami/nginx:latest
```

Since the NGINX server is only going to read the data, we will not run into any of the locking errors that we encountered for MySQL.

Now that we have been talking about volumes and have created a few of them, you might recognize that when you have many volumes on a host, it can become difficult to remember what volumes exist. The next section will discuss some basic management options for our volumes.

Listing Docker volumes

Remember that volumes are managed by Docker, so the daemon knows about every volume that was created. If you want to list every volume that you or the Docker daemon has created, use the `docker volume list` option:

```
[root@localhost docker]# docker volume list
DRIVER              VOLUME NAME
local               01a33357ddacce87762e4e84bafac11240b3c1ea9280e308891d059c65fa2c0c
local               8e8c2cd1771d6299d90ed666bb781ed01403e11a1d3972482178a11089a0ada6
local               26b5842b0247bb306bafb36acc5fa5d40ae6b49677f3c8c72c85ef0a8090a884
local               59cad006b82cf2d51e8313bff7b0cb971d098b71eb32ca47360bcdbb76268b79
local               74c99b1f7497e135a3e9f98f9a2a86c5f4d7344e2f1a1ff7e3408b9ba6052c56
local               99b858541e0acc3acbc6985d6d644e8681a8b55acb5c5d9fa9cd49247463579d
local               34831338a1c81f568a5b725a07d35fbcfab6c5be1fd7fc9585c539bfb7b1c28f
local               a3d8b42a5bdb615b81aef2cc294c88bfa46d737139a475a5acbd32f66d8ab67a
local               bcbec7f0a0c6390a149f49dfae610cabdd2e8e670f9f6ba221fc6910865ee150
local               c4e1e56ec9af7e9dcdbb084ab7cb6e2f1c050078a818d24e183e99e7fe4983c9
local               c14c408cdae19757e985c6a4e0d6f6cbaf212e281891209c136cbd845867df79
local               da5eab82d7d424f2a3af1fdd43d9f6edea3ff5b3f690f5c748f7eeccd67650a7
local               e0f5c8cb418296b820de1594a2bee3fcdbe2aa36c4dc0d201133337b45650b2f
local               pv-mysql-data
```

Figure 2.6 – docker volume list output

This option will display all the volumes that are currently being managed by Docker.

Cleaning up volumes

By default, Docker never deletes the volumes that are created for containers. We already know that when we stop and start a container using a volume, the data persists, but what can we do about the data after we no longer need it?

Imagine that the amount of data in the /var/lib/docker/volumes folder can grow at a tremendous rate. Because of this, it is a best practice to prune or remove the volumes to free up disk space – we often refer to this as part of a garbage collection process.

The simplest way to delete the data from an image that's no longer required is to use the -v option when you remove the container from Docker. We have used docker rm <image name> a few times in this book to remove an image from the host. If you have a volume attached to the container and you want to delete the data when you remove the image, you can add the -v option to the rm command, which will delete all the volumes that were associated with the container. To delete our MySQL server and the persistent data, we would use the following command:

```
docker rm -v mysql
```

There will be times where you will not want to delete the data by removing the container. Deleting a volume cannot be undone, so a better practice is to remove the container and keep the volume for a set number of days. After a defined period of time, you may be more comfortable deleting the volume or volumes.

If you wanted to delete a single or multiple volumes, you can use the docker volume rm option. You can supply the volume name, or names, after the rm option. Each volume that is supplied will be delete by the system, freeing up disk space on the host system.

You may be nervous that you might delete a volume that is being used by a container. Fear not – Docker has you covered. If you attempt to delete any volume that is currently in use by a running container, or assigned to a stopped container, you will receive an error:

```
Error response from daemon: remove test-auto: volume is in
use - [51000e2f61c79ae705cdac78692fa5590fb2b26d3d0eb0a3916df230
daf1b617]
```

Docker will only allow you to delete a volume that has not been opened by a running container.

You may have many volumes that you want to delete. While you could supply each name using the remove command, Docker provides another option, known as pruning. Pruning will look at all the volumes and remove any volume that is not currently mounted on a running container.

Be careful using this option – only use it if you know that the volumes that are not in use do not contain data that you need for any reason. This process is final and once run, it will delete *all* the volumes that are not in use.

To delete unused volumes, we use the docker volume prune option. This command will look at all the volumes, and any volume that is not attached to a running container will be deleted. When you issue the command, it will warn you that it will delete any volume without at least one running container:

```
[root@localhost docker]# docker volume prune
WARNING! This will remove all local volumes not used by at least one container.
Are you sure you want to continue? [y/N]
```

Figure 2.7 – docker prune confirmation

Select y for yes carefully – there is no undo command for this action. Once executed, you will receive a summary of the deleted volumes, including their names and the total reclaimed disk space:

```
Deleted Volumes:
e0f5c8cb418296b820de1594a2bee3fcdbe2aa36c4dc0d201133337b45650b2f
bcbec7f0a0c6390a149f49dfae610cabdd2e8e670f9f6ba221fc6910865ee150
59cad006b82cf2d51e8313bff7b0cb971d098b71eb32ca47360bcdbb76268b79
a3d8b42a5bdb615b81aef2cc294c88bfa46d737139a475a5acbd32f66d8ab67a
74c99b1f7497e135a3e9f98f9a2a86c5f4d7344e2f1a1ff7e3408b9ba6052c56
26b5842b0247bb306bafb36acc5fa5d40ae6b49677f3c8c72c85ef0a8090a884
34831338a1c81f568a5b725a07d35fbcfab6c5be1fd7fc9585c539bfb7b1c28f

Total reclaimed space: 283.2MB
```

Figure 2.8 – docker prune results

That completes the Docker volume section of this chapter. Remember that volumes are just one way to provide data persistence to your containers. The other method is called a bind mount, and while it also uses the host filesystem like a volume, bind mounts have a very different use case.

Docker bind mounts

The second option you can use to provide persistent data to a container is called a bind mount. Overall, volumes and bind mounts may look similar; both use the local host's filesystem, and both are mounted using the docker -v option. While they do share many of the same characteristics, a bind mount differs from a volume mount in one main area: it is *not* managed by Docker.

Unlike a Docker volume, a bind mount cannot be created by Docker. You cannot create a bind mount using the docker volume create option; however, a bind mount can be created automatically by Docker when a container starts. Even though Docker can create the bind mount location on the host, it does not "manage" the mount.

Since Docker does not manage the bind mounts, they cannot be deleted using a Docker command. Docker does not track the location of bind mounts in a list. If you create bind mounts in different areas of the filesystem on the host, you need to track the location of each one to remove once you no longer need the data manually.

A bind mount is a directory located anywhere on the host's filesystem that is bound to the container using the docker -v option. Unlike a volume, which is always located in a predefined location usually, such as /var/lib/docker/volumes, a bind mount can be anywhere on the host's filesystem. Since the directory is on the filesystem, you may run into permission issues when trying to access a directory. This discussion is outside the scope of this book and moves into the realms of Linux file system permissions.

You can bind any existing directory or create a new directory either by pre-creating the directory or letting Docker create the directory on container startup.

Before we explain how to use a bind mount, you might be asking yourself, *"Why would I use a bind mount?"* or *"Why would I use a volume? Why do I care which one I should use?".* We'll explain why you may or may not want to use a bind mount and then compare them to volumes.

A bind mount can be beneficial when you need to share something on the host system with a running container. For example, you develop an application on your local laptop and you want to test the application before finalizing the code. Rather than running it on your local console, you want to test it in a container. You could store your source code in /source and then, when you compile, you could store the executable and any libraries in /apps/testapp. Let's take a look:

1. You start a container with the -v option, which will bind mount the local host's /apps/testapp folder in the container. This doesn't change very much from using a volume in a container. In fact, the syntax to mount a bind location is the same as mounting a volume to a container when using the docker run -v option. However, rather than providing a volume name in the -v option, you need to provide the local host directory instead; for example:

    ```
    docker run -d -v /apps/testapp:/bin/testapp ubuntu:latest
    ```

    This will start a container running Ubuntu with a mount inside the container that binds to the local host's /apps/testapp path, where the compiled application is located.

2. To test the application, you would attach to the running image and execute the application by running /bin/testapp/testapp. Since the container's mount is using the local hosts directory, you can test the app and if any errors are encountered, you can fix the code and simply recompile the executable.

3. Once recompiled, you can run the new executable in the container again to test the application. This saves you from creating multiple test images, iterating through images after an issue is discovered. Once you have successfully tested the application, you can stop the container and create the final container image that includes the application.

Docker volumes cannot provide the same solution since they are all located in a directory on the host and cannot be pointed to an existing directory.

There are other example use cases for using bind mounts. The main point to remember is that bind mounts can be used to share data anywhere on the host system with a container. When used in the correct scenario, bind mounts are very useful, but when used incorrectly, their use can lead to an unstable system or a security breach.

It should go without saying that you should be careful when using any existing directory on the host system with a container. Binding your host's /etc directory in a container may lead to unexpected results. Someone running a shell in a container could easily delete or edit a file, or multiple files, making the host's system unstable.

Docker tmpfs mounts

At the beginning of this chapter, we mentioned that Docker allows you to use the host's RAM as a temporary storage location for container data. This type of mount will not persist data but for the right workload, it can be a very useful storage location. tmpfs offers a few unique advantages that are not available in volumes or bind mounts:

- The size can be pre-defined to limit the amount of RAM that is consumed for storage.

- Offers very fast data access.

There are also some limitations to tmpfs mounts:

- They are only available on Linux; Windows is not supported.

- A single tmpfs can only be mounted to one container.

Using a tmpfs mount in a container

A container can be started with a tmpfs mount by adding either --mount or using the --tmpfs option. In general, you should use the --mount option by default since --tmpfs does not allow for any customizations on the mount. If you use --tmpfs, you will not be able to set a size limit, or any file mode security. Since this type of mount will use an expensive resource, namely the host's RAM, you will want to create a size for your mount. Due to these limitations, we highly suggest that you do not use --tmpfs to create your tmpfs mounts.

To use a tmpfs mount for a NGINX container, you need to use the --mount option when you start the image:

```
docker run --mount type=tmpfs,target=/opt/html,tmpfs-
mode=1770,tmpfs-size=1000000 --name nginx-test -d bitnami/
nginx:latest
```

The mount option allows you to add multiple options after specifying --mount in your run command. In our example, we are adding options for the type of mount, the target mount in the container, the file mode, and the size. The following table shows the details for each option:

Docker Tmpfs Options	
Option	Description
type	Specifies tmpfs as the mount type. Other options include volume or bind.
target	Target mount point in the container. We are mounting the tmpfs at /opt/html.
tmpfs-mode	This option allows you to set security on the mount in octal format. Defaults to 1777.
tmpfs-size	Sets the size of the tmpfs volume. The value is in bytes, but you can specify it using bytes or (m) for megabytes. Defaults to ½ the RAM of the host.

Table 2.2 – Docker tmpfs optiond

Now that we have created a tmpfs mount, we want to list the volumes on the host to verify we have a tmpfs mount. You may recall that we can list the volumes using the docker volume ls command. The output after creating the tmpfs mount is shown here:

Figure 2.9 – Docker volume list

Notice that the list is empty; there are no volumes in use according to the Docker daemon. tmpfs mounts will not appear in the volume list since they are not "true" volumes; only volumes appear when using the docker volume ls command.

If you want to verify the tmpfs mount in the container, you can look at the `docker inspect` command's output from the container and look for the `"Mounts"` section:

```
"Mounts": [
    {
        "Type": "tmpfs",
        "Target": "/opt/html",
        "TmpfsOptions": {
            "SizeBytes": 1000000,
            "Mode": 1016
        }
    }
],
```

Figure 2.10 – Docker inspect output

You can also verify the mount inside the running container by executing a Linux `df` command when using the `docker exec` command:

```
root@Blade:~# docker exec nginx-test df -h
Filesystem      Size  Used Avail Use% Mounted on
overlay         251G  6.0G  233G   3% /
tmpfs            64M     0   64M   0% /dev
tmpfs            13G     0   13G   0% /sys/fs/cgroup
shm              64M     0   64M   0% /dev/shm
/dev/sdb        251G  6.0G  233G   3% /etc/hosts
tmpfs           980K     0  980K   0% /opt/html
tmpfs            13G     0   13G   0% /proc/acpi
tmpfs            13G     0   13G   0% /sys/firmware
```

Figure 2.11 – tmpfs mount in Linux

As you can see in the highlighted section of the `df` command's output, the mount exists in the container and the size is correct.

We want to show one last example of using a mount where we do not specify a size for the tmpfs space. If you do not specify a size, Docker will create a mount using half the RAM of the host. Our example server has **26 GB** of RAM and we have executed a `docker run` command with the same container without specifying a size.

Notice that we do specify a size in the `mount` command. To verify the container has the `/opt/html` target, we can execute a `df -u` command using `docker exec` and confirm that the `/opt/html` mount was created. As you may have noticed, the volume size is **13 GB**, which is **half** of the **26 GB** of RAM for the host. It is important to point out that while the volume is set to 26 GB, it has no data at this time, so it is not consuming any RAM yet. RAM is not consumed until data is stored in the container, so you need to be very careful with tmpfs volumes or you may run out of RAM on your host and may crash your system.

Summary

In this chapter, you learned multiple ways you can handle data in a container. After reading this chapter you should know how to decide on the appropriate type of storage to use for your containers.

In the next chapter, we'll learn about Docker networking by learning about the Docker default bridge network. We'll also learn how to use and create user-defined bridges and expose container services on the network.

Questions

1. Which of the following volumes provides persistent storage for containers?

   A. tmpfs

   B. Bind mounts

   C. Volumes

   D. SAN

2. Docker volumes must be created before they can be mounted.

   A. True

   B. False

3. You create a tmpfs volume on a host that has 64 GB of RAM. During its creation, you failed to set a size. What size volume will Docker create?

   A. 1 GB

   B. 64 GB

   C. 20 GB

   D. 32 GB

4. Docker volumes are automatically deleted when you remove a container.

   A. True

   B. False

5. Which volume type is managed by the Docker daemon?

    A. Bind volumes

    B. Named volumes

    C. All volumes

    D. None

6. How do you delete an unused bind volume?

    A. There is no need to; Docker will delete it automatically

    B. `docker volume prune`

    C. `docker volume bind prune`

    D. You must manually delete the bind folder

3
Understanding Docker Networking

So far, we have focused on how to access a container when we are local on the host system. There are use cases where local container access is all that may be required, but often, you will want to expose your containers to external users or systems. Exposing your containers to external users is not always as simple as just running a container. You will need to consider various options that Docker offers to connect your containers to the network. To avoid frustration, you should also understand how systems communicate using IP, including any limitations in regard to exposing IP ports.

In this chapter, we will cover the following topics:

- Exploring Docker networking
- Creating user-defined bridge networks

Let's get started!

Technical requirements

This chapter does not have any technical requirements.

If you want to create networks using the examples in this chapter, you can use the Docker host that we created in *Chapter 1, Docker and Container Essentials*. The networks that we'll be using for the examples in this chapter are not required for future chapters.

You can access the code to create a Docker host from *Chapter 1, Docker and Containers Essentials* by going to the following GitHub repository: `https://github.com/PacktPublishing/Kubernetes-and-Docker-The-Complete-Guide`.

Exploring Docker networking

In this section, we will discuss the networking options that are available in Docker and how you can use them to expose your containers to external users and systems. Docker includes various networking options to connect containers to your network, and if none of the included networking options fit your requirements, you can select from a number of third-party networking add-ons that offer features that may not be included in the base networking stack. By default, Docker networking focuses on a single host, but for more complex use cases, it includes networking features to facilitate cross-host networking by using Docker Swarm. Since the industry has moved away from using Docker Swarm to other offerings such as Kubernetes, this chapter will focus on single-host networking.

To avoid potential frustration when you expose containers, you should have a good understanding of how IP uses ports for communication. Many of you may know IP well, but we thought it would be beneficial to provide a short refresher on how TCP/IP uses ports to communicate.

A quick TCP/IP port refresher

We do assume that you have a working knowledge of TCP/IP, but for those of you who are new to this, it's important to highlight some networking topics that will be referenced in this chapter. Understanding ports is a vital concept to fully understand the limitations of exposing services in Docker.

As you may know, when you configure IP on a system, you assign a unique IP address to each network adapter in the system. When an incoming or outgoing connection is made, the request includes the IP address and a port between `1` and `65535`. You may not always see the port in the request since many applications will automatically include it in the default request, based on the protocol being used. When you are in a browser and enter a URL, you usually just enter the URL using the protocol and hostname. As an example, let's say you want to open the main Kubernetes page, so you enter `http://kubernetes.io` in your browser. What is not shown or required is the port. HTTP has a default port of 80, and all browsers will default the request to use port `80` – behind the scenes, the browser is requesting `http://kubernetes.io:80`.

This combination of the IP address and the port is called a socket, represented as **<IP address>:<port>** (that is, `192.168.1.1:443`). A socket is required for communication that occurs in both directions. When you request a web page, your computer will make an outgoing request using a port that is randomly selected from between `49152` and `65535`. This can be a little confusing if you are new to IP, so the following is an example of a connection from a workstation to two different web servers:

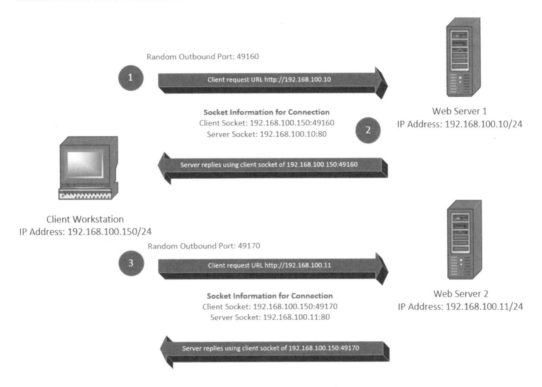

Figure 3.1 – Socket example

In *step 1*, a request is sent to a web server running on `192.168.100.10` from a workstation. The workstation uses a randomly generated port to initiate the outgoing request to the web server on port `80`. Next, in *step 2*, the web server replies to the client using the client IP of `192.168.100.150` on port `49160`.

We added *step 3* to show that a simultaneous connection to another web server will generate a different outgoing port, targeting a second web server on port `80`.

Binding a port to a service

On the server side, where you may be running a server such as NGINX to host a website, you must bind a socket to the web server process. The bound IP address can be a single IP, or it can be bound to all the IP addresses by using an address of 0.0.0.0, which binds the port to all the available IP addresses on the server.

As an example, we will use a host with a single network card and a single IP address. When you want to bind a port to a process, you configure the process so that it uses the IP of the server and an assign a port of 80. We want to highlight a key word in the last sentence, *bind* – by definition, to bind something is to tie or fasten tightly. When you bind a port to an IP address, it is exclusively bound and cannot be bound to any other running process using that IP address. In other words, since the socket has been tied, it cannot be tied to any other process on the host.

If you try to configure a process on a port that has been bound, you will receive an error similar to the following:

```
Bind for 192.168.1.1:443 failed: port is already allocated
```

If you wanted to run another process on the host, you only need to specify a unique port. On the same server running NGINX, you could run a MySQL server running on port 3306. Since the port is different from the web server running on port 80, it creates a unique socket.

How you expose a container using ports differs based on the Docker networking driver you are using for the container. In this chapter, we will explain the common networking options and how to configure and use each of them on your host. Once you understand these options, we will finish this chapter by looking at how to expose your containers to users outside the local host system using port assignments.

To begin, let's start by discussing the various network drivers that Docker includes.

Docker networking drivers

The networking system for Docker is modular. A base Docker installation includes a few network drivers and if you require a specialized networking driver, there are options available from other vendors. For the purpose of this book, we will only use the included networking drivers for our networks.

By default, you have the option of using five networking options. In reality, you have four options with a fifth option of none; that is, to disable networking. The options that are included with Docker are detailed in the following table:

Docker Networking Drivers

Driver Name	Description
Bridge	This is the most commonly used driver on a standalone Docker host system. It is the default driver that will be used if you do not specify another option when you start a container.
Host	If you wanted your containers to access the host network directly, you would use the host driver. This removes the need for your containers to go through a connection controlled by Docker. A container using the host network driver will not get an IP address and does not require exposing ports to allow incoming traffic.
Overlay	An overlay network is used by Docker to connect multiple Docker servers together. It provides a communication path between hosts and containers that is not dependent on the underlying network infrastructure.
Macvlan	The Macvlan is useful for an application that requires a direct connection to the network. It allows you to assign a MAC address to a container, which allows the container to bypass Docker networking. Even though it is bypassing the Docker networking stack, the Docker daemon is still used to route packets to the correct container, based on the MAC address.
None	You may need to disable the network for a container that needs to be used locally or may contain sensitive information. If you set the container network to none, it will not have **any** network access.

Figure 3.2 – Docker networking drivers

A default Docker installation will include a few preconfigured networks:

- A default bridge network
- A default host network
- None

Most Docker users simply use the default bridge network, which will work for most use cases, but it does have some limitations that need to be considered.

In this section, we will go over the default bridge network, a custom bridge network, and the no networking options. The host networking option is primarily used when your host is part of Docker Swarm, but it can be used without Swarm if you understand the limits of how ports are exposed when using it.

The default bridge network

In the preceding table, you learned that a bridge network only provides networking to containers running on the same Docker host. Unless you are running multiple Docker hosts by using Docker Swarm, you will usually use a bridged network with your Docker containers. When you install Docker, it will create what's known as the default Docker bridge network. By supplying the default bridge for all installations, Docker has made using a network in a container very simple. Many users simply start using Docker with the default networking settings and options, thereby starting up containers without knowing the limitations and potential security risks of the default bridge. Before using a Docker host, you should always consider creating a user-defined bridge, or multiple bridges, depending on your requirements.

Docker includes an easy to use default network, so why should you consider creating a user-defined bridge? Since the default bridge maintains backward compatibility, many of the bridge features had to be limited. Due to these limitations, the default bridge is considered to be inferior compared to a user-defined bridge. While that may sound a little harsh, consider the following list, which details items to consider when using the default bridge:

- When a container is started **without** a network specified, it will use the default bridge. This means that multiple containers will be able to communicate by default, without any consideration being given to the workloads.

  Consider: If you are running multiple containers and you want to isolate some containers from others, you may inadvertently allow communications between containers since they are using the default bridge.

- The default bridge limits communications between containers to IP addresses only. Containers connected to user-defined bridges can communicate using container names or IP addresses. Containers that use a user-defined bridge can communicate using IP addresses or host names.

  Consider: When you start up a container, the IP address may be different from the last time you ran the image.

  If you wanted to configure an application that has multiple containers that interact, you can use the container names, which will remain constant through restarts. If you were using the default bridge, you may need to change the configuration files due the containers starting with a different IP address.

- Containers that use the default bridge need to be stopped before you can move them to a different network. However, on a container using a user-defined switch, you can change the network without restarting the container.

  Consider: Depending on your workloads, you may not be able to stop a running container without an agreed maintenance window. While a networking change would still require a change request in most companies, it can be done without stopping the container if you are using a user-defined bridge. This will limit any potential impact to the application and offers a quick failback if something is misconfigured on the new network bridge.

- Using a single default bridge limits networking options for all containers. Since all the containers are on a single network, all networking settings are the same for all containers.

  Consider: You may have a requirement for some containers to run jumbo frames, while other containers will use a standard MTU size. If you only used the single default bridge, you can only set one MTU size. However, you could create a user-defined bridge that sets the MTU to 9000 and another that keeps the default MTU size of 1500.

With this, you can see why we mentioned that the default bridge is inferior to a user-defined bridge. Depending on your use case, you may be able to use the default bridge for all your needs, and for the purposes of this book, we will use the default bridge for our exercises. However, in a production environment running Docker, you should **always** create a new user-defined bridge.

Now that you know about the various networking options and the pros and cons of each type, it's time to dig into managing and creating Docker networks. Before we create a network, we'll take a look at the default networks that Docker includes by default and how to look at the details of a network using the Docker CLI.

Viewing the available networks

To view all the existing networks on a Docker host, we can use the `network` management option in the Docker CLI with the `ls` option. When you execute a list of Docker networks, your output will look similar to the following:

```
[root@localhost ~]# docker network ls
NETWORK ID          NAME                DRIVER              SCOPE
bdf7d93f8545        bridge              bridge              local
9e17e1e628b2        host                host                local
ad0665c8c456        none                null                local
```

Figure 3.3 – Default Docker network list

The preceding list is from a base Docker installation, so only the three default networks options are available.

The `docker network ls` command does not contain a lot of information; it is meant to provide you with a quick summary of the available networks. To dig a little deeper into the details of a network, you can ask Docker to inspect the network, which will provide all the network settings.

Retrieving details on a network

Once you have created multiple user-defined networks, you may start to lose track of the settings for each network, or what containers are running on each network. You can look at the details of each network on the host using the `docker network inspect <network name>` option. The output from an `inspect` command contains detailed information about the network, including the subnet, gateway, driver type, and all connected containers:

```
[
    {
        "Name": "backend",
        "Id": "0ea2374cc48b54daa6fc4f149d0e9db5ff5363f1d78a6be6ebde4ce5e62245de",
        "Created": "2020-03-03T18:55:09.067535801-05:00",
        "Scope": "local",
        "Driver": "bridge",
        "EnableIPv6": false,
        "IPAM": {
            "Driver": "default",
            "Options": {},
            "Config": [
                {
                    "Subnet": "192.168.10.0/24",
                    "Gateway": "192.168.10.1"
                }
            ]
        },
        "Internal": false,
        "Attachable": false,
        "Ingress": false,
        "ConfigFrom": {
            "Network": ""
        },
        "ConfigOnly": false,
        "Containers": {
            "505b3036dad4ec09f01f62d02470ba2980960f33c4e8f972d4e9fe10dd0d9591": {
                "Name": "nginx1",
                "EndpointID": "6fdd84bc9b1ef5ae76483bd02a1fe76f2da3a8b794826a0a9a5c00a93b674e29",
                "MacAddress": "02:42:c0:a8:0a:03",
                "IPv4Address": "192.168.10.3/24",
                "IPv6Address": ""
            },
            "9c72477cf304d8d0a6e8b6184a0da4f99b5b506b7f474bef2892efad45727f7d": {
                "Name": "frontend",
                "EndpointID": "a3e8286247e23a21e6c7350bcb8aef8786cd6bcc8d85f77d4e392ca08c71cdce",
                "MacAddress": "02:42:c0:a8:0a:02",
                "IPv4Address": "192.168.10.2/24",
                "IPv6Address": ""
            }
        },
        "Options": {},
        "Labels": {}
    }
]
```

Figure 3.4 – network inspect output

The preceding screenshot shows that the network is a bridge, but we already know that from the "Driver": "bridge" section of the output. In the containers section of the output, you can see that the bridge has two containers attached to it. The first container is named NGINX1 and has an IP address of 192.168.10.3, while the second container is named frontend and has an IP address of 192.168.10.2. The inspect command also shows the assigned MAC address for each container and, if enabled, the IPV6 address.

Now that you know how to keep track of the networks on the host, let's dive into user-defined bridges.

Creating user-defined bridge networks

When you create a new user-defined network, you can supply most of the standard IP options that you would use when creating a new network outside of Docker. You can set options for the subnet, IP range, and gateway. Remember that the network you define here is only internal to your Docker host and that the IP addresses you assign will not be addressable outside the host. To read about more advanced options, you can visit the advanced Docker networking page at https://docs.docker.com/engine/reference/commandline/network_create/#specify-advanced-options.

To create a user-defined network, we use the network management option in the Docker CLI, along with the create option. The syntax is very simple; you only need to provide the desired network name for the new network and Docker will create the new network. To create a new network called frontend, we simply need to execute the following command:

```
[root@localhost ~]# docker network create frontend
9435231d9c251aa073ede3169728756bdae1d94fb04cd5a2e362ccd15d001343
```

Figure 3.5 – Output from creating a Docker network

This will return the network ID. If you list the networks again, you will see a new bridge network is available:

```
[root@localhost ~]# docker network ls
NETWORK ID          NAME                DRIVER              SCOPE
bdf7d93f8545        bridge              bridge              local
9435231d9c25        frontend            bridge              local
9e17e1e628b2        host                host                local
ad0665c8c456        none                null                local
```

Figure 3.6 – Docker network list

Since we did not specify any options other than the network name, Docker will assign a non-overlapping IP range to the network.

If you wanted to create a second network called backend that used the
192.168.10.0/24 subnet using a gateway of 192.168.10.1, you just need to add
--subnet and --gateway to the docker network create command:

```
[root@localhost ~]# docker network create backend --subnet=192.168.10.0/24 --gateway=192.168.10.1
eac1de9dc37555d2599195670fc295e545f46cad2718434b04e402af19b66a72
```

Figure 3.7 – Adding options example

When you create a new network, like we did for the backend network example, Docker
binds a new IP on the host equal to the gateway address we used in the create
command. The following is the output of using ip addr on our host:

```
inet 192.168.10.1/24 brd 192.168.10.255 scope global br-0ea2374cc48b
```

Figure 3.8 – Host IP added after network creation

This will allow your host to route network traffic to any container that attaches to the
switch. Containers can access network resources outside the host by using the hosts IP
as the default gateway.

Now that you have created a user-defined network, let's look at how to assign the new
network to a container when running an image.

Connecting a container to a user-defined network

You can connect a container to a specific network when starting the container by
adding the --network option to your docker run command. To attach a new
NGINX container to the frontend network we created earlier, we only need to add
--network=frontend when we start the container:

```
[root@localhost ~]# docker run --network=frontend --name nginx1 -d bitnami/nginx:latest
505b3036dad4ec09f01f62d02470ba2980960f33c4e8f972d4e9fe10dd0d9591
```

Figure 3.9 – Connecting a network at startup

The preceding command will start a new NGINX container named frontend, on the
user-defined network named frontend.

Changing the network on a running container

We mentioned that one advantage of using a user-defined network over the default
network was the ability to change the container's network on the fly, without stopping
the container.

To change the network of a running container, you can use the Docker network options known as connect and disconnect, along with the network name and the container name. When you use the connect option, you add a network to the container, while if you use the disconnect option, you remove a network from a container, all without the need to stop the container.

In our NGINX example, we assigned the frontend network, but if we wanted to change that to the backend network, we only need to add one network and remove the other. The first step would be to attach the backend network using the docker network connect command:

```
[root@localhost ~]# docker network connect backend nginx1
```

Figure 3.10 – Connecting a network

This will connect the network named backend to our container named frontend.

The second step is to remove the frontend network using the disconnect option:

```
[root@localhost ~]# docker network disconnect frontend nginx1
```

Figure 3.11 – Disconnecting a network

You may be wondering if you can attach a container to more than one network, and the answer is yes. If you had a requirement for a container to access a network that requires jumbo frames but it also needs to access a standard network connection, you could connect the container to two different user-defined networks. Detailing this scenario is out of scope for this book and can become a complex topic since it may require custom routing to be created in the container, but it's good to know that it can be done and that there are specific use cases for it.

Removing a network

If you no longer need a user-defined network, you can delete the network from your host using the docker network rm <network name> command. To delete the frontend network we created earlier, we would execute the docker network rm command with the network name, frontend:

```
[root@localhost ~]# docker network rm frontend
frontend
```

Figure 3.12 – Removing a network

If you had multiple networks that you wanted to remove, then you can use the `prune` command, which will delete all unused networks on the host. This is similar to pruning the unused volumes. You only need to run `docker network prune` to remove the unused networks:

```
[root@localhost ~]# docker network prune
WARNING! This will remove all networks not used by at least one container.
Are you sure you want to continue? [y/N] y
Deleted Networks:
backend4
```

Figure 3.13 – Pruning a network

Once you've verified you want to continues, Docker will list the networks that were removed. In our example, it removed a network called `network4`.

Just like the `volume prune` command we discussed earlier, **this is a one-way process**. When you select yes to prune the networks, there is no undo, so always be **100%** sure that you want to delete the networks before verifying the action.

Running a container without networking

Remember that if you start a container without a network option, it will start connected to the default bridge network. You might have a requirement to test a container that may contain something suspicious, and having it connected to `network` could put the entire network at risk.

This is no different than the physical world. For example, if you had a machine that appeared to be acting in a malicious manner, you would down the network port or disconnect the network cable. In the container world, we may be running multiple containers on the host and we may not be able to simply pull the cable without effecting many workloads. We have two options available, depending on whether the container is already running, and if it is, you do not want to lose the running state.

If the container is stopped, you could simply start the container without an attached network by using the `--network=none` option when you start the container. This is the same process that you follow when you start a container with a user-defined network, except we specify the network name as `none`.

You may not be able to stop the container if you suspect it has something malicious running. If you needed to look at the running processes, RAM content, and so on, stopping the image would destroy anything running and you may lose valuable information. Rather than stopping and restarting the container using the network value of none, you could just disconnect the running container from the network. This would limit the container's ability to affect anything outside of the local image.

Exposing container services

Now that you know the networking options available in Docker, the next step is to expose any ports you want to accept traffic when you start a container. There are two options when it comes to exposing ports. The first is to use the `host network` option, while the second is to expose the port(s) on a bridge network when the container is started. Using the `host network` option is easier since you do not require any manual port mappings, but this makes it a challenge to keep track of ports as your number of running containers grows. We only suggest using the `host network` option if you plan to run a single container.

Exposing ports using a host network

As we stated in the table provided earlier in this chapter, *"A container using the host network driver will not get an IP address and does not need to expose ports to allow incoming traffic."* Since the container will start up directly on the host network, bypassing Docker's network stack completely, you do not need to expose any ports for the container.

As an example, to start a web server running NGINX on the host, using host networking, you would run the `docker run` command while providing `host` as the network type:

```
surovich@kind:~$ sudo docker run --network=host --name nginx -d bitnami/nginx:latest
aa2f7df70ff85021f7c039e5f4f93c525738e3448c6b39e66114373d7108414e
```

Figure 3.14 – Using the host network option

We want to verify the container is running and to look at any ports that may be exposed, so we'll run `docker ps` to list the running containers. The container shows as running, but under `PORTS`, we don't see anything listed:

```
PORTS                      NAMES
                           nginx
```

Figure 3.15 – Example port view from a host connection

Since the container was started using the `host network` option, we do not need to expose any ports. The NGINX container that we have been using runs on port `8080`, and since it bypasses Docker networking, the only method to prove it's using port `8080` is to run `netstat` on the host system:

```
Active Internet connections (servers and established)
Proto Recv-Q Send-Q Local Address          Foreign Address        State
tcp        0      0 0.0.0.0:8080           0.0.0.0:*              LISTEN
```

Figure 3.16 – Host netstat showing port 8080 in use

It looks like the container is running and listening on port 8080. From another machine on the network, we can open a browser and enter the IP address of the Docker host machine and use port 8080:

Welcome to nginx!

If you see this page, the nginx web server is successfully installed and working. Further configuration is required.

For online documentation and support please refer to nginx.org. Commercial support is available at nginx.com.

Thank you for using nginx.

Figure 3.17 – NGINX running on a host network

Here, we received the welcome page from NGINX, proving that the container is running.

Since the `docker ps` command did not list the ports that are in use, you can see where you may start to lose track of the assigned ports if your host is running multiple containers when using the `host network` option. This is why we suggest limiting use of the `host network` option, unless you are running a single container or a container that requires host networking.

> **Important Note**
>
> As we have stated, a socket must be unique on the host. In our example, we have been using a single NIC and a single IP address, which means a port can only be used one on the host. Since a socket is a combination of the IP address and the port, you could add a second IP address to the single NIC or add an additional NIC with a new IP address to create a new, unique socket. This will allow you to create a new binding of an already assigned port to another process since the socket will be unique.

Now, let's stop the NGINX container and look at `netstat` again to show that the port is no longer in use. We will use the following commands:

```
sudo docker stop nginx
sudo docker rm nginx
```

Then, we'll use netstat to show the active ports:

```
Active Internet connections (w/o servers)
Proto Recv-Q Send-Q Local Address          Foreign Address          State
tcp        0     64 10.2.1.145:ssh         10.2.1.125:33387         ESTABLISHED
```

Figure 3.18 – Host netstat showing port 8080 is not in use

As you can see, the only port open on the host is SSH; port 8080 has been closed since the container has been stopped.

Exposing ports using a bridge network

It may seem that using the host network option makes exposing ports easy, since you don't need to actually do anything to expose them. This may seem attractive initially, but if you were running multiple containers on a host and more than one was configured to run on the same port, such as port 8080 for our NGINX container, you would be limited to a single container due to the port conflict.

When an option seems easier, it is usually less robust or configurable, which is why it seems easier at the beginning. This is the case when exposing ports using host networking versus bridged networking, but once you understand how and why we expose ports using bridge networks, you will see why it offers a better all-round solution.

When you want to expose ports on a container that is using a bridge network, you only need to specify the ports you want to open when starting the container. If you have more than one bridge, you will need to provide the network name as well, but in our example, we will assume you are using the built-in bridge network.

When you expose a port in Docker, you need to supply the incoming (Docker host) port and the destination (the container) port using the incoming port:destination port syntax. Often, the numbers will be the same to keep things simple, but there will be scenarios where using a different port may be required.

If you only supply a port for the destination, a TCP connection will be assumed. You may need to expose UDP ports for a container, and to expose the port as a UDP port, just add /udp to the destination port assignment. So, your syntax would become incoming port:destination port/udp.

Using our example web server, we'll start the container using the default bridge network listening on port 8080 using the docker run command with the -p option for the port; that is, docker run -p 8080:8080 -p 8443:8443:

```
surovich@kind:~$ sudo docker run -p 8080:8080 --name nginx -d bitnami/nginx:latest
6e3d098d632343bd6062f2abbcc28b67643406900a77de56bc92cbc7d5f78579
```

Figure 3.19 – Exposing port 8080

To verify the container is running, we will use the docker ps command and take note of the PORTS column, which shows the mapped port(s) for the container:

```
PORTS
0.0.0.0:8080->8080/tcp, 0.0.0.0:8443->8443/tcp
```

Figure 3.20 – docker ps output showing assigned ports

Here, we can see that the container is running and that we have mapped the incoming host ports 8080 and 8443 to the container ports 8080 and 8443. Any incoming request to the Docker host on 8080 and 8443, on any interface (0.0.0.0), will be forwarded to the container.

Just like when we used the host network, we can see that the host is listening on both 8080 and 8443 using netstat:

```
Active Internet connections (servers and established)
Proto Recv-Q Send-Q Local Address           Foreign Address         State
tcp        0      0 0.0.0.0:22              0.0.0.0:*               LISTEN
tcp        0     64 10.2.1.145:22           10.2.1.125:33387        ESTABLISHED
tcp6       0      0 :::8080                 :::*                    LISTEN
tcp6       0      0 :::22                   :::*                    LISTEN
tcp6       0      0 :::8443                 :::*                    LISTEN
```

Figure 3.21 – Host netstat showing port 8080

Your project now calls for a second web server for another development site, and you want to deploy another NGINX container. The image uses ports 8080 and 8443 but both of those ports are in use by our first NGINX container. Attempting to run another container using 8080 and 8443 on the host will result in a port already allocated error:

```
surovich@kind:~$ sudo docker run -p 8080:8080 -p 8443:8443 --name nginx2 -d bitn
ami/nginx:latest
5262ec823d3bfa3dbabf8bafe0b5ce5e7097b97fe60d4aa3de5d225f196fdb4d
docker: Error response from daemon: driver failed programming external connectiv
ity on endpoint nginx2 (e9d5b4735153099d2761fde82397202d7d6270937b421ab4301ae5d6
0c211e3b): Bind for 0.0.0.0:8443 failed: port is already allocated.
```

Figure 3.22 – Port conflict example

One solution would be to create another container that listens on different ports, such as 8081 and 8444, but that starts to become difficult to maintain. Instead, remember that when you expose a port, you designate the incoming and the destination ports. We want to use the same NGINX image, so we can't change the container ports, but we can change the incoming ports on the host. When we start our second container, we will increase each port by one to avoid conflicts with the existing 8080 and 8443 rules, but we will still forward the ports to 8080 and 8433 on the new container. This may sound confusing, so it's easier to see an example docker run command; that is, docker run -p 8081:8080 -p 80444:8443 –name nginx2 bitnami/nginx:latest:

```
surovich@kind:~$ sudo docker run -p 8081:8080 -p 8444:8443 --name nginx2 -d bitnami/nginx:latest
9513e1c5821e9b77d286f7522bcee3b91eb87f430b745335f639f9d8fccf8b75
```

Figure 3.23 – Example of assigning ports 8081 and 8443

Since Docker returned the new container ID, we can see that, by increasing the incoming ports by one, we no longer have any conflicting ports.

Listing the currently running containers will show both NGINX containers and the port mappings:

```
surovich@kind:~$ sudo docker ps
CONTAINER ID       IMAGE                COMMAND            CREATED          STATUS              PORTS
                                        NAMES
9513e1c5821e       bitnami/nginx:latest "/entrypoint.sh /run…" 2 minutes ago    Up 2 minutes        0.0.0.0
:8081->8080/tcp, 0.0.0.0:8444->8443/tcp  nginx2
32d0bb32f337       bitnami/nginx:latest "/entrypoint.sh /run…" About an hour ago Up About an hour    0.0.0.0
:8080->8080/tcp, 0.0.0.0:8443->8443/tcp  nginx
```

Figure 3.24 – docker ps showing both running NGINX servers

Browsing to the host from another machine on the network on port 8081 will show the default NGINX welcome page:

←   →   C   ⓘ Not secure | 10.2.1.145:8081

Welcome to nginx!

If you see this page, the nginx web server is successfully installed and working. Further configuration is required.

For online documentation and support please refer to nginx.org.
Commercial support is available at nginx.com.

Thank you for using nginx.

Figure 3.25 – Browsing example to NGINX on port 8081

Looking at netstat, we can see that all four ports are listening on the host:

```
Active Internet connections (servers and established)
Proto Recv-Q Send-Q Local Address          Foreign Address         State
tcp        0      0 0.0.0.0:22             0.0.0.0:*               LISTEN
tcp        0     64 10.2.1.145:22          10.2.1.125:33387        ESTABLISHED
tcp6       0      0 :::8080                :::*                    LISTEN
tcp6       0      0 :::8081                :::*                    LISTEN
tcp6       0      0 :::22                  :::*                    LISTEN
tcp6       0      0 :::8443                :::*                    LISTEN
tcp6       0      0 :::8444                :::*                    LISTEN
udp        0      0 0.0.0.0:68             0.0.0.0:*
```

Figure 3.26 – Host netstat showing the four assigned NGINX ports

If you needed to run another NGINX container, you would just use another host port, potentially 8082 or 8445. The main takeaway is that the incoming port on the host must be unique to avoid port conflicts. The container's port can be the same since each container runs in its own namespace and each has its own resources and ports.

Summary

In this chapter, you learned about IP sockets and how hosts use ports to make a connection to a server. You learned that a socket is a combination of an IP address and the port and that it must be unique on the host. We then covered each networking type provided by Docker and use cases for each one, as well as when to use the default bridge network, a custom bridge network, host network, or no networking. Finally, you learned how to expose containers to external users.

In the next chapter, we'll begin to explore Kubernetes by exploring the Kubernetes cluster, looking at its control plane, understanding the differences between a kublet and an API, learning how the worker node functions, and reviewing over 25 Kubernetes objects.

Questions

1. Since Docker creates a default bridge network, there is no reason to create a custom bridge.

    A. True

    B. False

2. Which of the following is an example of a socket?

    A. http:192.168.100.10

    B. 192.168.100.10

    C. 192.168.100.10:80

    D. https://192.168.100.10

3. How would you start a container running a web server on port 8080 named
    nginx-web on a host that already has its host port (8080) bound to another
    container?

    A. docker run -d nginx-web bitnami/nginx

    B. docker run -p 8080:8080 -d nginx-web bitnami/nginx -
    force

    C. docker run -p 8081:8080 -d nginx-web bitnami/nginx

    D. Since port 8080 is bound on the host, you cannot run a container on port 8080

4. You suspect an image may contain malware. You need to run the image safely to
    look at its contents. What Docker command will mitigate any network impact?

    A. docker run -isolate -it badimage bash

    B. docker run -p 0:0 -it badimage bash

    C. docker run -it badimage bash

    D. docker run --network=none -it badimage bash

5. Once a container is connected to a custom bridge network, you cannot change the
    connected network.

    A. True

    B. False

6. What is the highest IP port number you can expose on a container?

    A. There is no limit

    B. 65535

    C. 65530

    D. 65532

    E. 65435

Section 2: Creating Kubernetes Development Clusters, Understanding objects, and Exposing Services

In this second section, we will move onto Kubernetes clusters and objects. The first chapter in this section will explain how to use a popular tool for creating Kubernetes clusters, called KinD. We will explain how to create differnet clusters that range from a single-node cluster to a multiple-node cluster that uses HAProxy as a load balancer for the worker nodes. With a working Kubernetes cluster, we move onto the next chapter, which will review the Kubernetes infrastructure components and the most commonly used Kubernetes objects. We close out this section by explaining a commonly misunderstood topic, exposing services in a cluster. We will look at Kubernetes service types, discuss how to use Layer 7 and Layer 4 load balancers, and see how to register dynamic names for services using External-DNS.

This part of the book comprises the following chapters:

4
Deploying Kubernetes Using KinD

One of the largest obstacles to learning Kubernetes is having enough resources to create a cluster for testing or development. Like most IT professionals, we like to have a Kubernetes cluster on our laptops for demonstrations and for testing products in general.

Often, you may have a need to run multiple clusters for a complex demonstration, such as a multi-cluster service mesh or testing kubefed2. These scenarios would require multiple servers to create the necessary clusters, which, in turn, would require a lot of RAM and a hypervisor.

To do full testing on a multiple cluster scenario, you would need to create six nodes for each cluster. If you created the clusters using virtual machines, you would need to have enough resources to run 6 virtual machines. Each of the machines would have an overhead including disk space, memory, and CPU utilization.

But what if you could create a cluster using just containers? Using containers, rather than full virtual machines, will give you the ability to run additional nodes due to the reduced system requirements, create and delete clusters in minutes with a single command, script cluster creation, and allow you to run multiple clusters on a single host.

Using containers to run a Kubernetes cluster provides you with an environment that would be difficult for most people to deploy using virtual machines, or physical hardware due to resource constraints. To explain how to run a cluster using only containers locally, we will use KinD to create a Kubernetes cluster on your Docker host. We will deploy a multi-node cluster that you will use in future chapters to test and deploy components such as Ingress controllers, authentication, RBAC, security policies, and more.

In this chapter, we will cover the following topics:

- Introducing Kubernetes components and objects
- Using development clusters
- Installing KinD
- Creating a KinD cluster
- Reviewing your KinD cluster
- Adding a custom load balancer for Ingress

Let's get started!

Technical requirements

This chapter has the following technical requirements:

- A Docker host installed using the steps from *Chapter 1, Docker and Container Essentials*
- Installation scripts from this book's GitHub repository

You can access the code for this chapter by going to this book's GitHub repository: `https://github.com/PacktPublishing/Kubernetes-and-Docker-The-Complete-Guide`.

> **Note**
>
> We thought it was important to point out that this chapter will reference multiple Kubernetes objects, some without a lot of context. *Chapter 5, Kubernetes Bootcamp*, goes over Kubernetes objects in detail, many with commands you can use to understand them, so we thought having a cluster to use while reading about this would be useful.
>
> Most of the base Kubernetes topics covered in this chapter will be discussed in future chapters, so if some topics are a bit foggy after you've read this chapter, don't fear! They will be discussed in detail in later chapters.

Introducing Kubernetes components and objects

Since this chapter will refer to common Kubernetes objects and components, we wanted to provide a short table of terms that you will see and a brief definition of each to provide context.

In *Chapter 5*, *Kubernetes Bootcamp*, we will go over the components of Kubernetes and the base set of objects that are included in a cluster. We will also discuss how to interact with a cluster using the kubectl executable:

Component	Description
Control Plane	API-Server:Frontend of the control plane that accepts requests from clients.
	kube-scheduler: Assigns workloads to nodes.
	etcd: Database that contains all cluster data.
	kube-controller-manager: Watches for node health, pod replicas, endpoints, service accounts, and tokens.
Node	kubelet: The agent that runs a pod based on instructions from the control plane.
	kube-proxy: Creates and deletes network rules for pod communication.
	Container runtime: Component responsible for running a container.
Object	**Description**
Container	A single immutable image that contains everything needed to run an application.
Pod	The smallest object that Kubernetes can control. A pod holds a container, or multiple containers. All containers in a pod are scheduled on the same server in a shared context (that is, each container in a pod can address other pods using 127.0.0.1).
Deployment	Used to deploy an application to a cluster based on a desired state, including the number of pods and rolling update configuration.
Storage Class	Defines storage providers and presents them to the cluster.
Persistent Volume (PV)	Provides a storage target that can be claimed by a Persistent Volume Request.
Persistent Volume Claim (PVC)	Connects (claims) a Persistent Volume so that it can be used inside a pod.
Container Network Interface (CNI)	Provides the network connection for pods. Common CNI examples include Flannel and Calico.
Container Storage Interface (CSI)	Provides the connection between pods and storage systems.

Table 4.1 – Kubernetes components and objects

While these are only a few of the objects that are available in a Kubernetes cluster, they are the main objects we will mention in this chapter. Knowing what each object is and having basic knowledge of their functionality will help you understand this chapter and deploy a KinD cluster.

Interacting with a cluster

To test our KinD installation, we will interact with the cluster using the kubectl executable. We will go over kubectl in *Chapter 5, Kubernetes Bootcamp*, but since we will be using a few commands in this chapter, we wanted to provide the commands we will use in a table with an explanation of what the options provide:

Kubectl command	Description
`kubectl get <object>`	Retrieves a list of the requested object. Example: `kubectl get nodes`.
`kubectl create -f <manifest-name>`	Creates the objects in the `include` manifest that is provided. `create` can only create the initial objects; it cannot update the objects.
`kubectl apply -f <manifest-name>`	Deploys the objects in the `include` manifest that is provided. Unlike the `create` option, the `apply` command can update objects, as well as create objects.
`kubectl patch <object-type> <object-name> -p {patching options}`	Patches the supplied `object-type` with the options provided.

Table 4.2 – Basic kubectl commands

In this chapter, you will use these basic commands to deploy parts of the cluster that we will use throughout this book.

Next, we will introduce the concept of development clusters and then focus on one of the most popular tools used to create development clusters: KinD.

Using development clusters

Over the years, various tools have been created to install development Kubernetes clusters, allowing admins and developers to perform testing on a local system. Many of these tools worked for basic Kubernetes tests, but they often had limitations that made them less than ideal for quick, advanced scenarios.

Some of the most common solutions available are as follows:

- Docker Desktop
- minikube
- kubeadm

Each solution has benefits, limitations, and use cases. Some solutions limit you to a single node that runs both the control plane and worker nodes. Others offer multi-node support but require additional resources to create multiple virtual machines. Depending on your development or testing requirements, these solutions may not fill your needs completely.

It seems that a new solution is coming out every few weeks, and one of the newest options for creating development clusters is a project from a **Kubernetes in Docker (KinD)** Kubernetes SIG.

Using a single host, KinD allows you to create multiple clusters, and each cluster can have multiple control plane and worker nodes. The ability to run multiple nodes allows advanced testing that would have required more resources using another solution. KinD has been very well received by the community and has an active Git community at `https://github.com/kubernetes-sigs/kind`, as well as a Slack channel (*#kind*).

> **Note**
>
> Do not use KinD as a production cluster or expose a KinD cluster to the internet. While KinD clusters offer most of the same features you would want in a production cluster, it has **not** been designed for production environments.

Why did we select KinD for this book?

When we started this book, we wanted to include theory, as well as hands-on experience. KinD allows us to provide scripts to spin up and spin down clusters, and while other solutions can do something similar, KinD can create a new multi-node cluster in minutes. We wanted to separate the control plane and worker nodes to provide a more "realistic" cluster. In order to limit the hardware requirements and to make Ingress easier to configure, we will only create a two-node cluster for the exercises in this book.

A multi-node cluster can be created in a few minutes and once testing has been completed, clusters can be torn down in a few seconds. The ability to spin up and spin down clusters makes KinD the perfect platform for our exercises. KinD's requirements are simple: you only need a running Docker daemon to create a cluster. This means that it is compatible with most operating systems, including the following:

- Linux
- macOS running Docker Desktop
- Windows running Docker Desktop
- Windows running WSL2

> **Important note**
> At the time of writing, KinD does not offer support for Chrome OS.

While KinD supports most operating systems, we have selected Ubuntu 18.04 as our host system. Some of the exercises in this book require files to be in specific directories and selecting a single Linux version helps us make sure the exercises work as designed. If you do not have access to an Ubuntu server at home, you can create a virtual machine in a cloud provider such as GCP. Google offers $300 in credit, which is more than enough to run a single Ubuntu server for a few weeks. You can view GCP's free options at `https://cloud.google.com/free/`.

Now, let's explain how KinD works and what a base KinD Kubernetes cluster looks like.

Working with a base KinD Kubernetes cluster

At a high level, you can think of a KinD cluster as consisting of a **single** Docker container that runs a control plane node and a worker node to create a Kubernetes cluster. To make the deployment easy and robust, KinD bundles every Kubernetes object into a single image, known as a node image. This node image contains all the required Kubernetes components to create a single-node cluster, or a multi-node cluster.

Once a cluster is running, you can use Docker to exec into a control plane node container and look at the process list. In the process list, you will see the standard Kubernetes components for the control plane nodes running:

```
UID        PID  PPID  C STIME  TTY          TIME CMD
root         1     0  0 12:34  ?        00:00:00 /sbin/init
root        70     1  0 12:34  ?        00:00:00 /lib/systemd/systemd-journald
root        79     1  0 12:34  ?        00:00:22 /usr/local/bin/containerd
root       794     1  1 12:35  ?        00:00:55 /usr/bin/kubelet --bootstrap-kubeconfig=/etc/kube
root       845     1  0 12:35  ?        00:00:00 /usr/local/bin/containerd-shim-runc-v2 -namespace
root       866   845  0 12:35  ?        00:00:00 /pause
root       893     1  0 12:35  ?        00:00:00 /usr/local/bin/containerd-shim-runc-v2 -namespace
root       919   893  0 12:35  ?        00:00:00 /pause
root       958   845  0 12:35  ?        00:00:01 /bin/kindnetd
root      1008   893  0 12:35  ?        00:00:01 /usr/local/bin/kube-proxy --config=/var/lib/kube-
root      1076     1  0 12:35  ?        00:00:00 /usr/local/bin/containerd-shim-runc-v2 -namespace
root      1098  1076  0 12:35  ?        00:00:00 /pause
root      1124     1  0 12:35  ?        00:00:00 /usr/local/bin/containerd-shim-runc-v2 -namespace
root      1149  1124  0 12:35  ?        00:00:00 /pause
root      1170     1  0 12:35  ?        00:00:00 /usr/local/bin/containerd-shim-runc-v2 -namespace
root      1191  1170  0 12:35  ?        00:00:00 /pause
root      1216     1  0 12:35  ?        00:00:00 /usr/local/bin/containerd-shim-runc-v2 -namespace
root      1240  1216  0 12:35  ?        00:00:00 /pause
root      1271  1076  0 12:35  ?        00:00:13 kube-scheduler --authentication-kubeconfig=/etc/
root      1328  1124  3 12:35  ?        00:02:05 kube-apiserver --advertise-address=172.17.0.6 --
root      1366  1170  0 12:35  ?        00:00:06 kube-controller-manager --allocate-node-cidrs=tr
root      1425  1216  3 12:35  ?        00:02:00 etcd --advertise-client-urls=https://172.17.0.6:
```

Figure 4.1 – Host process list showing control plane components

If you were to exec into a worker node to check the components, you would see all the standard worker node components:

```
UID        PID  PPID  C STIME  TTY          TIME CMD
root         1     0  0 12:34  ?        00:00:00 /sbin/init
root        72     1  0 12:34  ?        00:00:00 /lib/systemd/systemd-journald
root        79     1  0 12:34  ?        00:00:13 /usr/local/bin/containerd
root      1291     1  0 12:36  ?        00:00:35 /usr/bin/kubelet --bootstrap-kubeconfig=/etc/kube
root      1343     1  0 12:37  ?        00:00:00 /usr/local/bin/containerd-shim-runc-v2 -namespace
root      1373     1  0 12:37  ?        00:00:00 /usr/local/bin/containerd-shim-runc-v2 -namespace
root      1397  1343  0 12:37  ?        00:00:00 /pause
root      1404  1373  0 12:37  ?        00:00:00 /pause
root      1461  1373  0 12:37  ?        00:00:01 /bin/kindnetd
root      1467  1343  0 12:37  ?        00:00:01 /usr/local/bin/kube-proxy --config=/var/lib/kube-
root      3508     0  0 13:38  pts/1    00:00:00 bash
root      3516  3508  0 13:38  pts/1    00:00:00 ps -ef
```

Figure 4.2 – Host process list showing worker components

We will cover the standard Kubernetes components in *Chapter 5, Kubernetes Bootcamp*, including kube-apiserver, kubelets, kube-proxy, kube-scheduler, and kube-controller-manager.

In addition to standard Kubernetes components, both KinD nodes have an additional component that is not part of most standard installations: Kindnet. Kindnet is the included, default CNI when you install a base KinD cluster. While Kindnet is the default CNI, you have the option to disable it and use an alternative, such as Calico.

Now that you have seen each node and the Kubernetes components, let's take a look at what's included with a base KinD cluster. To show the complete cluster and all the components that are running, we can run the `kubectl get pods --all-namespaces` command. This will list all the running components for the cluster, including the base components we will discuss in *Chapter 5, Kubernetes Bootcamp*. In addition to the base cluster components, you may notice a running pod in a namespace called `local-path-storage`, along with a pod named `local-path-provisioner`. This pod is running one of the add-ons that KinD includes, providing the cluster with the ability to auto-provision `PersistentVolumeClaims`:

```
NAMESPACE            NAME                                              READY   STATUS    RESTARTS   AGE
kube-system          coredns-6955765f44-425sl                          1/1    Running   0          68m
kube-system          coredns-6955765f44-sclfh                          1/1    Running   0          68m
kube-system          etcd-config2-control-plane                        1/1    Running   0          68m
kube-system          etcd-config2-control-plane2                       1/1    Running   0          68m
kube-system          etcd-config2-control-plane3                       1/1    Running   0          67m
kube-system          kindnet-4lzz5                                      1/1    Running   0          68m
kube-system          kindnet-blcwt                                      1/1    Running   0          68m
kube-system          kindnet-bp6jj                                      1/1    Running   0          66m
kube-system          kindnet-p2jw8                                      1/1    Running   0          67m
kube-system          kindnet-pl2gg                                      1/1    Running   0          66m
kube-system          kindnet-vfcpm                                      1/1    Running   0          66m
kube-system          kube-apiserver-config2-control-plane              1/1    Running   0          68m
kube-system          kube-apiserver-config2-control-plane2             1/1    Running   0          68m
kube-system          kube-apiserver-config2-control-plane3             1/1    Running   1          67m
kube-system          kube-controller-manager-config2-control-plane     1/1    Running   1          68m
kube-system          kube-controller-manager-config2-control-plane2    1/1    Running   0          68m
kube-system          kube-controller-manager-config2-control-plane3    1/1    Running   0          66m
kube-system          kube-proxy-c77z6                                  1/1    Running   0          66m
kube-system          kube-proxy-fvvbb                                  1/1    Running   0          68m
kube-system          kube-proxy-llfpl                                  1/1    Running   0          66m
kube-system          kube-proxy-lpfnw                                  1/1    Running   0          68m
kube-system          kube-proxy-pfk46                                  1/1    Running   0          67m
kube-system          kube-proxy-rd26p                                  1/1    Running   0          66m
kube-system          kube-scheduler-config2-control-plane              1/1    Running   1          68m
kube-system          kube-scheduler-config2-control-plane2             1/1    Running   0          68m
kube-system          kube-scheduler-config2-control-plane3             1/1    Running   0          66m
local-path-storage   local-path-provisioner-7745554f7f-g5mj8           1/1    Running   1          68m
```

Figure 4.3 – kubectl get pods showing local-path-provisioner

Most development cluster offerings provide similar, common functions that people need to test deployments on Kubernetes. They all provide a Kubernetes control plane and worker nodes, and most include a default CNI for networking. Few offerings go beyond this base functionality, and as Kubernetes workloads mature, you may find the need for additional plugins such as `local-path-provisioner`. We will leverage this component heavily in some of the exercises in this book because without it, we will have a tougher time creating some of the procedures.

Why should you care about persistent volumes in your development cluster? Most production clusters running Kubernetes will provide persistent storage to developers. Usually, the storage will be backed by storage systems based on block storage, S3, or NFS. Aside from NFS, most home labs rarely have the resources to run a full-featured storage system. `local-path-provisioner` removes this limitation from users by providing all the functions to your KinD cluster that an expensive storage solution would provide.

In *Chapter 5, Kubernetes Bootcamp*, we will discuss a few API objects that are part of Kubernetes storage. We will discuss the `CSIdrivers`, `CSInodes`, and `StorageClass` objects. These objects are used by the cluster to provide access to the backend storage system. Once installed and configured, pods consume the storage using the `PersistentVolumes` and `PersistentVolumeClaims` objects. Storage objects are important to understand, but when they were first released, they were difficult for most people to test since they aren't included in most Kubernetes development offerings.

KinD recognized this limitation and chose to bundle a project from Rancher called `local-path-provisioner`, which is based on the Kubernetes local persistent volumes that were introduced in Kubernetes 1.10.

You may be wondering why anyone would need an add-on since Kubernetes has native support for local host persistent volumes. While support may have been added for local persistent storage, Kubernetes has not added auto-provisioning capabilities. CNCF does offer an auto-provisioner, but it must be installed and configured as a separate Kubernetes component. KinD makes it easy to auto-provision since the provisioner is included in all base installations.

Rancher's project provides the following to KinD:

- Auto-creation of `PersistentVolumes` when a PVC request is created
- A default `StorageClass` named standard

When the auto-provisioner sees a `PersistentVolumeClaim` request hit the API server, a `PersistentVolume` will be created and the pod's PVC will be bound to the newly created PVC.

`local-path-provisioner` adds a feature to KinD clusters that greatly expands the potential test scenarios that you can run. Without the ability to auto-provision persistent disks, it would be a challenge to test many pre-built deployments that require persistent disks.

With the help of Rancher, KinD provides you with a solution so that you can experiment with dynamic volumes, storage classes, and other storage tests that would otherwise be impossible to run outside a data center. We will use the provisioner in multiple chapters to provide volumes to different deployments. We will point these out to reinforce the advantages of using auto-provisioning.

Understanding the node image

The node image is what provides KinD the magic to run Kubernetes inside a Docker container. This is an impressive accomplishment since Docker relies on a `systemd` running system and other components that are not included in most container images.

KinD starts off with a base image, which is an image the team has developed that contains everything required for Docker, Kubernetes, and `systemd`. Since the base image is based on an Ubuntu image, the team removes services that are not required and configures `systemd` for Docker. Finally, the node image is created using the base image.

> **Tip**
>
> If you want to know the details of how the base image is created, you can look at the Dockerfile in the KinD team's GitHub repository at `https://github.com/kubernetes-sigs/kind/blob/control plane/images/base/Dockerfile`.

KinD and Docker networking

Since KinD uses Docker as the container engine to run the cluster nodes, all clusters are limited to the same network constraints that a standard Docker container is. In *Chapter 3, Understanding Docker Networking*, we had a refresher on Docker networking and the potential limitations of Docker's default networking stack. These limitations do not limit testing your KinD Kubernetes cluster from the local host, but they can lead to issues when you want to test containers from other machines on your network.

Along with the Docker networking considerations, we must consider the Kubernetes **Container Network Interface (CNI)** as well. Officially, the KinD team has limited the networking options to only two CNIs: Kindnet and Calico. Kindnet is the only CNI they will support but you do have the option to disable the default Kindnet installation, which will create a cluster without a CNI installed. After the cluster has been deployed, you can deploy a CNI manifest such as Calico.

Many Kubernetes installations for both small development clusters and enterprise clusters use Tigera's Calico for the CNI and as such, we have elected to use Calico as our CNI for the exercises in this book.

Keeping track of the nesting dolls

Running a solution such as KinD can get confusing due to the container-in-a-container deployment. We compare this to Russian nesting dolls, where one doll fits into another, then another, and so on. As you start to play with KinD for your own cluster, you may lose track of the communication paths between your host, Docker, and the Kubernetes nodes. To keep your sanity, you should have a solid understanding of where each component is running and how you can interact with each one.

The following diagram shows the three layers that must be running to form a KinD cluster. It's important to note that each layer can only interact with the layer directly above it. This means that the KinD container in layer 3 can only see the Docker image running in layer 2, and the Docker image can see the Linux host running in layer 1. If you wanted to communicate directly from the host to a container running in your KinD cluster, you would need to go through the Docker layer, and then to the Kubernetes container in layer 3.

This is important to understand so that you can use KinD effectively as a testing environment:

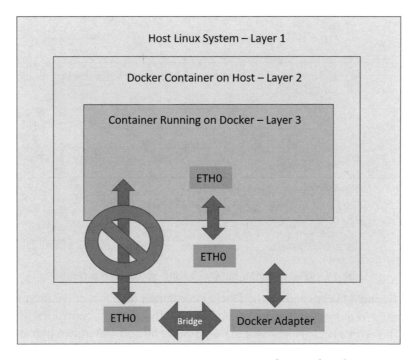

Figure 4.4 – Host cannot communicate with KinD directly

As an example, consider that you want to deploy a web server to your Kubernetes cluster. You deploy an Ingress controller in the KinD cluster and you want to test the site using Chrome on your Docker host or a different workstation on the network. You attempt to target the host on port 80 and receive a failure in the browser. Why would this fail?

The pod running the web server is in layer 3 and cannot receive direct traffic from the host or machines on the network. In order to access the web server from your host, you will need to forward the traffic from the Docker layer to the KinD layer. Remember that in *Chapter 3, Understanding Docker Networking*, we explained how to expose a container to the network by adding a listening port to the container. In our case, we need port 80 and port 443. When a container is started with a port, the Docker daemon will forward the incoming traffic from the host to the running Docker container:

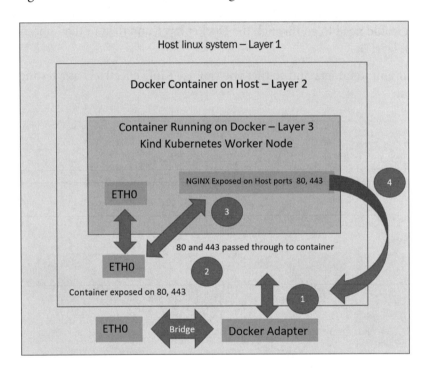

Figure 4.5 – Host communicates with KinD via an Ingress controller

With ports 80 and 443 exposed on the Docker container, the Docker daemon will now accept incoming requests for 80 and 443 and the NGINX Ingress controller will receive the traffic. This works because we have exposed ports 80 and 443 in two places on the Docker layer. We have exposed it in the Kubernetes layer by running our NGINX container using host ports 80 and 443. This installation process will be explained later in this chapter, but for now, you just need to understand the basic flow.

On the host, you make a request for a web server that has an Ingress rule in your Kubernetes cluster:

1. The request looks at the IP address that was requested (in this case, the local IP address).

2. The Docker container running our Kubernetes node is listening on the IP address for ports 80 and 443, so the request is accepted and sent to the running container.

3. The NGINX pod in your Kubernetes cluster has been configured to use the host ports 80 and 443, so the traffic is forwarded to the pod.

4. The user receives the requested web page from the web server via the NGINX Ingress controller.

This is a little confusing, but the more you use KinD and interact with it, the easier this becomes.

To use a KinD cluster for your development requirements, you need to understand how KinD works. So far, you have learned about the node image and how the image is used to create a cluster. You've also learned how KinD network traffic flows between the Docker host and the containers running the cluster. With this base knowledge, we will move on to creating a Kubernetes cluster using KinD.

Installing KinD

The files for this chapter are located in the KinD directory. You can use the provided files, or you can create your own files from this chapter's content. We will explain each step of the installation process in this section.

Note

At the time of writing, the current version of KinD is .0.8.1. Version .0.8.0 introduced a new feature; that is, maintaining cluster state between reboot and Docker restarts.

Installing KinD – prerequisites

KinD requires a few prerequisites before you can create a cluster. In this section, we will detail each requirement and what how to install each component.

Installing Kubectl

Since KinD is a single executable, it does not install kubectl. If you do not have kubectl installed and you are using an Ubuntu 18.04 system, you can install it by running a snap install:

```
sudo snap install kubectl --classic
```

Installing Go

Before we can create a KinD cluster, you will need to install Go on your host. If you already have Go installed and working, you can skip this step. Installing Go requires you to download the Go archive, extract the executable, and set a project path. The following commands can be used to install Go on your machine.

The script to install Go can be executed from this book's repository by running /chapter4/install-go.sh:

```
wget https://dl.google.com/go/go1.13.3.linux-amd64.tar.gz
tar -xzf go1.13.3.linux-amd64.tar.gz
sudo mv go /usr/local
mkdir -p $HOME/Projects/Project1


cat << 'EOF' >> ~/.bash_profile
export -p GOROOT=/usr/local/go
    export -p GOPATH=$HOME/Projects/Project1
export -p PATH=$GOPATH/bin:$GOROOT/bin:$PATH
EOF
source ~/.bash_profile
```

The commands in the preceding list will do the following:

- Download Go to your host, uncompress the archive, and move the files to /usr/local.

- Create a Go project folder in your home directory called Projects/Project1.

- Add Go environment variables to .bash_profile, which are required to execute Go applications.

Now that you have the prerequisites in place, we can move on to installing KinD.

Installing the KinD binary

Installing KinD is an easy process; it can be done with a single command. You can install KinD by running the included script in this book's repository, located at /chapter4/ install-kind.sh. Alternatively, you can execute the following command:

```
GO111MODULE="on" go get sigs.k8s.io/kind@v0.7.0
```

Once installed, you can verify that KinD has been installed correctly by typing kind version into the prompt:

```
kind version
```

This will return the installed version:

```
kind v0.7.0 go1.13.3 linux/amd64
```

The KinD executable provides every option you will need to maintain a cluster's life cycle. Of course, the KinD executable can create and delete clusters, but it also provides the following capabilites:

- The ability to create custom build base and node images

- Can export kubeconfig or log files

- Can retrieve clusters, nodes, or kubeconfig files

- Can load images into nodes

Now that you have installed the KinD utility, you are almost ready to create your KinD cluster. Before we execute a few create cluster commands, we will explain some of the creation options that KinD provides.

Creating a KinD cluster

Now that you have met all the requirements, you can create your first cluster using the KinD executable. The KinD utility can create a single-node cluster, as well as a complex cluster that's running multiple nodes for the control plane with multiple worker nodes. In this section, we will discuss the KinD executable options. By the end of the chapter, you will have a two-node cluster running – a single control plane node and a single worker node.

> **Important note**
> For the exercises in this book, we will install a multi-node cluster. The simple cluster configuration is an example and should not be used for our exercises.

Creating a simple cluster

To create a simple cluster that runs the control plane and a worker node in a single container, you only need to execute the KinD executable with the `create cluster` option.

Let's create a quick single-node cluster to see how quickly KinD creates a fast development cluster. On your host, create a cluster using the following command:

```
kind create cluster
```

This will quickly create a cluster with all the Kubernetes components in a single Docker container by using a cluster name of `kind`. It will also assign the Docker container a name of `kind-control-plane`. If you want to assign a cluster name, rather than the default name, you need to add the `--name <cluster name>` option to the `create cluster` command:

```
Creating cluster "kind" ...
   Ensuring node image (kindest/node:v1.18.2)
   Preparing nodes
   Writing configuration
   Starting control-plane
   Installing CNI
   Installing StorageClass
Set kubectl context to "kind-kind"
You can now use your cluster with:

kubectl cluster-info --context kind-kind
```

The `create` command will create the cluster and modify the kubectl `config` file. KinD will add the new cluster to your current kubectl `config` file, and it will set the new cluster as the default context.

We can verify that the cluster was created successfully by listing the nodes using the kubectl utility:

```
kubectl get nodes
```

This will return the running nodes, which, for a basic cluster, are single nodes:

```
NAME                STATUS   ROLES    AGE    VERSION
kind-control-plane Ready    master   130m   v1.18.2
```

The main point of deploying this single-node cluster was to show you how quickly KinD can create a cluster that you can use for testing. For our exercises, we want to split up the control plane and worker node so that we can delete this cluster using the steps in the next section.

Deleting a cluster

When you have finished testing, you can delete the cluster using the `delete` command:

```
kind delete cluster –name <cluster name>
```

The `delete` command will quickly delete the cluster, including any entries in your `kubeconfig` file.

A quick single-node cluster is useful for many use cases, but you may want to create a multi-node cluster for various testing scenarios. Creating a more complex cluster requires that you create a config file.

Creating a cluster config file

When creating a multi-node cluster, such as a two-node cluster with custom options, we need to create a cluster config file. The config file is a YAML file and the format should look familiar. Setting values in this file allows you to customize the KinD cluster, including the number of nodes, API options, and more. The config file we'll use to create the cluster for the book is shown here – it is included in this book's repository at `/chapter4/cluster01-kind.yaml`:

```
kind: Cluster
apiVersion: kind.x-k8s.io/v1alpha4
networking:
  apiServerAddress: "0.0.0.0"
  disableDefaultCNI: true
kubeadmConfigPatches:
- |
  apiVersion: kubeadm.k8s.io/v1beta2
  kind: ClusterConfiguration
  metadata:
    name: config
  networking:
    serviceSubnet: "10.96.0.1/12"
    podSubnet: "192.168.0.0/16"
```

```
nodes:
- role: control-plane
- role: worker
  extraPortMappings:
  - containerPort: 80
    hostPort: 80
  - containerPort: 443
    hostPort: 443
  extraMounts:
  - hostPath: /usr/src
    containerPath: /usr/src
```

Details about each of the custom options in the file are provided in the following table:

Config Options	Option Details
apiServerAddress	This tells the installation what IP address the API server will listen on. By default, it will use 127.0.0.1, but since we plan to use the cluster from other networked machines, we have selected to listen on all IP addresses.
disableDefaultCNI	This setting will enable or disable the Kindnet installation. The default value is false, but since we want to use Calico as our CNI, we are setting it to true.
kubeadmConfigPatches	This section allows you to set values for certain settings during the installation. For our control plane, we are setting the CIDRs for ServiceSubnet and podSubnet.
Nodes	This section is where you define your nodes. For our cluster, we will create a single control plane node and a single worker node.
- role: control-plane	This creates a control plane in our cluster, which is a single node. We can set options that are specific to the control plane in this section. These are covered in the next row.
kubeadmConfigPatches	This allows you to set options for the control plane. For our cluster, we are setting values for the API server to include the OIDC parameters that we will use in later chapters.
- role: worker	This section will create our worker node.
extraPortMappings	This setting will create extra port mappings for our worker node. It will tell Docker to bind port 80 and 443 to our worker node container.
extraMounts	This section tells Docker to create extra mounts between the host and the container. We're setting this value to allow a container that we'll create later in this book to use files from the host located at /usr/src.

Table 4.3 – KinD configuration options

If you plan to create a cluster that goes beyond a single-node cluster without using advanced options, you will need to create a configuration file. Understanding the options available to you will allow you to create a Kubernetes cluster that has advanced components such as Ingress controllers or multiple nodes to test failure and recovery procedures for deployments.

Now that you know how to create a simple all-in-one container for running a cluster and how to create a multi-node cluster using a config file, let's discuss a more complex cluster example.

Multi-node cluster configuration

If you only wanted a multi-node cluster without any extra options, you could create a simple configuration file that lists the number and node types you want in the cluster. The following `config` file will create a cluster with three control plane nodes and three worker nodes:

```
kind: Cluster
apiVersion: kind.x-k8s.io/v1alpha4
nodes:
- role: control-plane
- role: control-plane
- role: control-plane
- role: worker
- role: worker
- role: worker
```

Using multiple control plane servers introduces additional complexity since we can only target a single host or IP in our configuration files. To make this configuration usable, we need to deploy a load balancer in front of our cluster.

KinD has considered this, and if you do deploy multiple control plane nodes, the installation will create an additional container running a HAProxy load balancer. If we look at the running containers from a multi-node config, we will see six node containers running and a HAProxy container:

Container	ID	Port	Names
29b28504239b	kindest/node:v1.17.0		config2-worker2
ac3efb14fd51	kindest/node:v1.17.0		config2-worker
c1beba396fe8	kindest/node:v1.17.0	127.0.0.1:32792->6443/tcp	config2-control-plane3
26ceb0c672a5	kindest/node:v1.17.0	127.0.0.1:32794->6443/tcp	config2-control-plane
99dd75667824	kindest/haproxy:2.1.1-alpine	127.0.0.1:32791->6443/tcp	config2-external-load-balancer
25c9da1b7ffa	kindest/node:v1.17.0	127.0.0.1:32793->6443/tcp	config2-control-plane2
b8e201938cbe	kindest/node:v1.17.0		config2-worker3

Table 4.4 – KinD configuration options

Remember that, in *Chapter 3, Understanding Docker Networking*, we explained ports and sockets. Since we have a single host, each control plane node and the HAProxy container are running on unique ports. Each container needs to be exposed to the host so that they can receive incoming requests. In this example, the important one to note is the port assigned to HAProxy, since that's the target port for the cluster. If you were to look at the Kubernetes config file, you would see that it is targeting https://127.0.0.1:32791, which is the port that's been assigned to the HAProxy container.

When a command is executed using kubectl, it is sent to directly to the HAProxy server. Using a configuration file that was created by KinD during the cluster's creation, the HAProxy container knows how to route traffic between the three control plane nodes:

```
# generated by kind
global
  log /dev/log local0
```

```
    log /dev/log local1 notice
    daemon

defaults
    log global
    mode tcp
    option dontlognull
    # TODO: tune these
    timeout connect 5000
    timeout client 50000
    timeout server 50000

frontend control-plane
    bind *:6443

    default_backend kube-apiservers

backend kube-apiservers
    option httpchk GET /healthz
    # TODO: we should be verifying (!)

    server config2-control-plane 172.17.0.8:6443 check check-ssl
verify none
    server config2-control-plane2 172.17.0.6:6443 check check-ssl
verify none
    server config2-control-plane3 172.17.0.5:6443 check check-ssl
verify none
```

As shown in the preceding configuration file, there is a backend section called `kube-apiservers` that contains the three control plane containers. Each entry contains the Docker IP address of a control plane node with a port assignment of 6443, targeting the API server running in the container. When you request `https://127.0.0.1:32791`, that request will hit the HAProxy container. Using the rules in the HAProxy configuration file, the request will be routed to one of the three nodes in the list.

Since our cluster is now fronted by a load balancer, we have a highly available control plane for testing.

> **Note**
>
> The included HAProxy image is not configurable. It is only provided to handle the control plane and to load balance the API servers. Due to this limitation, if you needed to use a load balancer for the worker nodes, you will need to provide your own.
>
> An example use case for this would be if you wanted to use an Ingress controller on multiple worker nodes. You would need a load balancer in front of the worker nodes to accept incoming 80 and 443 requests that would forward the traffic to each node running NGINX. At the end of this chapter, we have provided an example configuration that includes a custom HAProxy configuration for load balancing traffic to the worker nodes.

Customizing the control plane and Kubelet options

You may want to go further than this to test features such as OIDC integration or Kubernetes feature gates. KinD uses the same configuration that you would use for a kubeadm installation. As an example, if you wanted to integrate a cluster with an OIDC provider, you could add the required options to the configuration patch section:

```
kind: Cluster
apiVersion: kind.x-k8s.io/v1alpha4
kubeadmConfigPatches:
- |
  kind: ClusterConfiguration
  metadata:
    name: config
  apiServer:
    extraArgs:
      oidc-issuer-url: "https://oidc.testdomain.com/auth/idp/
k8sIdp"
      oidc-client-id: "kubernetes"
      oidc-username-claim: sub
      oidc-client-id: kubernetes
      oidc-ca-file: /etc/oidc/ca.crt
nodes:
- role: control-plane
- role: control-plane
```

```
- role: control-plane
- role: worker
- role: worker
- rol: worker
```

For a list of available configuration options, take a look at *Customizing control plane configuration with kubeadm* on the Kubernetes site at `https://kubernetes.io/docs/setup/production-environment/tools/kubeadm/control-plane-flags/`.

Now that you have created the cluster file, you can create your KinD cluster.

Creating a custom KinD cluster

Finally! Now that you are familiar with KinD, we can move forward and create our cluster.

We need to create a controlled, known environment, so we will give the cluster a name and provide the config file that we discussed in the previous section.

Make sure that you are in your cloned repository under the `chapter4` directory.

To create a KinD cluster with our required options, we need to run the KinD installer with the following options:

```
kind create cluster --name cluster01 --config c
luster01-kind.yamlThe option --name will set the name of the
cluster to cluster01 and the --config tells the installer to
use the config file cluster01-kind.yaml.
```

When you execute the installer on your host, KinD will start the installation and tell you each step that is being performed. The entire cluster creation process should take less than 2 minutes:

Figure 4.6 – KinD cluster creation output

The final step in the deployment creates or edits an existing Kubernetes config file. In either case, the installer creates a new context with the name `kind-<cluster name>` and sets it as the default context.

While it may appear that the cluster installation procedure has completed its tasks, the cluster **is not** ready yet. Some of the tasks take a few minutes to fully initialize and since we disabled the default CNI to use Calico, we still need to deploy Calico to provide cluster networking.

Installing Calico

To provide networking to the pods in the cluster, we need to install a Container Network Interface, or CNI. We have elected to install Calico as our CNI and since KinD only includes the Kindnet CNI, we need to install Calico manually.

If you were to pause after the creation step and look at the cluster, you would notice that some pods are in a pending state:

```
coredns-6955765f44-86177   0/1   Pending   0   10m
coredns-6955765f44-bznjl   0/1   Pending   0   10m
local-path-provisioner-7   0/1   Pending   0   11m
745554f7f-jgmxv
```

The pods listed here require a working CNI to start. This puts the pods into a pending state, where they are waiting for a network. Since we did not deploy the default CNI, our cluster does not have networking support. To get these pods from pending to running, we need to install a CNI – and for our cluster, that will be Calico.

To install Calico, we will use the standard Calico deployment, which only requires a single manifest. To start deploying Calico, use the following command:

```
kubectl apply -f https://docs.projectcalico.org/v3.11/
manifests/calico.yaml
```

This will pull the manifests from the internet and apply them to the cluster. As it deploys, you will see that that a number of Kubernetes objects are created:

```
configmap/calico-config created
customresourcedefinition.apiextensions.k8s.io/felixconfigurations.crd.projectcalico.org created
customresourcedefinition.apiextensions.k8s.io/ipamblocks.crd.projectcalico.org created
customresourcedefinition.apiextensions.k8s.io/blockaffinities.crd.projectcalico.org created
customresourcedefinition.apiextensions.k8s.io/ipamhandles.crd.projectcalico.org created
customresourcedefinition.apiextensions.k8s.io/ipamconfigs.crd.projectcalico.org created
customresourcedefinition.apiextensions.k8s.io/bgppeers.crd.projectcalico.org created
customresourcedefinition.apiextensions.k8s.io/bgpconfigurations.crd.projectcalico.org created
customresourcedefinition.apiextensions.k8s.io/ippools.crd.projectcalico.org created
customresourcedefinition.apiextensions.k8s.io/hostendpoints.crd.projectcalico.org created
customresourcedefinition.apiextensions.k8s.io/clusterinformations.crd.projectcalico.org created
customresourcedefinition.apiextensions.k8s.io/globalnetworkpolicies.crd.projectcalico.org created
customresourcedefinition.apiextensions.k8s.io/globalnetworksets.crd.projectcalico.org created
customresourcedefinition.apiextensions.k8s.io/networkpolicies.crd.projectcalico.org created
customresourcedefinition.apiextensions.k8s.io/networksets.crd.projectcalico.org created
clusterrole.rbac.authorization.k8s.io/calico-kube-controllers created
clusterrolebinding.rbac.authorization.k8s.io/calico-kube-controllers created
clusterrole.rbac.authorization.k8s.io/calico-node created
clusterrolebinding.rbac.authorization.k8s.io/calico-node created
daemonset.apps/calico-node created
serviceaccount/calico-node created
deployment.apps/calico-kube-controllers created
serviceaccount/calico-kube-controllers created
```

Figure 4.7 – Calico installation output

The installation process will take about a minute and you can check on its status using `kubectl get pods -n kube-system`. You will see that three Calico pods were created. Two are `calico-node` pods, while the other is the `calico-kube-controller` pod:

NAME	READY	STATUS	RESTARTS	AGE
calico-kube-controllers -5b644bc49c-nm5wn	1/1	Running	0	64s
calico-node-4dqnv	1/1	Running	0	64s
calico-node-vwbpf	1/1	Running	0	64s

If you check the two CoreDNS pods in the `kube-system` namespace again, you will notice that they have changed from the pending state, from before we installed Calico, to being in a running state:

coredns-6955765f44-86177	1/1	Running	0	18m
coredns-6955765f44-bznjl	1/1	Running	0	18m

Now that the cluster has a working CNI installed, any pods that were dependent on networking will be in a running state.

Installing an Ingress controller

We have a chapter dedicated to Ingress to explain all the technical details. Since we are deploying a cluster and we require Ingress for future chapters, we need to deploy an Ingress controller to show a complete cluster build. All these details will be explained in more detail in *Chapter 6, Services, Load Balancing, and External DNS*.

Installing the NGINX Ingress controller requires only two manifests, which we will pull from the internet to make the installation easy. To install the controller, execute the following two lines:

```
kubectl apply -f https://raw.githubusercontent.com/kubernetes/
ingress-nginx/nginx-0.28.0/deploy/static/mandatory.yaml
kubectl apply -f https://raw.githubusercontent.com/kubernetes/
ingress-nginx/nginx-0.27.0/deploy/static/provider/baremetal/
service-nodeport.yaml
```

The deployment will create a few Kubernetes objects that are required for Ingress in a namespace called `ingress-nginx`:

```
namespace/ingress-nginx created
configmap/nginx-configuration created
configmap/tcp-services created
configmap/udp-services created
serviceaccount/nginx-ingress-serviceaccount created
clusterrole.rbac.authorization.k8s.io/nginx-ingress-clusterrole created
role.rbac.authorization.k8s.io/nginx-ingress-role created
rolebinding.rbac.authorization.k8s.io/nginx-ingress-role-nisa-binding created
clusterrolebinding.rbac.authorization.k8s.io/nginx-ingress-clusterrole-nisa-binding created
deployment.apps/nginx-ingress-controller created
limitrange/ingress-nginx created
```

Figure 4.8 – NGINX installation output

We have one more step so that we have a fully functioning Ingress controller: we need to expose ports 80 and 443 to the running pod. This can be done by patching the deployment. Here, we have included the patch to patch the deployment:

```
kubectl patch deployments -n ingress-nginx nginx-ingress-
controller -p '{"spec":{"template":{"spec":{"containers":[{"nam
e":"nginx-ingress-controller","ports":[{"containerPort":80,"hos
tPort":80},{"containerPort":443,"hostPort":443}]}]}}}}'
```

Congratulations! You now have a fully functioning, two-node Kubernetes cluster running Calico with an Ingress controller.

Reviewing your KinD cluster

With a Kubernetes cluster now available, we have the ability to look at Kubernetes objects first-hand. This will help you understand the previous chapter, where we covered many of the base objects included in a Kubernetes cluster. In particular, we will discuss the storage objects that are included with your KinD cluster.

KinD storage objects

Remember that KinD includes Rancher's auto-provisioner to provide automated persistent disk management for the cluster. In *Chapter 5, Kubernetes Bootcamp*, we went over the storage-related objects, and now that we have a cluster with a storage system configured, we can explain them in greater detail.

There is one object that the auto-provisioner does not require since it uses a base Kubernetes feature: it does not require a `CSIdriver`. Since the ability to use local host paths as PVCs is part of Kubernetes, we will not see any `CSIdriver` objects in our KinD cluster.

The first objects in our KinD cluster we will discuss are our `CSInodes`. In the bootcamp, we mentioned that this object was created to decouple any CSI objects from the base node object. Any node that can run a workload will have a `CSInode` object. On our KinD clusters, both nodes have a `CSInode` object. You can verify this by executing `kubectl get csinodes`:

```
NAME                          CREATED AT
cluster01-control-plane       2020-03-27T15:18:19Z
cluster01-worker              2020-03-27T15:19:01Z
```

If we were to describe one of the nodes using `kubectl describe csinodes <node name>`, you would see the details of the object:

```
[root@localhost yaml]# kubectl describe csinodes cluster01-worker
Name:           cluster01-worker
Namespace:
Labels:         <none>
Annotations:    <none>
API Version:    storage.k8s.io/v1
Kind:           CSINode
Metadata:
  Creation Timestamp:  2020-03-27T15:19:01Z
  Owner References:
    API Version:    v1
    Kind:           Node
    Name:           cluster01-worker
    UID:            85af82eb-0b55-45f7-8b18-12ed20ca9b40
  Resource Version:  480
  Self Link:        /apis/storage.k8s.io/v1/csinodes/cluster01-worker
  UID:              05ebab79-89e5-44d9-b04d-b80a70741002
Spec:
  Drivers:  <nil>
Events:     <none>
```

Figure 4.9 – CSInode describe

The main thing to point out is the Spec section of the output. This lists the details of any drivers that may be installed to support backend storage systems. Since we do not have a backend storage system, we do not require an additional driver on our cluster.

To show an example of what a node would list, here is the output from a cluster that has two drivers installed, supporting two different vendor storage solutions:

```
Name:              home-k8s-master3.k8shome.com
Namespace:
Labels:            <none>
Annotations:       <none>
API Version:       storage.k8s.io/v1beta1
Kind:              CSINode
Metadata:
  Creation Timestamp:  2019-10-29T12:38:05Z
  Owner References:
    API Version:       v1
    Kind:              Node
    Name:              home-k8s-master3.k8shome.com
    UID:               c7131855-e465-49e7-a700-debfcccc2ef2
  Resource Version:    28926386
  Self Link:           /apis/storage.k8s.io/v1beta1/csinodes/home-k8s-master3.k8shome.com
  UID:                 7487170e-d069-4b59-9589-8f12c9f6a98a
Spec:
  Drivers:
    Name:              csi.trident.netapp.io
    Node ID:           home-k8s-master3.k8shome.com
    Topology Keys:     <nil>
    Name:              reduxio.magellan
    Node ID:           home-k8s-master3.k8shome.com
    Topology Keys:     <nil>
Events:                <none>
```

Figure 4.10 – Multiple driver example

If you look at the spec.drivers section of this node, you will see two different name sections. The first shows that we have a driver installed to support NetApp SolidFire, while the second is a driver that supports Reduxio's storage solution.

Storage drivers

As we already mentioned, your KinD cluster does not have any additional storage drivers installed. If you execute kubectl get csidrivers, the API will not list any resources.

KinD storage classes

To attach to any cluster-provided storage, the cluster requires a `StorageClass` object. Rancher's provider creates a default storage class called standard. It also sets the class as the default `StorageClass`, so you do not need to provide a `StorageClass` name in your PVC requests. If a default `StorageClass` is not set, every PVC request will require a `StorageClass` name in the request. If a default class is not enabled and a PVC request fails to set a `StorageClass` name, the PVC allocation will fail since the API server won't be able to link the request to a `StorageClass`.

Note

On a production cluster, it is considered a good practice to omit assigning a default `StorageClass`. Depending on your users, you may have deployments that forget to set a class, and the default storage system may not fit the deployment needs. This issue may not occur until it becomes a production issue, and that may impact business revenue or the company's reputation. If you don't assign a default class, the developer will have a failed PVC request, and the issue will be discovered before any harm comes to the business.

To list the storage classes on the cluster, execute `kubectl get storageclasses`, or use the shortened version by using `sc` instead of `storageclasses`:

Figure 4.11 – Default storage class

Next, let's learn how to use the provisioner.

Using KinD's storage provisioner

Using the included provisioner is very simple. Since it can auto-provision the storage and is set as the default class, any PVC requests that are coming in are seen by the provisioning pod, which then creates `PersistentVolume` and `PersistentVolumeClaim`.

To show this process, let's go through the necessary steps. The following is the output of running `get pv` and `get pvc` on a base KinD cluster:

```
[root@localhost yaml]# kubectl get pv
No resources found in default namespace.
[root@localhost yaml]# kubectl get pvc --all-namespaces
No resources found
```

Figure 4.12 – PV and PVC example

Remember that `PersistentVolume` is not a namespaced object, so we don't need to add a namespace option to the command. PVCs are namespaced objects, so I told Kubernetes to show me the PVCs that are available in all the namespaces. Since this is a new cluster and none of the default workloads require persistent disk, there are no PV or PVC objects.

Without an auto-provisioner, we would need to create a PV before a PVC could claim the volume. Since we have the Rancher provisioner running in our cluster, we can test the creation process by deploying a pod with a PVC request like the one listed here:

```
kind: PersistentVolumeClaim
apiVersion: v1
metadata:
  name: test-claim
spec:
  accessModes:
    - ReadWriteOnce
  resources:
    requests:
      storage: 1Mi
---
kind: Pod
apiVersion: v1
metadata:
  name: test-pvc-claim
spec:
  containers:
  - name: test-pod
    image: busybox
    command:
      - "/bin/sh"
    args:
      - "-c"
      - "touch /mnt/test && exit 0 || exit 1"
    volumeMounts:
      - name: test-pvc
        mountPath: "/mnt"
  restartPolicy: "Never"
```

```
volumes:
  - name: test-pvc
    persistentVolumeClaim:
      claimName: test-claim
```

This PVC request will be named `test-claim` in the default namespace and it is requesting a 1 MB volume. We do need to include the `StorageClass` option since KinD has set a default `StorageClass` for the cluster.

To create the PVC, we can execute a `create` command using kubectl, such as `kubectl create -f pvctest.yaml` – Kubernetes will return, stating that the PVC has been created, but it's important to note that this does not mean that the PVC is fully working. The PVC object has been created, but if any dependencies are missing in the PVC request, it will still create the object, though it will fail to fully create the PVC request.

After creating a PVC, you can check the real status using one of two options. The first is a simple `get` command; that is, `kubectl get pvc`. Since my request is in the default namespace, I don't need to include a namespace value in the `get` command (note that we had to shorten the volume's name so that it fits the page):

```
NAME            STATUS         VOLUME
CAPACITY      ACCESS MODES    STORAGECLASS      AGE
test-claim      Bound       pvc-9c56cf65-d661-49e3-         1Mi
RWO             standard        2s
```

We know that we created a PVC request in the manifest, but we did not create a PV request. If we look at the PVs now, we will see that a single PV was created from our PVC request. Again, we shortened the PV name in order to fit the output on a single line:

```
NAME                        CAPACITY    ACCESS MODES    RECLAIM POLICY
STATUS      CLAIM
pvc-9c56cf65-d661-49e3-     1Mi             RWO
    Delete          Bound       default/test-claim
```

This completes the KinD storage section.

With so many workloads requiring persistent disks, it is very important to understand how Kubernetes workloads integrate with storage systems. In this section, you learned how KinD adds the auto-provisioner to the cluster. We will reinforce our knowledge of these Kubernetes storage objects in the next chapter, *Chapter 5, Kubernetes Bootcamp*.

Adding a custom load balancer for Ingress

> **Note**
>
> This section is a complex topic that covers adding a custom HAProxy container that you can use to load balance worker nodes in a KinD cluster. *You should not deploy these steps on the KinD cluster that we will use for the remaining chapters.*

We added this section for anybody that may want to know more about how to load balance between multiple worker nodes.

KinD does not include a load balancer for worker nodes. The included HAProxy container only creates a configuration file for the API server; the team does not officially support any modifications to the default image or configuration. Since you will interact with load balancers in your everyday work, we wanted to add a section on how to configure your own HAProxy container in order to load balance between three KinD nodes.

First, we will not use this configuration for any of chapters in this book. We want to make the exercises available to everyone, so to limit the required resources, we will always use the two-node cluster that we created earlier in this chapter. If you want to test KinD nodes with a load balancer, we suggest using a different Docker host or waiting until you have finished this book and deleting your KinD cluster.

Installation prerequisites

We assume that you have a KinD cluster based on the following configuration:

- Any number of control plane nodes
- Three worker nodes
- Cluster name is `cluster01`
- A working version of **Kindnet or Calico (CNI)**
- NGINX Ingress controller installed – patched to listen on ports 80 and 443 on the host

Creating the KinD cluster configuration

Since you will use an HAProxy container exposed on ports 80 and 443 on your Docker host, you do not need to expose any ports in your cluster `config` file.

To make a test deployment easier, you can use the example cluster config shown here, which will create a simple six-node cluster with Kindnet disabled:

```
kind: Cluster
apiVersion: kind.x-k8s.io/v1alpha4
networking:
  apiServerAddress: "0.0.0.0"
  disableDefaultCNI: true
kubeadmConfigPatches:
- |
  apiVersion: kubeadm.k8s.io/v1beta2
  kind: ClusterConfiguration
  metadata:
    name: config
  networking:
    serviceSubnet: "10.96.0.1/12"
    podSubnet: "192.168.0.0/16"
nodes:
- role: control-plane
- role: control-plane
- role: control-plane
- role: worker
- role: worker
- role: worker
```

You need to install Calico using the same manifest that we used earlier in this chapter. After installing Calico, you need to install the NGINX Ingress controller using the steps provided earlier in this chapter.

Once you've deployed Calico and NGINX, you should have a working base cluster. Now, you can move on to deploying a custom HAProxy container.

Deploying a custom HAProxy container

HAProxy offers a container on Docker Hub that is easy to deploy, requiring only a config file to start the container.

To create the configuration file, you will need you to know the IP addresses of each worker node in the cluster. In this book's GitHub repository, we have included a script file that will find this information for you, create the config file, and start the HAProxy container. It is located under the HAProxy directory and it's called HAProxy-ingress.sh.

To help you better understand this script, we will break out sections of the script and detail what each section is executing. Firstly, the following code block is getting the IP addresses of each worker node in our cluster and saving the results in a variable. We will need this information for the backend server list:

```
#!/bin/bash

worker1=$(docker inspect --format '{{ .NetworkSettings.
IPAddress }}' cluster01-worker)
worker2=$(docker inspect --format '{{ .NetworkSettings.
IPAddress }}' cluster01-worker2)
worker3=$(docker inspect --format '{{ .NetworkSettings.
IPAddress }}' cluster01-worker3)
```

Next, since we will use a bind mount when we start the container, we need to have the configuration file in a known location. We elected to store it in the current user's home folder, under a directory called HAProxy:

```
# Create an HAProxy directory in the current users home folder
mkdir ~/HAProxy
```

Next, the following part of the script will create the HAProxy directory:

```
# Create the HAProxy.cfg file for the worker nodes
tee ~/HAProxy/HAProxy.cfg <<EOF
```

The global section of the configuration sets process-wide security and performance settings:

```
global
   log /dev/log local0
   log /dev/log local1 notice
   daemon
```

The `defaults` section is used to configure values that will apply to all frontend and backend sections in the configuration value:

```
defaults
  log global
  mode tcp
  timeout connect 5000
  timeout client 50000
  timeout server 50000


frontend workers_https
  bind *:443
  mode tcp
  use_backend ingress_https

backend ingress_https
  option httpchk GET /healthz
  mode tcp
  server worker $worker1:443 check port 80
  server worker2 $worker2:443 check port 80
  server worker3 $worker3:443 check port 80
```

This tells HAProxy to create a frontend called `workers_https` and the IP addresses and ports to bind for incoming requests, to use TCP mode, and to use a backend named `ingress_https`.

The `ingress_https` backend includes the three worker nodes that are using port 443 as a destination. The check port is a health check that will test port 80. If a server replies on port 80, it will be added as a target for requests. While this is an HTTPS port 443 rule, we are only using port 80 to check for a network reply from the NGINX pod:

```
frontend workers_http
  bind *:80
  use_backend ingress_http

backend ingress_http
  mode http
```

```
option httpchk GET /healthz
server worker $worker1:80 check port 80
server worker2 $worker2:80 check port 80
server worker3 $worker3:80 check port 80
```

This `frontend` section creates a frontend that accepts incoming HTTP traffic on port 80. It then uses the list of servers in the backend, named `ingress_http`, for endpoints. Just like in the HTTPS section, we are using port 80 to check for any nodes that are running a service on port 80. Any endpoint that replies to the check will be added as a destination for HTTP traffic, and any nodes that do not have NGINX running on them will not reply, which means they won't be added as destinations:

```
EOF
```

This ends the creation of our file. The final file will be created in the `HAProxy` directory:

```
# Start the HAProxy Container for the Worker Nodes
docker run --name HAProxy-workers-lb -d -p 80:80 -p 443:443 -v
~/HAProxy:/usr/local/etc/HAProxy:ro HAProxy -f /usr/local/etc/
HAProxy/HAProxy.cfg
```

The final step is to start a Docker container running HAProxy with our created configuration file containing the three worker nodes, exposed on the Docker host on ports 80 and 443.

Now that you have learned how to install a custom HAProxy load balancer for your worker nodes, let's look at how the configuration works.

Understanding HAProxy traffic flow

The cluster will have a total of eight containers running. Six of these containers will be the standard Kubernetes components; that is, three control plane servers and three worker nodes. The other two containers are KinD's HAProxy server, and your own custom HAProxy container:

```
IMAGE                          PORTS                                          NAMES
haproxy                        0.0.0.0:80->80/tcp, 0.0.0.0:443->443/tcp       haproxy-workers-lb
kindest/haproxy:2.1.1-alpine   0.0.0.0:32776->6443/tcp                        cluster01-external-load-balance

kindest/node:v1.17.0                                                          cluster01-worker
kindest/node:v1.17.0           127.0.0.1:32801->6443/tcp                      cluster01-control-plane
kindest/node:v1.17.0           127.0.0.1:32799->6443/tcp                      cluster01-control-plane3
kindest/node:v1.17.0                                                          cluster01-worker2
kindest/node:v1.17.0           127.0.0.1:32800->6443/tcp                      cluster01-control-plane2
kindest/node:v1.17.0                                                          cluster01-worker3
```

Figure 4.13 – Custom HAProxy container running

There are a few differences between this cluster output versus our two-node cluster for the exercises. Notice that the worker nodes are not exposed on any host ports. The worker nodes do not need any mappings since we have our new HAProxy server running. If you look at the HAProxy container we created, it is exposed on host ports 80 and 443. This means that any incoming requests to the host on port 80 or 443 will be directed to the custom HAProxy container.

The default NGINX deployment only has a single replica, which means that the Ingress controller is running on a single node. If we look at the logs for the HAProxy container, we will see something interesting:

```
[NOTICE] 093/191701 (1) : New worker #1 (6) forked
[WARNING] 093/191701 (6) : Server ingress_https/worker is DOWN,
reason: Layer4 connection problem, info: "SSL handshake failure
(Connection refused)", check duration: 0ms. 2 active and 0
backup servers left. 0 sessions active, 0 requeued, 0 remaining
in queue.
[WARNING] 093/191702 (6) : Server ingress_https/worker3 is
DOWN, reason: Layer4 connection problem, info: "SSL handshake
failure (Connection refused)", check duration: 0ms. 1 active
and 0 backup servers left. 0 sessions active, 0 requeued, 0
remaining in queue.
[WARNING] 093/191702 (6) : Server ingress_http/worker is DOWN,
reason: Layer4 connection problem, info: "Connection refused",
check duration: 0ms. 2 active and 0 backup servers left. 0
sessions active, 0 requeued, 0 remaining in queue.
[WARNING] 093/191703 (6) : Server ingress_http/worker3 is DOWN,
reason: Layer4 connection problem, info: "Connection refused",
check duration: 0ms. 1 active and 0 backup servers left. 0
sessions active, 0 requeued, 0 remaining in queue.
```

You may have noticed a few errors in the log, such as SSL handshake failure and Connection refused. While these do look like errors, they are actually failed checked events on the worker nodes. Remember that NGINX is only running in a single pod, and since we have all three nodes in our HAProxy backend configuration, it will check for the ports on each node. Any nodes that fail to reply will not be used to load balance traffic. In our current config, this does load balance, since we only have NGINX on one node. It does, however, provide high availability to the Ingress controller.

If you look carefully at the log output, you will see how many servers are active on a defined backend; for example:

```
check duration: 0ms. 1 active and 0 backup servers left.
```

Each server pool in the log output shows 1 active endpoint, so we know that the HAProxy has successfully found a NGINX controller on both port 80 and 443.

To find out what worker the HAProxy server has connected to, we can use the failed connections in the log. Each backend will list the failed connections. For example, we know that the node that is working is cluster01-worker2 based on the logs that the other two worker nodes show as DOWN:

```
Server ingress_https/worker is DOWN
Server ingress_https/worker3 is DOWN
```

Let's simulate a node failure to prove that HAProxy is providing high availability to NGINX.

Simulating a Kubelet failure

Remember that KinD nodes are ephemeral and that stopping any container may cause it to fail on restart. So, how can we simulate a worker node failure since we can't simply stop the container?

To simulate a failure, we can stop the kubelet service on a node, which will alert kube-apisever so that it doesn't schedule any additional pods on the node. In our example, we want to prove that HAProxy is providing HA support for NGINX. We know that the running container is on worker2, so that's the node we want to "take down."

The easiest way to stop kubelet is to send a docker exec command to the container:

```
docker exec cluster01-worker2 systemctl stop kubelet
```

You will not see any output from this command, but if you wait a few minutes for the cluster to receive the updated node status, you can verify the node is down by looking at a list of nodes:

```
kubectl get nodes.
```

You will receive the following output:

```
NAME                        STATUS    ROLES    AGE   VERSION
cluster01-control-plane     Ready     master   45m   v1.17.0
cluster01-control-plane2    Ready     master   45m   v1.17.0
cluster01-control-plane3    Ready     master   43m   v1.17.0
cluster01-worker            Ready     <none>   43m   v1.17.0
cluster01-worker2           NotReady  <none>   43m   v1.17.0
cluster01-worker3           Ready     <none>   43m   v1.17.0
```

Figure 4.14 – worker2 is in a NotReady state

This verifies that we just simulated a kubelet failure and that `worker2` is in a `NotReady` status.

Any pods that were running before the kubelet "failure" will continue to run, but `kube-scheduler` will not schedule any workloads on the node until the kubelet issue is resolved. Since we know the pod will not restart on the node, we can delete the pod so that it can be rescheduled on a different node.

You need to get the pod name and then delete it to force a restart:

```
kubectl get pods -n ingress-nginx
nginx-ingress-controller-7d6bf88c86-r7ztq
kubectl delete pod nginx-ingress-controller-7d6bf88c86-r7ztq -n
ingress-nginx
```

This will force the scheduler to start the container on another worker node. It will also cause the HAProxy container to update the backend list, since the NGINX controller has moved to another worker node.

If you look at the HAProxy logs again, you will see that HAProxy has updated the backends to include `cluster01-worker3` and that it removed `cluster01-worker2` from the active servers list:

```
[WARNING] 093/194006 (6) : Server ingress_https/worker3 is
UP, reason: Layer7 check passed, code: 200, info: "OK", check
duration: 4ms. 2 active and 0 backup servers online. 0 sessions
requeued, 0 total in queue.
[WARNING] 093/194008 (6) : Server ingress_http/worker3 is UP,
reason: Layer7 check passed, code: 200, info: "OK", check
duration: 0ms. 2 active and 0 backup servers online. 0 sessions
requeued, 0 total in queue.
[WARNING] 093/195130 (6) : Server ingress_http/worker2 is DOWN,
reason: Layer4 timeout, check duration: 2000ms. 1 active and 0
backup servers left. 0 sessions active, 0 requeued, 0 remaining
```

```
in queue.
[WARNING] 093/195131 (6) : Server ingress_https/worker2 is
DOWN, reason: Layer4 timeout, check duration: 2001ms. 1 active
and 0 backup servers left. 0 sessions active, 0 requeued, 0
remaining in queue.
```

If you plan to use this HA cluster for additional tests, you will want to restart the kubelet on `cluster01-worker2`. If you plan to delete the HA cluster, you can just run a KinD cluster delete and all the nodes will be deleted.

Deleting the HAProxy container

Once you have deleted your KinD cluster, you will need to manually remove the HAProxy container we added. Since KinD didn't create our custom load balancer, deleting the cluster will not remove the container.

To delete the custom HAProxy container, run the `docker rm` command to force remove the image:

```
docker rm HAProxy-workers-lb –force
```

This will stop the container and remove it from Docker's list, allowing you to run it again using the same name with a future KinD cluster.

Summary

In this chapter, you learned about the Kubernetes SIG project called KinD. We went into details on how to install optional components in a KinD cluster, including Calico as the CNI and NGINX as the Ingress controller. Finally, we covered the details of the Kubernetes storage objects that are included with a KinD cluster.

Hopefully, with the help of this chapter, you now understand the power that using KinD can bring to you and your organization. It offers an easy to deploy, fully configurable Kubernetes cluster. The number of running clusters on a single host is theoretically limited only by the host resources.

In the next chapter, we will dive into Kubernetes objects. We've called the next chapter *Kubernetes Bootcamp* since it will cover the majority of the base Kubernetes objects and what each one is used for. The next chapter can be considered a "Kubernetes pocket guide." It contains a quick reference to Kubernetes objects and what they do, as well as when to use them.

It's a packed chapter and is designed to be a refresher for those of you who have experience with Kubernetes, or as a crash course for those of you who are new to Kubernetes. Our intention for this book is to go beyond the base Kubernetes objects since there are many books on the market today that cover the basics of Kubernetes very well.

Questions

1. What object must be created before you can create a `PersistentVolumeClaim`?

    A. PVC

    B. Disk

    C. `PersistentVolume`

    D. `VirtualDisk`

2. KinD includes a dynamic disk provisioner. What company created the provisioner?

    A. Microsoft

    B. CNCF

    C. VMware

    D. Rancher

3. If you create a KinD cluster with multiple worker nodes, what would you install to direct traffic to each node?

    A. Load balancer

    B. Proxy server

    C. Nothing

    D. Network load balancer

4. True or false: A Kubernetes cluster can only have one CSIdriver installed.

    A. True

    B. False

5
Kubernetes Bootcamp

We are sure that many of you have used Kubernetes in some capacity—you may have clusters running in production or you may have kicked the tires using kubeadm, Minikube, or Docker Desktop. Our goal for this book is to go beyond the basics of Kubernetes and, as such, we didn't want to rehash all of the basics of Kubernetes. Instead, we added this chapter as a bootcamp for anyone that may be new to Kubernetes or might have only played around with it a bit.

Since it is a bootcamp chapter we will not get in-depth on every topic, but by the end, you should know enough about the basics of Kubernetes to understand the remaining chapters. If you have a strong Kubernetes background, you may still find this chapter useful as a refresher, and we will get into more complex topics starting in *Chapter 6, Services, Load Balancing, and External DNS*.

In this chapter, we will cover the components of a running Kubernetes cluster, which include the control plane and the worker node(s). We will detail each Kubernetes object and its use cases. If you have used Kubernetes in the past and are comfortable using `kubectl` and fully understand Kubernetes objects (such as `DaemonSets`, `StatefulSets`, `ReplicaSets`, and so on…), you may want to jump to *Chapter 6, Services, Load Balancing, and External DNS*, where we will install Kubernetes using KinD.

In this chapter, we will cover the following topics:

- An overview of Kubernetes components

- Exploring the control plane

- Understanding the worker node components

- Interacting with the API server

- Introducing Kubernetes objects

Technical requirements

This chapter has the following technical requirements:

- An Ubuntu 18.04 server with a minimum of 4 **gigabytes** (**GB**) of **random-access memory** (**RAM**)

- A KinD Kubernetes cluster

You can access the code for this chapter at the following GitHub repository: `https://github.com/PacktPublishing/Kubernetes-and-Docker-The-Complete-Guide`.

An overview of Kubernetes components

In any infrastructure, it is always a good idea to understand how the systems work together to provide services. With so many installer options out there today, many Kubernetes users have not had the need to understand how Kubernetes components integrate.

A few short years ago, if you wanted to run a Kubernetes cluster, you needed to install and configure each component manually. It was a steep learning curve to install a functioning cluster, which often led to frustration, causing many people and companies to say *"Kubernetes is just too difficult"*. The advantage of installing manually was that you truly understood how each component interacted, and if your cluster ran into issues after installation, you knew what to look for.

Nowadays, most people will click a button on a cloud provider and have a fully functioning Kubernetes cluster in minutes. On-premise installations have become just as easy, with options from Google, RedHat, Rancher, and more, removing the complexities of installing a Kubernetes cluster. The issues we see occur when you run into a problem or have questions after the installation. Since you didn't configure the Kubernetes components, you may not be able to explain to a developer how a Pod is scheduled on a worker node. Lastly, since you are running an installer provided by a third party, they may enable or disable features that you are not aware of, leading to an installation that may be against your company's security standards.

To understand how Kubernetes components work together, you must first understand the different components of a Kubernetes cluster. The following diagram is from the Kubernetes.io site and shows a high-level overview of a Kubernetes cluster component:

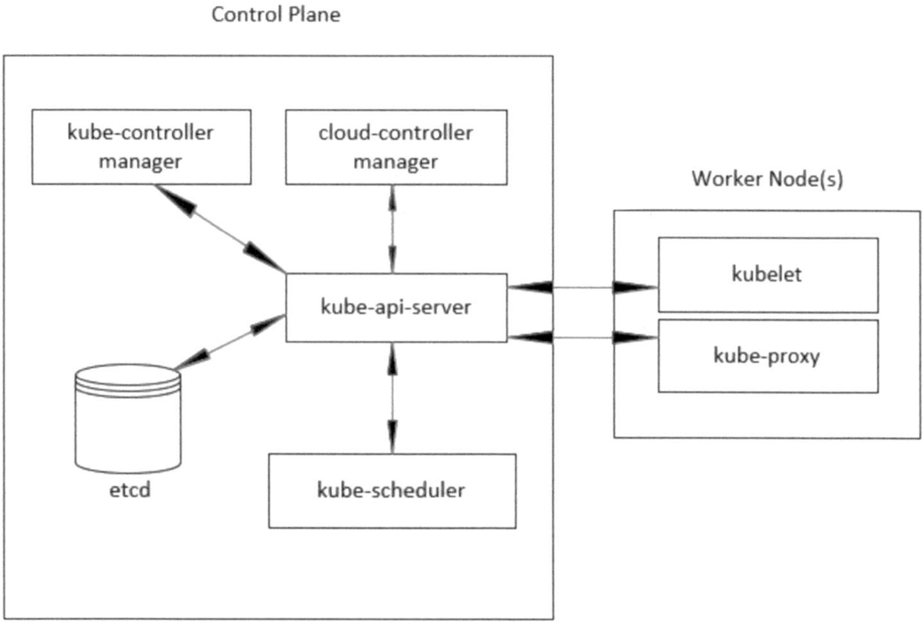

Figure 5.1 – Kubernetes cluster components

As you can see, the Kubernetes cluster is made up of several components. As we progress through the chapter, we'll discuss these components and the role they play in a Kubernetes cluster.

Exploring the control plane

As its name suggests, the control plane controls every aspect of a cluster. If your control plane goes down, you can probably imagine that your cluster will encounter issues. Without a control plane, a cluster will not have any scheduling abilities, which means that workloads that are running will remain running unless they are stopped and restarted. Since the control plane is extremely important, it is always suggested that you have at least three master nodes. Many production installations run more than three master nodes, but the number of installed nodes should always be an odd number. Let's look at why the control plane and its components are so vital to a running cluster by examining each one.

The Kubernetes API server

The first component to understand in a cluster is the `kube-apiserver` component. Since Kubernetes is **application programming interface** (**API**)-driven, every request that comes into a cluster goes through the API server. Let's look at a simple `get nodes` request using an API endpoint, as follows:

`https://10.240.100.100:6443/api/v1/nodes?limit=500`

One common method users of Kubernetes deploy to interact with the API server is the kubectl utility. Every command that is issued using kubectl calls an API endpoint behind the scenes. In the preceding example, we executed a `kubectl get nodes` command, which sent an API request to the `kube-apiserver` process on `10.240.100.100` on port `6443`. The API call requested the `/api/vi/nodes` endpoint, which returned a list of the nodes in the cluster, as shown in the following screenshot:

```
NAME                           STATUS    ROLES                              AGE     VERSION
home-k8s-master1.k8shome.com   Ready     controlplane,etcd,master           194d    v1.16.3
home-k8s-master2.k8shome.com   Ready     controlplane,etcd,master           194d    v1.16.3
home-k8s-master3.k8shome.com   Ready     controlplane,etcd,master,worker    194d    v1.16.3
home-k8s-worker1.k8shome.com   Ready     worker                             194d    v1.16.3
home-k8s-worker2.k8shome.com   Ready     worker                             194d    v1.16.3
home-k8s-worker3.k8shome.com   Ready     worker                             194d    v1.16.3
```

Figure 5.2 – List of Kubernetes nodes

Without a running API server, all requests to your cluster will fail. So, as you can see, it is very important to have a `kube-apiserver` component running at all times. By running three or more master nodes, we can limit any impact of losing a master node.

> **Note**
>
> When running more than one master node, you need to have a load balancer in front of the cluster. The Kubernetes API server can be fronted by most standard solutions, including F5, HAProxy, and Seesaw.

The Etcd database

It's not a stretch to say that Etcd is your Kubernetes cluster. Etcd is a fast and highly available distributed key-value database that Kubernetes uses to store all cluster data. Each resource in a cluster has a key in the database. If you logged in to the node—or Pod—running Etcd, you could use the `etcdctl` executable to look at all of the keys in the database. The following code snippet shows an example from a cluster running KinD:

```
EtcdCTL_API=3 etcdctl --endpoints=https://127.0.0.1:2379
--cacert=/etc/kubernetes/pki/etcd/ca.crt --key=/etc/kubernetes/
pki/etcd/server.key --cert=/etc/kubernetes/pki/etcd/server.crt
get / --prefix --keys-only
```

The output from the preceding command contains too much data to list it all in this chapter. A base KinD cluster will return approximately 317 entries. All keys start with `/registry/<object>`. For example, one of the keys that were returned is the `ClusterRole` for the `cluster-admin` key, as follows: `/registry/clusterrolebindings/cluster-admin`.

We can use the key name to retrieve the value using the `etcdctl` utility by slightly modifying our previous command, as follows:

```
EtcdCTL_API=3 etcdctl --endpoints=https://127.0.0.1:2379
--cacert=/etc/kubernetes/pki/etcd/ca.crt --key=/etc/kubernetes/
pki/etcd/server.key --cert=/etc/kubernetes/pki/etcd/server.crt
get /registry/clusterrolebindings/cluster-admin
```

The output will contain characters that cannot be interpreted by your shell, but you will get the idea of the data stored in Etcd. For the `cluster-admin` key, the output shows us the following:

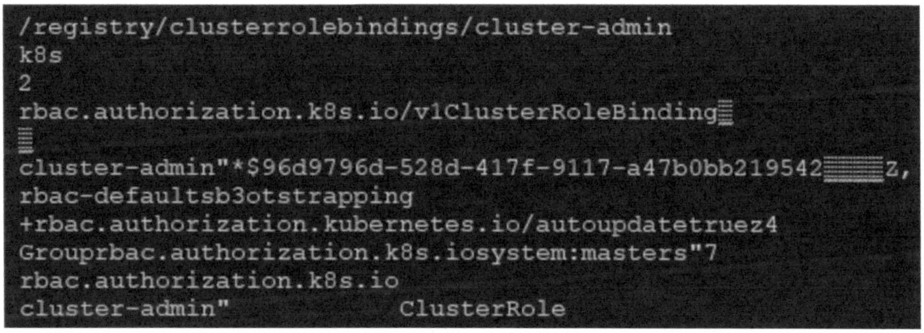

Figure 5.3 – etcdctl ClusterRoleBinding output

The reason we explain the entries in Etcd is to provide a background on how Kubernetes uses it to run a cluster. You have seen the output for the `cluster-admin` key directly from the database, but in everyday life you would query the API server using `kubectl get clusterrolebinding cluster-admin -o yaml`, which would return the following:

```
apiVersion: rbac.authorization.k8s.io/v1
kind: ClusterRoleBinding
metadata:
  annotations:
    rbac.authorization.kubernetes.io/autoupdate: "true"
  creationTimestamp: "2020-03-22T18:50:48Z"
  labels:
    kubernetes.io/bootstrapping: rbac-defaults
  name: cluster-admin
  resourceVersion: "95"
  selfLink: /apis/rbac.authorization.k8s.io/v1/clusterrolebindings/cluster-admin
  uid: 96d9796d-528d-417f-9117-a47b0bb21954
roleRef:
  apiGroup: rbac.authorization.k8s.io
  kind: ClusterRole
  name: cluster-admin
subjects:
- apiGroup: rbac.authorization.k8s.io
  kind: Group
  name: system:masters
```

Figure 5.4 – kubectl ClusterRoleBinding output

If you look at the output from the `kubectl` command and compare it with the output from the `etcdctl` query, you will see matching information. When you execute `kubectl` commands, the request goes to the API server, which then queries the Etcd database for the object's information.

kube-scheduler

As the name suggests, the `kube-scheduler` component is in charge of scheduling running Pods. Whenever a Pod is started in a cluster, the API server receives the requests and decides where to run the workload, based on multiple pieces of criteria including host resources and cluster policies.

kube-controller-manager

The `kube-controller-manager` component is actually a collection of multiple controllers that are included in a single binary. Including the four controllers in a single executable reduces complexity by running all four in a single process. The four controllers included in the `kube-controller-manager` component are the node, replication, endpoints, and service account and token controller.

Each controller provides a unique function to a cluster, and each controller and its function is listed here:

Controller	Description
Node	Monitors each node's availability. If a node goes offline, the node controller will update the status so that the scheduler does not attempt to start a workload on a failed node.
Replication	Monitors the number of replicas for pods, and will add or remove replicas based on the defined desired state.
Endpoints	Responsible for creating endpoints to pods that are included with a service.
Serviceaccounts	Monitors all service accounts.
Namespace	Monitors all namespaces.

Each controller runs a non-terminating (never-ending) control loop. These control loops watch the state of each resource, making any changes required to normalize the state of the resource. For example, if you needed to scale a deployment from one to three nodes, the replication controller would notice that the current state has one Pod running, and the desired state is to have three Pods running. To move the current state to the desired state, two additional Pods will be requested by the replication controller.

cloud-controller-manager

This is one component that you may not have run into, depending on how your clusters are configured. Similar to the kube-controller-manager component, this controller containers four controllers in a single binary. The included controllers are the node, route, service, and volume controllers—each controller is responsible for interacting with their respective cloud service provider offering.

Understanding the worker node components

Worker nodes, as the name implies, are responsible for running workloads. When we discussed the kube-scheduler component of the control plane, we mentioned that when a new Pod is scheduled, the kube-scheduler component will decide which node to run the Pod on. It does this using information that has been sent to it from the worker nodes. This information is constantly updated to help spread Pods around a cluster to utilize resources efficiently. Here is a list of the worker node components.

kubelet

You may hear a worker node referred to as a `kubelet`. `kubelet` is an agent that runs on all worker nodes, and it is responsible for running the actual containers.

kube-proxy

Contrary to the name, `kube-proxy` is not a proxy server at all. `kube-proxy` is responsible for routing network communication between a Pod and the outside network.

Container runtime

This is not represented in the picture, but each node also needs a container runtime. A container runtime is responsible for running the containers. The first thing you might think of is Docker. While Docker is a container runtime, it is not the only runtime option available. Over the last year, other options have become available and are quickly replacing Docker as the preferred container runtime. The two most prominent Docker replacements are CRI-O and containerd.

For the book exercises, we will create a Kubernetes cluster using KinD. At the time of this writing, KinD only offers official support for Docker as the container runtime, with limited support for Podman.

Interacting with the API server

As we mentioned earlier, you interact with the API server using either direct API requests or the `kubectl` utility. We will focus on using `kubectl` for the majority of our interaction in this book, but we will call out using direct API calls where applicable.

Using the Kubernetes kubectl utility

`kubectl` is a single executable file that allows you to interact with the Kubernetes API using a **command-line interface (CLI)**. It is available for most major operating systems and architectures, including Linux, Windows, and Mac.

Installation instructions for most operating systems are located on the Kubernetes site at `https://kubernetes.io/docs/tasks/tools/install-kubectl/`. Since we are using Linux as our operating system for the exercises in the book, we will cover installing `kubectl` on a Linux machine. Follow these steps:

1. To download the latest version of `kubectl`, you can run a `curl` command that will download it, as follows:

    ```
    curl -LO https://storage.googleapis.com/kubernetes-
    release/release/`curl -s https://storage.googleapis.com/
    kubernetes-release/release/stable.txt`/bin/linux/amd64/
    kubectl
    ```

2. After downloading, you need to make the file executable by running the following command:

    ```
    chmod +x ./kubectl
    ```

3. Finally, we will move the executable to your path, as follows:

    ```
    sudo mv ./kubectl /usr/local/bin/kubectl
    ```

You now have the latest `kubectl` utility on your system and can execute `kubectl` commands from any working directory.

Kubernetes is updated every 3 months. This includes upgrades to the base Kubernetes cluster components and the `kubectl` utility. You may run into a version mismatch between a cluster and your `kubectl` command, requiring you to either upgrade or download your `kubectl` executable. You can always check the version of both by running a `kubectl version` command, which will output the version of both the API server and the `kubectl` client. The output from a version check is shown in the following code snippet:

```
Client Version: version.Info{Major:"1",
Minor:"17", GitVersion:"v1.17.1",
GitCommit:"d224476cd0730baca2b6e357d144171ed74192d6",
GitTreeState:"clean", BuildDate:"2020-01-14T21:04:32Z",
GoVersion:"go1.13.5", Compiler:"gc", Platform:"linux/amd64"}

Server Version: version.Info{Major:"1",
Minor:"17", GitVersion:"v1.17.0",
GitCommit:"70132b0f130acc0bed193d9ba59dd186f0e634cf",
GitTreeState:"clean", BuildDate:"2020-01-14T00:09:19Z",
GoVersion:"go1.13.4", Compiler:"gc", Platform:"linux/amd64"}
```

As you can see from the output, the kubectl client is running version 1.17.1 and the cluster is running 1.17.0. A minor version difference in the two will not cause any issues. In fact, the official supported version difference is within one major version release. So, if your client is running version 1.16 and the cluster is running 1.17, you would be within the supported version difference. While this may be supported, it doesn't mean that you won't run into issues if you are trying to use any new commands or objects included in the higher version. In general, you should try to keep your cluster and client version in sync to avoid any issues.

Through the remainder of this chapter, we will discuss Kubernetes objects and how you interact with the API server to manage each object. But before diving into the different objects, we wanted to mention one commonly overlooked option of the kubectl utility: the verbose option.

Understanding the verbose option

When you execute a kubectl command, the only outputs you will see by default are any direct responses to your command. If you were to look at all Pods in the kube-system namespace, you would receive a list of all Pods. In most cases this is the desired output, but what if you issued a get Pods request and received an error from the API server? How could you get more information about what might be causing the error?

By adding the verbose option to your kubectl command, you can get additional details about the API call itself and any replies from the API server. Often, the replies from the API server will contain additional information that may be useful to find the root cause of the issue.

The verbose option has multiple levels ranging from 0 to 9; the higher the number, the more output you will receive. The following screenshot has been taken from the Kubernetes site, detailing each level and what the output will include:

Verbosity	Description
--v=0	Generally useful for this to *always* be visible to a cluster operator.
--v=1	A reasonable default log level if you don't want verbosity.
--v=2	Useful steady state information about the service and important log messages that may correlate to significant changes in the system. This is the recommended default log level for most systems.
--v=3	Extended information about changes.
--v=4	Debug level verbosity.
--v=6	Display requested resources.
--v=7	Display HTTP request headers.
--v=8	Display HTTP request contents.
--v=9	Display HTTP request contents without truncation of contents.

Figure 5.5 – Verbosity description

You can experiment with the levels by adding the -v or --v option to any kubectl command.

General kubectl commands

The CLI allows you to interact with Kubernetes in an imperative and declarative manner. Using an imperative command involves you telling Kubernetes what to do—for example, kubectl run nginx –image nginx. This tells the API server to create a new deployment called nginx that runs an image called nginx. While imperative commands are useful for development and quick fixes or testing, you will use declarative commands more often in a production environment. In a declarative command, you tell Kubernetes what you want. To use declarative commands, you send a manifest to the API server, usually written in **YAML Ain't Markup Language** (**YAML**), which declares what you want Kubernetes to create.

`kubectl` includes commands and options that can provide general cluster information or information about an object. The following table contains a cheat-sheet of commands and what they are used for. We will use many of these commands in future chapters, so you will see them in action throughout the book:

Cluster Commands	
`api-resources`	List supported API resources
`api-versions`	List supported API versions
`cluster-info`	List cluster information, including the API server and other cluster endpoints
`cluster-info dump`	Get detailed cluster information to troubleshoot issues
Object Commands – Can be executed against most objects	
`get <object>`	Retrieves a list or a single object
`describe <object>`	Provides details on an object
`logs <pod name>`	Retrieves the logs for a pod
`edit <object>`	Edit an object interactively
`delete <object>`	Delete an object
`label <object>`	Create or delete a label for an object
`annotate <object>`	Create or delete an annotation for an object
`run`	Create a deployment, pod, or job depending on the `--restart` option provided in the command line. The default action is to create a deployment.

With an understanding of each Kubernetes component and how to interact with the API server using imperative commands, we can now move on to Kubernetes objects and how we use `kubectl` to manage them.

Introducing Kubernetes objects

This section will contain a lot of information and, since this is a bootcamp, we will not go into deep details on each object. As you can imagine, each object could have its own chapter, or multiple chapters, in a book. Since there are many books on Kubernetes that go into detail on the base objects, we will only cover the required details of each to have an understanding of each one. In the following chapters, we will include additional details for objects as we build out our cluster using the book exercises.

Before we go on to understand what Kubernetes objects really are, let's first explain Kubernetes manifests.

Kubernetes manifests

The files that we will use to create Kubernetes objects are referred to as manifests. A manifest can be created using YAML or **JavaScript Object Notation (JSON)**—most manifests use YAML, and that is the format we will use throughout the book.

The content of a manifest will vary depending on the object, or objects, that will be created. At a minimum, all manifests require a base configuration that include the `apiVersion`, object `KinD`, and `metadata` fields, as can be seen here:

```
apiVersion: apps/v1
KinD: Deployment
metadata:
  labels:
    app: grafana
  name: grafana
  namespace: monitoring
```

The preceding manifest alone is not complete; we are only showing the beginning of a full deployment manifest. As you can see in the file, we start with the three required fields that all manifests are required to have: the `apiVersion`, `KinD`, and `metadata` fields.

You may also notice that there are spaces in the file. YAML is very format-specific, and if the format of any line is off by even a single space, you will receive an error when you try to deploy the manifest. This takes time to get used to, and even after creating manifests for a long time, formatting issues will still pop up from time to time.

What are Kubernetes objects?

When you want to add or delete something from a cluster, you are interacting with a Kubernetes object. An object is what a cluster uses to keep a list of a desired state. The desired state may be to create, delete, or scale an object. Based on the desired state of the object, the API server will make sure that the current state equals the desired state.

To retrieve a list of objects a cluster supports, you can use the `kubectl api-resources` command. The API server will reply with a list of all objects, including any valid short name, namespace support, and supported API group. There are approximately 53 base objects included with a base cluster, but an abbreviated list of the most common objects is shown in the following screenshot:

NAME	SHORTNAMES	APIGROUP	NAMESPACED
configmaps	cm		TRUE
endpoints	ep		TRUE
events	ev		TRUE
namespaces	ns		FALSE
nodes	no		FALSE
persistentvolumeclaims	pvc		TRUE
persistentvolumes	pv		FALSE
pods	po		TRUE
replicationcontrollers	rc		TRUE
resourcequotas	quota		TRUE
secrets			TRUE
serviceaccounts	sa		TRUE
services	svc		TRUE
customresourcedefinitions	crd,crds	apiextensions.k8s.io	FALSE
daemonsets	ds	apps	TRUE
deployments	deploy	apps	TRUE
replicasets	rs	apps	TRUE
statefulsets	sts	apps	TRUE
horizontalpodautoscalers	hpa	autoscaling	TRUE
cronjobs	cj	batch	TRUE
jobs	batch		TRUE
events	ev	events.k8s.io	TRUE
ingresses	ing	extensions	TRUE
ingresses	ing	networking.k8s.io	TRUE
networkpolicies	netpol	networking.k8s.io	TRUE
podsecuritypolicies	psp	policy	FALSE
clusterrolebindings		rbac.authorization.k8s.io	FALSE
clusterroles		rbac.authorization.k8s.io	FALSE
rolebindings		rbac.authorization.k8s.io	TRUE
roles		rbac.authorization.k8s.io	TRUE
csidrivers		storage.k8s.io	FALSE
csinodes		storage.k8s.io	FALSE
storageclasses	sc	storage.k8s.io	FALSE

Figure 5.6 – Kubernetes API resources

Since this chapter is a bootcamp, we will offer a brief review of many of the objects in the list. In order to ensure that you can follow the remaining chapters, we will provide an overview of each object and how to interact with them. Some objects will also be explained in greater detail in future chapters, including `Ingress`, `RoleBindings`, `ClusterRoles`, `StorageClasses`, and more.

Reviewing Kubernetes objects

To make this section easier to follow, we will present each object in the order they were provided by the `kubectl api-services` command.

Most objects in a cluster are run in a namespace, and to create/edit/read them, you should supply the `-n <namespace>` option to any `kubectl` command. To find a list of objects that accept a namespace option, you can reference the output from our previous `get api-server` command. If an object can be referenced by a namespace, the namespaced column will show `true`. If the object is only referenced by the cluster level, the namespaced column will show `false`.

ConfigMaps

A ConfigMap stores data in key-value pairs, providing a way to keep your configuration separate from your application. ConfigMaps may contain data from a literal value, files, or directories.

Here is an imperative example:

```
kubectl create configmap <name> <data>
```

The `name` option will vary based on the source of the ConfigMap. To use a file or a directory, you supply the `--from-file` option and either the path to a file or an entire directory, as shown here:

```
kubectl create configmap config-test --from-file=/apps/nginx-
config/nginx.conf
```

This would create a new ConfigMap named `config-test`, with the `nginx.conf` key containing the content of the `nginx.conf` file as the value.

If you needed to have more than one key added in a single ConfigMap, you could put each file into a directory and create the ConfigMap using all of the files in the directory. As an example, you have three files in a directory located at `~/config/myapp`. In the directory are three files, each containing data, called `config1`, `config2`, and `config3`. To create a ConfigMap that would add each file into a key, you need to supply the `--from-file` option and point to the directory, as follows:

```
kubectl create configmap config-test --from-file=/apps/config/
myapp
```

This would create a new `ConfigMap` with three key values called `config1`, `config2`, and `config3`. Each key would contain a value equal to the content of each file in the directory.

To quickly show a `ConfigMap`, using the example to create a `ConfigMap` from a directory, we can retrieve the `ConfigMap` using the get command, `kubectl get configmaps config-test`, resulting in the following output:

```
NAME            DATA    AGE
config-test     3       7s
```

We can see that the ConfigMap contains three keys, shown as a 3 under the DATA column. To look in greater detail, we can use the same `get` command and output the value of each key as YAML by adding the `-o yaml` option to the `kubectl get configmaps config-test -o yaml` command, resulting in the following output:

```
apiVersion: v1
data:
  config1: |
    Value for Config1
    We have multiple lines to show that a value isnt limited to a single entry
    A config key can have a large amount of data in each key
  config2: |
    Config2 Example
  config3: |
    and last - Config3
kind: ConfigMap
```

Figure 5.7 – kubectl ConfigMap output

Looking at the preceding output, you can see each key matches the filenames, and the value for each key contains the data in each respective file.

One limitation of ConfigMaps that you should keep in mind is that the data is easily accessible to anyone with permissions to the object. As you can see from the preceding output, a simple get command shows the data in cleartext. Due to this design, you should never store sensitive information such as a password in a ConfigMap. Later in this section, we will cover an object that was designed to store sensitive information, called a Secret.

Endpoints

An endpoint maps a service to a Pod or Pods. This will make more sense when we explain the Service object. For now, you only need to know that you can use the CLI to retrieve endpoints by using the kubectl get endpoints command. In a new KinD cluster, you will see a value for the Kubernetes API server in the default namespace, as illustrated in the following code snippet:

```
NAMESPACE    NAME       ENDPOINTS          AGE
default      kubernetes 172.17.0.2:6443    22h
```

The output shows that the cluster has a service called kubernetes that has an endpoint at the **Internet Protocol** (**IP**) address 172.17.0.2 on port 6443. Later, you will see when looking at endpoints that they can be used to troubleshoot service and ingress issues.

Events

The Events object will display any events for a namespace. To get a list of events for the kube-system namespace, you would use the kubectl get events -n kube-system command.

Namespaces

A namespace is an object to divide a cluster into logical units. Each namespace allows granular management of resources, including permissions, quotas, and reporting.

The namespace object is used for namespace tasks, which are cluster-level operations. Using the namespace object, you can execute commands including create, delete, edit, and get.

The syntax for the command is kubectl <verb> ns <namespace name>.

For example, to describe the `kube-system` namespace, we would execute a `kubectl describe namespaces kube-system` command. This will return information for the namespace, including any labels, annotations, and assigned quotas, as illustrated in the following code snippet:

```
Name:            kube-system
Labels:          <none>Annotations:   <none>
Status:          Active


No resource quota.


No LimitRange resource.
```

In the preceding output, you can see that this namespace does not have any labels, annotations, or resource quotas assigned.

This section is only meant to introduce the concept of namespaces as a management unit in multi-tenant clusters. If you plan to run clusters with multiple tenants, you need to understand how namespaces can be used to secure a cluster.

Nodes

The `nodes` object is a cluster-level resource that is used to interact with the cluster's nodes. This object can be used with various actions including `get`, `describe`, `label`, and `annotate`.

To retrieve a list of all of the nodes in a cluster using `kubectl`, you need to execute a `kubectl get nodes` command. On a new KinD cluster running a simple one-node cluster, this would display as follows:

```
NAME                    STATUS ROLES    AGE    VERSION
KinD-control-plane Ready   master   22h    v1.17.0
```

You can also use the nodes object to get details of a single node using the `describe` command. To get a description of the KinD node listed previously, we can execute `kubectl describe node KinD-control-plane`, which would return details on the node, including consumed resources, running Pods, IP **classless inter-domain routing (CIDR)** ranges, and more.

Persistent Volume Claims

We will describe **Persistent Volume Claims** (**PVCs**) in more depth in a later chapter, but for now you just need to know that a PVC is used by a Pod to consume persistent storage. A PVC uses a **persistent volume** (**PV**) to map the storage resource. As with most other objects we have discussed, you can issue `get`, `describe`, and `delete` commands on a PVC object. Since these are used by Pods, they are a `namespaced` object, and must be created in the same namespace as the Pod(s) that will use the PVC.

PVs

PVs are used by PVCs to create a link between the PVC and the underlying storage system. Manually maintaining PVs is a messy task and in the real world it should be avoided, since Kubernetes includes the ability to manage most common storage systems using the **Container Storage Interface** (**CSI**). As mentioned in the **PVC** object section, we will discuss how Kubernetes can automatically create the PVs that will be linked to PVCs.

Pods

The Pod object is used to interact with the Pods that are running your container(s). Using the `kubectl` utility you can use commands such as `get`, `delete`, and `describe`. For example, if you wanted to get a list of all Pods in the `kube-system` namespace, you would execute a `kubectl get Pods -n kube-system` command that would return all Pods in the namespace, as follows:

```
NAME                                          READY   STATUS    RESTARTS   AGE
coredns-6955765f44-brxbz                      1/1     Running   0          23h
coredns-6955765f44-zmkqk                      1/1     Running   0          23h
etcd-kind-control-plane                       1/1     Running   0          23h
kindnet-7q8gm                                 1/1     Running   0          23h
kube-apiserver-kind-control-plane             1/1     Running   0          23h
kube-controller-manager-kind-control-plane    1/1     Running   0          23h
kube-proxy-vvjzx                              1/1     Running   0          23h
kube-scheduler-kind-control-plane             1/1     Running   0          23h
```

Figure 5.8 – All Pods in the kube-system namespace

While you can create a Pod directly, you should avoid doing so unless you are using a Pod for quick troubleshooting. Pods that are created directly cannot use many of the features provided by Kubernetes, including scaling, automatic restarts, or rolling upgrades. Instead of creating a Pod directly, you should use a Deployment, or in some rare cases a `ReplicaSet` object or replication controller.

Replication controllers

Replication controllers will manage the number of running Pods, keeping the desired replicas specified running at all times. If you create a replication controller and set the replica count to 5, the controller will always keep five Pods of the application running.

Replication controllers have been replaced by the `ReplicaSet` object, which we will discuss in its own section. While you can still use replication controllers, you should consider using a Deployment or a `ReplicaSet` object.

ResourceQuotas

It is becoming very common to share a Kubernetes cluster between multiple teams, referred to as a multi-tenant cluster. Since you will have multiple teams working in a single cluster, you should consider creating quotas to limit any potential of a single tenant consuming all the resources in a cluster or on a node. Limits can be set on most cluster objects, including the following:

- **Central processing unit (CPU)**
- Memory
- PVCs
- ConfigMaps
- Deployments
- Pods, and more

Setting a limit will stop any additional objects being created once the limit is hit. If you set a limit of 10 Pods for a namespace and a user creates a new Deployment that attempts to start 11 Pods, the 11th Pod will fail to start up and the user will receive an error.

A basic manifest file to create a quota for memory and CPU would look this:

```
apiVersion: v1
KinD: ResourceQuota
metadata:
  name: base-memory-cpu
spec:
  hard:
    requests.cpu: "2"
```

```
requests.memory: 8Gi
limits.cpu: "4"
limits.memory: 16Gi
```

This will set a limit on the total amount of resources the namespace can use for CPU and memory requests and limits.

Once a quota has been created, you can view the usage using the `kubectl describe` command. In our example, we named the `ResourceQuota base-memory-cpu`. To view the usage, we would execute the `kubectl get resourcequotas base-memory-cpu` command, resulting in the following output:

```
Name:                 base-memory-cpu
Namespace:            default
Resource              Used      Hard
--------              ----      ----
limits.cpu            0         4
limits.memory         0         16Gi
requests.cpu          0         2
requests.memory       0         8Gi
```

`ResourceQuota` objects are used to control a cluster's resources. By allocating the resources to a namespace, you can guarantee that a single tenant will have the required CPU and memory to run their application, while limiting the impact that a poorly written application can have on other applications.

Secrets

Earlier we described how to use a `ConfigMap` object to store configuration information. We mentioned that `ConfigMap` objects should never be used to store any type of sensitive data. This is the job of a Secret.

Secrets are stored as Base64-encoded strings, which aren't a form of encryption. So, why separate Secrets from `ConfigMap` objects? Providing a separate object type offers an easier way to maintain access controls and the ability to inject sensitive information using an external system.

Secrets can be created using a file, directory, or from a literal string. As an example, we have a MySQL image we want to execute, and we would like to pass the password to the Pod using a Secret. On our workstation, we have a file called dbpwd in our current working directory that has our password in it. Using the kubectl command, we can create a Secret by executing kubectl create secret generic mysql-admin --from-file=./dbpwd.

This would create a new a Secret called mysql-admin in the current namespace, with the content of the dbpwd file. Using kubectl, we can get the output of the Secret by running the kubectl get secret mysql-admin -o yaml command, which would output the following:

```
apiVersion: v1
data:
  dbpwd: c3VwZXJzZWNyZXQtcGFzc3dvcmQK
KinD: Secret
metadata:
  creationTimestamp: "2020-03-24T18:39:31Z"
  name: mysql-admin
  namespace: default
  resourceVersion: "464059"
  selfLink: /api/v1/namespaces/default/secrets/mysql-admin
  uid: 69220ebd-c9fe-4688-829b-242ffc9e94fc
type: Opaque
```

Looking at the preceding output, you can see that the data section contains the name of our file and then a Base64-encoded value, which was created from the content of the file.

If we copy the Base64 value from the Secret and pipe it out to the base64 utility, we can easily decode the password, as follows:

```
echo c3VwZXJzZWNyZXQtcGFzc3dvcmQK | base64 -d
supersecret-password
```

> **Tip**
>
> When using the echo command to Base64-encode strings, add the -n flag to avoid adding an additional \n. Instead of echo 'test' | base64, use echo -n 'test' | base64.

Everything is stored in Etcd, but we are concerned that someone may be able to hack into the master server and steal a copy of the Etcd database. Once someone has a copy of the database, they could easily use the `etcdctl` utility to look through the content to retrieve all of our Base64-encoded Secrets. Luckily, Kubernetes added a feature to encrypt Secrets when they are written to a database.

Enabling this feature can be fairly complex for many users, and while it sounds like a good idea, it does present some potential issues that you should consider before implementing it. If you would like to read the steps on encrypting your Secrets at rest, you can view these on the Kubernetes site at `https://kubernetes.io/docs/tasks/administer-cluster/encrypt-data/`.

Another option to secure Secrets is to use a third-party Secrets management tool such as HashiCorp's Vault or CyberArk's Conjur.

Service accounts

Kubernetes uses service accounts to enable access controls for workloads. When you create a Deployment, you may need to access other services or Kubernetes objects. Since Kubernetes is a secure system, each object or service your application tries to access will evaluate **role-based access control** (**RBAC**) rules to accept or deny the request.

Creating a service account using a manifest is a straightforward process, requiring only a few lines in the manifest. The following code snippet shows a service account manifest to create a service account for a Grafana Deployment:

```
apiVersion: v1
KinD: ServiceAccount
metadata:
  name: grafana
  namespace: monitoring
```

You combine the service account with role bindings and roles to allow access to the required services or objects.

Services

In order to make an application running in a Pod(s) available to the network, you need to create a service. A service object stores information about how to expose the application, including which Pods are running on the application and the network ports to reach them.

Each service has a network type that is assigned when they are created, and they include the following:

- `ClusterIP`: A network type that is only accessible inside the cluster itself. This type can still be used for external requests using an ingress controller, which will be discussed in a later chapter.

- `NodePort`: A network type that exposes the service to a random port between ports `30000-32767`.This port becomes accessible by targeting any worker node in a cluster on the assigned `NodePort`. Once created, each node in the cluster will receive the port information and incoming requests will be routed via `kube-proxy`.

- `LoadBalancer`: This type requires an add-on to use inside a cluster. If you are running Kubernetes on a public cloud provider, this type will create an external load balancer that will assign an IP address to your service. Most on-premise Kubernetes installations do not include support for the `LoadBalancer` type, but some offerings such as Google's Anthos do offer support for it. In a later chapter, we will explain how to add an open source project called `MetalLB` to a Kubernetes cluster to provide support for the `LoadBalancer` type.

- `ExternalName`: This type is different from the other three. Unlike the other three options, this type will not assign an IP address to the service. Instead, this is used to map the internal Kubernetes **Domain Name System** (**DNS**) name to an external service.

As an example, we have deployed a Pod running Nginx on port `80`. We want to create a service that will allow this Pod to receive incoming requests on port `80` from within the cluster. The code for this can be seen in the following snippet:

```
apiVersion: v1
KinD: Service
metadata:
  labels:
    app: nginx-web-frontend
  name: nginx-web
spec:
  ports:
  - name: http
    port: 80
```

```
    targetPort: 80
  selector:
    app: nginx-web
```

In our manifest, we create a label with a value of app and assign a value of nginx-web-frontend. We have called the service itself nginx-web and we exposed the service on port 80, targeting the Pod port of 80. The last two lines of the manifest are used to assign the Pods that the service will forward to, also known as endpoints. In this manifest, any Pod that has the label of app with a value of nginx-web in the namespace will be added as an endpoint to the service.

CustomResourceDefinitions

CustomResourceDefinitions (**CRDs**) allow anyone to extend Kubernetes by integrating your application into a cluster as a standard object. Once a CRD is created, you can reference it using an API endpoint, and it can be interacted with using standard kubectl commands.

DaemonSets

A DaemonSet allows you to deploy a Pod on every node in a cluster, or a subset of nodes. A common use for a DaemonSet is to deploy a log forwarding Pod such as FluentD to every node in a cluster. Once deployed, the DaemonSet will create a FluentD Pod on all existing nodes. Since a DaemonSet deploys to all nodes, any additional nodes that are added to a cluster will have a FluentD Pod started once the node has joined the cluster.

Deployments

We mentioned earlier that you should never deploy a Pod directly, and we also introduced the ReplicationContoller object as an alternative to creating Pods directly. While both of these will create your Pods, each comes with the following limitation: Pods created directly cannot be scaled and cannot be upgraded using rolling updates.

Pods created by a ReplicationController can be scaled, and can perform rolling updates. However, they do not support rollbacks, and upgrades cannot be done declaratively.

Deployments offer you a few advantages, including a way to manage your upgrades declaratively and the ability to roll back to previous revisions. Creating a Deployment is actually a three-step process executed by the API server: a Deployment is created, which creates a ReplicaSet object, which then creates the Pod(s) for the application.

Even if you don't plan to use these features, you should use Deployments by default so that you can leverage the features at a future date.

ReplicaSets

ReplicaSets can be used to create a Pod or a set of Pods (replicas). Similar to the `ReplicationController` object, a `ReplicaSet` object will maintain the set number of Pods defined in the replica count of the object. If there are too few Pods, Kubernetes will reconcile the difference and create the missing Pods. If there are too many Pods for a ReplicaSet, Kubernetes will delete Pods until the number is equal to the replica count set in the object.

In general, you should avoid creating ReplicaSets directly. Instead, you should create a Deployment, which will create and manage a ReplicaSet.

StatefulSets

StatefulSets offer some unique features when creating Pods. They provide features that none of the other Pod creation methods offer, including the following:

- Known Pod names
- Ordered Deployment and scaling
- Ordered updates
- Persistent storage creation

The best way to understand the advantages of a StatefulSet is to review an example manifest from the Kubernetes site, shown in the following screenshot:

```
apiVersion: apps/v1
kind: StatefulSet
metadata:
  name: web
spec:
  selector:
    matchLabels:
      app: nginx
  serviceName: "nginx"
  replicas: 3 ──────────────────────────────  Create Three Pods
  template:
    metadata:
      labels:
        app: nginx
    spec:
      terminationGracePeriodSeconds: 10
      containers:
      - name: nginx ─────────────────────────  Name that will be
        image: k8s.gcr.io/nginx-slim:0.8       used for the pods
        ports:
        - containerPort: 80
          name: web
        volumeMounts: ───────────────────────  Mount PVC at
        - name: www                            /usr/share/nginx/html
          mountPath: /usr/share/nginx/html
  volumeClaimTemplates: ─────────────────────
  - metadata:
      name: www
    spec:
      accessModes: [ "ReadWriteOnce" ]
      storageClassName: nfs ─────────────────  PVC Creation - Using
      resources:                               the storage class
        requests:                              named nfs
          storage: 1Gi
```

Figure 5.9 – StatefulSet manifest example

Now, we can look at the objects that the StatefulSet object created.

The manifest specifies that there should be three replicas of a Pod named `nginx`. When we get a list of Pods, you will see that three Pods were created using the `nginx` name, with an additional dash and an incrementing number. This is what we meant in the overview when we mentioned that Pods will be created with known names, as illustrated in the following code snippet:

NAME	READY	STATUS	RESTARTS	AGE
web-0	1/1	Running	0	4m6s
web-1	1/1	Running	0	4m2s
web-2	1/1	Running	0	3m52s

The Pods are also created in order – web-0 must be fully deployed before web-1 is created, and then finally web-2.

Finally, for this example, we also added a PVC to each Pod using the `VolumeClaimTemplate` in the manifest. If you look at the output of the `kubectl get pvc` command, you would see that three PVCs were created with names we expected (note that we removed the VOLUME column due to space), as illustrated in the following code snippet:

NAME AGE	STATUS	CAPACITY	ACCESS MODES	STORAGECLASS
www-web-0 nfs	Bound	1Gi 13m		RWO
www-web-1 nfs	Bound	1Gi 13m		RWO
www-web-2 nfs	Bound	1Gi 12m		RWO

In the `VolumeClaimTemplate` section of the manifest, you will see that we assigned the name www to the PVC claim. When you assign a volume in a StatefulSet, the PVC name will combine the name used in the claim template, combined with the name of the Pod. Using this naming, you can see why Kubernetes assigned the PVC names www-web-0, www-web-1, and www-web-2.

HorizontalPodAutoscalers

One of the biggest advantages of running a workload on a Kubernetes cluster is the ability to easily scale your Pods. While you can scale using the `kubectl` command or by editing a manifest's replica count, these are not automated and require manual intervention.

HorizontalPodAutoscalers (**HPAs**) provide the ability to scale an application based on a set of criteria. Using metrics such as CPU and memory usage, or your own custom metrics, you can set a rule to scale your Pods up when you need more Pods to maintain your service level. After a cooldown period, Kubernetes will scale the application back to the minimum number of Pods defined in the policy.

To quickly create an HPA for an `nginx` Deployment, we can execute a `kubectl` command using the `autoscale` option, as follows:

```
kubectl autoscale deployment nginx --cpu-percent=50 --min=1
--max=5
```

You can also create a Kubernetes manifest to create your HPAs. Using the same options as those we did in the CLI, our manifest would look like this:

```
apiVersion: autoscaling/v1
KinD: HorizontalPodAutoscaler
metadata:
  name: nginx-deployment
spec:
  maxReplicas: 5
  minReplicas: 1
  scaleTargetRef:
    apiVersion: apps/v1
    KinD: Deployment
    name: nginx-deployment
  targetCPUUtilizationPercentage: 50
```

Both options will create an HPA that will scale our `nginx-deployment nginx` Deployment up to five replicas when the Deployment hits a CPU utilization of 50%. Once the Deployment usage falls below 50% and the cooldown period is reached (by default, 5 minutes), the replica count will be reduced down to 1.

CronJobs

If you have used Linux cronjobs in the past, then you already know what a Kubernetes `CronJob` object is. If you don't have a Linux background, a cronjob is used to create a scheduled task. As another example, if you are a Windows person, it's similar to Windows scheduled tasks.

An example manifest that creates a `CronJob` is shown in the following code snippet:

```yaml
apiVersion: batch/v1beta1
KinD: CronJob
metadata:
  name: hello-world
spec:
  schedule: "*/1 * * *"
  jobTemplate:
    spec:
      template:
        spec:
          containers:
          - name: hello-world
            image: busybox
            args:
            - /bin/sh
            - -c
            - date; echo Hello World!
          restartPolicy: OnFailure
```

The `schedule` format follows the standard `cron` format. From left to right, each * represents the following:

- Minute (0 – 59)
- Hour (0 -23)
- Day (1 -31)
- Month (1 – 12)
- Day of the week (0 – 6) (Sunday = 0, Saturday = 6)

Cron jobs accept step values, which allow you to create a schedule that can execute every minute, every 2 minutes, or every hour.

Our example manifest will create a `cronjob` that runs an image called `hello-world` every minute and outputs `Hello World!` in the Pod log.

Jobs

Jobs allow you to execute a specific number of executions of a Pod or Pods. Unlike a `cronjob` object, these Pods are not run on a set schedule, but rather they will execute once created. Jobs are used to execute a task that may only need to be executed at the initial Deployment stage.

An example use case would be an application that may require the creation of Kubernetes CRDs that must exist before the main application is deployed. The Deployment would wait until the job execution completed successfully.

Events

Events objects store information about events for Kubernetes objects. You do not create events; rather, you can only retrieve events. For example, to retrieve events for the `kube-system` namespace, you would execute `kubectl get events -n kube-system`, or to show events for all namespaces, you'd execute `kubectl get events --all-namespaces`.

Ingresses

You may have noticed that the `Ingress` object was listed twice in our `api-server` output. This will happen to objects as Kubernetes upgrades are released and objects changed in the API server. In the case of Ingress, it was original part of the extensions API and was moved to the `networking.k8s.io` API in version 1.16. The project will wait a few releases before deprecating the old API call, so in our example cluster running Kubernetes 1.17, using either API will work. In version 1.18, they have plans to fully deprecate the Ingress extensions.

NetworkPolicies

`NetworkPolicy` objects let you define how network traffic can flow through your cluster. They allow you to use Kubernetes native constructs to define which Pods can talk to other Pods. If you've ever used Security Groups in **Amazon Web Services** (**AWS**) to lock down access between two groups of systems, it's a similar concept. As an example, the following policy will allow traffic on port 443 to Pods in the `myns` namespace from any namespace with the `app.kubernetes.io/name: ingress-nginx` label on it (which is the default label for the `nginx-ingress` namespace):

```
apiVersion: networking.k8s.io/v1
KinD: NetworkPolicy
metadata:
  name: allow-from-ingress
  namespace: myns
spec:
  PodSelector: {}
  policyTypes:
  - Ingress
  ingress:
  - from:
    - namespaceSelector:
        matchLabels:
          app.kubernetes.io/name: ingress-nginx    ports:
    - protocol: TCP
      port: 443
```

A `NetworkPolicy` object is another object that you can use to secure a cluster. They should be used in all production clusters, but in a multi-tenant cluster they should be considered a **must-have** to secure each namespace in the cluster.

PodSecurityPolicies

`PodSecurityPolicies` (**PSPs**) are how your cluster protects your nodes from your containers. They allow you to limit the actions that a Pod can execute in a cluster. Some examples include denying access to the HostIPC and HostPath, and running a container in a privileged mode.

We'll get into the details of PSPs in *Chapter 10*, *Creating Pod Security Policies*. The key point to remember about PSPs is that without them, your containers can do almost anything on your nodes.

ClusterRoleBindings

Once you have defined a `ClusterRole`, you bind it to a subject via a `ClusterRoleBinding`. A `ClusterRole` can be bound to a User, Group, or ServiceAccount.

We'll explore `ClusterRoleBinding` details in *Chapter 8, RBAC Policies and Auditing*.

ClusterRoles

A `ClusterRole` combines a set of permissions for interacting with your cluster's API. A `ClusterRole` combines a verb or action with an API group to define a permission. For instance, if you only want your **continuous integration/continuous delivery (CI/CD)** pipeline to be able to patch your Deployments so that it can update your image tag, you might use a `ClusterRole` like this:

```
apiVersion: rbac.authorization.k8s.io/v1
KinD: ClusterRole
metadata:
  name: patch-deployment
rules:
- apiGroups: ["apps/v1"]
  resources: ["deployments"]
  verbs: ["get", "list", "patch"]
```

A `ClusterRole` can apply to APIs at both the cluster and namespace level.

RoleBindings

The `RoleBinding` object is how you associate a Role or `ClusterRole` to a subject and namespace. For instance, the following `RoleBinding` object will allow the `aws-codebuild` user to apply the `patch-openunison` ClusterRole to the `openunison` namespace:

```
apiVersion: rbac.authorization.k8s.io/v1
KinD: RoleBinding
metadata:
  name: patch-openunison
  namespace: openunison
subjects:
```

```
- KinD: User
  name: aws-codebuild
  apiGroup: rbac.authorization.k8s.io
roleRef:
  KinD: ClusterRole
  name: patch-deployment
  apiGroup: rbac.authorization.k8s.io
```

Even though this references a ClusterRole, it will only apply to the openunison namespace. If the aws-codebuild user tries to patch a Deployment in another namespace, the API server will stop it.

Roles

As with a ClusterRole, Roles combine API groups and actions to define a set of permissions that can be assigned to a subject. The difference between a ClusterRole and a Role is that a Role can only have resources defined at the namespace level and applies only within a specific namespace.

CsiDrivers

Kubernetes uses the CsiDriver object to connect nodes to a storage system.

You can list all CSI drivers that are available on a cluster by executing the kubectl get csidriver command. In one of our clusters we are using Netapp's SolidFire for storage, so our cluster has the Trident CSI driver installed, as can be seen here:

NAME	CREATED AT
csi.trident.netapp.io	2019-09-04T19:10:47Z

CsiNodes

To avoid storing storage information in the node API object, the CSINode object was added to the API server to store information generated by the CSI drivers. The information that is stored includes mapping Kubernetes node names to CSI node names, CSI driver availability, and the volume topology.

StorageClasses

Storage classes are used to define a storage endpoint. Each storage class can be assigned labels and policies, allowing a developer to select the best storage location for their persistent data. You may create a storage class for a backend system that has all **Non-Volatile Memory Express (NVMe)** drives, assigning it the name `fast`, while assigning a different class to a Netapp **Network File System (NFS)** volume running standard drives, using the name `standard`.

When a PVC is requested, the user can assign a `StorageClass` that they wish to use. When the API server receives the request, it finds the matching name and uses the `StorageClass` configuration to create the volume on the storage system using a provisioner.

At a very high level, a `StorageClass` manifest does not require a lot of information. Here is an example of a storage class using a provisioner from the Kubernetes incubator project to provide NFS auto-provisioned volumes, named `nfs`:

```
apiVersion: storage.k8s.io/v1
KinD: StorageClass
metadata:
  name: nfs
provisioner: nfs
```

Storage classes allow you to offer multiple storage solutions to your users. You may create a class for cheaper, slower storage while offering a second class that supports high throughput for high data requirements. By providing a different class to each offering, you allow developers to select the best choice for their application.

Summary

In this chapter, you were thrown into a Kubernetes bootcamp that presented a lot of technical material in a short amount of time. Try to remember that this will all become easier as you get into the Kubernetes world in more depth. We realize that this chapter had a lot of information on many objects. Many of the objects will be used in later chapters, and they will be explained in greater detail.

You learned about each Kubernetes component and how they interact to create a cluster. With this knowledge, you have the required skills to look at errors in a cluster and determine which component may be causing an error or issue. We covered the control plane of a cluster where the `api-server`, `kube-scheduler`, Etcd, and control managers run. The control plane is how users and services interact with a cluster; using the `api-server` and the `kube-scheduler` will decide which worker node to schedule your Pod(s) on. You also learned about Kubernetes nodes that run the `kubelet` and `kube-proxy` components, and a container runtime.

We covered the `kubectl` utility that you will use to interact with a cluster. You also learned some common commands that you will use on a daily basis, including `logs` and `describe`.

In the next chapter, we will create a development Kubernetes cluster that we will use as the base cluster for the remaining chapters. Throughout the remainder of the book, we will reference many of the objects that were presented in this chapter, helping to explain them by using them in real-world examples.

Questions

1. A Kubernetes control plane does not include which of the following components?

   A. `api-server`

   B. `kube-scheduler`

   C. Etcd

   D. Ingress controller

2. What is the name of the component that keeps all of the cluster information?

   A. `api-server`

   B. Master controller

   C. `kubelet`

   D. Etcd

3. Which component is responsible for selecting the node that will run a workload?

   A. `kubelet`

   B. `api-server`

   C. `kube-scheduler`

   D. `Pod-scheduler`

4. Which option would you add to a `kubectl` command to see additional output from a command?

   A. `Verbose`

   B. `-v`

   C. `–verbose`

   D. `-log`

5. Which service type creates a randomly generated port, allowing incoming traffic to any worker node on the assigned port to access the service?

   A. `LoadBalancer`

   B. `ClusterIP`

   C. None—it's the default for all services

   D. `NodePort`

6. If you need to deploy an application on a Kubernetes cluster that requires known node names and a controlled startup of each Pod, which object would you create?

   A. `StatefulSet`

   B. `Deployment`

   C. `ReplicaSet`

   D. `ReplicationController`

6
Services, Load Balancing, and External DNS

When you deploy an application to a Kubernetes cluster, your pods are assigned ephemeral IP addresses. Since the assigned addresses are likely to change as pods are restarted, you should never target a service using a pod IP address; instead, you should use a service object, which will map a service IP address to backend pods based on labels. If you need to offer service access to external requests, you can deploy an Ingress controller, which will expose your service to external traffic on a per-URL basis. For more advanced workloads, you can deploy a load balancer, which provides your service with an external IP address, allowing you to expose any IP-based service to external requests.

We will explain how to implement each of these by deploying them on our KinD cluster. To help us understand how the Ingress works, we will deploy a NGINX Ingress controller to the cluster and expose a web server. Since Ingress rules are based on the incoming URL name, we need to be able to provide stable DNS names. In an enterprise environment, this would be accomplished using standard DNS. Since we are using a development environment without a DNS server, we will use a popular service from nip.io.

To end the chapter, we will explain how you can dynamically register service names using an ETCD-integrated DNS zone with the Kubernetes incubator project, external-dns.

In this chapter, we will cover the following topics:

- Exposing workloads to requests
- Introduction to load balancers
- Layer 7 load balancers
- Layer 4 load balancers
- Making service names available externally

Technical requirements

This chapter has the following technical requirements:

- A new Ubuntu 18.04 server with a minimum of 4 GB of RAM.
- A KinD cluster configured using the configuration from Chapter 4, Deploying Kubernetes using KinD.

You can access the code for this chapter at GitHub repository `https://github.com/PacktPublishing/Kubernetes-and-Docker-The-Complete-Guide`.

Exposing workloads to requests

Three of the most misunderstood objects in Kubernetes are services, Ingress controllers, and load balancers. In order to expose your workloads, you need to understand how each object works and the options that are available to you. Let's look at these in detail.

Understanding how services work

As we mentioned in the introduction, any pod that is running a workload is assigned an IP address at pod startup. Many events will cause a deployment to restart a pod, and when the pod is restarted, it will likely receive a new IP address. Since the addresses that are assigned to pods may change, you should never target a pod's workload directly.

One of the most powerful features that Kubernetes offers is the ability to scale your deployments. When a deployment is scaled, Kubernetes will create additional pods to handle any additional resource requirements. Each pod will have an IP address, and as you may know, most applications only target a single IP address or name. If your application were to scale from a single pod to ten pods, how would you utilize the additional pods?

Services use Kubernetes labels to create a dynamic mapping between the service itself and the pods running the workload. The pods that are running the workload are labeled when they start up. Each pod has the same label that is defined in the deployment. For example, if we were using a NGINX web server in our deployment, we would create a deployment with the following manifest:

```
apiVersion: apps/v1
kind: Deployment
metadata:
  creationTimestamp: null
  labels:
    run: nginx-frontend
  name: nginx-frontend
spec:
  replicas: 3
  selector:
    matchLabels:
      run: nginx-frontend
  strategy: {}
  template:
    metadata:
      labels:
        run: nginx-frontend
    spec:
      containers:
      - image: bitnami/nginx
        name: nginx-frontend
```

This deployment will create three NGINX servers and each pod will be labeled with run=nginx-frontend. We can verify whether the pods are labeled correctly by listing the pods using kubectl, adding the --show-labels option, kubectl get pods --show-labels.

This will list each pod and any associated labels:

```
nginx-frontend-6c4dbf86d4-72cbc              1/1        Running
0           19s    pod-template-hash=6c4dbf86d4,run=nginx-
frontend
nginx-frontend-6c4dbf86d4-8zlwc              1/1        Running
0           19s    pod-template-hash=6c4dbf86d4,run=nginx-
frontend
nginx-frontend-6c4dbf86d4-xfz6m              1/1        Running
0           19s    pod-template-hash=6c4dbf86d4,run=nginx-
frontend
```

As you can see from the preceding output, each pod has a label, `run=nginx-frontend`. You will use this label when you create your service for the application, configuring the service to use the label to create the endpoints.

Creating a service

Now that you know how a service will use labels to create endpoints, let's discuss the service options we have in Kubernetes.

This section will introduce each service type and show you how to create a service object. Each type will be detailed in its own section after the general introduction.

Kubernetes services can be created using one of four types:

Service Type	Description
ClusterIP	Creates a service that is accessible from inside of the cluster.
NodePort	Creates a service that is accessible from inside or outside of the cluster using an assigned port.
LoadBalancer	Creates a service that is accessible from inside or outside of the cluster. For external access, an additional component is required to create the load-balanced object.
ExternalName	Creates a service that does not target an endpoint in the cluster. Instead, it is used to provide a service name that targets any external DNS name as an endpoint.

Table 6.1: Kubernetes service types

To create a service, you need to create a service object that includes the `kind`, a `selector`, a `type`, and any `ports` that will be used to connect to the service. For our NGINX deployment, we want to expose the service on ports 80 and 443. We labeled the deployment with `run=nginx-frontend`, so when we create a manifest, we will use that name as our selector:

```
apiVersion: v1
kind: Service
metadata:
  labels:
    run: nginx-frontend
  name: nginx-frontend
spec:
  selector:
    run: nginx-frontend
  ports:
  - name: http
    port: 80
    protocol: TCP
    targetPort: 80
  - name: https
    port: 443
    protocol: TCP
    targetPort: 443
  type: ClusterIP
```

If a type is not defined in a service manifest, Kubernetes will assign a default type of `ClusterIP`.

Now that a service has been created, we can verify that it was correctly defined using a few `kubectl` commands. The first check we will perform is to verify that the service object was created. To check our service, we use the `kubectl get services` command:

```
NAME                     TYPE          CLUSTER-IP     EXTERNAL-IP
PORT(S)                  AGE
nginx-frontend    ClusterIP    10.43.142.96    <none>
80/TCP,443/TCP    3m49s
```

After verifying that the service has been created, we can verify that the endpoints were created. Using kubectl, we can verify the endpoints by executing `kubectl get ep <service name>`:

```
NAME                   ENDPOINTS
AGE
nginx-frontend    10.42.129.9:80,10.42.170.91:80,10.42.183.124:
80 + 3 more...     7m49s
```

We can see that the service shows three endpoints, but it also shows a `+3 more` in the endpoint list. Since the output is truncated, the output from a get is limited and it cannot show all of the endpoints. Since we cannot see the entire list, we can get a more detailed list if we describe the endpoints. Using kubectl, you can execute the `kubectl describe ep <service name>` command:

```
Name:           nginx-frontend
Namespace:      default
Labels:         run=nginx-frontend
Annotations:    endpoints.kubernetes.io/last-change-trigger-time:
2020-04-06T14:26:08Z
Subsets:
  Addresses:              10.42.129.9,10.42.170.91,10.42.183.124
  NotReadyAddresses:   <none>
  Ports:
    Name    Port  Protocol
    ----          ----  --------
    http         80         TCP
    https  443  TCP

Events:   <none>
```

If you compare the output from our `get` and `describe` commands, it may appear that there is a mismatch in endpoints. The `get` command showed a total of six endpoints: it showed three IP endpoints and because it was truncated, it also listed a `+3`, for a total of six endpoints. The output from the `describe` command shows only three IP addresses, not six. Why do the two outputs appear to show different results?

The `get` command will list each endpoint and port in the list of addresses. Since our service is defined to expose two ports, each address will have two entries, one for each exposed port. The address list will always contain every socket for the service, which may list the endpoint addresses multiple times, once for each socket.

The `describe` command handles the output differently, listing the addresses on one line with all of the ports listed below the addresses. At first glance, it may look like the `describe` command is missing three address, but since it breaks the output into multiple sections, it will only list the addresses once. All ports are broken out below the address list; in our example, it shows port 80 and 443.

Both commands show the same data, but it's presented in a different format.

Now that the service is exposed to the cluster, you could use the assigned service IP address to connect to the application. While this would work, the address may change if the service object is deleted and recreated. Rather than target an IP address, you should use the DNS that was assigned to the service when it was created. In the next section, we will explain how to use internal DNS names to resolve services.

Using DNS to resolve services

In the world of physical machines and virtual servers, you have probably targeted a DNS record to communicate with a server. If the IP address of the server changed, then assuming you had dynamic DNS enabled, it would not have any effect on the application. This is the advantage of using names rather than IP addresses as endpoints.

When you create a service, an internal DNS record is created that can be queried by other workloads in the cluster. If all pods are in the same namespace, then we can target the services using a simple, short name like, `mysql-web`; however, you may have some services that will be used by multiple namespaces, and when workloads need to communicate to a service outside of their own namespace, you must target the service using the full name. The following is an example table showing how a service may be targeted from namespaces:

Cluster name: `cluster.local` Target Service: `mysql-web` Target Service Namespace: `database`	
Pod Namespace	Valid Names to Connect to the MySQL Service
`database`	`mysql-web`
`kube-system`	`mysql-web.database.svc` `mysql-web.database.svc.cluster.local`
`production-web`	`mysql-web.database.svc` `mysql-web.database.svc.cluster.local`

Table 6.2: Internal DNS examples

As you can see from the preceding table, you can target a service that is in another namespace by using a standard naming convention, .*<namespace>.svc.<cluster name>*. In most cases, when you are accessing a service in a different namespace, you do not need to add the cluster name since it should be appended automatically.

To build on the general services concept, let's get into the details of each of the types and how we can use them to access our workloads.

Understanding different service types

When you create a service, you need to specify a service type. The service type that is assigned will configure how the service is exposed to either the cluster or external traffic.

The ClusterIP service

The most commonly used, and misunderstood, service type is ClusterIP. If you look back at our table, you can see that the description for the ClusterIP type states that the service allows connectivity to the service from within the cluster. The ClusterIP type does not allow any external traffic to the exposed service.

The idea of exposing a service to only internal cluster workloads can be a confusing concept. Why would you expose a service that can only be used by workloads in the cluster?

For a minute, let's forget about external traffic entirely. We need to concentrate on our current deployment and how each component interacts to create our application. Using the NGINX example, we will expand the deployment to include a backend database that services the web server.

Our application will have two deployments, one for the NGINX servers and one for the database server. The NGINX deployment will create five replicas while the database server will consist of a single replica. The NGINX servers need to connect to the database server to pull data for the web pages.

So far, this is a simple application: we have our deployments created, a service for the NGINX servers called the web frontend, and a database service called `mysql-web`. To configure the database connection from the web servers, we have decided to use a ConfigMap that will target the database service. What do we use in the ConfigMap as the destination for the database?

You may be thinking that since we are using a single database server, we could simply use the IP address. While this would initially work, any restarts to the pod would change the address and the web servers would fail to connect to the database. A service should always be used, even if you are only targeting a single pod. Since the database deployment is called mysql-web, our ConfigMap should use that name as the database server.

By using the service name, we will not run into issues when the pod is restarted since the service targets the labels rather than an IP address. Our web servers will simply query the Kubernetes DNS server for the service name, which will contain the endpoints of any pod that has a matching label.

The NodePort service

A NodePort service will expose your service internally to the cluster, as well as externally to the network. At a first glance, this may look like the go-to service when you want to expose a service. It exposes your service to everybody, but it does this by using something called a NodePort, and using it for external service access can become difficult to maintain. It is also very confusing for users to use a NodePort or remember when they need to access a service over the network.

To create a service that uses the NodePort type, you just need to set the type to NodePort in your manifest. We can use the same manifest that we used earlier to expose a NGINX deployment from the ClusterIP example, only changing the `type` to `NodePort`:

```
apiVersion: v1
kind: Service
metadata:
  labels:
    run: nginx-frontend
  name: nginx-frontend
spec:
  selector:
    run: nginx-frontend
  ports:
  - name: http
    port: 80
    protocol: TCP
    targetPort: 80
  - name: https
    port: 443
```

```
    protocol: TCP
    targetPort: 443
  type: NodePort
```

We can view the endpoints in the same way that we did for a ClusterIP service, using kubectl. Running a `kubectl get services` will show you the newly created service:

```
NAME                        TYPE
CLUSTER-IP        EXTERNAL-IP      PORT(S)
AGE

nginx-frontend       NodePort     10.43.164.118      <none>
80:31574/TCP,443:32432/TCP    4s
```

The output shows that the type is NodePort and that we have exposed the service IP address and the ports. If you look at the ports, you will notice that unlike a ClusterIP service, a NodePort service shows two ports rather than one. The first port is the exposed port that the internal cluster services can target and the second port number is the randomly generated port that is accessible from outside of the cluster.

Since we exposed both ports 80 and 443 for the service, we will have two NodePorts assigned. If someone needs to target the service from outside of the cluster, they can target any worker node with the supplied port to access the service:

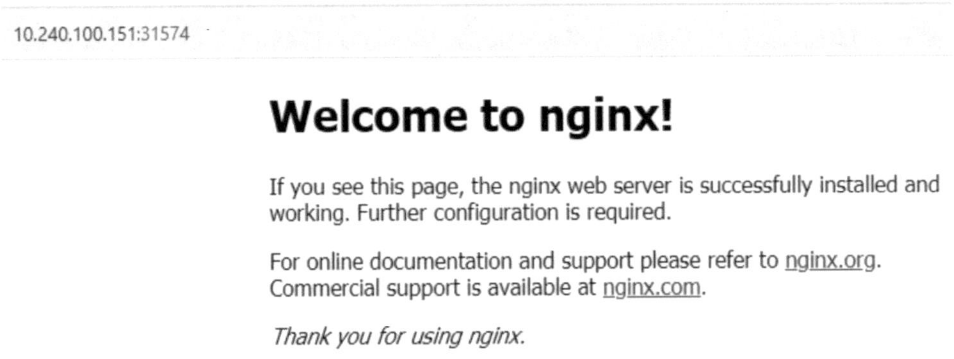

10.240.100.151:31574

Welcome to nginx!

If you see this page, the nginx web server is successfully installed and working. Further configuration is required.

For online documentation and support please refer to nginx.org. Commercial support is available at nginx.com.

Thank you for using nginx.

Figure 6.1 – NGINX service using NodePort

Each node maintains a list of the NodePorts and their assigned services. Since the list is shared with all nodes, you can target any functioning node using the port and Kubernetes will route it to a running pod.

To visualize the traffic flow, we have created a graphic showing the web request to our NGINX pod:

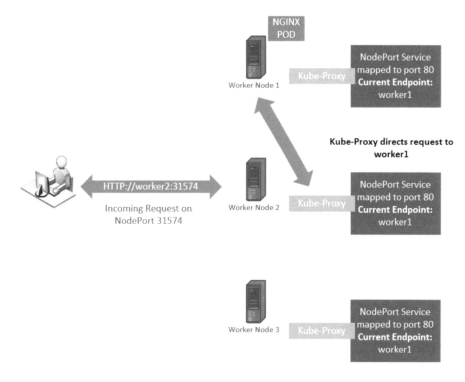

Figure 6.2 – NodePort traffic flow overview

There are some issues to consider when using a NodePort to expose a service:

- If you delete and recreate the service, the assigned NodePort will change.

- If you target a node that is offline or having issues, your request will fail.

- Using NodePort for too many services may get confusing. You need to remember the port for each service, and remember that there are no *external* names associated with the service. This may get confusing for users that are targeting services in the cluster.

Because of the limitations listed here, you should limit using NodePort services.

The LoadBalancer service

Many people starting out in Kubernetes read about services and discover that the LoadBalancer type will assign an external IP address to a service. Since an external IP address can be addressed directly by any machine on the network, this is an attractive option for a service, which is why many people try to use it first. Unfortunately, since many users start by using an on-premise Kubernetes cluster, they run into headaches trying to create a LoadBalancer service.

The LoadBalancer service relies on an external component that integrates with Kubernetes to create the IP address assigned to the service. Most on-premise Kubernetes installations do not include this type of service. When you try to use a LoadBalancer service without the support infrastructure, you will find that your service shows `<pending>` in the EXTERNAL-IP status column.

We will explain the LoadBalancer service and how to implement it later in the chapter.

The ExternalName service

The ExternalName service is a unique service type with a specific use case. When you query a service that uses an ExternalName type, the final endpoint is not a pod that is running in the cluster, but an external DNS name.

To use an example that you may be familiar with outside of Kubernetes, this is similar to using c-name to alias a host record. When you query a c-name record in DNS, it resolves to a host record rather than an IP address.

Before using this service type, you need to understand potential issues that it may cause for your application. You may run into issues if the target endpoint is using SSL certificates. Since the hostname you are querying may not be the same as the name on the destination server's certificate, your connection may not succeed because of the name mismatch. If you find yourself in this situation, you may be able to use a certificate that has **subject alternative names (SAN)** added to the certificate. Adding alternative names to a certificate allow you to associate multiple names with a certificate.

To explain why you may want to use an ExternalName service, let's use the following example:

FooWidgets Application Requirements
FooWidgets is running an application on their Kubernetes cluster that needs to connect to a database server running on a Windows 2019 server called sqlserver1. foowidgets.com (192.168.10.200).   The current application is deployed to a namespace called finance.   The SQL server will be migrated to a container in the next quarter.   You have two requirements: • Configure the application to use the external database server using only the cluster's DNS server.   • FooWidgets cannot make any configuration changes to the applications after the SQL server is migrated.

Based on the requirements, using an ExternalName service is the perfect solution. So, how would we accomplish the requirements? (This is a theoretical exercise; you do not need to execute anything on your KinD cluster)

1. The first step is to create a manifest that will create the ExternalName service for the database server:

```
apiVersion: v1
kind: Service
metadata:
  name: sql-db
  namespace: finance
spec:
  type: ExternalName
  externalName: sqlserver1.foowidgets.com
```

2. With the service created, the next step is to configure the application to use the name of our new service. Since the service and the application are in the same namespace, you can configure the application to target the name `sql-db`.

3. Now, when the application queries for `sql-db`, it will resolve to `sqlserver1.foowidgets.com`, and, ultimately, the IP address of 192.168.10.200.

This accomplishes the initial requirement, connecting the application to the external database server using only the Kubernetes DNS server.

You may be wondering why we didn't simply configure the application to use the database server name directly. The key is the second requirement, limiting any reconfiguration when the SQL server is migrated to a container.

Since we cannot reconfigure the application after the SQL server is migrated to the cluster, we will not be able to change the name of the SQL server in the application settings. If we configured the application to use the original name, `sqlserver1.foowidgets.com`, the application would not work after the migration. By using the ExternalName service, we have the ability to change the internal DNS service name by replacing the ExternalHost service name with a standard Kubernetes service that points to the SQL server.

To accomplish the second goal, go through the following steps:

1. Delete the `ExternalName` service.

2. Create a new service using the name `ext-sql-db` that uses `app=sql-app` as the selector. The manifest would look like the one shown here:

```
apiVersion: v1
kind: Service
metadata:
  labels:
    app: sql-db
  name: sql-db
  namespace: finance
ports:
- port: 1433
  protocol: TCP
  targetPort: 1433
  name: sql
selector:
  app: sql-app
type: ClusterIP
```

Since we are using the same service name for the new service, no changes need to be made to the application. The app will still target the name `sql-db`, which will now use the SQL server deployed in the cluster.

Now that you know about services, we can move on to load balancers, which will allow you to expose services externally using standard URL names and ports.

Introduction to load balancers

Before discussing different types of load balancers, it's important to understand the **Open Systems Interconnection** (**OSI**) model. Understanding the different layers of the OSI model will help you to understand how different solutions handle incoming requests.

Understanding the OSI model

When you hear about different solutions to expose an application in Kubernetes, you will often here a reference to layer 7 or layer 4 load balancing. These designations refer to where each operates in the OSI model. Each layer offers different functionality; a component that runs at layer 7 offers different functionality than a component in layer 4.

To begin, let's look at a brief overview of the seven layers and a description of each. For this chapter, we are interested in the two highlighted sections, **layer 4 and layer 7**:

OSI Layer	Name	Description
7	Application	Provides application traffic, including HTTP and HTTPS
6	Presentation	Forms data packets and encryption
5	Session	Controls traffic flow
4	Transport	Communication traffic between devices, including TCP and UDP
3	Network	Routing between devices, including IP
2	Data Link	Performs error checking for physical connection (MAC address)
1	Physical	Physical connection of devices

Table 6.3 OSI model layers

You don't need to be an expert in the OSI layers, but you should understand what a layer 4 and layer 7 load balancer provide and how each may be used with a cluster.

Let's go deeper into the details of layer 4 and 7:

- **Layer 4**: As the description states in the chart, layer 4 is responsible for the communication traffic between devices. Devices that run at layer 4 have access to TCP/UPD information. Load balancers that are layer-4 based provide your applications with the ability to service incoming requests for any TCP/UDP port.

- **Layer 7**: Layer 7 is responsible for providing network services to applications. When we say application traffic, we are not referring to applications such as Excel or Word; instead, we are referring to the protocols that support the applications, such as HTTP and HTTPS.

In the next section, we will explain each load balancer type and how to use them in a Kubernetes cluster to expose your services.

Layer 7 load balancers

Kubernetes provides layer 7 load balancers in the form of an Ingress controller. There are a number of solutions to provide Ingress to your clusters, including the following:

- NGINX

- Envoy

- Traefik

- Haproxy

Typically, a layer 7 load balancer is limited in the functions it can perform. In the Kubernetes world, they are implemented as Ingress controllers that can route incoming HTTP/HTTPS requests to your exposed services. We will go into detail on implementing NGINX as a Kubernetes Ingress controller in the *Creating Ingress rules* section.

Name resolution and layer 7 load balancers

To handle layer 7 traffic in a Kubernetes cluster, you deploy an Ingress controller. Ingress controllers are dependent on incoming names to route traffic to the correct service. In a legacy server deployment model, you would create a DNS entry and map it to an IP address.

Applications that are deployed on a Kubernetes cluster are no different—the user will use a DNS name to access the application.

Oftentimes, you will create a new wildcard domain that will target the Ingress controller via an external load balancer, such as an F5, HAproxy, or SeeSaw.

Let's assume that our company is called FooWidgets and we have three Kubernetes clusters, fronted by an external load balancer with multiple Ingress controller endpoints. Our DNS server would have entries for each cluster, using a wildcard domain that points to the load balancer's virtual IP address:

Domain Name	IP Address	K8s Cluster
`*.cluster1.` `foowidgets.com`	`192.168.200.100`	Production001
`*.cluster2.` `foowidgets.com`	`192.168.200.101`	Production002
`*.cluster3.` `foowidgets.com`	`192.168.200.102`	Development001

Table 6.4 Example wildcard domain names for Ingress

The following diagram shows the entire flow of the request:

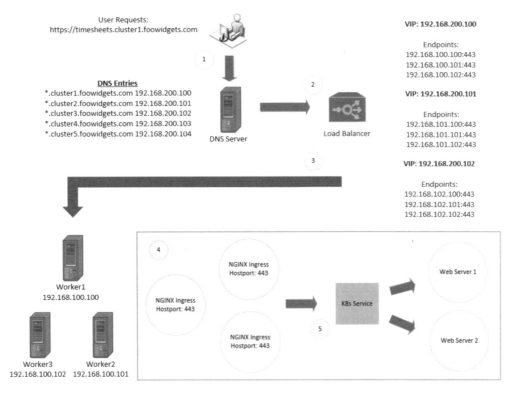

Figure 6.3 – Multiple-name Ingress traffic flow

Each of the steps in diagram 6.3 are detailed here:

1. Using a browser, the user requests the URL `https://timesheets.cluster1.foowidgets.com`.

2. The DNS query is sent to a DNS server. The DNS server looks up the zone details for `cluster1.foowidgets.com`. There is a single entry in the DNS zone that resolves to the VIP assigned on the load balancer for the domain.

3. The load balancer's VIP for `cluster1.foowidgets.com` has three backend servers assigned, pointing to three worker nodes where we have deployed Ingress controllers.

4. Using one of the endpoints, the request is sent to the Ingress controller.

5. The Ingress controller will compare the requested URL to a list of Ingress rules. When a matching request is found, the Ingress controller will forward the request to the service that was assigned to the Ingress rule.

To help reinforce how Ingress works, it will help to create Ingress rules on a cluster to see them in action. Right now, the key takeaways are that Ingress uses the requested URL to direct traffic to the correct Kubernetes services.

Using nip.io for name resolution

Most personal development clusters, such as our KinD installation, may not have enough access to add records to a DNS server. To test Ingress rules, we need to target unique host names that are mapped to Kubernetes services by the Ingress controller. Without a DNS server, you need to create a local host file with multiple names pointing to the IP address of the Ingress controller.

For example, if you deployed four web servers, you need to add all four names to your local hosts. An example of this is shown here:

```
192.168.100.100 webserver1.test.local
192.168.100.100 webserver2.test.local
192.168.100.100 webserver3.test.local
192.168.100.100 webserver4.test.local
```

This can also be represented on a single line rather than multiple lines:

```
192.168.100.100 webserver1.test.local webserver2.test.local
webserver3.test.local webserver4.test.local
```

If you use multiple machines to test your deployments, you will need to edit the host file on every machine that you plan to use for testing. Maintaining multiple files on multiple machines is an administrative nightmare and will lead to issues that will make testing a challenge.

Luckily, there are free services available that provide DNS services that we can use without configuring a complex DNS infrastructure for our KinD cluster.

Nip.io is the service that we will use for our KinD cluster name resolution requirements. Using our previous web server example, we will not need to create any DNS records. We still need to send the traffic for the different servers to the NGINX server running on 192.168.100.100 so that Ingress can route the traffic to the appropriate service. Nip.io uses a naming format that includes the IP address in the hostname to resolve the name to an IP. For example, say that we have four web servers that we want to test called webserver1, webserver2, webserver3, and webserver4, with Ingress rules on an Ingress controller running on 192.168.100.100.

As we mentioned earlier, we do not need to create any records to accomplish this. Instead, we can use the naming convention to have nip.io resolve the name for us. Each of the web servers would use a name with the following naming standard:

```
<desired name>.<INGRESS IP>.nip.io
```

The names for all four web servers are listed in the following table:

Web Server Name	Nip.io DNS Name
webserver1	webserver1.192.168.100.100.nip.io
webserver2	webserver2.192.168.100.100.nip.io
webserver3	webserver3.192.168.100.100.nip.io
webserver4	webserver4.192.168.100.100.nip.io

Table 6.5 – Nip.io example domain names

When you use any of the preceding names, nip.io will resolve them to 192.168.100.100. You can see an example ping for each name in the following screenshot:

```
[root@localhost /]# ping webserver1.192.168.100.100.nip.io
PING webserver1.192.168.100.100.nip.io (192.168.100.100) 56(84) bytes of data.
[root@localhost /]# ping webserver2.192.168.100.100.nip.io
PING webserver2.192.168.100.100.nip.io (192.168.100.100) 56(84) bytes of data.
[root@localhost /]# ping webserver3.192.168.100.100.nip.io
PING webserver3.192.168.100.100.nip.io (192.168.100.100) 56(84) bytes of data.
[root@localhost /]# ping webserver4.192.168.100.100.nip.io
PING webserver4.192.168.100.100.nip.io (192.168.100.100) 56(84) bytes of data.
```

Figure 6.4 – Example name resolution using nip.io

This may look like it has very little benefit, since you are supplying the IP address in the name. Why would you need to bother using nip.io if you know the IP address?

Remember that the Ingress rules require a unique name to route traffic to the correct service. While the name may not be required for you to know the IP address of the server, the name is required for the Ingress rules. Each name is unique, using the first part of the full name—in our example, that is webserver1, webserver2, webserver3, and webserver4.

By providing this service, nip.io allows you to use any name for Ingress rules without the need to have a DNS server in your development cluster.

Now that you know how to use nip.io to resolve names for your cluster, let's explain how to use a nip.io name in an Ingress rule.

Creating an Ingress rules

Remember, Ingress rules use names to route the incoming request to the correct service. The following is a graphical representation of an incoming request, showing how Ingress routes the traffic:

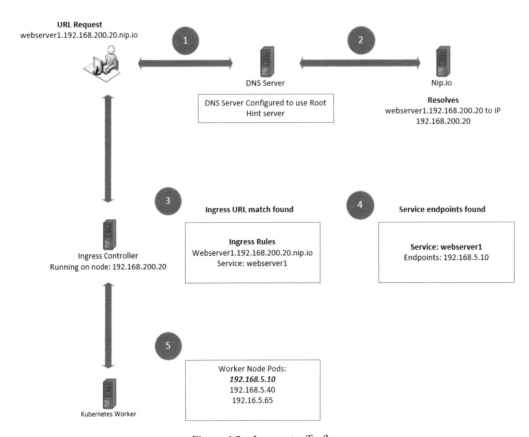

Figure 6.5 – Ingress traffic flow

Figure 6.5 shows a high-level overview of how Kubernetes handles incoming Ingress requests. To help explain each step in more depth, let's go over the five steps in greater detail. Using the graphic provided in Figure 6.5, we will explain each numbered step in detail to show how Igress processes the request:

1. The user requests a URL in their browser named webserver1.192.168.200.20.nio.io. A DNS request is sent to the local DNS server, which is ultimately sent to the nip.io DNS server.

2. The nip.io server resolves the domain name to the IP address of 192.168.200.20, which is returned to the client.

3. The client sends the request to the Ingress controller, which is running on 192.168.200.20. The request contains the complete URL name, **webserver1.192.168.200.20.nio.io**.

4. The Ingress controller looks up the requested URL name in the configured rules and matches the URL name to a service.

5. The service endpoint(s) will be used to route traffic to the assigned pods.

6. The request is routed to an endpoint pod running the web server.

Using the preceding example traffic flow, let's go over the Kubernetes objects that need to be created:

1. First, we need a simple webserver running in a namespace. We will simply deploy a base NGINX webserver in the default namespace. Rather than create a manifest manually, we can create a deployment quickly using the following `kubectl run` command:

    ```
    kubectl run nginx-web --image bitnami/nginx
    ```

2. Using the `run` option is a shortcut that will create a deployment called `nginx-web` in the default namespace. You may notice that the output will give you a warning that the run is being deprecated. This is just a warning; it will still create our deployment, although using `run` to create a deployment may not work in future Kubernetes versions.

3. Next, we need to create a service for the deployment. Again, we will create a service using a kubectl command, `kubectl expose`. The Bitnami NGINX image runs on port 8080, so we will use the same port to expose the service:

    ```
    kubectl expose deployment nginx-web --port 8080 --target-
    port 8080
    ```

    This will create a new service called nginx-web for our deployment, called nginx-web.

4. Now that we have our deployment and service created, the last step is to create the Ingress rule. To create an Ingress rule, you create a manifest using the object type `Ingress`. The following is an example Ingress rule that assumes that the Ingress controller is running on 192.168.200.20. If you are creating this rule on your host, you should use the **IP address of your Docker host**.

Create a file called `nginx-ingress.yaml` with the following content:

```
apiVersion: networking.k8s.io/v1beta1
kind: Ingress
metadata:
  name: nginx-web-ingress
spec:
  rules:
  - host: webserver1.192.168.200.20.nip.io
    http:
      paths:
      - path: /
        backend:
            serviceName: nginx-web
            servicePort: 8080
```

5. Create the Ingress rune using `kubectl apply`:

```
kubectl apply -f nginx-ingress.yaml
```

6. You can test the deployment from any client on your internal network by browsing to the Ingress URL, `http:// webserver1.192.168.200.20.nip.io`.

7. If everything was created successfully, you should see the NGINX welcome page:

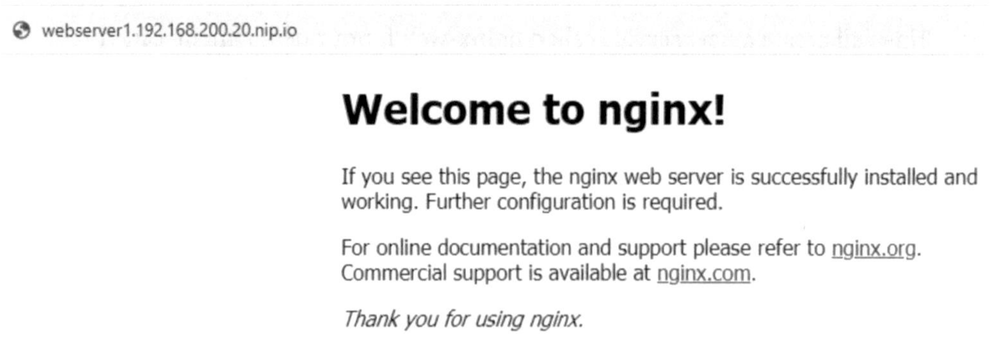

webserver1.192.168.200.20.nip.io

Welcome to nginx!

If you see this page, the nginx web server is successfully installed and working. Further configuration is required.

For online documentation and support please refer to nginx.org.
Commercial support is available at nginx.com.

Thank you for using nginx.

Figure 6.6 – NGINX web server using nip.io for Ingress

Using the information in this section, you can create Ingress rules for multiple containers using different hostnames. Of course, you aren't limited to using a service like nip.io to resolve names; you can use any name resolution method that you have available in your environment. In a production cluster, you will have an enterprise DNS infrastructure, but in a lab environment, such as our KinD cluster, nip.io is the perfect tool to test scenarios that require proper naming conventions.

We will use nip.io naming standards throughout the book, so it's important to understand the naming convention before moving on to the next chapter.

Layer 7 load balancers, such as NGINX Ingress, are used by many standard workloads, such as like web servers. There will be deployments that will require a more complex load balancer, one that runs at a lower layer of the OIS model. As we move down the model, we gain lower-level features. In our next section, we will discuss layer 4 load balancers.

> **Note**
>
> If you deployed the NGINX example on your cluster, you should delete the service and the Ingress rules:
>
> • To delete the Ingress rule, execute the following: `kubectl delete ingress nginx-web-ingress`
>
> • To delete the service, execute the following: `kubectl delete service nginx-web`
>
> You can leave the NGINX deployment running for the next section.

Layer 4 load balancers

Layer 4 of the OSI model is responsible for protocols such as TCP and UDP. A load balancer that is running in layer 4 accepts incoming traffic based on the only IP address and port. The incoming request is accepted by the load balancer, and based on a set of rules, the traffic is sent to the destination IP address and port.

There are lower-level networking operations in the process that are out of the scope of this book. HAproxy has a good summary of the terminology and example configurations on their website at `https://www.haproxy.com/fr/blog/loadbalancing-faq/`.

Layer 4 load balancer options

There are multiple options available to you if you want to configure a layer 4 load balancer for a Kubernetes cluster. Some of the options include the following:

- HAproxy
- NGINX Pro
- SeeSaw
- F5 Networks
- MetalLB
- And more...

Each option provides layer 4 load balancing, but for the purpose of this book, we felt that MetalLB was the best choice.

Using MetalLB as a layer 4 load balancer

> **Important note**
>
> Remember that in *Chapter 4 Deploying Kubernetes using KinD* we had a diagram showing the flow of traffic between a workstation and the KinD nodes. Because KinD was running in a nested Docker container, a layer 4 load balancer would have had certain limitations when it came to networking connectivity. Without additional network configuration on the Docker host, you will not be able to target the services that use the LoadBalancer type outside of the Docker host itself.
>
> If you deploy MetalLB to a standard Kubernetes cluster running on a host, you will not be limited to accessing services outside of the host itself.

MetalLB is a free, easy to configure layer 4 load balancer. It includes powerful configuration options that give it the ability to run in a development lab or an enterprise cluster. Since it is so versatile, it has become a very popular choice for clusters requiring layer 4 load balancing.

In this section, we will focus on installing MetalLB in layer 2 mode. This is an easy installation and works for development or small Kubernetes clusters. MetalLB also offers the option to deploy using BGP mode, which allows you to establish peering partners to exchange networking routes. If you would like to read about MetalLB's BGP mode, you can read about it on MetalLB's site at `https://metallb.universe.tf/concepts/bgp/`.

Installing MetalLB

To deploy MetalLB on your KinD cluster, use the manifests from MetalLB's GitHub repository. To install MetalLB, go through the following steps:

1. The following will create a new namespace called `metallb-system` with a label of `app: metallb`:

    ```
    kubectl apply -f https://raw.githubusercontent.com/
    metallb/metallb/v0.9.3/manifests/namespace.yaml
    ```

2. This will deploy MetalLB to your cluster. It will create all required Kubernetes objects, including `PodSecurityPolicies`, `ClusterRoles`, `Bindings`, `DaemonSet`, and a `deployment`:

    ```
    kubectl apply -f https://raw.githubusercontent.com/
    metallb/metallb/v0.9.3/manifests/metallb.yaml
    ```

3. The last command will create a secret in the `metalb-system` namespace that has a randomly generated value. This secret is used by MetalLB to encrypt communications between speakers:

    ```
    kubectl create secret generic -n metallb-system
    memberlist --from-literal=secretkey="$(openssl rand
    -base64 128)"
    ```

Now that MetalLB has been deployed to the cluster, you need to supply a configuration file to complete the setup.

Understanding MetalLB's configuration file

MetalLB is configured using a ConfigMap that contains the configuration. Since we will be using MetalLB in layer 2 mode, the required configuration file is fairly simple and only requires one piece of information: the IP range that you want to create for services.

To keep the configuration simple, we will use a small range from the Docker subnet in which KinD is running. If you were running MetalLB on a standard Kubernetes cluster, you could assign any range that is routable in your network, but we are limited with our KinD clusters.

To get the subnet that Docker is using, we can inspect the default bridge network that we are using:

```
docker network inspect bridge
```

In the output, you will see the assigned subnet, similar to following:

```
"Subnet": "172.17.0.0/16"
```

This is an entire class-B address range. We know that we will not use all of the IP addresses for running containers, so we will use a small range from the subnet in our MetalLB configuration.

Let's create a new file called `metallb-config.yaml` and add the following to the file:

```yaml
apiVersion: v1
kind: ConfigMap
metadata:
  namespace: metallb-system
  name: config
data:
  config: |
    address-pools:
    - name: default
      protocol: layer2
      addresses:
      - 172.17.200.100-172.17.200.125
```

The manifest will create a ConfigMap in the `metallb-system` namespace called `config`. The configuration file will set MetalLB's mode to layer 2 with an IP pool called `default`, using the range of 172.16.200-100 through 172.16.200.125 for LoadBalancer services.

You can assign different addresses based on the configuration names. We will show this when we explain how to create a LoadBalancer service.

Finally, deploy the manifest using kubectl:

```
kubectl apply -f metallb-config.yaml
```

To understand how MetalLB works, you need to know the installed components and how they interact to assign IP addresses to services.

MetalLB components

The second manifest in our deployment is what installs the MetalLB components to the cluster. It deploys a DaemonSet that includes the speaker image and a DaemonSet that includes the controller image. These components communicate with each other to maintain a list of services and assigned IP addresses:

The speaker

The speaker component is what MetalLB uses to announce the LoadBalancer services on the node. It is deployed as a DaemonSet since the deployments can be on any worker node, and therefore, each worker node needs to announce the workloads that are running. As services are created using a LoadBalancer type, the speaker will announce the service.

If we look at the speaker log from a node, we can see the announcements following:

```
{"caller":"main.go:176","event":"startUpdate","msg":"start
of service update","service":"my-grafana-operator/grafana-
operator-metrics","ts":"2020-04-21T21:10:07.437231123Z"}
{"caller":"main.go:189","event":"endUpdate","msg":"end of
service update","service":"my-grafana-operator/grafana-
operator-metrics","ts":"2020-04-21T21:10:07.437516541Z"}
{"caller":"main.go:176","event":"startUpdate","msg":"start
of service update","service":"my-grafana-operator/grafana-
operator-metrics","ts":"2020-04-21T21:10:07.464140524Z"}
{"caller":"main.
go:246","event":"serviceAnnounced","ip":"10.2.1.72","msg":
"service has IP, announcing","pool":"default","protocol":
"layer2","service":"my-grafana-operator/grafana-operator-
metrics","ts":"2020-04-21T21:10:07.464311087Z"}
{"caller":"main.go:249","event":"endUpdate","msg":"end of
service update","service":"my-grafana-operator/grafana-
operator-metrics","ts":"2020-04-21T21:10:07.464470317Z"}
```

The preceding announcement is for Grafana. After the announcement, you can see that it has been assigned an IP address of 10.2.1.72.

The controller

The controller will receive the announcements from the speaker on each worker node. Using the same service announcement shown previously, the controller log shows the announcement and the IP address that the controller assigned to the service:

```
{"caller":"main.go:49","event":"startUpdate","msg":"start
of service update","service":"my-grafana-operator/grafana-
operator-metrics","ts":"2020-04-21T21:10:07.437701161Z"}
{"caller":"service.
go:98","event":"ipAllocated","ip":"10.2.1.72","msg":"IP address
assigned by controller","service":"my-grafana-operator/grafana-
operator-metrics","ts":"2020-04-21T21:10:07.438079774Z"}
{"caller":"main.go:96","event":"serviceUpdated","msg":"updated
service object","service":"my-grafana-operator/grafana-
operator-metrics","ts":"2020-04-21T21:10:07.467998702Z"}
```

In the second line of the log, you can see that the controller assigned the IP address of 10.2.1.72.

Creating a LoadBalancer service

Now that you have installed MetalLB and understand how the components create the services, let's create our first LoadBalancer service on our KinD cluster.

In the layer 7 load balancer section, we created a deployment running NGINX that we exposed by creating a service and an Ingress rule. At the end of the section, we deleted the service and the Ingress rule, but we kept the NGINX deployment for this section. If you followed the steps in the Ingress section and have not deleted the service and Ingress rule, please do so before creating the LoadBalancer service. If you did not create the deployment at all, you will need an NGINX deployment for this section:

1. You can create a quick NGINX deployment by executing the following command:

    ```
    kubectl run nginx-web --image bitnami/nginx
    ```

2. To create a new service that will use the LoadBalancer type, you can create a new manifest or you can expose the deployment using only kubectl.

    To create a manifest, create a new file called `nginx-lb.yaml` and add the following:

    ```
    apiVersion: v1
    kind: Service
    ```

```
metadata:
  name: nginx-lb
spec:
  ports:
  - port: 8080
    targetPort: 8080
  selector:
    run: nginx-web
  type: LoadBalancer
```

3. Apply the file to the cluster using kubectl:

```
kubectl apply -f nginx-lb.yaml
```

4. To verify that the service was created correctly, list the services using kubectl get services:

```
NAME         TYPE           CLUSTER-IP     EXTERNAL-IP      PORT(S)          AGE
kubernetes   ClusterIP      10.96.0.1      <none>           443/TCP          24m
nginx-lb     LoadBalancer   10.96.18.33    172.16.200.100   8080:30924/TCP   19s
```

Figure 6.7 – Kubectl service output

You will see that a new service was created using the LoadBalancer type and that MetalLB assigned an IP address from the configured pool we created earlier.

A quick look at the controller log will verify that the MetalLB controller assigned the service the IP address:

```
{"caller":"service.
go:114","event":"ipAllocated","ip":"172.16.200.100",
"msg":"IP address assigned by
controller","service":"default/nginx-lb","ts":"2020-04-
25T23:54:03.668948668Z"}
```

5. Now you can test the service by using curl on the Docker host. Using the IP address that was assigned to the service and port 8080, enter the following command:

```
curl 172.17.200.100:8080
```

You will receive the following output:

```
<!DOCTYPE html>
<html>
<head>
<title>Welcome to nginx!</title>
<style>
    body {
        width: 35em;
        margin: 0 auto;
        font-family: Tahoma, Verdana, Arial, sans-serif;
    }
</style>
</head>
<body>
<h1>Welcome to nginx!</h1>
<p>If you see this page, the nginx web server is successfully installed and
working. Further configuration is required.</p>

<p>For online documentation and support please refer to
<a href="http://nginx.org/">nginx.org</a>.<br/>
Commercial support is available at
<a href="http://nginx.com/">nginx.com</a>.</p>

<p><em>Thank you for using nginx.</em></p>
</body>
</html>
```

Figure 6.8 – Curl output to the LoadBalancer service running NGINX

Adding MetalLB to a cluster allows you to expose applications that otherwise could not be exposed using a layer 7 balancer. Adding both layer 7 and layer 4 services to your clusters allows you to expose almost any application type you can think of, including databases. What if you wanted to offer different IP pools to services? In the next section, we will explain how to create multiple IP pools that can be assigned to services using an annotation, allowing you to assign an IP range to services.

Adding multiple IP pools to MetalLB

There may be scenarios where you need to provide different subnets to specific workloads on a cluster. One scenario may be that when you created a range on the network for your services, you underestimated how many services would be created and you ran out of IP addresses.

Depending on the original range that you used, you may be able to just increase the range on your configuration. If you cannot extend the existing range, you will need to create a new range before any new LoadBalancer services can be created. You can also add additional IP ranges to the default pool, but for this example, we will create a new pool.

We can edit the configuration file and add the new range information to the file. Using the original YAML file, `metallb-config.yaml`, we need to add the text in bold in the following code:

```yaml
apiVersion: v1
kind: ConfigMap
metadata:
  namespace: metallb-system
  name: config
data:
  config: |
    address-pools:
    - name: default
      protocol: layer2
      addresses:
      - 172.17.200.100-172.17.200.125
    - name: subnet-201
      protocol: layer2
      addresses:
      - 172.17.201.100-172.17.201.125
```

Apply the updated ConfigMap using `kubectl`:

```
kubectl apply -f metallb-config.yaml
```

The updated ConfigMap will create a new pool called subnet-201. MetalLB now has two pools that can be used to assign IP addresses to services: the default and subnet-201.

If a user creates a LoadBalancer service and does not specify a pool name, Kubernetes will attempt to use the default pool. If the requested pool is out of address, the service will sit in a pending state until an address is available.

To create a new service from the second pool, you need to add an annotation to your service request. Using our NGINX deployment, we will create a second service called nginx-web2 that will request an IP address from the subnet-201 pool:

1. Create a new file called nginx-lb2.yaml with the following content:

```
apiVersion: v1
kind: Service
metadata:
  name: nginx-lb2
  annotations:
    metallb.universe.tf/address-pool: subnet-201
spec:
  ports:
  - port: 8080
    targetPort: 8080
  selector:
    run: nginx-web
  type: LoadBalancer
```

2. To create the new service, deploy the manifest using kubectl:

```
kubectl apply -f nginx-lb2.yaml
```

3. To verify that the service was created with an IP address from the subnet-201 pool, list all of the services:

```
kubectl get services
```

You will receive the following output:

```
NAME         TYPE          CLUSTER-IP       EXTERNAL-IP       PORT(S)           AGE
kubernetes   ClusterIP     10.96.0.1        <none>            443/TCP           114m
nginx-lb     LoadBalancer  10.96.53.164     172.17.200.100    8080:30405/TCP    49m
nginx-lb2    LoadBalancer  10.96.215.203    172.17.201.100    8080:30744/TCP    11m
```

Figure 6.9 – Example services using LoadBalancer

The last service in the list is our newly created nginx-lb2 service. We can confirm that it has been assigned an external IP address of 172.17.20.100, which is from the subnet-201 pool.

4. And finally, we can test the service by using a curl command on the Docker host, to the assigned IP address on port 8080:

```
root@kind:/# curl 172.17.201.100:8080
<!DOCTYPE html>
<html>
<head>
<title>Welcome to nginx!</title>
<style>
    body {
        width: 35em;
        margin: 0 auto;
        font-family: Tahoma, Verdana, Arial, sans-serif;
    }
</style>
</head>
<body>
<h1>Welcome to nginx!</h1>
<p>If you see this page, the nginx web server is successfully installed and
working. Further configuration is required.</p>

<p>For online documentation and support please refer to
<a href="http://nginx.org/">nginx.org</a>.<br/>
Commercial support is available at
<a href="http://nginx.com/">nginx.com</a>.</p>

<p><em>Thank you for using nginx.</em></p>
</body>
</html>
```

Figure 6.10 – Curl NGINX on a LoadBalancer using a second IP pool

Having the ability to offer different address pools allows you to assign a known IP address block to services. You may decide that address pool 1 will be used for web services, address pool 2 for databases, address pool 3 for file transfers, and so on. Some organizations do this to identify traffic based on the IP assignment, making it easier to track communication.

Adding a layer 4 load balancer to your cluster allows you to migrate applications that may not work with simple layer 7 traffic.

As more applications are migrated or refactored for containers, you will run into many applications that require multiple protocols for a single service. Natively, if you attempt to create a service with both TCP and UDP port mapping, you will receive an error that multiple protocols are not supported for the service object. This may not affect many applications, but why should you be limited to a single protocol for a service?

Using multiple protocols

All of our examples so far have used a TCP as the protocol. Of course, MetalLB supports using UDP as the service protocol as well, but what if you had a service that required you to use both protocols?

Multiple protocol issues

Not all service types support assigning multiple protocols to a single service. The following table shows the three service types and their support for multiple protocols:

Service Type	Supports Multiple Protocols
ClusterIP	Yes
NodePort	Yes
LoadBalancer	No

Table 6.6 – Service type protocol support

If you attempt to create a service that uses both protocols, you will receive an error message. We have highlighted the error in the following error message:

```
The Service "kube-dns-lb" is invalid: spec.ports: Invalid
value: []core.ServicePort{core.ServicePort{Name:"dns",
Protocol:"UDP", Port:53, TargetPort:intstr.IntOrString{Type:0,
IntVal:53, StrVal:""}, NodePort:0}, core.ServicePort{Name:"dns-
tcp", Protocol:"TCP", Port:53, TargetPort:intstr.
IntOrString{Type:0, IntVal:53, StrVal:""}, NodePort:0}}: cannot
create an external load balancer with mix protocols
```

The service we were attempting to create would expose our CoreDNS service to an external IP using a LoadBalancer service. We need to expose the service on port 50 for both TCP and UDP.

MetalLB includes support for multiple protocols bound to a single IP address. The configuration requires the creation of two different services rather than a single service, which may seem a little odd at first. As we have shown previously, the API server will not allow you to create a service object with multiple protocols. The only way to work around this limitation is to create two different services: one that has the TCP ports assigned and another that has the UDP ports assigned.

Using our CoreDNS example, we will go through the steps to create an application that requires multiple protocols.

Using multiple protocols with MetalLB

To enable support for an application that requires both TCP and UDP you need to create two separate services. If you have been paying close attention to how services are created, you may have noticed that each service receives an IP address. Logically, this means that when we create two services for our application, we would receive two different IP addresses.

In our example, we want to expose CoreDNS as a LoadBalancer service, which requires both TCP and UDP protocols. If we created two standard services, one with each protocol defined, we would receive two different IP address. How would you configure a system to use a DNS server that requires two different IP addresses for a connection?

The simple answer is, **you can't**.

But we just told you that you MetalLB supports this type of configuration. Stay with us—we are building up to explaining this by first explaining the issues that MetalLB will solve for us.

When we created the NGINX service that pulled from the subnet-201 IP pool earlier, we did so by adding an annotation to the load-balancer manifest. MetalLB has added support for multiple protocols by adding an annotation for **shared-IPs.**

Using shared-IPs

Now that you understand the limitations around multiple protocol support in Kubernetes, let's use MetalLB to expose our CoreDNS service to external requests, using both TCP and UDP.

As we mentioned earlier, Kubernetes will not allow you to create a single service with both protocols. To have a single load-balanced IP use both protocols, you need to create a service for both protocols, one for TCP and another for UDP. Each of the services will need an annotation that MetalLB will use to assign the same IP to both services.

 For each service, you need to set the same value for the `metallb.universe.tf/ allow-shared-ip` annotation. We will cover a complete example to expose CoreDNS to explain the entire process.

> **Important note**
>
> Most Kubernetes distributions use CoreDNS as the default DNS provider, but some of them still use the service name from when kube-dns was the default DNS provider. KinD is one of the distributions that may confuse you at first, since the service name is kube-dns, but rest assured, the deployment is using CoreDNS.

So, let's begin:

1. First, look at the services in the `kube-system` namespace:

Figure 6.11 – Default service list for kube-system

The only service we have is the default `kube-dns` service, using the ClusterIP type, which means that it is only accessible internally to the cluster.

You might have noticed that the service has multiple protocol support, having both port UDP and TCP assigned. Remember that, unlike the LoadBalancer service, a ClusterIP service **can** be assigned multiple protocols.

2. The first step to add LoadBalancer support to our CoreDNS server is to create two manifests, one for each protocol.

We will create the TCP service first. Create a file called `coredns-tcp.yaml` and add the content from the following example manifest. Note that the internal service for CoreDNS is using the `k8s-app: kube-dns` selector. Since we are exposing the same service, that's the selector we will use in our manifests:

```yaml
apiVersion: v1
kind: Service
metadata:
  name: coredns-tcp
  namespace: kube-system
  annotations:
    metallb.universe.tf/allow-shared-ip: "coredns-ext"
spec:
  selector:
    k8s-app: kube-dns
  ports:
  - name: dns-tcp
    port: 53
    protocol: TCP
    targetPort: 53
  type: LoadBalancer
```

This file should be familiar by now, with the one exception in the annotations being the addition of the `metallb.universe.tf/allow-shared-ip` value. The use for this value will become clear when we create the next manifest for the UDP services.

3. Create a file called `coredns-udp.yaml` and add the content from the following example manifest.

```
apiVersion: v1
kind: Service
metadata:
  name: coredns-udp
  namespace: kube-system
  annotations:
    metallb.universe.tf/allow-shared-ip: "coredns-ext"
spec:
  selector:
    k8s-app: kube-dns
  ports:
  - name: dns-tcp
    port: 53
    protocol: UDP
    targetPort: 53
  type: LoadBalancer
```

Note that we used the same annotation value from the TCP service manifest, `metallb.universe.tf/allow-shared-ip: "coredns-ext"`. This is the value that MetalLB will use to create a single IP address, even though two separate services are being requested.

4. Finally, we can deploy the two services to the cluster using `kubectl apply`:

```
kubectl apply -f coredns-tcp.yaml
kubectl apply -f coredns-udp.yaml
```

5. Once deployed, get the services in the `kube-system` namespace to verify that our services were deployed:

```
NAME          TYPE           CLUSTER-IP     EXTERNAL-IP      PORT(S)                               AGE
coredns-tcp   LoadBalancer   10.96.37.159   172.17.200.101   53:30121/TCP                          25s
coredns-udp   LoadBalancer   10.96.191.45   172.17.200.101   53:32329/UDP                          19s
kube-dns      NodePort       10.96.0.10     <none>           53:32207/UDP,53:30962/TCP,9153:31882/TCP   17h
```

Figure 6.12 – Multiple protocols assigned using MetalLB

You should see that two new services were created: the `coredns-tcp` and `coredns-udp` services. Under the `EXTERNAL-IP` column, you can see that both services have been assigned the same IP address, which allows the service to accept both protocols on the same IP address.

Adding MetalLB to a cluster gives your users the ability to deploy any application that they can containerize. It uses IP pools that dynamically assign an IP address for the service so that it is instantly accessible for servicing external requests.

One issue is that MetalLB does not provide name resolution for the service IPs. Users prefer to target an easy-to-remember name rather than random IP addresses when they want to access a service. Kubernetes does not provide the ability to create externally accessible names for services, but it does have an incubator project to enable this feature.

In the next section, we will learn how to use CoreDNS to create service name entries in DNS using an incubator project called external-dns.

Making service names available externally

You may have been wondering why we were using the IP addresses to test the NGINX services that we created while we used domain names for our Ingress tests.

While a Kubernetes load balancer provides a standard IP address to a service, it does not create an external DNS name for users to connect to the service. Using IP addresses to connect to applications running on a cluster is not very efficient, and manually registering names in DNS for each IP assigned by MetalLB would be an impossible method to maintain. So how would you provide a more cloud-like experience to adding name resolution to our LoadBalancer services?

Similar to the team that maintains KinD, there is a Kubernetes SIG that is working on this feature to Kubernetes called `external-dns`. The main project page is found on the SIG's Github at `https://github.com/kubernetes-sigs/external-dns`.

At the time of writing, the `external-dns` project supports a long list of compatible DNS servers, including the following:

- Google's cloud DNS
- Amazon's Route 53
- AzureDNS
- Cloudflare
- CoreDNS

- RFC2136

- And more…

As you know, our Kubernetes cluster is running CoreDNS to provide cluster DNS name resolution. Many people are not aware that CoreDNS is not limited to providing only internal cluster DNS resolution. It can also provide external name resolution, resolving names for any DNS zone that is managed by a CoreDNS deployment.

Setting up external-dns

Right now, our CoreDNS is only resolving names for internal cluster names, so we need to set up a zone for our new DNS entries. Since FooWidgets wanted all applications to go into `foowidgets.k8s`, we will use that as our new zone.

Integrating external-dns and CoreDNS

The final step to providing dynamic service registration to our cluster is to deploy and integrate `external-dns` with CoreDNS.

To configure `external-dns` and CoreDNS to work in the cluster, we need to configure each to use ETCD for the new DNS zone. Since our clusters are running KinD with a preinstalled ETCD, we will deploy a new ETCD pod dedicated to `external-dns` zones.

The quickest method to deploy a new ETCD service is to use the official ETCD operator Helm chart. Using the following single command, we can install the operator and a three-node ETCD cluster.

First, we need install the Helm binary. We can install Helm quickly using the script provided by the Helm team:

```
curl -fsSL -o get_helm.sh https://raw.githubusercontent.com/
helm/helm/master/scripts/get-helm-3
chmod 700 get_helm.sh
./get_helm.sh
```

Now, using Helm, we can create the ETCD cluster that we will integrate with CoreDNS. The following command will deploy the ETCD operator and create the ETCD cluster:

```
helm install etcd-dns --set customResources.
createEtcdClusterCRD=true stable/etcd-operator --namespace
kube-system
```

It will take a few minutes to deploy the operator and the ETCD nodes. You can check on the status by looking at the pods in the kube-system namespace. Once fully installed, you will see three ETCD operator pods and three ETCD cluster pods:

```
NAME                                                            READY   STATUS    RESTARTS   AGE
coredns-66bff467f8-fq7lf                                        1/1     Running   0          11d
coredns-66bff467f8-w52qp                                        1/1     Running   0          11d
etcd-cluster-67thf88ktl                                         1/1     Running   0          77s
etcd-cluster-dccdn6pk6c                                         1/1     Running   0          36s
etcd-cluster-sbtfh9bfzq                                         1/1     Running   0          96s
etcd-dns-etcd-operator-etcd-backup-operator-756d9b664c-kg7sd    1/1     Running   0          111s
etcd-dns-etcd-operator-etcd-operator-d76f944fd-tlt29            1/1     Running   0          111s
etcd-dns-etcd-operator-etcd-restore-operator-59b6c9486c-vkrn8   1/1     Running   0          111s
etcd-kind-control-plane                                         1/1     Running   0          11d
```

Figure 6.13 – ETCD operator and nodes

Once the deployment has completed, view the services in the kube-system namespace to get the IP address of the new ETCD service called etcd-cluster-client:

```
etcd-cluster-client    ClusterIP    10.96.181.53    <none>    2379/TCP
```

Figure 6.14 – ETCD service IP

We will need the assigned IP address to configure external-dns and the CoreDNS zone file in the next section.

Adding an ETCD zone to CoreDNS

external-dns requires the CoreDNS zone to be stored on an ETCD server. Earlier, we created a new zone for foowidgets, but that was just a standard zone that would require manually adding new records for new services. Users do not have time to wait to test their deployments, and using an IP address may cause issues with proxy servers or internal policies. To help the users speed up their delivery and testing of application, we need to provide dynamic name resolution for their services. To enable an ETCD-integrated zone for foowidgets, edit the CoreDNS configmap, and add the following bold lines.

You may need to change the **endpoint** to the IP address of the new ETCD service that was retrieved on the previous page:

```
apiVersion: v1
data:
  Corefile: |
    .:53 {
        errors
        health {
```

```
            lameduck 5s
        }
        ready
        kubernetes cluster.local in-addr.arpa ip6.arpa {
            pods insecure
            fallthrough in-addr.arpa ip6.arpa
            ttl 30
        }
        prometheus :9153
        forward . /etc/resolv.conf
                    etcd foowidgets.k8s {
                    stubzones
                        path /skydns
                        endpoint http://10.96.181.53:2379
                }

        cache 30
        loop
        reload
        loadbalance
    }
kind: ConfigMap
```

The next step is to deploy `external-dns` to the cluster.

We have provided a manifest in the GitHub repository in the `chapter6` directory that will patch the deployment with your ETCD service endpoint. You can deploy `external-dns` using this manifest by executing the following command, from the `chapter6` directory. The following command will query the service IP for the ETCD cluster and create a deployment file using that IP as the endpoint.

The newly created deployment will then install `external-dns` in your cluster:

```
ETCD_URL=$(kubectl -n kube-system get svc etcd-cluster-client
-o go-template='{{ .spec.clusterIP }}')
cat external-dns.yaml | sed -E "s/<ETCD_URL>/${ETCD_URL}/" >
external-dns-deployment.yaml
kubectl apply -f external-dns-deployment.yaml
```

To deploy `external-dns` to your cluster manually, create a new manifest called `external-dns-deployment.yaml` with the following content, using your ETCD service IP address on the last line:

```yaml
apiVersion: rbac.authorization.k8s.io/v1beta1
kind: ClusterRole
metadata:
  name: external-dns
rules:
- apiGroups: [""]
  resources: ["services","endpoints","pods"]
  verbs: ["get","watch","list"]
- apiGroups: ["extensions"]
  resources: ["ingresses"]
  verbs: ["get","watch","list"]
- apiGroups: [""]
  resources: ["nodes"]
  verbs: ["list"]
---
apiVersion: rbac.authorization.k8s.io/v1beta1
kind: ClusterRoleBinding
metadata:
  name: external-dns-viewer
roleRef:
  apiGroup: rbac.authorization.k8s.io
  kind: ClusterRole
  name: external-dns
subjects:
- kind: ServiceAccount
  name: external-dns
  namespace: kube-system
---
apiVersion: v1
kind: ServiceAccount
metadata:
  name: external-dns
```

```
    namespace: kube-system
---
apiVersion: apps/v1
kind: Deployment
metadata:
  name: external-dns
  namespace: kube-system
spec:
  strategy:
    type: Recreate
  selector:
    matchLabels:
      app: external-dns
  template:
    metadata:
      labels:
        app: external-dns
    spec:
      serviceAccountName: external-dns
      containers:
      - name: external-dns
        image: registry.opensource.zalan.do/teapot/external-
dns:latest
        args:
        - --source=service
        - --provider=coredns
        - --log-level=info
        env:
        - name: ETCD_URLS
          value: http://10.96.181.53:2379
```

Remember, if your ETCD server's IP address is not 10.96.181.53, change it before deploying the manifest.

Deploy the manifest using `kubectl apply -f external-dns-deployment.yaml`.

Creating a LoadBalancer service with external-dns integration

You should still have the NGINX deployment from the beginning of this chapter running. It has a few services tied to it. We will add another one to show you how to create a dynamic registration for the deployment:

1. To create a dynamic entry in the CoreDNS zone, you need to add an annotation in your service manifest. Create a new file called `nginx-dynamic.yaml` with the following content:

    ```
    apiVersion: v1
    kind: Service
    metadata:
      annotations:
        external-dns.alpha.kubernetes.io/hostname: nginx.
    foowidgets.k8s
      name: nginx-ext-dns
      namespace: default
    spec:
      ports:
      - port: 8080
        protocol: TCP
        targetPort: 8080
      selector:
        run: nginx-web
      type: LoadBalancer
    ```

    Note the annotation in the file. To instruct `external-dns` to create a record, you need to add an annotation that has the key `external-dns.alpha.kubernetes.io/hostname` with the desired name for the service—in this example, `nginx.foowidgets.k8s`.

2. Create the service using `kubectl apply -f nginx-dynamic.yaml`.

    It takes about a minute for the `external-dns` to pick up on DNS changes.

3. To verify that the record was created, check the `external-dns` pod logs using `kubectl logs -n kube-system -l app=external-dns`. Once the record has been picked up by `external-dns`, you will see an entry similar to the following:

```
time="2020-04-27T18:14:38Z" level=info msg="Add/
set key /skydns/k8s/foowidgets/nginx/03ebf8d8 to
Host=172.17.201.101, Text=\"heritage=external-
dns,external-dns/owner=default,external-dns/
resource=service/default/nginx-lb\", TTL=0"
```

4. The last step to confirm that external-dns is fully working is to test a connection to the application. Since we are using a KinD cluster, we must test this from a pod in the cluster. We will use a Netshoot container, as we have been doing throughout this book.

> **Important note**
>
> At the end of this section, we will show the steps to integrate a Windows DNS server with our Kubernetes CoreDNS servers. The steps are being provided to provide you with a complete understanding of how you fully integrate the enterprise DNS server with delegation to our CoreDNS service.

5. Run a Netshoot container:

```
kubectl run --generator=run-pod/v1 tmp-shell --rm -i
--tty --image nicolaka/netshoot -- /bin/bash
```

6. To confirm that the entry has been created successfully, execute a `nslookup` for the host in a Netshoot shell:

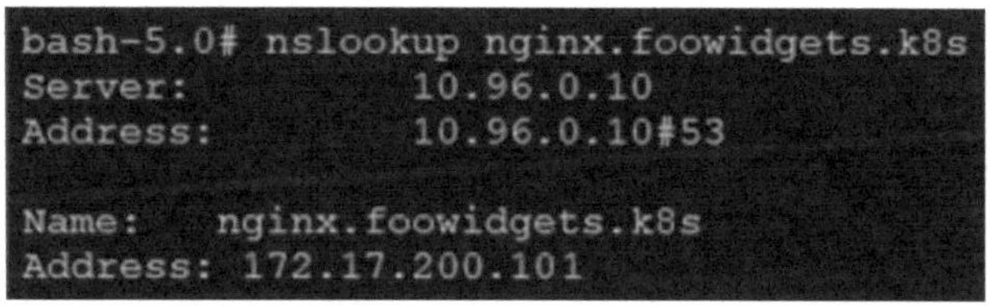

```
bash-5.0# nslookup nginx.foowidgets.k8s
Server:         10.96.0.10
Address:        10.96.0.10#53

Name:    nginx.foowidgets.k8s
Address: 172.17.200.101
```

Figure 6.15 – Nslookup for new record

We can confirm that the DNS server in use is CoreDNS, based on the IP address, which is the assigned IP to the kube-dns service. (Again, the service is kube-dns, but the pods are running CoreDNS).

The 172.17.201.101 address is the IP that was assigned to the new NGINX service; we can confirm this by listing the services in the default namespace:

```
NAME            TYPE           CLUSTER-IP      EXTERNAL-IP     PORT(S)            AGE
kubernetes      ClusterIP      10.96.0.1       <none>          443/TCP            42h
nginx-ext-dns   LoadBalancer   10.96.5.169     172.17.201.101  8080:31602/TCP     104s
nginx-lb        LoadBalancer   10.96.53.164    172.17.200.100  8080:30405/TCP     41h
nginx-lb2       LoadBalancer   10.96.215.203   172.17.201.100  8080:30744/TCP     41h
```

Figure 6.16 – NGINX external IP address

7. Finally, let's confirm that the connection to NGINX works by connecting to the container using the name. Using a curl command in the Netshoot container, curl to the DNS name on port 8080:

```
bash-5.0# curl nginx.foowidgets.k8s:8080
<!DOCTYPE html>
<html>
<head>
<title>Welcome to nginx!</title>
<style>
    body {
        width: 35em;
        margin: 0 auto;
        font-family: Tahoma, Verdana, Arial, sans-serif;
    }
</style>
</head>
<body>
<h1>Welcome to nginx!</h1>
<p>If you see this page, the nginx web server is successfully installed and
working. Further configuration is required.</p>

<p>For online documentation and support please refer to
<a href="http://nginx.org/">nginx.org</a>.<br/>
Commercial support is available at
<a href="http://nginx.com/">nginx.com</a>.</p>

<p><em>Thank you for using nginx.</em></p>
</body>
</html>
```

Figure 6.17 – Curl test using the external-dns name

The `curl` output confirms that we can use the dynamically created service name to access the NGINX web server.

We realize that some of these tests aren't very exciting, since you can test them using a standard browser. In the next section, we will integrate the CoreDNS running in our cluster with a Windows DNS server.

Integrating CoreDNS with an enterprise DNS

This section will show you how to forward the name resolution of the `foowidgets.k8s` zone to a CoreDNS server running on a Kubernetes cluster.

> **Note**
>
> This section has been included to provide an example of integrating an enterprise DNS server with a Kubernetes DNS service.
>
> Because of the external requirements and additional setup, the steps provided are for reference and **should not be executed** on your KinD cluster.

For this scenario, the main DNS server is running on a Windows 2016 server.

The components deployed are as follows:

- Windows 2016 Server running DNS
- A Kubernetes cluster
- Bitnami NGINX deployment
- LoadBalancer service created, assigned IP 10.2.1.74
- CoreDNS service configured to use hostPort 53
- Deployed add-ons, using the configuration from this chapter such as external-dns, ETCD cluster for CoreDNS, CoreDNS ETCD zone added, and MetalLB using an address pool of 10.2.1.60-10.2.1.80

Now, let's go through the configuration steps to integrate our DNS servers.

Configuring the primary DNS server

The first step is to create a conditional forwarder to the node running the CoreDNS pod.

On the Windows DNS host, we need to create a new conditional forwarder for `foowidgets.k8s` pointing to the host that is running the CoreDNS pod. In our example, the CoreDNS pod has been assigned to the host 10.240.100.102:

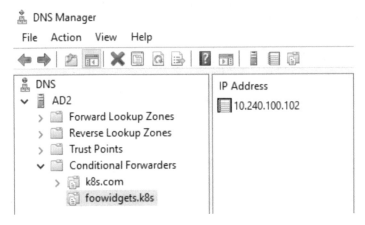

Figure 6.18 – Windows conditional forwarder setup

This configures the Windows DNS server to forward any request for a host in the `foowidgets.k8s` domain to CoreDNS pod.

Testing DNS forwarding to CoreDNS

To test the configuration, we will use a workstation on the main network that has been configured to use the Windows DNS server.

The first test we will run is a `nslookup` of the NGINX record that was created by the MetalLB annotation:

From a command prompt, we execute a `nslookup nginx.foowidgets.k8s`:

```
PS C:\> nslookup nginx.foowidgets.k8s
Server:   AD2.hyper-vplanet.com
Address:  10.2.1.14

Non-authoritative answer:
Name:     nginx.foowidgets.k8s
Address:  10.2.1.74
```

Figure 6.19 – Nslookup confirmation for registered name

Since the query returned the IP address we expected for the record, we can confirm that the Windows DNS server is forwarding requests to CoreDNS correctly.

We can do one more additional NGINX test from the laptop's browser:

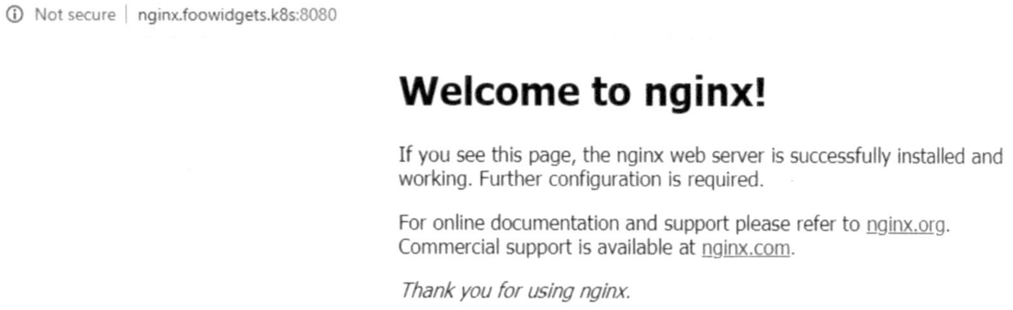

Figure 6.20 – Success browsing from an external workstation using CoreDNS

One test confirms that the forwarding works, but we aren't comfortable that the system is fully working.

To test a new service, we deploy a different NGINX server called microbot, with a service that has an annotation assigning the name `microbot.foowidgets.k8s`. MetalLB has assigned the service the IP address of 10.2.1.65.

Like our previous test, we test the name resolution using nslookup:

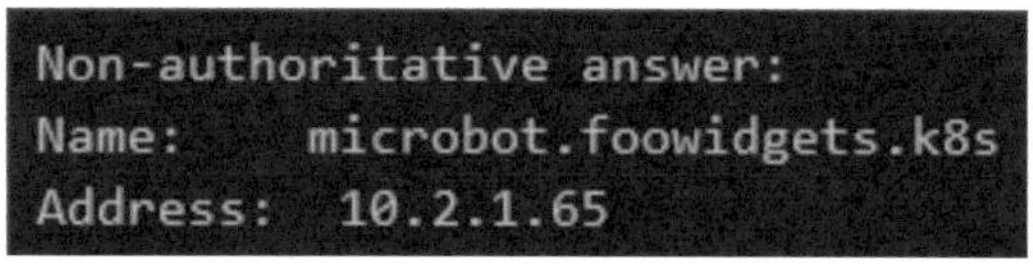

Figure 6.21 – Nslookup confirmation for an additional registered name

To confirm that the web server is running correctly, we browse to the URL from a workstation:

ⓘ Not secure | microbot.foowidgets.k8s/

Container hostname: microbot-5b8559b777-h6tpp

Figure 6.22 – Successful browsing from an external workstation using CoreDNS

Success! We have now integrated an enterprise DNS server with a CoreDNS server running on a Kubernetes cluster. This integration provides users with the ability to register service names dynamically by simply adding an annotation to the service.

Summary

In this chapter, you learned about two important objects in Kubernetes that expose your deployments to other cluster resources and users.

We started the chapter by going over services and the multiple types that can be assigned. The three major service types are ClusterIP, NodePort, and LoadBalancer. Selecting the type of service will configure how your application is accessed.

Typically, services alone are not the only objects that are used to provide access to applications running in the cluster. You will often use a ClusterIP service along with an Ingress controller to provide access to services that use layer 7. Some applications may require additional communication, that is not provided by a layer-7 load balancer. These applications may need a layer-4 load balancer to expose their services to the users. In the load balancing section, we demonstrated the installation and use of MetalLB, a commonly used open source layer-7 load balancer.

In the last section, we explained how to integrate a dynamic CoreDNS zone with an external enterprise DNS server using conditional forwarding. Integrating the two naming systems provides a method to allow the dynamic registration of any layer-4 load-balanced service in the cluster.

Now that you know how to expose services on the cluster to users, how do we control who has access to the cluster to create a new service? In the next chapter, we will explain how to integrate authentication with your cluster. We will deploy an OIDC provider into our KinD clusters and connect with an external SAML2 lab server for identities.

Questions

1. How does a service know what pods should be used as endpoints for the service?

    A. By the service port

    B. By the namespace

    C. By the author

    D. By the selector label

2. What kubectl command helps you to troubleshoot services that may not be working properly?

    A. `kubectl get services <service name>`

    B. `kubectl get ep <service name>`

    C. `kubectl get pods <service name>`

    D. `kubectl get servers <service name>`

3. All Kubernetes distributions include support for services that use the
    `LoadBalancer` type.

    A. True

    B. False

4. Which load balancer type supports all TCP/UDP ports and accepts traffic regardless
    of the packet's contents?

    A. Layer 7

    B. Cisco layer

    C. Layer 2

    D. Layer 4

5. Without any added components, you can use multiple protocols using which of the
    following service types?

    A. `NodePort` and `ClusterIP`

    B. `LoadBalancer` and `NodePort`

    C. `NodePort`, `LoadBalancer`, and `ClusterIP`

    D. `LoadBalancer` and `ClusterIP`

Section 3: Running Kubernetes in the Enterprise

In this last section, we will dive into the add-on components that a cluster requires for the enterprise. The first topic will explain how to integrate identity and access management using an enterprise directory. We will then focus on securing a cluster, starting with how to deploy a secure Kubernetes dashboard, which is commonly viewed as a security issue. Using the dashboard as an example, we will explain how to use an identity provider to secure a cluster using **role-based access control** (**RBAC**).

Going beyond basic RBAC, we will then see how to secure a cluster by using Pod Security Policies and Open Policy Agent. Finally, we will expain how to close a commonly overlooked audit point in a cluster, pod-level auditing, by implementing Falco and EFK.

The last part of this section will provide details on how to back up workloads for disaster recovery and cluster migrations. Finally, we will close out the book by creating a new cluster that we will use to explain how to provision a platform using various CI/CD tools.

This part of the book comprises the following chapters:

- *Chapter 7, Integrating Authentication into Your Cluster*
- *Chapter 8, Deploying a Secured Kubernetes Dashboard*
- *Chapter 9, RBAC Policies and Auditing*
- *Chapter 10, Creating Pod Security Policies*
- *Chapter 11, Extending Security Using Open Policy Agent*
- *Chapter 12, Auditing Using Falco and EFK*
- *Chapter 13, Backing Up Workloads*
- *Chapter 14, Provisioning a Platform*

7
Integrating Authentication into Your Cluster

Once a cluster has been built, users will need to interact with it securely. For most enterprises, this means authenticating individual users and making sure they can only access what they need in order to do their jobs. With Kubernetes, this can be challenging because a cluster is a collection of APIs, not an application with a frontend that can prompt for authentication.

In this chapter, you'll learn how to integrate enterprise authentication into your cluster using the OpenID Connect protocol and Kubernetes impersonation. We'll also cover several anti-patterns and explain why you should avoid using them.

In this chapter, we will cover the following topics:

- Understanding how Kubernetes knows who you are
- Understanding OpenID Connect
- What are the other options?
- Configuring KinD for OpenID Connect

- How cloud Kubernetes knows who you are

- Configuring your cluster for impersonation

- Configuring impersonation without OpenUnison

- Let's get started!

Technical requirements

To complete the exercises in this chapter, you will require the following:

- An Ubuntu 18.04 server with 8 GB of RAM

- A KinD cluster running with the configuration from *Chapter 5*, *Deploying a Cluster Using KinD*

You can access the code for this chapter at the following GitHub repository: `https://github.com/PacktPublishing/Kubernetes-and-Docker-The-Complete-Guide/tree/master/chapter7`.

Understanding how Kubernetes knows who you are

There Is No Spoon

– The Matrix, 1999

In the 1999 sci-fi film *The Matrix*, Neo talks to a child about the Matrix as he waits to see the Oracle. The child explains to him that the trick to manipulating the Matrix is to realize that *"There is no spoon"*.

This is a great way to look at users in Kubernetes because they don't exist. With the exception of service accounts, which we'll talk about later, there are no objects in Kubernetes called "User" or "Group". Every API interaction must include enough information to tell the API server who the user is and what groups the user is a member of. This assertion can take different forms, depending on how you plan to integrate authentication into your cluster.

In this section, we will get into the details of the different ways Kubernetes can associate a user with a cluster.

External users

Users who are accessing the Kubernetes API from outside the cluster will usually do so using one of a two authentication methods:

- **Certificate**: You can assert who you are using a client certificate that has information about you, such as your username and groups. The certificate is used as part of the TLS negotiation process.

- **Bearer token**: Embedded in each request, a bearer token can either be a self-contained token that contains all the information needed to verify itself or a token that can be exchanged by a webhook in the API server for that information.

You can also use service accounts to access the API server outside the cluster, though it's strongly discouraged. We'll cover the risks and concerns around using service accounts in the *What are the other options?* section.

Groups in Kubernetes

Different users can be assigned the same permissions without creating `RoleBinding` `objects` for each user individually via groups. Kubernetes includes two types of groups:

- **System assigned**: These groups start with the `system:` prefix and are assigned by the API server. An example group is `system:authenticated`, which is assigned to all authenticated users. Other examples of system assigned groups are the `system:serviceaccounts:namespace` group, where `Namespace` is the name of the namespace that contains all the service accounts for the namespace named in the group.

- **User asserted groups**: These groups are asserted by the authentication system either in the token provided to the API server or via the authentication webhook. There are no standards or requirements for how these groups are named. Just as with users, groups don't exist as objects in the API server. Groups are asserted at authentication time by external users and tracked locally for system generated groups. When asserting a user's groups, the primary difference between a user's unique ID and groups is that the unique ID is expected to be unique, whereas groups are not.

You may be authorized for access by groups, but all access is still tracked and audited based on your user's unique ID.

Service accounts

Service accounts are objects that exist in the API server to track which pods can access the various APIs. Service account tokens are called **JSON Web Tokens**, or **JWTs**. Depending on how the token was generated, there are two ways to obtain a service account:

- The first is from a secret that was generated by Kubernetes when the service account was created.

- The second is via the `TokenRequest` API, which is used to inject a secret into pods via a mount point or used externally from the cluster. All service accounts are used by injecting the token as a header in the request into the API server. The API server recognizes it as a service account and validates it internally.

Unlike users, service accounts can **NOT** be assigned to arbitrary groups. Service accounts are members of pre-built groups, but you can't create a group of specific service accounts for assigning roles.

Now that we explored the fundamentals of how Kubernetes identifies users, we'll explore how this framework fits into the **OpenID Connect** (**OIDC**) protocol. OIDC provides the security most enterprises require and is standards-based, but Kubernetes doesn't use it in a way that is typical of many web applications. Understanding these differences and why Kubernetes needs them is an important step in integrating a cluster into an enterprise security environment.

Understanding OpenID Connect

OpenID Connect is a standard identity federation protocol. It's built on the OAuth2 specification and has some very powerful features that make it the preferred choice for interacting with Kubernetes clusters.

The main benefits of OpenID Connect are as follows:

- **Short-lived tokens**: If a token is leaked, such as via a log message or breach, you want the token to expire as quickly as possible. With OIDC, you're able to specify tokens that can live for 1-2 minutes, which means the token will likely be expired by the time an attacker attempts to use it.

- **User and group memberships**: When we start talking about authorizations, we'll see quickly that it's important to manage access by groups instead of managing access by referencing users directly. OIDC tokens can embed both the user's identifier and their groups, leading to easier access management.

- **Refresh tokens scoped to timeout policies**: With short-lived tokens, you need to be able to refresh them as needed. The time a refresh token is valid for can be scoped to your enterprise's web application idle timeout policy, keeping your cluster in compliance with other web-based applications.

- **No plugins required for kubectl**: The kubectl binary supports OpenID Connect natively, so there's no need for any additional plugins. This is especially useful if you need to access your cluster from a jump box or VM because you're unable to install the **Command-Line Interface** (**CLI**) tools directly onto your workstation.

- **More multi-factor authentication options**: Many of the strongest multi-factor authentication options require a web browser. Examples include FIDO U2F and WebAuth, which use hardware tokens.

OIDC is a peer reviewed standard that has been in use for several years and is quickly becoming the preferred standard for identity federation.

> **Important Note**
>
> Identity federation is the term used to describe the assertion of identity data and authentication without sharing the user's confidential secret or password. A classic example of identity federation is logging into your employee website and being able to access your benefits provider without having to log in again. Your employee website doesn't share your password with your benefits provider. Instead, your employee website *asserts* that you logged in at a certain date and time and provides some information about you. This way, your account is *federated* across two silos (your employee website and benefits portal), without your benefits portal knowing your employee website password.

The OpenID Connect protocol

As you can see, there are multiple components to OIDC. To fully understand how OIDC works, let's begin the OpenID connect protocol.

The two aspects of the OIDC protocol we will be focusing on are as follows:

- Using tokens with kubectl and the API server
- Refreshing tokens to keep your tokens up to date

We won't focus too much on obtaining tokens. While the protocol to get a token does follow a standard, the login process does not. How you obtain tokens from an identity provider will vary, based on how you choose to implement the OIDC **Identity Provider (IdP)**.

There are three tokens that are generated from an OIDC login process:

- `access_token`: This token is used to make authenticated requests to web services your identity provider may provide, such as obtaining user information. It is **NOT** used by Kubernetes and can be discarded.

- `id_token`: This token is a JWT that encapsulates your identity, including your unique identifier (sub), groups, and expiration information about you that the API server can use to authorize your access. The JWT is signed by your identity provider's certificate and can be verified by Kubernetes simply by checking the JWT's signature. This is the token you pass to Kubernetes for each request to authenticate yourself.

- `refresh_token`: kubectl knows how to refresh your `id_token` for you automatically once it expires. To do this, it makes a call to your IdP's token endpoint using `refresh_token` to obtain a new `id_token`. A `refresh_token` can only be used once and is opaque, meaning that you, as the holder of the token, have no visibility into its format and it really doesn't matter to you. It either works, or it doesn't *refresh_token never goes to Kubernetes (or any other application). It is only used in communications with the IdP.*

Once you have your tokens, you can use them to authenticate with the API server. The easiest way to use your tokens is to add them to the kubectl configuration using command-line parameters:

```
kubectl config set-credentials username --auth-provider=oidc
--auth-provider-arg=idp-issuer-url=https://host/uri --auth-
provider-arg=client-id=kubernetes --auth-provider-arg=refresh-
token=$REFRESH_TOKEN --auth-provider-arg=id-token=$ID_TOKEN
```

`config set-credentials` has a few options that need to be provided. We have already explained `id-token` and `refresh_token`, but there are two additional options:

- `idp-issuer-url`: This is the same URL we will use to configure the API server and points to the base URL used for the IdP's discovery URL.

- `client-id`: This is used by your IdP to identify your configuration. This is unique to a Kubernetes deployment and is not considered secret information.

The OpenID Connect protocol has an optional element, known as a `client_secret`, that is shared between an OIDC client and the IdP. It is used to "authenticate" the client prior to making any requests, such as refreshing a token. While it's supported by Kubernetes as an option, its recommended to not use it and instead configure your IdP to use a public endpoint (which doesn't use a secret at all).

The client secret has no practical value since you'd need to share it with every potential user and since it's a password, your enterprise's compliance framework will likely require that it is rotated regularly, causing support headaches. Overall, it's just not worth any potential downsides in terms of security.

> **Important Note**
> Kubernetes requires that your identity provider supports the discovery URL endpoint, which is a URL that provides some JSON to tell you where you can get keys to verify JWTs and the various endpoints available. Take any issuer URL and add `/.well-known/openid-configuration` to see this information.

Following OIDC and the API's interaction

Once `kubectl` has been configured, all of your API interactions will follow the following sequence:

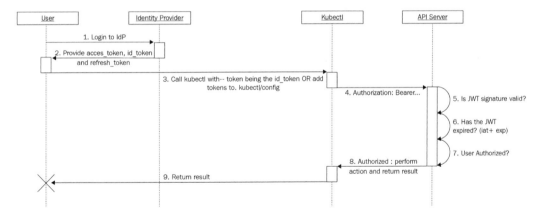

Figure 7.1 – Kubernetes/kubectl OpenID Connect sequence diagram

The preceding diagram is from Kubernetes' authentication page at `https://kubernetes.io/docs/reference/access-authn-authz/authentication/#openid-connect-tokens`. Authenticating a request involves doing the following:

1. **Log in to your Identity Provider (IdP):** This will be different for each IdP. This could involve providing a username and password to a form in a web browser, a multi-factor token, or a certificate. This will be implementation-specific to every implementation.

2. **Provide tokens to the user:** Once authenticated, the user needs a way to generate the tokens needed by `kubectl` to access the Kubernetes APIs. This can take the form of an application that makes it easy for the user to copy and paste them into the configuration file, or can be a new file to download.

3. This step is where `id_token` and `refresh_token` are added to the `kubectl` configuration. If the tokens were presented to the user in the browser, they can be manually added to the configuration. If a new configuration is provided so that it can be downloaded, it can be. There are also `kubectl` plugins that will launch a web browser to start the authentication process and, once completed, generate your configuration for you.

4. **Inject id_token:** Once the `kubectl` command has been called, each API call includes an addition header, called the `Authorization` header, that includes `id_token`.

5. **JWT signature validation:** Once the API server receives `id_token` from the API call, it validates the signature against the public key provided by the identity provider. The API server will also validate whether the issuer matches the issuer for the API server configuration, and also that the recipient matches the client ID from the API server configuration.

6. **Check the JWT's expiration:** Tokens are only good for a limited amount of time. The API server ensures that the token hasn't expired.

7. **Authorization check:** Now that the user has been authenticated, the API server will determine whether the user identified by the provided `id_token` is able to perform the requested action by matching the user's identifier and asserted groups to internal policies.

8. **Execute the API**: All checks are complete and the API server executes the request, generating a response that will be sent back to `kubectl`.

9. **Format the response for the user**: Once the API call is complete (or a series of API calls), the JSON is formatted for the user by `kubectl`.

> **Important Note**
>
> In general terms, authentication is the process of validating you are you. Most of us encounter this when we put our username and password into a website. We're proving who we are. In the enterprise world, authorization then becomes the decision of whether we're allowed to do something. First, we authenticate and then we authorize. The standards built around API security don't assume authentication and go straight to authorization based on some sort of token. It's not assumed that the caller has to be identified. For instance, when you use a physical key to open a door, the door doesn't know who you are, only that you have the right key. This terminology can become very confusing, so don't feel bad if you get a bit lost. You're in good company!

`id_token` is self-contained; everything the API server needs to know about you is in that token. The API server verifies `id_token` using the certificate provided by the identity provider and verifies that the token hasn't expired. As long as that all lines up, the API server will move on to authorizing your request based on its own RBAC configuration. We'll cover the details of that process later. Finally, assuming you're authorized, the API server provides a response.

Notice that Kubernetes never sees your password or any other secret information that you, and only you, know. The only thing that's shared is `id_token`, and that's ephemeral. This leads to several important points:

- Since Kubernetes never sees your password or other credentials, it can't compromise them. This can save you a tremendous amount of time working with your security team, because all the tasks related to securing passwords can be skipped!

- `id_token` is self-contained, which means that if it's compromised, there is nothing you can do, short of re-keying your identity provider, to stop it from being abused. This is why it's so important for your `id_token` to have a short lifespan. At 1-2 minutes, the likelihood that an attacker will be able to obtain an `id_token`, realize what it is, and abuse it, is very low.

If, while performing its calls, kubectl finds that id_token has expired, it will attempt to refresh it by calling the IdP's token endpoint using refresh_token. If the user's session is still valid, the IdP will generate a new id_token and refresh_token, which kubectl will store for you in the kubectl configuration. This happens automatically with no user intervention. Additionally, a refresh_token has a one-time use, so if someone tries to use a previously used refresh_token, your IdP will fail the refresh process.

> **Important Note**
>
> It's bound to happen. Someone may need to be locked out immediately. It may be that they're being walked out or that their session has been compromised. This is dependent on your IdP, so when choosing an IdP, make sure it supports some form of session revocation.

Finally, if refresh_token has expired or the session has been revoked, the API server will return a **401 Unauthorized** message to indicate that it will no longer support the token.

We've spent a considerable amount of time examining the OIDC protocol. Now, let's take an in-depth look at id_token.

id_token

An id_token is a JSON web token that is base64-encoded and is digitally signed. The JSON contains a series of attributes, known as claims, in OIDC. There are some standard claims in id_token, but for the most part, the claims you will be most concerned with are as follows:

- iss: The issuer, which **MUST** line up with the issuer in your kubectl configuration
- aud: Your client ID
- sub: Your unique identifier
- groups: Not a standard claim, but should be populated with groups specifically related to your Kubernetes deployment

> **Important Note**
>
> Many deployments attempt to identify you by your email address. This is an anti-pattern as your email address is generally based on your name, and names change. The sub claim is supposed to be a unique identifier that is immutable and will never change. This way, it doesn't matter if your email changes because your name changes. This can make it harder to debug *"who is cd25d24d-74b8-4cc4-8b8c-116bf4abbd26?"* but will provide a cleaner and easier to maintain cluster.

There are several other claims that indicate when an `id_token` should no longer be accepted. These claims are all measured in seconds from epoch (January 1, 1970) UTC time:

- `exp`: When `id_token` expires

- `iat`: When `id_token` was created

- `nbf`: The absolute earliest an `id_token` should be allowed

Why doesn't a token just have a single expiration time?

It's unlikely that the clock on the system that created `id_token` has the exact same time as the system that is evaluating it. There's often a skew and depending on how the clock is set, it may be a few minutes. Having a not-before in addition to an expiration gives some room for standard time deviation.

There are other claims in an `id_token` that don't really matter but are there for additional context. Examples include your name, contact information, organization, and so on.

While the primary use for tokens is to interact with the Kubernetes API server, they are not limited to only API interaction. In addition to going to the API server, webhook calls may also receive your `id_token`.

You may have deployed OPA as a validating webhook on a cluster. When someone submits a pod creation request, the webhook will receive the user's `id_token`, which can be used for other decisions.

One example is that you want to ensure that the PVCs are mapped to specific PVs based on the submitter's organization. The organization is included in `id_token`, which is passed to Kubernetes, and then onto OPA webhook. Since the token has been passed to the webhook, the information can then be used in your OPA policies.

Other authentication options

In this section, we focused on OIDC and presented reasons why it's the best mechanism for authentication. It is certainly not the only option, and we will cover the other options in this section and when they're appropriate.

Certificates

This is generally everyone's first experience authenticating to a Kubernetes cluster.

Once a Kubernetes installation is complete, a pre-built kubectl `config` file that contains a certificate and private key is created and ready to be use. This file should only be used in "break glass in case of emergency" scenarios, where all other forms of authentication are not available. It should be controlled by your organization's standards for privileged access. When this configuration file is used, it doesn't identify the user and can easily be abused since it doesn't allow for an easy audit trail.

While this is a standard use case for certificate authentication, it's not the only use case for certificate authentication. Certificate authentication, when done correctly, is one of the strongest recognized credentials in the industry.

Certificate authentication is used by the US Federal Government for its most important tasks. At a high level, certificate authentication involves using a client key and certificate to negotiate your HTTPS connection to the API server. The API server can get the certificate you used to establish the connection and validate it against a **Certificate Authority (CA)** certificate. Once verified, it maps attributes from the certificate to a user and groups the API server can recognize.

To get the security benefits of certificate authentication, the private key needs to be generated on isolated hardware, usually in the form of a smartcard, and never leave that hardware. A certificate signing request is generated and submitted to a CA that signs the public key, thus creating a certificate that is then installed on the dedicated hardware. At no point does the CA get the private key, so even if the CA were compromised, you couldn't gain the user's private key. If a certificate needs to be revoked, it's added to a revocation list that can either be pulled from an LDAP directory, a file, or can be checked using the OCSP protocol.

This may look like an attractive option, so why shouldn't you use certificates with Kubernetes?

- Smartcard integration uses a standard called PKCS11, which neither `kubectl` or the API server support.

- The API server has no way of checking certificate revocation lists or using OCSP, so once a certificate has been minted, there's no way to revoke it so that the API server can use it.

Additionally, the process to correctly generate a key pair is rarely used. It requires a complex interface to be built that is difficult for users to use combine with command-line tools that need to be run. To get around this, the certificate and key pair are generated for you and you download it or it's emailed to you, negating the security of the process.

The other reason you shouldn't use certificate authentication for users is that it's difficult to leverage groups. While you can embed groups into the subject of the certificate, you can't revoke a certificate. So, if a user's role changes, you can give them a new certificate but you can't keep them from using the old one.

As stated in the introduction to this section, using a certificate to authenticate in "break glass in case of emergencies" situations is a good use of certificate authentication. It may be the only way to get into a cluster if all other authentication methods are experiencing issues.

Service accounts

Service accounts appear to provide an easy access method. Creating them is easy. The following command creates a service account object and a secret to go with it that stores the service account's token:

```
kubectl create sa mysa -n default
```

Next, the following command will retrieve the service account's token in JSON format and return only the value of the token. This token can then be used to access the API server:

```
kubectl get secret $(kubectl get sa mysa -n default -o json
 | jq -r '.secrets[0].name') -o json | jq -r '.data.token' |
base64 -d
```

To show an example of this, let's call the API endpoint directly, without providing any credentials:

```
curl -v --insecure https://0.0.0.0:32768/api
```

You will receive the following:

```
  .

  .

  .

{
  "kind": "Status",
  "apiVersion": "v1",
  "metadata": {
  },
  "status": "Failure",
  "message": "forbidden: User \"system:anonymous\" cannot get
path \"/api\"",
  "reason": "Forbidden",
  "details": {
  },
  "code": 403
* Connection #0 to host 0.0.0.0 left intact
```

By default, most Kubernetes distributions do not allow anonymous access to the API server, so we receive a *403 error* because we didn't specify a user.

Now, let's add our service account to an API request:

```
export KUBE_AZ=$(kubectl get secret $(kubectl get sa mysa -n
default -o json | jq -r '.secrets[0].name') -o json | jq -r
'.data.token' | base64 -d)
curl  -H "Authorization: Bearer $KUBE_AZ" --insecure
https://0.0.0.0:32768/api
{
  "kind": "APIVersions",
  "versions": [
    "v1"
  ],
```

```
  "serverAddressByClientCIDRs": [
    {
      "clientCIDR": "0.0.0.0/0",
      "serverAddress": "172.17.0.3:6443"
    }
  ]
}
```

Success! This was an easy process, so you may be wondering, *"Why do I need worry about all the complicated OIDC mess?"* This solution's simplicity brings multiple security issues:

- **Secure transmission of the token**: Service accounts are self-contained and need nothing to unlock them or verify ownership, so if a token is taken in transit, you have no way of stopping its use. You could set up a system where a user logs in to download a file with the token in it, but you now have a much less secure version of OIDC.

- **No expiration**: When you decode a service account token, there is nothing that tell you when the token expires. That's because the token never expires. You can revoke a token by deleting the service account and recreating it, but that means you need a system in place to do that. Again, you've built a less capable version of OIDC.

- **Auditing**: The service account can easily be handed out by the owner once the key has been retrieved. If there are multiple users using a single key, it becomes very difficult to audit use of the account.

In addition to these issues, you can't put a service account into arbitrary groups. This means that RBAC bindings have to either be direct to the service account or use one of the pre-built groups that service accounts are a member of. We'll explore why this is an issue when we talk about authorization, so just keep it in mind for now.

Finally, service accounts were never designed to be used outside of the cluster. It's like using a hammer to drive in a screw. With enough muscle and aggravation, you will drive it in, but it won't be pretty and no one will be happy with the result.

TokenRequest API

At the time of writing, the TokenRequest API is still a **beta** feature.

The TokenRequest API lets you request a short-lived service account for a specific scope. While it provides slightly better security since it will expire and has a limited scope, it's still bound to a service account, which means no groups, and there's still the issue of securely getting the token to the user and auditing its use.

Tokens generated by the `TokenRequest` API are built for other systems to talk to your cluster; they are not meant to be used by users.

Custom authentication webhooks

If you already have an identity platform that doesn't use an existing standard, a custom authentication webhook will let you integrate it without having to customize the API server. This feature is commonly used by cloud providers who host managed Kubernetes instances.

You can define an authentication webhook that the API server will call with a token to validate it and get information about the user. Unless you manage a public cloud with a custom IAM token system that you are building a Kubernetes distribution for, don't do this. Writing your own authentication is like writing your own encryption – just don't do it. Every custom authentication system we've seen for Kubernetes boils down to either a pale imitation of OIDC or "pass the password". Much like the analogy of driving a screw in with a hammer, you could do it, but it will be very painful. This is mostly because instead of driving the screw through a board, you're more likely to drive it into your own foot.

Keystone

Those familiar with OpenStack will recognize the name Keystone as an identity provider. If you are not familiar with Keystone, it is the default identity provider used in an OpenStack deployment.

Keystone hosts the API that handles authentication and token generation. OpenStack stores users in Keystone's database. While using Keystone is more often associated with OpenStack, Kubernetes can also be configured to use Keystone for username and password authentication, with some limitations:

- The main limitation of using Keystone as an IdP for Kubernetes is that it only works with Keystone's LDAP implementation. While you could use this method, you should consider that only username and password are supported, so you're creating an identity provider with a non-standard protocol to authenticate to an LDAP server, which pretty much any OIDC IdP can do out of the box.

- You can't leverage SAML or OIDC with Keystone, even though Keystone supports both protocols for OpenStack, which limits how users can authenticate, thus cutting you off from multiple multi-factor options.

- Few, if any, applications know how to use the Keystone protocol outside of OpenStack. Your cluster will have multiple applications that make up your platform, and those applications won't know how to integrate with Keystone.

Using Keystone is certainly an appealing idea, especially if you're deploying on OpenStack, but ultimately, it's very limiting and you will likely put in just as much working getting Keystone integrated as just using OIDC.

The next section will take the details we've explored here and apply them to integrating authentication into a cluster. As you move through the implementation, you'll see how `kubectl`, the API server, and your identity provider interact to provide secure access to the cluster. We'll tie these features back to common enterprise requirements to illustrate why the details for understanding the OpenID Connect protocol are important.

Configuring KinD for OpenID Connect

For our example deployment, we will use a scenario from our customer, FooWidgets. Foowidgets has a Kubernetes cluster that they would like integrated using OIDC. The proposed solution needs to address the following requirements:

- Kubernetes must use our central authentication system, Active Directory Federation Services.
- We need to be able map Active Directory groups into our RBAC `RoleBinding` objects.
- Users need access to the Kubernetes Dashboard.
- Users need to be able to use the CLI.
- All enterprise compliance requirements must be met.

Let's explore each of these in detail and explain how we can address the customer's requirements.

Addressing the requirements

Our enterprise's requirements require multiple moving parts, both inside and outside our cluster. We'll examine each of these components and how they relate to building an authenticated cluster.

Use Active Directory Federation Services

Most enterprises today use Active Directory from Microsoft™ to store information about users and their credentials. Depending on the size of your enterprise, it's not unusual to have multiple domain or forests where users live. If your IdP is well integrated into a Microsoft's Kerberos environment, it may know how to navigate these various systems. Most non-Microsoft applications are not, including most identity providers. **Active Directory Federation Services** (**ADFS**) is Microsoft's IdP that supports both SAML2 and OpenID Connect, and it knows how to navigate the domains and forest of an enterprise implementation. It's common in many large enterprises.

The next decision with ADFS is whether to use SAML2 or OpenID Connect. At the time of writing, SAML2 is much easier to implement and most enterprise environments with ADFS prefer to use SAML2. Another benefit of SAML2 is that it doesn't require a connection between our cluster and the ADFS servers; all of the important information is transferred through the user's browser. This cuts down on potential firewall rules that need to be implemented in order to get our cluster up and running.

> **Important Note**
> Don't worry – you don't need ADFS ready to go to run this exercise. We have a handy SAML testing identity provider we'll use. You won't need to install anything to use SAML2 with your KinD cluster.

Mapping Active Directory Groups to RBAC RoleBindings

This will become important when we start talking about authorization. What's important to point out here is that ADFS has the capability to put a user's group memberships in the SAML assertion, which our cluster can then consume.

Kubernetes Dashboard access

The dashboard is a powerful way to quickly access information about your cluster and make quick updates. When deployed correctly, the dashboard does not create any security issues. The proper way to deploy the dashboard is with no privileges, instead relying on the user's own credentials. We'll do this with a reverse proxy that injects the user's OIDC token on each request, which the dashboard will then use when it makes calls to the API server. Using this method, we'll be able to constrain access to our dashboard the same way we would with any other web application.

There are a few reasons why using the kubectl built-in proxy and port-forward aren't a great strategy for accessing the dashboard. Many enterprises will not install CLI utilities locally, forcing you to use a jump box to access privileged systems such as Kubernetes, meaning port forwarding won't work. Even if you can run kubectl locally, opening a port on loopback (127.0.0.1) means anything on your system can use it, not just you from your browser. While browsers have controls in place to keep you from accessing ports on loopback using a malicious script, that won't stop anything else on your workstation. Finally, it's just not a great user experience.

We'll dig into the details of how and why this works in *Chapter 9, Deploying a Secured Kubernetes Dashboard.*

Kubernetes CLI access

Most developers want to be able to access kubectl and other tools that rely on the kubectl configuration. For instance, the Visual Studio Code Kubernetes plugin doesn't require any special configuration. It just uses the kubectl built-in configuration. Most enterprises tightly constrain what binaries you're able to install, so we want to minimize any additional tools and plugins we want to install.

Enterprise compliance requirements

Being cloud-native doesn't mean you can ignore your enterprise's compliance requirements. Most enterprises have requirements such as having 20-minute idle timeouts, may require multi-factor authentication for privileged access, and so on. Any solution we put in place has to make it through the control spreadsheets needed to go live. Also, this goes without saying, but everything needs to be encrypted (and I do mean everything).

Pulling it all together

To fulfill these requirements, we're going to use OpenUnison. It has prebuilt configurations to work with Kubernetes, the dashboard, the CLI, and SAML2 identity providers such as ADFS. It's also pretty quick to deploy, so we don't need to concentrate on provider-specific implementation details and instead focus on Kubernetes' configuration options. Our architecture will look like this:

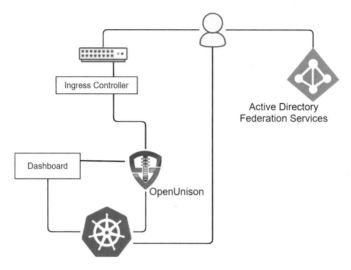

Figure 7.2 – Authentication architecture

For our implementation, we're going to use two hostnames:

- **k8s.apps.X-X-X-X.nip.io**: Access to the OpenUnison portal, where we'll initiate our login and get our tokens

- **k8sdb.apps.X-X-X-X.nip.io**: Access to the Kubernetes dashboard

> **Important Note**
>
> As a quick refresher, `nip.io` is a public DNS service that will return an IP address from the one embedded in your hostname. This is really useful in a lab environment where setting up DNS can be painful. In our examples, X-X-X-X is the IP of your Docker host.

When a user attempts to access `https://k8s.apps.X-X-X-X.nip.io/`, they'll be redirected to ADFS, which will collect their username and password (and maybe even a multi-factor authentication token). ADFS will generate an assertion that will be digitally signed and contain our user's unique ID, as well as their group assignments. This assertion is similar to `id_token`, which we examined earlier, but instead of being JSON, it's XML. The assertion is sent to the user's browser in a special web page that contains a form that will automatically submit the assertion back to OpenUnison. At that point, OpenUnison will create user objects in the OpenUnison namespace to store the user's information and create OIDC sessions.

Earlier, we described how Kubernetes doesn't have user objects. Kubernetes lets you extend the base API with **Custom Resource Definitions** (**CRDs**). OpenUnison defines a User CRD to help with high availability and to avoid needing a database to store state in. These user objects can't be used for RBAC.

Once the user is logged into OpenUnison, they can get their `kubectl` configuration to use the CLI or use the Kubernetes dashboard, `https://kubernetes.io/docs/tasks/access-application-cluster/web-ui-dashboard/`, to access the cluster from their browser. Once the user is ready, they can log out of OpenUnison, which will end their session and invalidate their `refresh_token`, making it impossible for them to use `kubectl` or the dashboard until after they log in again. If they walk away from their desk for lunch without logging out, when they return, their `refresh_token` will have expired, so they'll no longer be able to interact with Kubernetes without logging back in.

Now that we have walked through how users will log in and interact with Kubernetes, we'll deploy OpenUnison and integrate it into the cluster for authentication.

Deploying OIDC

We have included two installation scripts to automate the deployment steps. These scripts, `install-oidc-step1.sh` and `install-oidc-step2.sh`, are located in this book's GitHub repository, in the `chapter7` directory.

This section will explain all of the manual steps that the script automates.

> **Important Note**
>
> If you install OIDC using the scripts, you **must** follow this process for a successful deployment:
>
> Step 1: Run the `./install-oidc-step1.sh` script.
>
> Step 2: Register for an SAML2 test lab by following the procedure in the *Registering for a SAML2 test lab* section.
>
> Step3: Run the `./install-oidc-step2.sh` script to complete the OIDC deployment.

Deploying OIDC to a Kubernetes cluster using OpenUnison is a five-step process:

1.   Deploy the dashboard.

2.   Deploy the OpenUnison operator.

3.   Create a secret.

4.   Create a `values.yaml` file.

5.   Deploy the chart.

Let's perform these steps one by one.

Deploying OpenUnison

The dashboard is a popular feature for many users. It provides a quick view into resources without us needing to use the kubectl CLI. Over the years, it has received some bad press for being insecure, but when deployed correctly, it is very secure. Most of the stories you may have read or heard about come from a dashboard deployment that was not set up correctly. We will cover this topic in *Chapter 9, Securing the Kubernetes Dashboard*:

1.   First, we'll deploy the dashboard from `https://github.com/kubernetes/dashboard`:

```
kubectl apply -f https://raw.githubusercontent.com/
kubernetes/dashboard/v2.0.0/aio/deploy/recommended.yaml
namespace/kubernetes-dashboard created
serviceaccount/kubernetes-dashboard created
service/kubernetes-dashboard created
secret/kubernetes-dashboard-certs created
secret/kubernetes-dashboard-csrf created
```

```
secret/kubernetes-dashboard-key-holder created
configmap/kubernetes-dashboard-settings created
role.rbac.authorization.k8s.io/kubernetes-dashboard
created
clusterrole.rbac.authorization.k8s.io/kubernetes-
dashboard created
rolebinding.rbac.authorization.k8s.io/kubernetes-
dashboard created
clusterrolebinding.rbac.authorization.k8s.io/kubernetes-
dashboard created
deployment.apps/kubernetes-dashboard created
service/dashboard-metrics-scraper created
deployment.apps/dashboard-metrics-scraper created
```

2. Next, we need to add the repository that contains OpenUnison to our Helm list. To add the Tremolo chart repository, use the Helm repo add command:

```
Helm repo add tremolo https://nexus.tremolo.io/
repository/Helm/
https://nexus.tremolo.io/repository/Helm/
"tremolo" has been added to your repositories
```

> **Important Note**
>
> Helm is a package manager for Kubernetes. Helm provides a tool that
> will deploy a "Chart" to your cluster and help you manage the state of the
> deployment. We're using Helm v3, which does not require you to deploy any
> components, such as Tiller, to your cluster to work.

3. Once added, you need to update the repository using the Helm repo update command:

```
helm repo update

Hang tight while we grab the latest from your chart
repositories...
...Successfully got an update from the "tremolo" chart
repository
Update Complete. Happy Helming!
```

You are now ready to deploy the OpenUnison operator using the Helm chart.

4. First, we want to deploy OpenUnison in a new namespace called `openunison`. We need to create the namespace before deploying the Helm chart:

```
kubectl create ns openunison

namespace/openunison created
```

5. With the namespace created, you can deploy the chart into the namespace using Helm. To install a chart using Helm, use `Helm install <name> <chart> <options>`:

```
helm install openunison tremolo/openunison-operator
--namespace openunison

NAME: openunison
LAST DEPLOYED: Fri Apr 17 15:04:50 2020
NAMESPACE: openunison
STATUS: deployed
REVISION: 1
TEST SUITE: None
```

The operator will take a few minutes to finish deploying.

Important Note

An operator is a concept that was pioneered by CoreOS with the goal of encapsulating many of the tasks an administrator may perform that can be automated. Operators are implemented by watching for changes to a specific CRD and acting accordingly. The OpenUnison operator looks for objects of the OpenUnison type and will create any objects that are needed. A secret is created with a PKCS12 file; Deployment, Service and Ingress objects are all created too. As you make changes to an OpenUnison object, the operator makes updates to the Kubernetes object as needed. For instance, if you change the image in the OpenUnison object, the operator updates the Deployment, which triggers Kubernetes to rollout new pods. For SAML, the operator also watches metadata so that if it changes, the updated certificates are imported.

---

6. Once the operator has been deployed, we need to create a secret that will store passwords used internally by OpenUnison. Make sure to use your own values for the keys in this secret (remember to base64 encode them):

```
kubectl create -f - <<EOF
  apiVersion: v1
  type: Opaque
  metadata:
    name: orchestra-secrets-source
    namespace: openunison
  data:
    K8S_DB_SECRET: cGFzc3dvcmQK
    unisonKeystorePassword: cGFzc3dvcmQK
  kind: Secret
EOF

secret/orchestra-secrets-source created
```

> **Important Note**
>
> From here on out, we'll assume you're using Tremolo Security's testing identity provider. This tool will let you customize the user's login information without having to stand up a directory and identity provider. Register by going to `https://portal.apps.tremolo.io/` and clicking on **Register**.

To provide the accounts for the OIDC environment, we will use a SAML2 testing lab, so be sure to register before moving on.

7. First, we need to need to log into the testing identity provider by going to `https://portal.apps.tremolo.io/` and clicking on the **SAML2 Test Lab** badge:

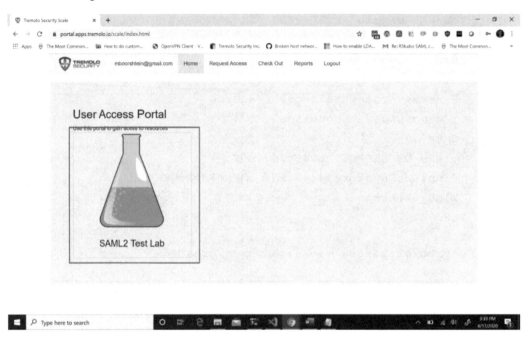

Figure 7.3 – SAML2 Test Lab badge

8. Once you've clicked on the badge, you'll be presented with a screen that shows your test IdP metadata URL:

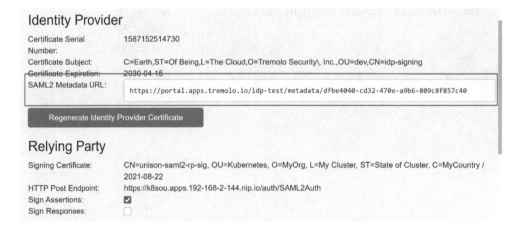

Figure 7.4 – Testing identity provider's page, highlighting the SAML2 metadata URL

Copy this value and store it in a safe place.

9. Now, we need to create a values.yaml file that will be used to supply configuration information when we deploy OpenUnison. This book's GitHub repository contains a base file in the chapter7 directory:

```yaml
network:
  openunison_host: "k8sou.apps.XX-XX-XX-XX.nip.io"
  dashboard_host: "k8sdb.apps.XX-XX-XX-XX.nip.io"
  api_server_host: ""
  session_inactivity_timeout_seconds: 900
  k8s_url: https://0.0.0.0:6443
cert_template:
  ou: "Kubernetes"
  o: "MyOrg"
  l: "My Cluster"
  st: "State of Cluster"
  c: "MyCountry"

image: "docker.io/tremolosecurity/openunison-k8s-login-saml2:latest"
myvd_config_path: "WEB-INF/myvd.conf"
k8s_cluster_name: kubernetes
enable_impersonation: false
dashboard:
  namespace: "kubernetes-dashboard"
  cert_name: "kubernetes-dashboard-certs"
  label: "k8s-app=kubernetes-dashboard"
  service_name: kubernetes-dashboard
certs:
  use_k8s_cm: false
trusted_certs: []
monitoring:
  prometheus_service_account: system:serviceaccount:monitoring:prometheus-k8s
saml:
  idp_url: https://portal.apps.tremolo.io/idp-test/metadata/dfbe4040-cd32-470e-a9b6-809c840
  metadata_xml_b64: ""
```

You need to change the following values for your deployment:

- `Network: openunison_host`: This value should use the IP address of your cluster, which is the IP address of your Docker host; for example, `k8sou.apps.192-168-2=131.nip.io`.

- `Network: dashboard_host`: This value should use the IP address of your cluster, which is the IP address of your Docker host; for example, `k8sdb.apps.192-168-2-131.nip.io`.

- `saml: idp url`: This value should be the SAML2 metadata URL that you retrieved from the SAML2 lab page in the previous step.

    After you've edited or created the file using your own entries, save the file and move on to deploying your OIDC provider.

10. To deploy OpenUnison using your `values.yaml` file, execute a `Helm install` command that uses the `-f` option to specify the `values.yaml` file:

```
helm install orchestra tremolo/openunison-k8s-login-saml2
--namespace openunison -f ./values.yaml


NAME: orchestra
LAST DEPLOYED: Fri Apr 17 16:02:00 2020
NAMESPACE: openunison
STATUS: deployed
REVISION: 1
TEST SUITE: None
```

11. In a few minutes, OpenUnison will be up and running. Check the deployment status by getting the pods in the `openunison` namespace:

```
kubectl get pods -n openunison


NAME                                         READY    STATUS
RESTARTS     AGE
openunison-operator-858d496-zzvvt            1/1      Running
0           5d6h
openunison-orchestra-57489869d4-88d2v        1/1      Running
0           85s
```

There is one more step you need to follow to complete the OIDC deployment: you need to update the SAML2 lab with the relying party for your deployment.

12. Now that OpenUnison is running, we need to get the SAML2 metadata from OpenUnison using the host in `network.openunison_host` in our `values.yaml` file and the `/auth/forms/saml2_rp_metadata.jsp` path:

```
curl --insecure https://k8sou.apps.192-168-2-131.nip.io/
auth/forms/saml2_rp_metadata.jsp
<?xml version="1.0" encoding="UTF-8"?><md:EntityDescriptor
xmlns:md="urn:oasis:names:tc:SAML:2.0:metadata"
ID="fc334f48076b7b13c3fcc83d1d116ac2decd7d665"
entityID="https://k8sou.apps.192-168-2-131.nip.io/auth/
SAML2Auth">
.
.
.
```

13. Copy the output, paste it into the testing identity provider where it says **Meta Data**, and click **Update Relying Party**:

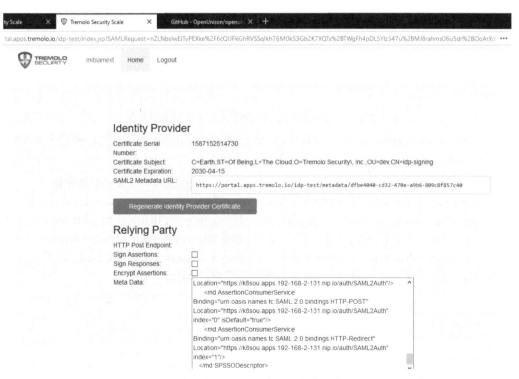

Figure 7.5 – Testing the identity provider with the relying party metadata

14. Finally, we need to add some attributes to our test user. Add the attributes shown in the following screenshot:

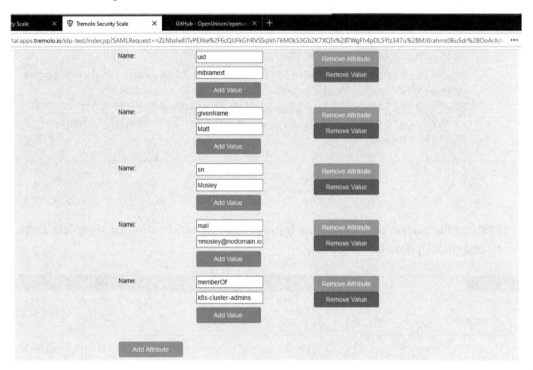

Figure 7.6 – Identity provider test user configuration

15. Next, click **Update Test User Data** to save your attributes. With that, you're ready to log in.

16. You can log into the OIDC provider using any machine on your network by using the assigned nip.io address. Since we will test access using the dashboard, you can use any machine with a browser. Navigate your browser to `network.openunison_host` in your `values.yaml` file. Enter your testing identity provider credentials, if needed, and then click **Finish Login** at the bottom of the screen. You should now be logged into OpenUnison:

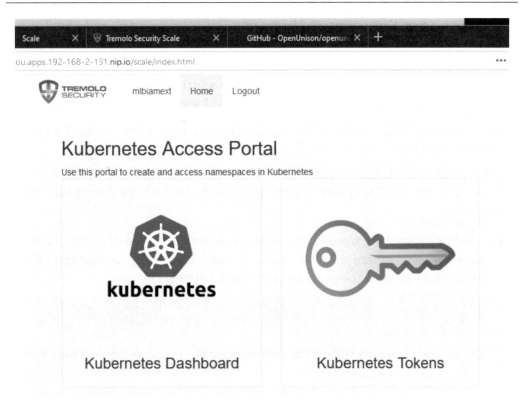

Figure 7.7 – OpenUnison home screen

17. Let's test the OIDC provider by clicking on the **Kubernetes Dashboard** link. Don't panic when you look at the initial dashboard screen – you'll see something like the following:

Figure 7.8 – Kubernetes Dashboard before SSO integration has been completed with the API server

That looks like a lot of errors! We're in the dashboard, but nothing seems to be authorized. That's because the API server doesn't trust the tokens that have been generated by OpenUnison yet. The next step is to tell Kubernetes to trust OpenUnison as its OpenID Connect Identity Provider.

Configuring the Kubernetes API to use OIDC

At this point, you have deployed OpenUnison as an OIDC provider and it's working, but your Kubernetes cluster has not been configured to use it as a provider yet. To configure the API server to use an OIDC provider, you need to add the OIDC options to the API server and provide the OIDC certificate so that the API will trust the OIDC provider.

Since we are using KinD, we can add the required options using a few `kubectl` and `docker` commands.

To provide the OIDC certificate to the API server, we need to retrieve the certificate and copy it over to the KinD master server. We can do this using two commands on the Docker host:

1. The first command extracts OpenUnison's TLS certificate from its secret. This is the same secret referenced by OpenUnison's Ingress object. We use the `jq` utility to extract the data from the secret and then base64 decode it:

    ```
    kubectl get secret ou-tls-certificate -n openunison -o
    json | jq -r '.data["tls.crt"]' | base64 -d > ou-ca.pem
    ```

2. The second command will copy the certificate to the master server into the `/etc/Kubernetes/pki` directory:

    ```
    docker cp ou-ca.pem cluster01-control-plane:/etc/
    kubernetes/pki/ou-ca.pem
    ```

3. As we mentioned earlier, to integrate the API server with OIDC, we need to have the OIDC values for the API options. To list the options we will use, describe the `api-server-config` ConfigMap in the `openunison` namespace:

    ```
    kubectl describe configmap api-server-config -n
    openunison


    Name:          api-server-config
    Namespace:     openunison
    Labels:        <none>
    Annotations:   <none>


    Data
    ====
    ```

```
oidc-api-server-flags:
----
--oidc-issuer-url=https://k8sou.apps.192-168-2-131.nip.
io/auth/idp/k8sIdp
--oidc-client-id=kubernetes
--oidc-username-claim=sub
--oidc-groups-claim=groups
--oidc-ca-file=/etc/kubernetes/pki/ou-ca.pem
```

4. Next, edit the API server configuration. OpenID Connect is configured by changing flags on the API server. This is why managed Kubernetes generally doesn't offer OpenID Connect as an option, but we'll cover that later in this chapter. Every distribution handles these changes differently, so check with your vendor's documentation. For KinD, shell into the control plane and update the manifest file:

```
docker exec -it cluster-auth-control-plane bash
apt-get update
apt-get install vim
vi /etc/kubernetes/manifests/kube-apiserver.yaml
```

5. Look for two options under command called --oidc-client and –oidc-issuer-url. Replace those two with the output from the preceding command that produced the API server flags. Make sure to add spacing and a dash (-) in front. It should look something like this when you're done:

```
    - --kubelet-preferred-address-types=InternalIP,Extern
alIP,Hostname
    - --oidc-issuer-url=https://k8sou.apps.192-168-2-131.
nip.io/auth/idp/k8sIdp
    - --oidc-client-id=kubernetes
    - --oidc-username-claim=sub
    - --oidc-groups-claim=groups
    - --oidc-ca-file=/etc/kubernetes/pki/ou-ca.pem
    - --proxy-client-cert-file=/etc/kubernetes/pki/front-
proxy-client.crt
```

6. Exit vim and the Docker environment (*ctl+d*) and then take a look at the
    `api-server` pod:

    ```
    kubectl get pod kube-apiserver-cluster-auth-control-plane
    -n kube-system
    NAME                                      READY   STATUS    RESTARTS   AGE
    kube-apiserver-cluster-auth-control-plane   1/1   Running
    0 73s
    ```

Notice that it's only 73 s old. That's because KinD saw that there was a change in the
manifest and restarted the API server.

> **Important Note**
>
> The API server pod is known as a "static pod". This pod can't be changed
> directly; its configuration has to be changed from the manifest on disk. This
> gives you a process that's managed by the API server as a container, but without
> giving you a situation where you need to edit pod manifests in EtcD directly if
> something goes wrong.

Verifying OIDC integration

Once OpenUnison and the API server have been integrated, we need to test that the
connection is working:

1. To test the integration, log back into OpenUnison and click on the **Kubernetes
    Dashboard** link again.

2. Click on the bell in the upper right and you'll see a different error:

Figure 7.9 – SSO enabled but the user is not authorized to access any resources

SSO between OpenUnison and you'll see that Kubernetes is working! However, the
new error, `service is forbidden: User https://...`, is an authorization
error, **not** an authentication error. The API server knows who we are, but isn't
letting us access the APIs.

3. We'll dive into the details of RBAC and authorizations in the next chapter, but for now, create this RBAC binding:

```
kubectl create -f - <<EOF
  apiVersion: rbac.authorization.k8s.io/v1
  kind: ClusterRoleBinding
  metadata:
    name: ou-cluster-admins
  subjects:
  - kind: Group
    name: k8s-cluster-admins
    apiGroup: rbac.authorization.k8s.io
  roleRef:
    kind: ClusterRole
    name: cluster-admin
    apiGroup: rbac.authorization.k8s.io
EOF
clusterrolebinding.rbac.authorization.k8s.io/ou-cluster-
admins created
```

4. Finally, go back to the dashboard and you'll see that you have full access to your cluster and all that of error messages are gone.

The API server and OpenUnison are now connected. Additionally, an RBAC policy has been created to enable our test user to manage the cluster as an administrator. Access was verified by logging into the Kubernetes dashboard, but most interactions will take place using the kubectl command. The next step is to verify we're able to access the cluster using kubectl.

Using your tokens with kubectl

> **Important Note**
> This section assumes you have a machine on your network that has a browser and kubectl running.

Using the Dashboard has its use cases, but you will likely interact with the API server using kubectl, rather than the dashboard, for the majority of your day. In this section, we will explain how to retrieve your JWT and how to add it to your Kubernetes config file:

1. You can retrieve you token from the OpenUnison dashboard. Navigate to the OpenUnison home page and click on the key that says **Kubernetes Tokens**. You'll see a screen that looks as follows:

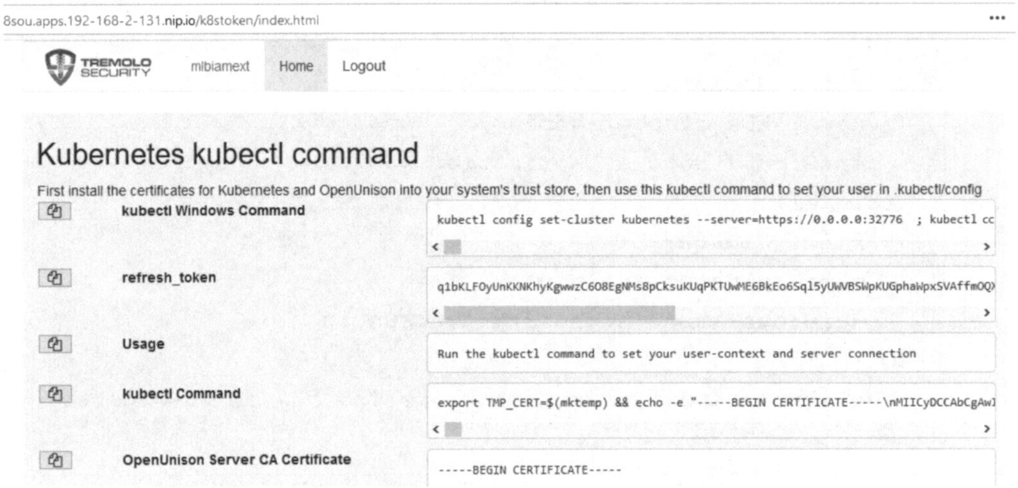

Figure 7.10 – OpenUnison kubectl configuration tool

OpenUnison provides a command line that you can copy and paste into your host session that adds all the required information to your config.

2. First, click on the double documents button next to the kubectl command to copy your kubectl command into your buffer. Leave the web browser open in the background.

3. You may want to back up your original config file before pasting the kubectl command from OpenUnison:

```
cp .kube/config .kube/config.bak

export KUBECONFIG=/tmp/k
kubectl get nodes
W0423 15:46:46.924515       3399 loader.go:223] Config not
found: /tmp/k
error: no configuration has been provided, try setting
KUBERNETES_MASTER environment variable
```

4. Then, go to your host console and paste the command into the console (the following output has been shortened, but your paste will start with the same output):

```
export TMP_CERT=$(mktemp) && echo -e "-----BEGIN CER. . .
Cluster "kubernetes" set.
Context "kubernetes" modified.
User "mlbiamext" set.
Switched to context "kubernetes".
```

5. Now, verify that you can view the cluster nodes using kubectl get nodes:

```
kubectl get nodes
NAME                         STATUS    ROLES     AGE
VERSION
cluster-auth-control-plane   Ready     master    47m
v1.17.0
cluster-auth-worker          Ready     <none>    46m
v1.17.0
```

6. You are now using your login credentials instead of the master certificate! As you work, the session will refresh. Log out of OpenUnison and watch the list of nodes. Within a minute or two, your token will expire and no longer work:

```
$ kubectl get nodes
Unable to connect to the server: failed to refresh token:
oauth2: cannot fetch token: 401 Unauthorized
```

Congratulations! You've now set up your cluster so that it does the following:

- Authenticate using SAML2 using your enterprise's existing authentication system.

- Use groups from your centralized authentication system to authorize access to Kubernetes (we'll get into the details of how in the next chapter).

- Give access to your users to both the CLI and the dashboard using the centralized credentials.

- Maintain your enterprise's compliance requirements by having short-lived tokens that provide a way to time out.

- Everything uses TLS from the user's browser, to the Ingress Controller, to OpenUnison, the dashboard, and finally the API server.

Next, you'll learn how to integrate centralized authentication into your managed clusters.

Introducing impersonation to integrate authentication with cloud-managed clusters

It's very popular to use managed Kubernetes services from cloud vendors such as Google, Amazon, Microsoft, and DigitalOcean (among many others). When it comes to these services, its generally very quick to get up and running, and they all share a common thread: they don't support OpenID Connect.

Earlier in this chapter, we talked about how Kubernetes supports custom authentication solutions through webhooks and that you should never, ever, use this approach unless you are a public cloud provider or some other host of Kubernetes systems. It turns out that pretty much every cloud vendor has its own approach to using these webhooks that uses their own identity and access management implementations. In that case, why not just use what the vendor provides? There are several reasons why you may not want to use a cloud vendor's IAM system:

- **Technical**: You may want to support features not offered by the cloud vendor, such as the dashboard, in a secure fashion.

- **Organizational**: Tightly coupling access to managed Kubernetes with that cloud's IAM puts an additional burden on the cloud team, which means that they may not want to manage access to your clusters.

- **User Experience**: Your developers and admins may have to work across multiple clouds. Providing a consistent login experience makes it easier on them and requires learning fewer tools.

- **Security and Compliance**: The cloud implementation may not offer choices that line up with your enterprise's security requirements, such as short-lived tokens and idle timeouts.

All that being said, there may be reasons to use the cloud vendor's implementation. You'll need to balance out the requirements, though. If you want to continue to use centralized authentication and authorization with hosted Kubernetes, you'll need to learn how to work with Impersonation.

What is Impersonation?

Kubernetes Impersonation is a way of telling the API server who you are without knowing your credentials or forcing the API server to trust an OpenID Connect IdP. When you use kubectl, instead of the API server receiving your id_token directly, it will receive a service account or identifying certificate that will be authorized to impersonate users, as well as a set of headers that tell the API server who the proxy is acting on behalf of:

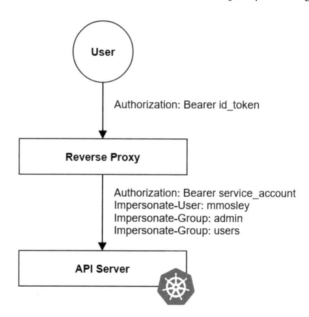

Figure 7.11 – Diagram of how a user interacts with the API server when using Impersonation

The reverse proxy is responsible for determining how to map from `id_token`, which the user provides (or any other token, for that matter), to the `Impersonate-User` and `Impersonate-Group` HTTP headers. The dashboard should never be deployed with a privileged identity, which the ability to impersonate falls under. To allow Impersonation with the 2.0 dashboard, use a similar model, but instead of going to the API server, you go to the dashboard:

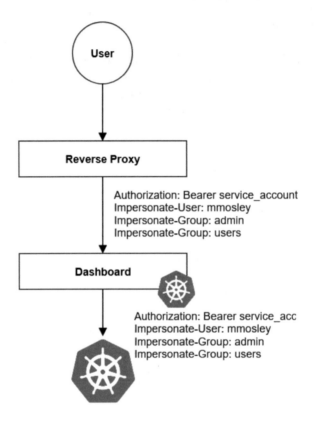

Figure 7.12 – Kubernetes Dashboard with Impersonation

The user interacts with the reverse proxy just like any web application. The reverse proxy uses its own service account and adds the impersonation headers. The dashboard passes this information through to the API server on all requests. The dashboard never has its own identity.

Security considerations

The service account has a certain superpower: it can be used to impersonate **anyone** (depending on your RBAC definitions). If you're running your reverse proxy from inside the cluster, a service account is OK, especially if combined with the `TokenRequest` API to keep the token short-lived. Earlier in the chapter, we talked about `ServiceAccount` objects having no expiration. That's important here because if you're hosting your reverse proxy off cluster, then if it were compromised, someone could use that service account to access the API service as anyone. Make sure you're rotating that service account often. If you're running the proxy off cluster, it's probably best to use a shorter-lived certificate instead of a service account.

When running the proxy on a cluster, you want to make sure it's locked down. It should run in its own namespace at a minimum. Not `kube-system` either. You want to minimize who has access. Using multi-factor authentication to get to that namespace is always a good idea, as are network policies that control what pods can reach out to the reverse proxy.

Based on the concepts we've just learned about regarding impersonation, the next step is to update our cluster's configuration to use impersonation instead of using OpenID Connect directly. You don't need a cloud-managed cluster to work with impersonation.

Configuring your cluster for impersonation

Let's deploy an impersonating proxy for our cluster. Assuming you're reusing your existing cluster, we first need to delete our orchestra Helm deployment (this will not delete the operator; we want to keep the OpenUnison operator). So, let's begin:

1. Run the following command to delete our `orchestra` Helm deployment:

    ```
    $ helm delete orchestra --namespace openunison
    release "orchestra" uninstalled
    ```

    The only pod running in the `openunison` namespace is our operator. Notice that all the Secrets, Ingress, Deployments, Services, and other objects that were created by the operator when the orchestra Helm chart was deployed are all gone.

2. Next, redeploy OpenUnison, but this time, update our Helm chart to use impersonation. Edit the `values.yaml` file and add the two bold lines shown in the following example file:

    ```
    network:
        openunison_host: "k8sou.apps.192-168-2-131.nip.io"
        dashboard_host: "k8sdb.apps.192-168-2-131.nip.io"
    ```

```
  api_server_host: "k8sapi.apps.192-168-2-131.nip.io"
  session_inactivity_timeout_seconds: 900
  k8s_url: https://192.168.2.131:32776

cert_template:
  ou: "Kubernetes"
  o: "MyOrg"
  l: "My Cluster"
  st: "State of Cluster"
  c: "MyCountry"

image: "docker.io/tremolosecurity/openunison-k8s-login-
saml2:latest"
myvd_config_path: "WEB-INF/myvd.conf"
k8s_cluster_name: kubernetes
enable_impersonation: true

dashboard:
  namespace: "kubernetes-dashboard"
  cert_name: "kubernetes-dashboard-certs"
  label: "k8s-app=kubernetes-dashboard"
  service_name: kubernetes-dashboard
certs:
  use_k8s_cm: false

trusted_certs: []

monitoring:
  prometheus_service_account: system:serviceaccount:monit
oring:prometheus-k8s

saml:
  idp_url: https://portal.apps.tremolo.io/idp-test/
metadata/dfbe4040-cd32-470e-a9b6-809c8f857c40
  metadata_xml_b64: ""
```

We have made two changes here:

- Added a host for the API server proxy
- Enabled impersonation

These changes enable OpenUnison's impersonation features and generate an additional RBAC binding to enable impersonation on OpenUnison's service account.

3. Run the Helm chart with the new `values.yaml` file:

```
helm install orchestra tremolo/openunison-k8s-login-saml2
-namespace openunison -f ./values.yaml


NAME: orchestra
LAST DEPLOYED: Thu Apr 23 20:55:16 2020
NAMESPACE: openunison
STATUS: deployed
REVISION: 1
TEST SUITE: None
```

4. Just like with our OpenID Connect integration with Kubernetes, finish the integration with the testing identity provider. First, get the metadata:

```
$ curl --insecure https://k8sou.apps.192-168-2-131.nip.
io/auth/forms/saml2_rp_metadata.jsp


<?xml version="1.0" encoding="UTF-8"?><md:EntityDescriptor
xmlns:md="urn:oasis:names:tc:SAML:2.0:metadata"
ID="f4a4bacd63709fe486c30ec536c0f552a506d0023"
entityID="https://k8sou.apps.192-168-2-131.nip.io/auth/
SAML2Auth">
    <md:SPSSODescriptor WantAssertionsSigned="true"
protocolSupportEnumeration="urn:oasis:names:tc:SAML:2.0:
protocol">
    .
    .
    .
```

5. Next, log into `https://portal.apps.tremolo.io/`, choose the testing identity provider, and copy and paste the resulting metadata into the testing identity provider where it says **Meta Data**.

6. Finally, to update the change, click **Update Relying Party**.

The new OpenUnison deployment is configured as a reverse proxy for the API server and has been re-integrated with our SAML2 identity provider. There are no cluster parameters to set because impersonation doesn't need any cluster-side configuration. The next step is to test the integration.

Testing impersonation

Now, let's test our impersonation setup. Follow these steps:

1. In a browser, enter the URL for your OpenUnison deployment. This is the same URL you used for your initial OIDC deployment.

2. Log into OpenUnison and then click on the dashboard. You should recall that the first time you opened the dashboard on the your initial OpenUnison deployment, you received a lot of errors until you created the new RBAC role, which granted access to the cluster.

    After you've enabled impersonation and opened the dashboard, you shouldn't see any error messages, even though you were prompted for new certificate warnings and didn't tell the API server to trust the new certificates you're using with the dashboard.

3. Click on the little circular icon in the upper right-hand corner to see who you're logged in as.

4. Next, go back to the main OpenUnison dashboard and click on the **Kubernetes Tokens** badge.

    Notice that the --server flag being passed to kubectl no longer has an IP. Instead, it has the hostname from network.api_server_host in the values.yaml file. This is impersonation. Instead of interacting directly with the API server, you're now interacting with OpenUnison's reverse proxy.

5. Finally, let's copy and paste our kubectl command into a shell:

```
export TMP_CERT=$(mktemp) && echo -e "-----BEGIN
CERTIFI...


Cluster "kubernetes" set.
Context "kubernetes" created.
User "mlbiamext" set.
Switched to context "kubernetes".
```

6. To verify you have access, list the cluster nodes:

```
kubectl get nodes
NAME                          STATUS    ROLES     AGE
VERSION
cluster-auth-control-plane    Ready     master    6h6m
v1.17.0
cluster-auth-worker           Ready     <none>    6h6m
v1.17.0
```

7. Just like when you integrated the original deployment of OpenID Connect, once you've logged out of the OpenUnison page, within a minute or two, the tokens will expire and you won't be able to refresh them:

```
kubectl get nodes


Unable to connect to the server: failed to refresh token:
oauth2: cannot fetch token: 401 Unauthorized
```

You've now validated that your cluster is working correctly with impersonation. Instead of authenticating directly to the API server, the impersonating reverse proxy (OpenUnison) is forwarding all requests to the API server with the correct impersonation headers. You're still meeting your enterprise's needs by providing both a login and logout process and integrating your Active Directory groups.

Configuring Impersonation without OpenUnison

The OpenUnison operator automated a couple of key steps to get impersonation working. There are other projects designed specifically for Kubernetes, such as JetStack's OIDC Proxy (https://github.com/jetstack/kube-oidc-proxy), that are designed to make using impersonation easier. You can use any reverse proxy that can generate the correct headers. There are two critical items to understand when doing this on your own.

Impersonation RBAC policies

RBAC will be covered in the next chapter, but for now, the correct policy to authorize a service account for impersonation is as follows:

```
apiVersion: rbac.authorization.k8s.io/v1
kind: ClusterRole
metadata:
  name: impersonator
rules:
- apiGroups:
  - ""
  resources:
  - users
  - groups
  verbs:
  - impersonate
```

To constrain what accounts can be impersonated, add `resourceNames` to your rule.

Default groups

When impersonating a user, Kubernetes does not add the default group, `system:authenticated`, to the list of impersonated groups. When using a reverse proxy that doesn't specifically know to add the header for this group, configure the proxy to add it manually. Otherwise, simple acts such as calling the `/api` endpoint will fail as this will be unauthorized for anyone except cluster administrators.

Summary

This chapter detailed how Kubernetes identifies users and what groups their members are in. We detailed how the API server interacts with identities and explored several options for authentication. Finally, we detailed the OpenID Connect protocol and how it's applied to Kubernetes.

Learning how Kubernetes authenticates users and the details of the OpenID Connect protocol are an important part of building security into a cluster. Understanding the details and how they apply to common enterprise requirements will help you decide the best way to authenticate to clusters, and also provide justification regarding why the anti-patterns we explored should be avoided.

In the next chapter, we'll apply our authentication process to authorizing access to Kubernetes resources. Knowing who someone is isn't enough to secure your clusters. You also need to control what they have access to.

Questions

1. OpenID Connect is a standard protocol with extensive peer review and usage.

   A. True

   B. False

2. Which token does Kubernetes use to authorize your access to an API?

   A. `access_token`

   B. `id_token`

   C. `refresh_token`

   D. `certificate_token`

3. In which situation is certificate authentication a good idea?

   A. Day-to-day usage by administrators and developers

   B. Access from external CI/CD pipelines and other services

   C. Break glass in case of emergency when all other authentication solutions are unavailable

4. How should you identify users accessing your cluster?

   A. Email address

   B. Unix login ID

   C. Windows login ID

   D. An immutable ID not based on a user's name

5. Where are OpenID Connect configuration options set in Kubernetes?

   A. Depends on the distribution

   B. In a ConfigMap object

   C. In a Secret

   D. Set as flags on the Kubernetes API server executable

6. When using impersonation with your cluster, the groups your user brings are the only ones needed.

    A. True

    B. False

7. The dashboard should have its own privileged identity to work properly.

    A. True

    B. False

8
RBAC Policies and Auditing

Authentication is only the first step in managing access in a cluster. Once access to a cluster is granted, it's important to limit what accounts can do, depending on whether an account is for an automated system or a user. Authorizing access to resources is an important part of both protecting against accidental issues and bad actors looking to abuse a cluster.

In this chapter, we're going to detail how Kubernetes authorizes access via its **Role-Based Access Control** (**RBAC**) model. The first part of this chapter will be a deep dive into how Kubernetes RBAC is configured, what options are available, and mapping the theory into practical examples. Debugging and troubleshooting RBAC policies will be the focus of the second half.

In this chapter, we will cover the following topics:

- Introduction to RBAC
- Mapping enterprise identities to Kubernetes to authorize access to resources
- Namespace multi-tenancy
- Kubernetes auditing
- Using `audit2rbac` to debug policies

Technical requirements

This chapter has the following technical requirements:

- A KinD cluster running with the configuration from *Chapter 7, Integrating Authentication into Your Cluster*

- Access to the SAML2 lab from *Chapter 6, Services, Load Balancing, and External DNS*

You can access the code for this chapter at the following GitHub repository: `https://github.com/PacktPublishing/Kubernetes-and-Docker-The-Complete-Guide`.

Introduction to RBAC

Before we jump into RBAC, let's take a quick look at the history of Kubernetes and access controls.

Before Kubernetes 1.6, access controls were based on **Attribute-Based Access Control** (**ABAC**). As the name implies, ABAC provides access by comparing a rule against attributes, rather than roles. The assigned attributes can be assigned any type of data, including user attributes, objects, environments, locations, and so on.

In the past, to configure a Kubernetes cluster for ABAC, you had to set two values on the API server:

- `--authorization-policy-file`
- `--authorization-mode=ABAC`

`authorization-policy-file` is a local file on the API server. Since it's a local file on each API server, any changes to the file require privileged access to the host and will require you to restart the API server. As you can imagine, the process to update ABAC policies becomes difficult and any immediate changes will require a short outage as the API servers are restarted.

Starting in Kubernetes 1.6, **RBAC** became the preferred method of authorizing access to resources. Unlike **ABAC**, **RBAC** uses Kubernetes native objects, and updates are reflected without restarts to the API servers. **RBAC** is also compatible with different authentication methods. From here, our focus will be on how to develop RBAC policies and applying them to your cluster.

What's a Role?

In Kubernetes, a Role is a way to tie together permissions into an object that can be described and configured. Roles have rules, which are a collection of resources and verbs. Working backward, we have the following:

- **Verbs**: The actions that can be taken on an API, such as reading (`get`), writing (`create`, `update`, `patch`, and `delete`), or listing and watching.

- **Resources**: Names of APIs to apply the verbs to, such as `services`, `endpoints`, and so on. Specific sub-resources may be listed as well. Specific resources can be named to provide very specific permissions on an object.

A Role does not say who can perform the verbs on the resources—that is handled by `RoleBindings` and `ClusterRoleBindings`. We will learn more about these in the *RoleBindings and ClusterRoleBindings* section.

> **Important Note**
>
> The term "role" can have multiple meanings, and RBAC is often used in other contexts. In the enterprise world, the term "role" is often associated with a business role and used to convey entitlements to that role instead of a specific person. As an example, an enterprise may assign all accounts' payable staff the ability to issue checks instead of creating a specific assignment for each member of the accounts' payable department the specific permission in order to issue a check. When someone moves between roles, they lose the permissions from their old role and gain permissions for their new role. In the instance of moving from accounts payable to accounts receivable the user would lose the ability to make payments and gain the ability to accept payment. By tying the permissions to roles, instead of individuals, the change in permissions happens automatically with the role change instead of having to manually toggle permissions for each user. This is the more "classic" use of the term RBAC.

Each resource that a rule will be built of is identified by the following:

- `apiGroups`: A list of groups the resources are a member of

- `resources`: The name of the object type for the resource (and potentially sub-resources)

- `resourceNames`: An optional list of specific objects to apply this rule to

Each rule *must* have a list of **apiGroups** and **resources**. **resourceNames** is optional.

> **Important Note**
>
> If you find yourself authorizing access to specific objects in a namespace from within that namespace, it's time to rethink your authorization strategy. Kubernetes' tenant boundary is the namespace. Except for very specific reasons, naming specific Kubernetes objects in an RBAC Role is an anti-pattern and should be avoided. When specific objects are being named by RBAC Roles, consider breaking up the namespace they're in to create separate namespaces.

Once the resource is identified in a rule, verbs can be specified. A verb is an action that can be taken on the resource, providing access to the object in Kubernetes.

If the desired access to an object should be `all`, you do not need to add each verb; instead, the wildcard character may be used to identify all the **verbs**, **resources**, or **apiGroups**.

Identifying a Role

The Kubernetes authorization page (`https://kubernetes.io/docs/reference/access-authn-authz/rbac/`) uses the following Role as an example to allow someone to get the details of a pod and its logs:

```
apiVersion: rbac.authorization.k8s.io/v1
kind: Role
metadata:
  namespace: default
  name: pod-and-pod-logs-reader
rules:
- apiGroups: [""]
  resources: ["pods", "pods/log"]
  verbs: ["get", "list"]
```

Working backward to determine how this Role was defined, we will start with `resources`, since it is the easiest aspect to find. All objects in Kubernetes are represented by URLs. If you want to pull all the information about the pods in the default namespace, you would call the `/api/v1/namespaces/default/pods` URL, and if you wanted the logs for a specific pod, you would call the `/api/v1/namespaces/default/pods/mypod/log` URL.

The URL pattern will be true of all namespace-scoped objects. pods lines up to resources, as does pods/log. When trying to identify which resources you want to authorize, use the api-reference document from the Kubernetes API documentation at https://kubernetes.io/docs/reference/#api-reference.

If you are trying to access an additional path component after the name of the object (such as with status and logs on pods), it needs to be explicitly authorized. Authorizing pods does not immediately authorize logs or status.

Based on the use of URL mapping to resources, your next thought may be that verbs is going to be HTTP verbs. This is not the case. There is no GET verb in Kubernetes. Verbs are instead defined by the schema of the object in the API server. The good news is that there's a static mapping between HTTP verbs and RBAC verbs (https://kubernetes.io/docs/reference/access-authn-authz/authorization/#determine-the-request-verb). Looking at this URL, notice that there are verbs on top of the HTTP verbs for PodSecurityPolicies and impersonation. That's because the **RBAC** model is used beyond authorizing specific APIs and is also used to authorize who can impersonate users and how to assign a PodSecurityPolicy object. The focus of this chapter is going to be on the standard HTTP verb mappings.

The final component to identify is apiGroups. This is an additional area of inconsistency from the URL model. pods is part of the "core" group, but the apiGroups list is just an empty string (""). These are legacy APIs that were part of the original Kubernetes. Most other APIs will be in an API group and that group will be part of their URL. You can find the group by looking at the API documentation for the object you are looking to authorize.

The inconsistencies in the RBAC model can make debugging difficult, to say the least. The last lab in this chapter will walk through the debugging process and take much of the guesswork out of defining your rules.

Now that we've defined the contents of a Role and how to define specific permissions, it's important to note that Roles can be applied at both the namespace and cluster level.

Roles versus ClusterRoles

RBAC rules can be scoped either to specific namespaces or to the entire cluster. Taking our preceding example, if we defined it as a ClusterRole instead of a Role, and removed the namespace, we would have a Role that authorizes someone to get the details and logs of all pods across the cluster. This new role could alternatively be used in individual namespaces to assign the permissions to the pods in a specific namespace:

```
apiVersion: rbac.authorization.k8s.io/v1
kind: ClusterRole
metadata:
  name: cluster-pod-and-pod-logs-reader
rules:
- apiGroups: [""]
  resources: ["pods", "pods/log"]
  verbs: ["get", "list"]
```

Whether this permission is applied globally across a cluster or within the scope of a specific namespace depends on how it's bound to the subjects it applies to. This will be covered in the *RoleBindings and ClusterRoleBindings* section.

In addition to applying a set of rules across the cluster, ClusterRoles are used to apply rules to resources that aren't mapped to a namespace, such as PersistentVolume and StorageClass objects.

After understanding how a Role is defined, let's understand the different ways Roles can be designed for specific purposes. In the next sections, we'll look at different patterns for defining Roles and their application in a cluster.

Negative Roles

One of the most common requests for authorization is *"can I write a Role that lets me do everything EXCEPT xyz?"*. In RBAC, the answer is *NO*. RBAC requires either every resource to be allowed or specific resources and verbs to be enumerated. There are two reasons for this in RBAC:

- **Better security through simplicity**: Being able to enforce a rule that says *every Secret except this one* requires a much more complex evaluation engine than RBAC provides. The more complex an engine, the harder it is to test and validate, and the easier it is to break. A simpler engine is just simpler to code and keep secure.

- **Unintended consequences**: Allowing someone to do everything *except* xyz leaves the door open for issues in unintended ways as the cluster grows and new capabilities are added.

On the first point, building an engine with this capability is difficult to build and maintain. It also makes the rules much harder to keep track of. To express this type of rule, you need to not only have authorization rules but also an order to those rules. For instance, to say *I want to allow everything except this Secret*, you would first need a rule that says *allow everything* and then a rule that says *deny this secret*. If you switch the rules to say *deny this secret* then *allow everything*, the first rule would be overridden. You could assign priorities to different rules, but that now makes it even more complex.

There are ways to implement this pattern, either by using a custom authorization webhook or by using a controller to dynamically generate RBAC `Role` objects. These should both be considered security anti-patterns and so won't be covered in this chapter.

The second point deals with unintended consequences. It's becoming more popular to support the provisioning of infrastructure that isn't Kubernetes using the operator pattern, where a custom controller looks for new instances of a **CustomResourceDefinition (CRD)** to provision infrastructure such as databases. Amazon Web Services publishes an operator for this purpose (`https://github.com/aws/aws-controllers-k8s`). These operators run in their own namespaces with administrative credentials for their cloud looking for new instances of their objects to provision resources. If you have a security model that allows everything "except…", then once deployed, anyone in your cluster can provision cloud resources that have real costs and can create security holes. Enumerating your resources, from a security perspective, is an important part of knowing what is running and who has access.

The trend of Kubernetes clusters is to provide more control over infrastructure outside of the cluster via the custom resource API. You can provision anything from VMs to additional nodes, to any kind of API-driven cloud infrastructure. There are other tools you can use besides RBAC to mitigate the risk of someone creating a resource they shouldn't, but these should be secondary measures.

Aggregated ClusterRoles

ClusterRoles can become confusing quickly and be difficult to maintain. It's best to break them up into smaller ClusterRoles that can be combined as needed. Take the admin ClusterRole, which is designed to let someone do generally anything inside of a specific namespace. When we look at the admin ClusterRole, it enumerates just about every resource there is. You may think someone wrote this ClusterRole so that it would contain all those resources, but that would be really inefficient, and what happens as new resource types get added to Kubernetes? The admin ClusterRole is an aggregated ClusterRole. Take a look at the ClusterRole:

```
kind: ClusterRole
apiVersion: rbac.authorization.k8s.io/v1
metadata:
  name: admin
  labels:
    kubernetes.io/bootstrapping: rbac-defaults
  annotations:
    rbac.authorization.kubernetes.io/autoupdate: 'true'
rules:

  .

  .

  .

aggregationRule:
  clusterRoleSelectors:
    - matchLabels:
        rbac.authorization.k8s.io/aggregate-to-admin: 'true'
```

The key is the aggregationRule section. This section tells Kubernetes to combine the rules for all ClusterRoles where the rbac.authorization.k8s.io/aggregate-to-admin label is true. When a new CRD is created, an admin is not able to create instances of that CRD without adding a new ClusterRole that includes this label. To allow namespace admin users to create an instance of the new myapi/superwidget objects, create a new ClusterRole:

```
apiVersion: rbac.authorization.k8s.io/v1
kind: ClusterRole
metadata:
  name: aggregate-superwidget-admin
  labels:
```

```
     # Add these permissions to the "admin" default role.
     rbac.authorization.k8s.io/aggregate-to-admin: "true"
rules:
- apiGroups: ["myapi"]
  resources: ["superwidgets"]
  verbs: ["get", "list", "watch", "create", "update", "patch",
"delete"]
```

The next time you look at the admin ClusterRole, it will include `myapi/superwidgets`. You can also reference this ClusterRole directly for more specific permissions.

RoleBindings and ClusterRoleBindings

Once a permission is defined, it needs to be assigned to something to enable it. "Something" can be a user, a group, or a service account. These options are referred to as subjects. Just as with Roles and ClusterRoles, a RoleBinding binds a Role or ClusterRole to a specific namespace and a ClusterRoleBinding will apply a ClusterRole across the cluster. A binding can have many subjects but may only reference a single Role or ClusterRole. To assign the `pod-and-pod-logs-reader` Role created earlier in this chapter to a service account called `mysa` in the default namespace, a user named `podreader`, or anyone with the `podreaders` group, create a `RoleBinding`:

```
apiVersion: rbac.authorization.k8s.io/v1
kind: RoleBinding
metadata:
  name: pod-and-pod-logs-reader
  namespace: default
subjects:
- kind: ServiceAccount
  name: mysa
  namespace: default
  apiGroup: rbac.authorization.k8s.io
- kind: User
  name: podreader
- kind: Group
  name: podreaders
roleRef:
  kind: Role
  name: pod-and-pod-logs-reader
  apiGroup: rbac.authorization.k8s.io
```

The preceding `RoleBinding` lists three different subjects:

- `ServiceAccount`: Any service account in the cluster can be authorized to a RoleBinding. The namespace must be included since a RoleBinding could authorize a service account in any namespace, not just the one the RoleBinding is defined in.

- `User`: A user is asserted by the authentication process. Remember from *Chapter 7, Integrating Authentication into Your Cluster*, that there are no objects in Kubernetes that represent users.

- `Group`: Just as with users, groups are asserted as part of the authentication process and have an object associated with them.

Finally, the Role we created earlier is referenced. In a similar fashion, to assign the same subjects the ability to read pods and their logs across the cluster, a ClusterRoleBinding can be created to reference the `cluster-pod-and-pod-logs-reader` ClusterRole created earlier in the chapter:

```
apiVersion: rbac.authorization.k8s.io/v1
kind: ClusterRoleBinding
metadata:
  name: cluster-pod-and-pod-logs-reader
subjects:
- kind: ServiceAccount
  name: mysa
  namespace: default
  apiGroup: rbac.authorization.k8s.io
- kind: User
  name: podreader
- kind: Group
  name: podreaders
roleRef:
  kind: ClusterRole
  name: cluster-pod-and-pod-logs-reader
  apiGroup: rbac.authorization.k8s.io
```

The `ClusterRoleBinding` is bound to the same subjects, but is instead bound to a ClusterRole instead of a namespace-bound Role. Now, instead of having the ability to read pod details and pod/logs in the default namespace, these users can read all pod details and pod/logs in all namespaces.

Combining ClusterRoles and RoleBindings

We have a use case where a log aggregator wants to pull logs from pods in multiple namespaces, but not all namespaces. A ClusterRoleBinding is too broad. While the Role could be recreated in each namespace, this is inefficient and a maintenance headache. Instead, define a ClusterRole but reference it from a RoleBinding in the applicable namespaces. This allows the reuse of permission definitions while still applying those permissions to specific namespaces. In general, note the following:

- ClusterRole + ClusterRoleBinding = cluster-wide permission

- ClusterRole + RoleBinding = namespace-specific permission

To apply our ClusterRoleBinding in a specific namespace, create a Role, referencing the `ClusterRole` instead of a namespaced `Role` object:

```
apiVersion: rbac.authorization.k8s.io/v1
kind: RoleBinding
metadata:
  name: pod-and-pod-logs-reader
  namespace: default
subjects:
- kind: ServiceAccount
  name: mysa
  namespace: default
  apiGroup: rbac.authorization.k8s.io
- kind: User
  name: podreader
- kind: Group
  name: podreaders
roleRef:
  kind: ClusterRole
  name: cluster-pod-and-pod-logs-reader
  apiGroup: rbac.authorization.k8s.io
```

The preceding `RoleBinding` lets us reuse the existing `ClusterRole`. This cuts down on the number of objects that need to be tracked in the cluster and makes it easier to update permissions cluster-wide if the ClusterRole permissions need to change.

Having built our permissions and defined how to assign them, next we'll look at how to map enterprise identities into cluster policies.

Mapping enterprise identities to Kubernetes to authorize access to resources

One of the benefits of centralizing authentication is leveraging the enterprise's existing identities instead of having to create new credentials that users that interact with your clusters need to remember. It's important to know how to map your policies to these centralized users. In *Chapter 7, Integrating Authentication into Your Cluster,* you created a cluster and integrated it with either **Active Directory Federation Services (ADFS)** or Tremolo Security's testing identity provider. To finish the integration, the following ClusterRoleBinding was created:

```
apiVersion: rbac.authorization.k8s.io/v1
kind: ClusterRoleBinding
metadata:
  name: ou-cluster-admins
subjects:
- kind: Group
  name: k8s-cluster-admins
  apiGroup: rbac.authorization.k8s.io
roleRef:
  kind: ClusterRole
  name: cluster-admin
  apiGroup: rbac.authorization.k8s.io
```

This binding allows all users that are members of the k8s-cluster-admins group to have full cluster access. At the time, the focus was on authentication, so there weren't many details provided as to why this binding was created.

What if we wanted to authorize our users directly? That way, we have control over who has access to our cluster. Our RBAC ClusterRoleBinding would look different:

```
apiVersion: rbac.authorization.k8s.io/v1
kind: ClusterRoleBinding
metadata:
  name: ou-cluster-admins
subjects:
- kind: User
  name: https://k8sou.apps.192-168-2-131.nip.io/auth/idp/
k8sIdp#mlbiamext
```

```
    apiGroup: rbac.authorization.k8s.io
 roleRef:
   kind: ClusterRole
   name: cluster-admin
   apiGroup: rbac.authorization.k8s.io
```

Using the same ClusterRole as before, this ClusterRoleBinding will assign the `cluster-admin` privileges only to my testing user.

The first issue to point out is that the user has the URL of our OpenID Connect issuer in front of the username. When OpenID Connect was first introduced, it was thought that Kubernetes would integrate with multiple identity providers and different types of identity providers, so the developers wanted you to be able to easily distinguish between users from different identity sources. For instance, `mlbiamext` in domain 1 is a different user then `mlbiamext` in domain 2. To ensure that a user's identity doesn't collide with another user across identity providers, Kubernetes requires the identity provider's issuer to be prepended to your user. This rule doesn't apply if the username claim defined in your API server flags is mail. It also doesn't apply if you're using certificates or impersonation.

Beyond the inconsistent implementation requirements, this approach can cause problems in a few ways:

- **Changing your identity provider URL**: Today, you're using an identity provider at one URL, but tomorrow you decide to move it. Now, you need to go through every ClusterRoleBinding and update them.

- **Audits**: You can't query for all RoleBindings associated with a user. You need to instead enumerate every binding.

- **Large bindings**: Depending on how many users you have, your bindings can get quite large and difficult to track.

While there are tools you can use to help manage these issues, it's much easier to associate your bindings with groups instead of individual users. You could use the `mail` attribute to avoid the URL prefix, but that is considered an anti-pattern and will result in equally difficult changes to your cluster if an email address changes for any reason.

So far in this chapter, we have learned how to define access policies and map those policies to enterprise users. Next, we need to determine how clusters will be divided into tenants.

Implementing namespace multi-tenancy

Clusters deployed for multiple stakeholders, or tenants, should be divided up by namespace. This is the boundary that was designed into Kubernetes from the very beginning. When deploying namespaces, there are generally two ClusterRoles that are assigned to users in the namespace:

- `admin`: This aggregated ClusterRole provides access to every verb and nearly every resource that ships with Kubernetes, making the admin user the ruler of their namespace. The exception to this is any namespace-scoped object that could affect the entire cluster, such as `ResourceQuotas`.

- `edit`: Similar to `admin`, but without the ability to create RBAC Roles or RoleBindings.

It's important to note that the `admin` ClusterRole can't make changes to the namespace object by itself. Namespaces are cluster-wide resources, so they can only be assigned permissions via a ClusterRoleBinding.

Depending on your strategy for multi-tenancy, the `admin` ClusterRole may not be appropriate. The ability to generate RBAC Role and RoleBinding objects means that a namespace admin may grant themselves the ability to change resource quotas or run elevated PodSecurityPolicy privileges. This is where RBAC tends to fall apart and needs some additional options:

- **Don't grant access to Kubernetes**: Many cluster owners want to keep Kubernetes out of the hands of their users and limit their interaction to external CI/CD tools. This works well with microservices but begins to fall apart on multiple lines. First, more legacy applications being moved into Kubernetes means more legacy administrators needing to directly access their namespace. Second, if the Kubernetes team keeps users out of the clusters, they are now responsible. The people who own Kubernetes may not want to be the reason things aren't happening the way application owners want them to and often, the application owners want to be able to control their own infrastructure to ensure they can handle any situation that impacts their own performance.

- **Treat access as privileged**: Most enterprises require a privileged user to access infrastructure. This is typically done using a privileged access model where an admin has a separate account that needs to be "checked out" in order to use it and is only authorized at certain times as approved by a "change board" or process. The use of these accounts is closely monitored. This is a good approach if you already have a system in place, especially one that integrates with your enterprise's central authentication system.

- **Give each tenant a cluster**: This model moves multi-tenancy from the cluster to the infrastructure layer. You haven't eliminated the problem, only moved where it is addressed. This can lead to sprawl that becomes unmanageable and can skyrocket costs depending on how you are implementing Kubernetes.

- **Admission controllers**: These augment RBAC by limiting which objects can be created. For instance, an admission controller can decide to block an RBAC policy from being created, even if RBAC explicitly allows it. This topic will be covered in *Chapter 11, Extending Security Using Open Policy Agent*.

In addition to authorizing access to namespaces and resources, a multi-tenant solution needs to know how to provision tenants. This topic will be covered in the final chapter, *Chapter 14, Provisioning a Platform*.

Now that we have a strategy for implementing authorization policies, we'll need a way to debug those policies as we create them and also to know when those policies are violated. Kubernetes provides an audit capability that will be the focus of the next section where we will add the audit log to our KinD cluster and debug the implementation of RBAC policies.

Kubernetes auditing

The Kubernetes audit log is where you track what is happening in your cluster from an API perspective. It's in JSON format, which makes reading it directly more difficult, but makes it much easier to parse using tools such as Elasticsearch. In *Chapter 12, Pod Auditing Using Falco and EFK*, we will cover how to create a full logging system using the **Elasticsearch, Fluentd, and Kibana (EFK)** stack.

Creating an audit policy

A policy file is used to control what events are recorded and where to store the logs, which can be a standard log file or a webhook. We have included an example audit policy in the `chapter8` directory of the GitHub repository and we will apply it to the KinD cluster that we have been using throughout the book.

An audit policy is a collection of rules that tell the API server which API calls to log and how. When Kubernetes parses the policy file, all rules are applied in order and only the initial matching policy event will be applied. If you have more than one rule for a certain event, you may not receive the expected data in your log files. For this reason, you need to be careful that your events are created correctly.

Policies use the audit.k8s.io API and the manifest kind of Policy. The following example shows the beginning of a policy file:

```
apiVersion: audit.k8s.io/v1beta1
kind: Policy
rules:
  - level: Request
    userGroups: ["system:nodes"]
    verbs: ["update","patch"]
    resources:
      - group: "" # core
        resources: ["nodes/status", "pods/status"]
    omitStages:
      - "RequestReceived"
```

> **Important Note**
>
> While a policy file may look like a standard Kubernetes manifest, you do not apply it using kubectl. A policy file is used with the --audit-policy-file API flag on the API server(s). This will be explained in the *Enabling auditing on a cluster* section.

To understand the rule and what it will log, we will go through each section in detail.

The first section of the rule is level, which determines the type of information that will be logged for the event. There are four levels that can be assigned to events:

Audit level	Logging details
None	Does not log any data
Metadata	Only logs metadata – does not include the request or the request response
Request	Logs metadata and the request, but not the request response
RequestResponse	Logs metadata, the request, and the request response

Table 8.1 – Kubernetes auditing levels

The userGroups, verbs, and resources values tell the API server the object and action that will trigger the auditing event. In this example, only requests from system:nodes that attempt an action of update or patch on a node/status or pod/status on the core API will create an event.

`omitStages` tells the API server to skip any logging events during a *stage*, which helps you to limit the amount of data that is logged. There are four stages that an API request goes through:

API stage	Stage details
RequestReceived	This is the stage where the API receives a request.
ResponseStarted	This stage is only used with certain requests and it starts before the response is sent in the ResponseComplete stage.
ResponseComplete	This is the stage where the API server responds to a request.
Panic	Event created if a panic occurs.

Table 8.2 – Auditing stages

In our example, we have set the event to ignore the RequestReceived event, which tells the API server not to log any data for the incoming API request.

Every organization has its own auditing policy, and policy files can become long and complex. Don't be afraid to set up a policy that logs everything until you get a handle on the types of events that you can create. Logging everything is not a good practice since the log files become very large. Fine-tuning an audit policy is a skill that is learned over time and as you learn more about the API server, you will start to learn what events are most valuable to audit.

Policy files are just the start of enabling cluster auditing, and now that we have an understanding of the policy file, let's explain how to enable auditing on a cluster.

Enabling auditing on a cluster

Enabling auditing is specific to each distribution of Kubernetes. In this section, we will enable the audit log in KinD to understand the low-level steps. As a quick refresher, the finished product of the last chapter was a KinD cluster with impersonation enabled (instead of directly integrating with OpenID Connect). The rest of the steps and examples in this chapter assume this cluster is being used.

You can follow the steps in this section manually or you can execute the included script, `enable-auditing.sh`, in the `chapter8` directory of the GitHub repository:

1. First, copy the example audit policy from the `chapter8` directory to the API server:

    ```
    k8s@book:~/kind-oidc-ldap-master$ docker cp k8s-audit-
    policy.yaml cluster01-control-plane:/etc/kubernetes/
    audit/
    ```

2. Next, create the directories to store the audit log and policy configuration on the API server. We will exec into the container since we need to modify the API server file in the next step:

    ```
    k8s@book:~/kind-oidc-ldap-master$ docker exec -ti
    cluster01-control-plane bash
    root@cluster01-control-plane:/# mkdir /var/log/k8s
    root@cluster01-control-plane:/# mkdir /etc/kubernetes/
    audit
    root@cluster01-control-plane:/# exit
    ```

    At this point, you have the audit policy on the API server and you can enable the API options to use the file.

3. On the API server, edit the `kubeadm` configuration file, `/etc/kubernetes/manifests/kube-apiserver.yaml`, which is the same file that we updated to enable OpenID Connect. To enable auditing, we need to add three values. It's important to note that many Kubernetes clusters may only require the file and the API options. We need the second and third steps since we are using a KinD cluster for our testing.

4. First, add command-line flags for the API server that enable the audit logs. Along with the policy file, we can add options to control the log file rotation, retention, and maximum size:

    ```
        - --tls-private-key-file=/etc/kubernetes/pki/
    apiserver.key
        - --audit-log-path=/var/log/k8s/audit.log
        - --audit-log-maxage=1
        - --audit-log-maxbackup=10
        - --audit-log-maxsize=10
        - --audit-policy-file=/etc/kubernetes/audit/
    k8s-audit-policy.yaml
    ```

Notice that the option is pointing to the policy file that you copied over in the previous step.

5. Next, add the directories that store the policy configuration and the resulting logs to the `volumeMounts` section:

```
- mountPath: /usr/share/ca-certificates
  name: usr-share-ca-certificates
  readOnly: true
- mountPath: /var/log/k8s
  name: var-log-k8s
  readOnly: false
- mountPath: /etc/kubernetes/audit
  name: etc-kubernetes-audit
  readOnly: true
```

6. Finally, add the `hostPath` configurations to the `volumes` section so that Kubernetes knows where to mount the local paths to:

```
- hostPath:
    path: /usr/share/ca-certificates
    type: DirectoryOrCreate
  name: usr-share-ca-certificates
- hostPath:
    path: /var/log/k8s
    type: DirectoryOrCreate
  name: var-log-k8s
- hostPath:
    path: /etc/kubernetes/audit
    type: DirectoryOrCreate
  name: etc-kubernetes-audit
```

7. Save and exit the file.

8. Like all API option changes, you need to restart the API server for the changes to take effect; however, KinD will detect that the file has changed and restart the API server's pod automatically.

Exit from the attached shell and check the pods in the kube-system namespace:

```
k8s@book:~/kind-oidc-ldap-master$ kubectl get pods -n
kube-system
NAME                                                        READY
STATUS      RESTARTS    AGE
calico-kube-controllers-5b644bc49c-q68q7                    1/1
Running     0           28m
calico-node-2cvm9                                           1/1
Running     0           28m
calico-node-n29tl                                           1/1
Running     0           28m
coredns-6955765f44-gzvjd                                    1/1
Running     0           28m
coredns-6955765f44-r567x                                    1/1
Running     0           28m
etcd-cluster01-control-plane                                1/1
Running     0           28m
kube-apiserver-cluster01-control-plane                      1/1
Running     0           14s
kube-controller-manager-cluster01-control-plane    1/1
Running     0           28m
kube-proxy-h62mj                                            1/1
Running     0           28m
kube-proxy-pl4z4                                            1/1
Running     0           28m
kube-scheduler-cluster01-control-plane                      1/1
Running     0           28m
```

The API server is highlighted to have been running for only 14 seconds, showing that it successfully restarted.

9. Having verified that the API server is running, let's look at the audit log to verify that it's working correctly. To check the log, you can use docker exec to tail audit.log:

```
$ docker exec cluster01-control-plane  tail /var/log/
k8s/audit.log
```

This command generates the following log data:

```
{"kind":"Event","apiVersion":"audit.k8s.io/v1","level"
:"Metadata","auditID":"473e8161-e243-4c5d-889c-42f478
025cc2","stage":"ResponseComplete","requestURI":"/
apis/crd.projectcalico.org/v1/clusterinformations/
default","verb":"get","user":{"usernam

e":"system:serviceaccount:kube-system:calico-kube-
controllers","uid":"38b96474-2457-4ec9-a146-9a63c2
b8182e","groups":["system:serviceaccounts","system-
:serviceaccounts:kube-system","system:authenticated"]},"s
ourceIPs":["172.17.0.2"],"userAgent":"

Go-http-client/2.0","objectRef":{"resource":"clusterinfo
rmations","name":"default","apiGroup":"crd.projectcalico.
org","apiVersion":"v1"},"responseStatus":{"metadata"
:{},"code":200},"requestReceivedTimestamp":"2020-05-
20T00:27:07.378345Z","stageT

imestamp":"2020-05-20T00:27:07.381227Z","annotations":{
"authorization.k8s.io/decision":"allow","authorization.
k8s.io/reason":"RBAC: allowed by ClusterRoleBinding
\"calico-kube-controllers\" of ClusterRole \"calico-kube-
controllers\" to ServiceAc

count \"calico-kube-controllers/kube-system\""}}
```

There is quite a bit of information in this JSON, and it would be challenging to find a specific event looking at a log file directly. Luckily, now that you have auditing enabled, you can forward events to a central logging server. We will do this in *Chapter 12, Auditing Using Falco and EFK*, where we will deploy an EFK stack.

Now that we have auditing enabled, the next step is to practice debugging RBAC policies.

Using audit2rbac to debug policies

There is a tool called `audit2rbac` that can reverse engineer errors in the audit log into RBAC policy objects. In this section, we'll use this tool to generate an RBAC policy after discovering that one of our users can't perform an action they need to be able to do. This is a typical RBAC debugging process and learning how to use this tool can save you hours trying to isolate RBAC issues:

1. In the previous chapter, a generic RBAC policy was created to allow all members of the `k8s-cluster-admins` group to be administrators in our cluster. If you're logged into OpenUnison, log out.

2. Now, log in again, but before hitting the **Finish Login** button at the bottom of the screen, remove the `k8s-cluster-admins` group and add `cn=k8s-create-ns,cn=users,dc=domain,dc=com`:

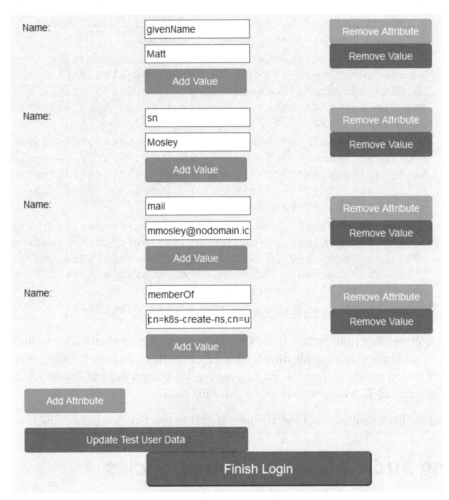

Figure 8.1 – Updated login attributes

3. Next, click on **Finish Login**. Once logged in, go to the dashboard. Just as when OpenUnison was first deployed, there won't be any namespaces or other information because the RBAC policy for cluster administrators doesn't apply anymore.

> **Important Note**
>
> The format of the `memberOf` attribute was changed from a simple name to an LDAP distinguished name because this is the format that's most often presented by ADFS or Active Directory. A **distinguished name**, or **DN**, is read from left to right with the leftmost component being the name of the object and each component to its right being its placement in the LDAP tree. For example, the name `cn=k8s-create-ns,cn=users,dc=domain,dc=com` group is read as "The group `k8s-create-ns` in the `users` container (`cn`) in the `domain.com` domain (`dc`)." While ADFS can generate more user-friendly names, that requires specific configuration or scripting, so most implementations just add the `memberOf` attributes, which list all the groups the user is a member of.

4. Next, copy your `kubectl` configuration from the token screen, making sure to paste it into a window that isn't your main KinD terminal so as to not overwrite your master configuration.

5. Once your tokens are set, attempt to create a namespace called `not-going-to-work`:

```
PS C:\Users\mlb> kubectl create ns not-going-to-work
Error from server (Forbidden): namespaces is forbidden:
User "mlbiamext" cannot create resource "namespaces" in
API group "" at the cluster scope
```

There's enough information here to reverse engineer an RBAC policy.

6. In order to eliminate this error message, create a `ClusterRole` with a resource for `"namespaces"`, `apiGroups` set to `""`, and a verb of `"create"`:

```
apiVersion: rbac.authorization.k8s.io/v1
kind: ClusterRole
metadata:
  name: cluster-create-ns
rules:
- apiGroups: [""]
  resources: ["namespaces"]
  verbs: ["create"]
```

7. Next, create a `ClusterRoleBinding` for the user and this ClusterRole:

```
apiVersion: rbac.authorization.k8s.io/v1
kind: ClusterRoleBinding
metadata:
  name: cluster-create-ns
subjects:
- kind: User
  name: mlbiamext
  apiGroup: rbac.authorization.k8s.io
roleRef:
  kind: ClusterRole
  name: cluster-create-ns
  apiGroup: rbac.authorization.k8s.io
```

8. Once the ClusterRole and ClusterRoleBinding are created, try running the command again and it will work:

```
PS C:\Users\mlb> kubectl create ns not-going-to-work
namespace/not-going-to-work created
```

Unfortunately, this is not likely how most RBAC debugging will go. Most of the time, debugging RBAC will not be this clear or simple. Typically, debugging RBAC means getting unexpected error messages between systems. For instance, if you're deploying the `kube-Prometheus` project for monitoring, you'll generally want to monitor by `Service` objects, not by explicitly naming pods. In order to do this, the Prometheus ServiceAccount needs to be able to list the `Service` objects in the namespace of the service you want to monitor. Prometheus won't tell you this needs to happen; you just won't see your services listed. A better way to debug is to use a tool that knows how to read the audit log and can reverse engineer a set of roles and bindings based on the failures in the log.

The `audit2rbac` tool is the best way to do this. It will read the audit log and give you a set of policies that will work. It may not be the exact policy that's needed, but it will provide a good starting point. Let's try it out:

1. First, attach a shell to the `control-plane` container of your cluster and download the tool from GitHub (https://github.com/liggitt/audit2rbac/releases):

```
root@cluster01-control-plane:/# curl -L https://github.
com/liggitt/audit2rbac/releases/download/v0.8.0/
```

```
audit2rbac-linux-amd64.tar.gz 2>/dev/null > audit2rbac-
linux-amd64.tar.gz
root@cluster01-control-plane:/# tar -xvzf audit2rbac-
linux-amd64.tar.gz
```

2. Before using the tool, make sure to close the browser with the Kubernetes dashboard in it to keep from polluting the logs. Also, remove the `cluster-create-ns` ClusterRole and ClusterRoleBinding created previously. Finally, try creating the `still-not-going-to-work` namespace:

```
PS C:\Users\mlb> kubectl create ns still-not-going-to-
work
Error from server (Forbidden): namespaces is forbidden:
User "mlbiamext" cannot create resource "namespaces" in
API group "" at the cluster scope
```

3. Next, use the `audit2rbac` tool to look for any failures for your test user:

```
root@cluster01-control-plane:/# ./audit2rbac --filename=/
var/log/k8s/audit.log  --user=mlbiamext
Opening audit source...
Loading events...
Evaluating API calls...
Generating roles...
apiVersion: rbac.authorization.k8s.io/v1
kind: ClusterRole
metadata:
  annotations:
    audit2rbac.liggitt.net/version: v0.8.0
  labels:
    audit2rbac.liggitt.net/generated: "true"
    audit2rbac.liggitt.net/user: mlbiamext
  name: audit2rbac:mlbiamext
rules:
- apiGroups:
  - ""
  resources:
  - namespaces
```

```
    verbs:
    - create
---
apiVersion: rbac.authorization.k8s.io/v1
kind: ClusterRoleBinding
metadata:
  annotations:
    audit2rbac.liggitt.net/version: v0.8.0
  labels:
    audit2rbac.liggitt.net/generated: "true"
    audit2rbac.liggitt.net/user: mlbiamext
  name: audit2rbac:mlbiamext
roleRef:
  apiGroup: rbac.authorization.k8s.io
  kind: ClusterRole
  name: audit2rbac:mlbiamext
subjects:
- apiGroup: rbac.authorization.k8s.io
  kind: User
  name: mlbiamext
Complete!
```

This command generated a policy that will exactly allow the test user to create namespaces. This becomes an anti-pattern, though, of explicitly authorizing access to users.

4. In order to better leverage this policy, it would be better to use our group:

```
apiVersion: rbac.authorization.k8s.io/v1
kind: ClusterRole
metadata:
  name: create-ns-audit2rbac
rules:
- apiGroups:
  - ""
  resources:
  - namespaces
```

```
    verbs:
    - create
---
apiVersion: rbac.authorization.k8s.io/v1
kind: ClusterRoleBinding
metadata:
  name: create-ns-audit2rbac
roleRef:
  apiGroup: rbac.authorization.k8s.io
  kind: ClusterRole
  name: create-ns-audit2rbac
subjects:
- apiGroup: rbac.authorization.k8s.io
  kind: Group
  name: cn=k8s-create-ns,cn=users,dc=domain,dc=com
```

The major change is highlighted. Instead of referencing the user directly, the
ClusterRoleBinding is now referencing the cn=k8s-create-ns,cn=users,
dc=domain,dc=com group so that any member of that group can now create namespaces.

Summary

This chapter's focus was on RBAC policy creation and debugging. We explored how
Kubernetes defines authorization policies and how it applies those policies to enterprise
users. We also looked at how these policies can be used to enable multi-tenancy in your
cluster. Finally, we enabled the audit log in our KinD cluster and learned how to use the
audit2rbac tool to debug RBAC issues.

Using Kubernetes' built-in RBAC policy management objects lets you enable access that's
needed for operational and development tasks in your clusters. Knowing how to design
policies can help limit the impact of issues, providing the confidence to let users do more
on their own.

In the next chapter, we'll be learning about how to secure the Kubernetes dashboard,
as well as how to approach security for other infrastructure applications that make up
your cluster. You'll learn how to apply what we've learned about authentication and
authorization to the applications that make up your cluster, providing your developers
and infrastructure team with a better and more secure experience.

Questions

1. True or false – ABAC is the preferred method of authorizing access to Kubernetes clusters.

   A. True

   B. False

2. What are the three components of a Role?

   A. Subject, noun, and verb

   B. Resource, action, and group

   C. `apiGroups`, resources, and verbs

   D. Group, resource, and sub-resource

3. Where can you go to look up resource information?

   A. Kubernetes API reference

   B. The library

   C. Tutorials and blog posts

4. How can you reuse Roles across namespaces?

   A. You can't; you need to re-create them.

   B. Define a ClusterRole and reference it in each namespace as a RoleBinding.

   C. Reference the Role in one namespace with the RoleBindings of other namespaces.

   D. None of the above.

5. How should bindings reference users?

   A. Directly, listing every user.

   B. RoleBindings should only reference service accounts.

   C. Only ClusterRoleBindings should reference users.

   D. Whenever possible, RoleBindings and ClusterRoleBindings should reference groups.

6. True or false – RBAC can be used to authorize access to everything except for one resource.

   A. True

   B. False

7. True or false – RBAC is the only method of authorization in Kubernetes.

   A. True

   B. False

9
Deploying a Secured Kubernetes Dashboard

Kubernetes clusters are made up of more than the API server and the kubelet. Clusters are generally made up of additional applications that need to be secured, such as container registries, source control systems, pipeline services, GitOps applications, and monitoring systems. The users of your cluster will often need to interact with these applications directly.

While many clusters are focused on authenticating access to user-facing applications and services, cluster solutions are not given the same first-class status. Users often are asked to use kubectl's **port-forward** or **proxy** capability to access these systems. This method of access is an anti-pattern from a security and user experience standpoint. The first exposure users and administrators will have to this anti-pattern is the Kubernetes Dashboard. This chapter will detail why this method of access is an anti-pattern and how to properly access the Dashboard. We'll walk you through how not to deploy a secure web application and point out the issues and risks.

We'll use the Kubernetes Dashboard as a way to learn about web application security and how to apply those patterns in your own cluster. These lessons will work with not just the dashboard, but other cluster focused applications such as the Kiali dashboard for Istio, Grafana, Prometheus, and other cluster management applications.

Finally, we'll spend some time talking about local dashboards and how to evaluate their security. This is a popular trend, but not universal. It's important to understand the security of both approaches, and we'll explore them in this chapter.

In this chapter, we will cover the following topics:

- How does the dashboard know who you are?
- Is the dashboard insecure?
- Deploying the dashboard with a reverse proxy
- Integrating the dashboard with OpenUnison

Technical requirements

To follow the exercises in this chapter you will require a KinD cluster running with OIDC integration. We created this in *Chapter 7, Integrating Authentication into Your Cluster*.

You can access the code for this chapter at the following GitHub repository: `https://github.com/PacktPublishing/Kubernetes-and-Docker-The-Complete-Guide`.

How does the dashboard know who you are?

The Kubernetes Dashboard is a powerful web application for quickly accessing your cluster from inside a browser. It lets you browse your namespaces and view the status of nodes, and even provides a shell you can use to access Pods directly. There is a fundamental difference between using the dashboard and kubectl. The dashboard, being a web application, needs to manage your session, whereas kubectl does not. This leads to a different set of security issues during deployment that are often not accounted for, leading to severe consequences. In this section, we'll explore how the dashboard identifies users and interacts with the API server.

Dashboard architecture

Before diving into the specifics of how the dashboard authenticates a user, it's important to understand the basics of how the dashboard works. The dashboard at a high level has three layers:

- **User Interface**: This is the Angular + HTML frontend that is displayed in your browser and that you interact with.

- **Middle Tier**: The frontend interacts with a set of APIs hosted in the dashboard's container to translate calls from the frontend into Kubernetes API calls.

- **API Server**: The middle tier API interacts directly with the Kubernetes API server.

This three-layered architecture of the Kubernetes Dashboard can be seen in the following diagram:

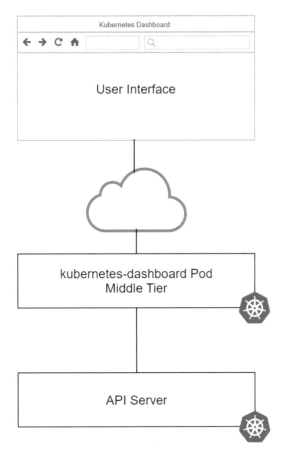

Figure 9.1 – Kubernetes Dashboard architecture

When a user interacts with the dashboard, the user interface makes calls to the middle tier, which in turn makes calls to the API server. The dashboard doesn't know how to collect credentials, with which most of the applications users would generally get access. There's no place to put a username or password. It has a very simple session mechanism system based on cookies, but for the most part the dashboard doesn't really know, or care, who the currently logged in user is. The only thing the dashboard cares about is what token to use when communicating with the API server.

So, how does the dashboard know who you are?

Authentication methods

There are three ways that the dashboard can determine who a user is:

- **No credentials**: The dashboard can be told not to collect any tokens or credentials. When this happens, the dashboard will interact with the API server using the container's own service account with whatever privileges it is assigned via RBAC.

- **Token from login/uploaded kubectl configuration**: The dashboard can prompt the user for their kubectl configuration file or for a bearer token to use. Once a token is provided (or extracted from the configuration file uploaded to the dashboard), an encrypted cookie is created to store the token. This cookie is decrypted by the middle tier, and the token inside is passed to the API server.

- **Token from a reverse proxy**: If there's an authorization header containing a bearer token in requests from the user interface to the middle tier, the middle tier will use that bearer token in requests to the API server. This is the most secure option and the implementation that will be detailed in this chapter.

Throughout the rest of this chapter, the first two options will be explored as anti-patterns for accessing the dashboard, and we will explain why the reverse proxy pattern is the best option for accessing a cluster's dashboard implementation from a security standpoint and a user experience standpoint.

Understanding dashboard security risks

The question of the dashboard's security often comes up when setting up a new cluster. Securing the dashboard boils down to how the dashboard is deployed, rather than if the dashboard itself is secure. Going back to the architecture of the dashboard application, there is no sense of "security" being built in. The middle tier simply passes a token to the API server.

When talking about any kind of IT security, it's important to look at it through the lens of *defense in depth*. This is the idea that any system should have multiple layers of security. If one fails, there are other layers to fill the gap until the failed layers can be addressed. A single failure doesn't give an attacker direct access.

The most often cited incident related to the dashboard's security was the breach of Tesla in 2018 by crypto-miners. Attackers were able to access Pods running in Tesla's clusters because the dashboard wasn't secured. The cluster's Pods had access to tokens that provided the attackers with access to Tesla's cloud providers where the attackers ran their crypto-mining systems.

Dashboards in general are often an attack vector because they make it easy to find what attackers are looking for and can easily be deployed insecurely. Illustrating this point, at KubeCon NA 2019 a **Capture the Flag** (**CTF**) was presented where one of the scenarios was a developer "accidentally" exposing the cluster's dashboard.

> **Note**
>
> The CTF is available as a home lab at `https://securekubernetes.com/`. It's a highly recommended resource for anyone learning Kubernetes security. In addition to being educational, and terrifying, it's also really fun!

Since the Tesla breach, it's become harder to deploy the dashboard without credentials. It's no longer the default and requires updates to both the dashboard and the cluster. To demonstrate just how dangerous this can be, let's go through the steps to do it and see what damage can be done.

Going through these steps might bring about the thought "does anyone really go through all these steps to get to the dashboard?" The answer is probably something no one wants to talk about. In the previous chapter, multiple options for authorizing access to a cluster and designing multi-tenancy were discussed. One of the options was tenancy at the cluster layer, where each tenant gets its own cluster. Unfortunately, many of these deployments include cluster-admin access for the tenants, which would give them the ability to perform these steps. Cluster administrators are a few Google searches away from instructions to easily bypass that pesky VPN developers don't like using from home.

Deploying an insecure dashboard

While this may sound crazy, it's something that we have seen in the wild far too often. The recommended dashboard installation states multiple times not to use this type of configuration outside of an isolated development lab. The downfall is that since it does make deploying the dashboard so easy, many newer administrators use it since it's easy to set up, and they often use the same deployment in a production cluster.

Now, let's show how easy it is to attack a dashboard that is deployed without security in mind:

1. The first step is to tell the dashboard to allow users to bypass authentication. Edit the `kubernetes-dashboard` deployment in the `kubernetes-dashboard` namespace:

    ```
    kubectl edit deployment kubernetes-dashboard -n
    kubernetes-dashboard
    ```

2. Look for the `args` option for the container, add `- --enable-skip-login`, then save:

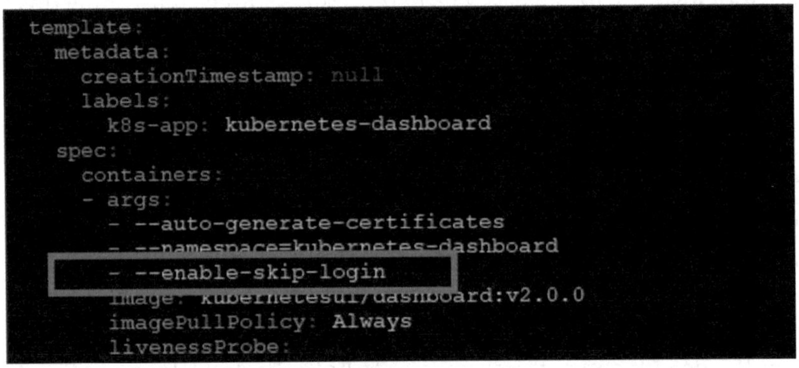

    Figure 9.2 – Enabling skip-login on the dashboard

3. Now we need to expose the dashboard to the network by creating a new Ingress rule. Create a new Ingress manifest called `insecure-dashboard.yaml` with the following YAML. Remember to replace the IP address in the `host` section with your Docker host's IP address:

    ```
    apiVersion: networking.k8s.io/v1beta1
    kind: Ingress
    metadata:
      name: dashboard-external-auth
      namespace: kubernetes-dashboard
      annotations:
        kubernetes.io/ingress.class: nginx
        nginx.ingress.kubernetes.io/affinity: cookie
        nginx.ingress.kubernetes.io/backend-protocol: https
        nginx.ingress.kubernetes.io/secure-backends: "true"
    ```

```
        nginx.org/ssl-services: kubernetes-dashboard
spec:
  rules:
  - host: k8s-secret-dashboard.apps.192-168-2-129.nip.io
    http:
      paths:
      - backend:
          serviceName: kubernetes-dashboard
          servicePort: 443
        path: /
```

4. Create the Ingress rule by deploying the manifest using `kubectl`. Since we added the namespace value to the manifest, we do need to add `-n` to the kubectl command:

    ```
    kubectl create -f insecure-dashboard.yaml
    ```

5. Once the Ingress is created, open a browser and go to your secret dashboard using the Nip.io name specified in the `host` section of the Ingress rule.

6. You will see an authentication screen that asks for a token or a Kubeconfig file, but since we enabled the option to skip the login when we edited the dashboard, you can simply skip the login by clicking on **Skip**:

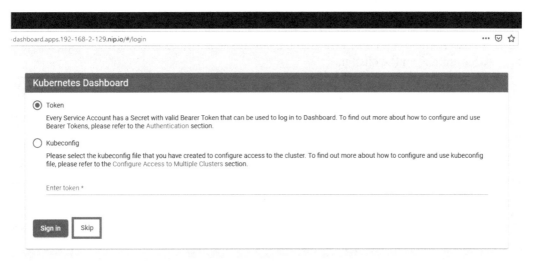

Figure 9.3 – Kubernetes Dashboard with login disabled

7. Once in the dashboard, the default service account doesn't have access to anything:

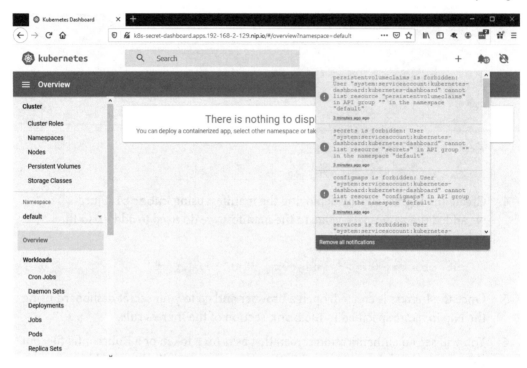

Figure 9.4 – Kubernetes Dashboard with the default service account

So far this may not look too bad. You will see *access forbidden* errors, so right now the dashboard will not allow you to do any damage. Unfortunately, many people get to this point and go the extra step to change the permissions that the default service account has on the cluster.

8. Right now, the service account isn't authorized for access to the cluster, so change that by creating a new ClusterRoleBinding to the cluster-admin ClusterRole.

Create a new file called dashboard-role.yaml with the following contents:

```
apiVersion: rbac.authorization.k8s.io/v1
kind: ClusterRoleBinding
metadata:
  name: secret-dashboard-cluster-admin
roleRef:
  apiGroup: rbac.authorization.k8s.io
  kind: ClusterRole
```

```
      name: cluster-admin
   subjects:
   - apiGroup: ""
     kind: ServiceAccount
     namespace: kubernetes-dashboard
     name: kubernetes-dashboard
```

9. Create the new `ClusterRoleBinding` by applying it using `kubectl`:

```
kubectl create -f dashboard-role.yaml
```

Congratulations! The secret dashboard is now available for anyone who may want to use it!

Now, you may be thinking *"Who can find my dashboard? They would need to know the URL, and I'm not telling anyone what it is."* You feel secure because nobody else knows the URL or the IP address to your dashboard. This is called Security by Obscurity and is generally accepted to be a terrible approach to securing a system.

Let's use a scenario of how someone may exploit the dashboard without you knowing.

You are a big Reddit fan, and one day you come across a Reddit post titled *This is a great tool for securing your Kubernetes Dashboard.* The post seems to be legit and you are excited to test this new tool out. After reading the post, you see the link at the bottom to the utility and the command to run it: You can download it from `https://raw.githubusercontent.com/PacktPublishing/Kubernetes-and-Docker-The-Complete-Guide/master/chapter9/kubectl-secure-my-dashboard.go` to give it a try!

To fully experience this example, you can run the tool on your KinD cluster by executing the following command from your cloned repository in the `chapter9` directory. Be sure to change the URL to your dashboard's Ingress host:

```
go run kubectl-secure-my-dashboard.go https://k8s-secret-
dashboard.apps.192-168-2-129.nip.io
Running analysis on https://k8s-secret-dashboard.apps.192-168-
2-129.nip.io
Your dashboard has been secured!
```

Now, let's see review what just happened. Open a browser and go to your secret dashboard site to view what's been changed:

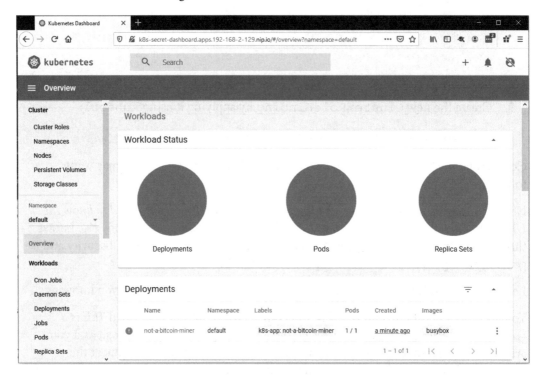

Figure 9.5 – Kubernetes Dashboard showing malware deployed

It appears our hardening plugin was a ruse to deploy a bitcoin miner. How rude!

Now that you have seen how easily an insecure dashboard can be exploited, delete the deployment using kubectl.

While this attack could be mitigated by preauthorizing registries with approved images (this topic will be covered when OpenPolicyAgent is covered in *Chapter 11*, *Extending Security Using Open Policy Manager*), at that point the security is reactive, trying to respond to threats instead of preventing them. Using an admission controller won't stop someone from extracting secrets from your dashboard either.

While this was the simplest way to get access to the dashboard insecurely, it's not the only way. The kubectl utility includes two features that can make accessing the dashboard easy. The port-forward utility is often used to create a tunnel to a pod inside the cluster. This utility creates a TCP stream to a specific port on your pod, making it accessible to your local host (or more if you wanted). This still bypasses authentication in the dashboard, requiring that the dashboard's service account has access via RBAC to perform whichever tasks are needed. While it is true that the user must have RBAC authorization to port-forward to a pod, this leaves the dashboard open via two attack vectors:

- **External**: Any script running on a user's local workstation can access the forwarded network tunnel.

- **Internal**: Any pod inside of the cluster can access the dashboard pod.

For internal access, network policies can be used to limit which namespaces and Pods can access the dashboard's API. It's a good idea to use network policies to begin with, but that's a single point of failure in this instance. One misconfigured policy will open the dashboard to attack.

Threats from external sources will likely come in the form of scripts you (or another tool you use) may decide to run. Web browsers aren't able to access the ports opened by port-forwarding from a page hosted outside your local system, but any script running on your workstation can. For instance, while you could access a port-forwarded host by opening your browser and going directly to that port, a web page with malicious JavaScript that loads from a remote site can't open a connection to your local host. Attempt to run the hardening script from earlier in the section against a forwarded port and the same result will occur, an unwanted pod on your infrastructure.

Another technique for providing access is to use the API server's integrated proxy utility. Running `kubectl proxy` creates a local network tunnel to the API server that can then be used to proxy HTTP requests to any pod, including the dashboard. This has the same drawbacks as `kubectl port-forward` and will open your cluster up to attacks from any script running locally.

The common thread among these methods is they have a single point of failure in their security. Even with mitigations put in place to limit what images can be deployed, an unsecured dashboard can still be used to access Secret objects, delete deployments, and even remote shell into Pods via the terminal integrated into the dashboard.

Having explored how to bypass all authentication on the dashboard, and its implications, next we'll look at how to provide a token to the dashboard without deploying additional infrastructure.

Using a token to log in

A user may upload a token or kubectl configuration file to the dashboard as a login to avoid the perils of a secret dashboard. As discussed earlier, the dashboard will take the user's bearer token and use it with all requests to the API server. While this may appear to solve the problem of giving the dashboard its own privileged service account, it brings its own issues. The dashboard isn't kubectl and doesn't know how to refresh tokens as they expire. This means that a token would need to be fairly long lived to be useful. This would require either creating service accounts that can be used or making your OpenID Connect id_tokens longer lived. Both options would negate much of the security put in place by leveraging OpenID Connect for authentication.

So far, we've only focused on the wrong way to deploy the dashboard. While it is important to understand this, what is the correct method? In the next section, we'll detail the correct way to deploy the dashboard using a reverse proxy.

Deploying the dashboard with a reverse proxy

Proxies are a common pattern in Kubernetes. There are proxies at every layer in a Kubernetes cluster. The proxy pattern is also used by most service mesh implementations on Kubernetes, creating side cars that will intercept requests. The difference between the reverse proxy described here and these proxies is in their intent. Microservice proxies often do not carry a session, whereas web applications need a session to manage state.

The following diagram shows the architecture of a Kubernetes Dashboard with a reverse proxy:

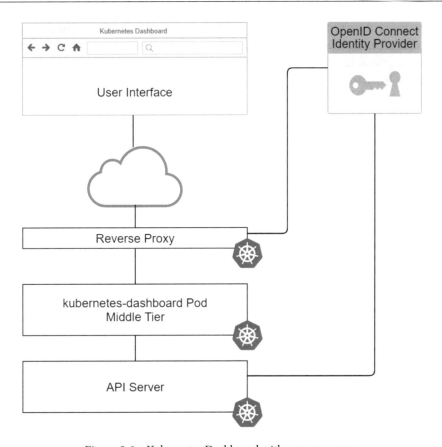

Figure 9.6 – Kubernetes Dashboard with a reverse proxy

The reverse proxy shown in *Figure 9.6* performs three roles:

- **Authentication**: The reverse proxy intercepts unauthenticated requests (or stale sessions) and triggers the authentication process with an OpenID Connect identity provider to authenticate the user.

- **Session management**: Kubernetes' Dashboard is a user-facing application. It should have the typical controls put in place to support session timeouts and revocation. Be wary of a reverse proxy that stores all session data in a cookie. These methods are difficult to revoke.

- **Identity injection**: Once the proxy has authenticated a user, it needs to be able to inject an HTTP authorization header on each request that is a JWT identifying the logged-in user, is signed by the same OpenID Connect identity provider, and has the same issuer and recipient as the API server. The exception to this is using impersonation, which, as discussed in *Chapter 7, Integrating Authentication into Your Cluster*, injects specific headers into the requests.

The reverse proxy does not need to run on the cluster. Depending on your setup, it may be advantageous to do so, especially when utilizing impersonation with your cluster. When using impersonation, the reverse proxy uses a service account's token, so it's best for that token to never leave the cluster.

The focus of this chapter has been on the Kubernetes project's dashboard. There are multiple options for dashboard functionality. Next, we'll explore how these dashboards interact with the API server and how to evaluate their security.

Local dashboards

A common theme among third-party dashboards is to run locally on your workstation and use a Kubernetes SDK to interact with the API server the same way kubectl would. These tools offer the benefit of not having to deploy additional infrastructure to secure them.

Visual Studio Code's Kubernetes plugin is an example of a local application leveraging direct API server connections. When launching the plugin Visual Studio Code accesses your current kubectl configuration and interacts with the API server using that configuration. It will even refresh an OpenID Connect token when it expires:

Figure 9.7 – Visual Studio Code with the Kubernetes plugin

The Kubernetes plugin for Visual Studio Code is able to refresh its OpenID Connect Token because it's built with the client-go SDK, the same client libraries used by kubectl. When evaluating client dashboards make sure it works with your authentication type even if it isn't OpenID Connect. Many of the SDKs for Kubernetes don't support OpenID Connect token refreshes. The Java and Python SDKs only recently (as of the published date of this book) began supporting the refresh of OpenID Connect tokens the way the client-go SDK does. When evaluating a local dashboard, make sure it's able to leverage your short-lived tokens and can refresh them as needed, just like kubectl can.

Other cluster-level applications

The introduction of this chapter discussed how a cluster is made up of several applications besides Kubernetes. Other applications will likely follow the same model as the dashboard for security, and the reverse proxy method is a better method for exposing those applications than kubectl port-forward, even when the application has no built-in security. Use the common Prometheus stack as an example. Grafana has support for user authentication, but Prometheus and Alert Manager do not. How would you track who had access to these systems or when they were accessed using port-forwarding?

There's no user context provided. Using a reverse proxy, logs of each URL and the user that was authenticated to access the URL can be forwarded to a central log management system and analyzed by a **Security Information and Event Manager** (**SIEM**) providing an additional layer of visibility into a cluster's usage.

Just as with the dashboard, using a reverse proxy with these applications provides a layered security approach. It offloads sessions management from the application in question and provides the capability to have enhanced authentication measures in place such as multi-factor authentication and session revocation. These benefits will lead to a more secure, and easier to use, cluster.

Integrating the dashboard with OpenUnison

The topic of how OpenUnison injected identity headers using impersonation was covered in *Chapter 7, Integrating Authentication into Your Cluster*, but not how OpenUnison injected user's identity into the dashboard with an OpenID Connect integrated cluster. It worked, but it wasn't explained. This section will use the OpenUnison implementation as an example of how to build a reverse proxy for the dashboard. Use the information in this section to get a better understanding of API security or to build your own solution for dashboard authentication.

The OpenUnison deployment comprises two integrated applications:

- **The OpenID Connect Identity Provider & Login Portal**: This application hosts the login process and the discovery URLs used by the API server to get the keys needed to validate an id_token. It also hosts the screens where you can obtain your token for kubectl.

- **The dashboard**: A reverse proxy application that authenticates to the integrated OpenID Connect identity provider and injects the user's id_token into each request.

This diagram shows how the dashboard's user interface interacts with its server side component with a reverse proxy injecting the user's id_token:

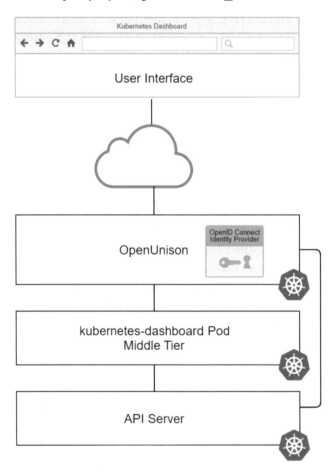

Figure 9.8 – OpenUnison integration with the dashboard

The dashboard uses the same OpenID Connect identity provider as the API server, but doesn't use the `id_token` provided by it. Instead, OpenUnison has a plugin that will generate a new `id_token` independent of the identity provider with the user's identity data in it. OpenUnison can do this because the key used to generate an `id_token` for the OpenID Connect identity provider, used by kubectl and the API server, is stored in OpenUnison.

A new, short-lived token is generated separate from the OpenID Connect session used with kubectl. This way, the token can be refreshed independently of a kubectl session. This process provides the benefits of 1- to 2-minute token life with the convenience of a direct login process.

If you have an eye for security, you may point out that this method has a glaring single-point-of-failure in the security model, a user's credentials! Just as with the Secret dashboard built earlier in this chapter in the *Understanding dashboard security risks section*, an attacker generally just needs to ask for credentials in order to get them. This is often done via email in an attack called phishing, where an attacker sends a victim a link to a page that looks like their login page but really just collects credentials. This is why multi-factor authentication is so important for infrastructure systems.

In a 2019 study, Google showed multi-factor authentication stopped 99% of automated and phishing attacks (`https://security.googleblog.com/2019/05/new-research-how-effective-is-basic.html`). Adding multi-factor authentication to the identity provider OpenUnison authenticates against, or integrating it directly into OpenUnison, is one of the most effective ways to secure the dashboard and your cluster.

Summary

In this chapter, we explored the security of the Kubernetes Dashboard in detail. First, we walked through the architecture and how the dashboard passes your identity information on to the API server. We then explored how the dashboard gets compromised, and finally we detailed how to correctly deploy the dashboard securely.

With this knowledge, you can now provide a secured tool to your users. Many users prefer the simplicity of accessing the dashboard via a web browser. Adding multi-factor authentication adds an additional layer of security and peace of mind. When your security team questions the security of the dashboard, you'll have the answers needed to satisfy their concerns.

The previous three chapters focused on the security of the Kubernetes APIs. Next, we'll explore securing the soft underbelly of every Kubernetes deployment, nodes!

Questions

1. The dashboard is insecure.

    A. True

    B. False

2. How can the dashboard identify a user?

    A. The options are either no authentication, or a token injected from a reverse proxy
    B. Username and password
    C. ServiceAccount
    D. Multi-factor authentication

3. How does the dashboard track session state?

    A. Sessions are stored in etcd.
    B. Sessions are stored in custom resource objects called `DashboardSession`.
    C. There are no sessions.
    D. If a token is uploaded, it's encrypted and stored in the browser as a cookie.

4. When using a token, how often can the dashboard refresh it?

    A. Once a minute
    B. Every thirty seconds
    C. When the token expires
    D. None of the above

5. What's the best way to deploy the dashboard?

    A. Using `kubectl port-forward`
    B. Using `kubectl proxy`
    C. With a secret ingress host
    D. Behind a reverse proxy

6. The dashboard doesn't support impersonation.

    A. True

    B. False

7. OpenUnison is the only reverse proxy that supports the dashboard.

    A. True

    B. False

10
Creating PodSecurityPolicies

Most of the security discussed so far has focused on protecting Kubernetes APIs. Authentication has meant the authentication of API calls. Authorization has meant authorizing access to certain APIs. Even the discussion on the dashboard centered mostly around how to securely authenticate to the API server by way of the dashboard.

This chapter will be different as we will now shift our focus to securing our nodes. We will learn how **PodSecurityPolicies** (**PSPs**) protect the nodes of a Kubernetes cluster. Our focus will be on how containers run on the nodes of your cluster and how to keep those containers from having more access than they should. We'll get into the details of impacts in this chapter by looking at how exploits can be used to gain access to a cluster when the nodes aren't protected. We'll also explore how these scenarios can be exploited even in code that doesn't need node access.

In this chapter, we will cover the following topics:

- What is a PSP?
- Aren't they going away?
- Enabling pod security policies
- Alternatives to PSPs

Technical requirements

To follow the examples in this chapter, make sure you have a KinD cluster running with the configuration from *Chapter 8, RBAC Policies and Auditing*.

You can access the code for this chapter at the following GitHub repository: `https://github.com/PacktPublishing/Kubernetes-and-Docker-The-Complete-Guide/tree/master/chapter10`.

What is a PodSecurityPolicy?

A PSP is a Kubernetes resource that allows you to set security controls for your workloads, allowing you to set limitations on what a pod can do. PSPs are evaluated before a pod is allowed to start up and if the pod attempts to do something that a PSP forbids, it will not be allowed to start.

Many people have experience with physical and virtual servers, and most know how to secure workloads running on them. Containers need to be considered differently when you talk about securing each workload. To understand why PSPs and other Kubernetes security tools such as the **Open Policy Agent** (**OPA**) exist, you need to understand how a container is different from a **virtual machine** (**VM**).

Understanding the difference between containers and VMs

"*A container is a lightweight VM*" is often how containers are described to those new to containers and Kubernetes. While this makes for a simple analogy, from a security standpoint, it's a dangerous comparison. A container at runtime is a process that runs on a node. On a Linux system, these processes are isolated by a series of Linux technologies that limit their visibility to the underlying system.

Go to any node in a Kubernetes cluster and run the `top` command and all of the processes from containers are listed. As an example, even though Kubernetes is running in KinD, running `ps -A -elf | grep java` will show the OpenUnison and operator container processes:

```
k8s@book:~$ ps -A -elf | grep java
4 S 431     18399 18346 0 80  0 - B75313 -     May28 ?     00:50:13 java -classpath /usr/local/openunison/work/webapp/WEB-INF/lib/*:/usr/local/openunison/work/webapp/
WEB-INF/classes:/tmp/quartz -Djava.awt.headless=true -Djava.security.egd=file:/dev/./urandom -DunisonEnvironmentFile=/etc/openunison/ou.env com.tremolosecurity.openunison.un
dertow.OpenUnisonOnUndertow /etc/openunison/openunison.yaml
4 S 431     23622 23514 0 80  0 - 770470 -     May19 ?     00:28:02 java -jar /usr/local/openunison/javascript-operator.jar -tokenPath /var/run/secrets/kubernetes.io/
serviceaccount/token -rootCaPath /var/run/secrets/kubernetes.io/serviceaccount/ca.crt -kubernetesURL https://kubernetes.default.svc.cluster.local -namespace NAMESPACE -apiGr
oup openunison.tremolo.io/v1 -objectType openunisons -jsPath /usr/local/openunison/js -configMaps /etc/extraMaps
0 S k8s     29943 29003 0 80  0 - 3607 pipe_w 09:12 pts/1   00:00:00 grep java
k8s@book:~$
```

Figure 10.1 – Pod processes from the system console

In contrast, a VM is, as the name implies, a complete virtual system. It emulates its own hardware, has an isolated kernel, and so on. The hypervisor provides isolation for VMs down to the silicone layer, whereas by comparison, there is very little isolation between every container on a node.

> **Note**
>
> There are container technologies that will run a container on their own VM. The container is still just a process.

When containers aren't running, they're simply a "tarball of tarballs," where each layer of the filesystem is stored in a file. The image is still stored on the host system, or multiple host systems, wherever the container has been run or pulled previously.

> **Note**
>
> A "tarball" is a file created by the `tar` Unix command. It can also be compressed.

A VM, on the other hand, has its own virtual disk that stores the entire OS. While there are some very lightweight VM technologies, there's often an order of magnitude's difference in the size between a VM and a container.

While some people refer to containers as lightweight VMs, that couldn't be further from the truth. They aren't isolated in the same way and require more attention to be paid to the details of how they are run on a node.

From this section, you may think that we are trying to say that containers are not secure. Nothing could be further from the truth. Securing a Kubernetes cluster, and the containers running on it, requires attention to detail and an understanding of how containers differ from VMs. Since so many people do understand VMs, it's easy to attempt to compare them to containers, but doing so puts you at a disadvantage since they are very different technologies.

Once you understand the limitations of a default configuration and the potential dangers that come from it, you can remediate the "issues."

Container breakouts

A container breakout is when the process of your container gets access to the underlying node. Once on the node, an attacker now has access to all the other pods and any capability the node has in your environment. A breakout can also be a matter of mounting the local filesystem into your container. An example from https://securekubernetes.com, originally pointed out by Duffie Cooley from VMware, uses a container to mount the local filesystem. Running this on a KinD cluster opens both reads and writes to the node's filesystem:

```
kubectl run r00t --restart=Never -ti --rm --image lol
--overrides '{"spec":{"hostPID": true, "containers":[
{"name":"1","image":"alpine","command":["nsenter","-
-mount=/proc/1/ns/mnt","--","/bin/bash"],"stdin":
true,"tty":true,"imagePullPolicy":"IfNotPresent",
"securityContext":{"privileged":true}}]}}'
If you don't see a command prompt, try pressing Enter.
```

The run command in the preceding code started a container that added an option that is key to the example, hostPID: true, which allows the container to share the host's process namespace. You may see a few other options, such as –mount and a security context setting that sets privileged to true. All of the options combined will allow us to write to the host's filesystem.

Now that you are in the container, execute the ls command to look at the filesystem. Notice how the prompt is root@r00t:/#, confirming you are in the container and not on the host:

```
root@r00t:/# ls
bin  boot  build  dev  etc  home  kind  lib  lib32  lib64
libx32  media  mnt  opt  proc  root  run  sbin  srv  sys  tmp
usr  var
```

To prove that we have mapped the host's filesystem to our container, create a file called this is from a container and exit the container:

```
root@r00t:/# touch this_is_from_a_container
root@r00t:/# exit
```

Finally, let's look at the host's filesystem to see whether the container created the file. Since we are running KinD with a single worker node, we need to use Docker to `exec` into the worker node. If you are using the KinD cluster from the book, the worker node is called `cluster01-worker`:

```
docker exec -ti cluster01-worker ls /
bin  boot  build  dev  etc  home  kind  lib  lib32  lib64
libx32  media  mnt  opt  proc  root  run  sbin  srv  sys  this_
is_from_a_container  tmp  usr  var
```

There it is! In this example, a container was run that mounted the local filesystem. From inside of the pod, the `this_is_from_a_container` file was created. After exiting the pod and entering the node container, the file was there. Once an attacker has access to the node's filesystem, they also have access to the kubelet's credentials, which can open the entire cluster up.

It's not hard to envision a string of events that can lead to a Bitcoin miner (or worse) running on a cluster. A phishing attack gets the credentials a developer is using for their cluster. Even though those credentials only have access to one namespace, a container is created to get the kubelet's credentials, and from there, containers are launched to stealthily deploy miners across the environment. There are certainly multiple mitigations that could be used to prevent this attack, including the following:

- Multi-factor authentication, which would have kept the phished credentials from being used

- Pre-authorizing only certain containers

- A PSP, which would have prevented this attack by stopping a container from running as `privileged`

- A properly secured base image

At the core of security is a properly designed image. In the case of physical machines and VMs, this is accomplished by securing the base OS. When you install an OS, you don't select every possible option during installation. It is considered poor practice to have anything running on a server that is not required for its role or function. This same practice needs to be carried over to the images that will run on your clusters, which should only contain the necessary binaries that are required for your application.

Given how important it is to properly secure images on your cluster, the next section explores container design from a security standpoint. Building a locked-down container makes managing the security of the nodes much easier.

Properly designing containers

Before exploring how to build a `PodSecurityPolicy`, it's important to address how containers are designed. Often, the hardest part of using a `PodSecurityPolicy` to mitigate attacks on the node is the fact that so many containers are built and run as root. Once a restricted policy is applied, the container stops running. This is problematic at multiple levels. System administrators have learned over the decades of networked computing not to run processes as root, especially services such as web servers that are accessed anonymously over untrusted networks.

> **Note**
>
> All networks should be considered "untrusted." Assuming all networks are hostile leads to a more secure approach to implementation. It also means that services that need security need to be authenticated. This concept is called zero trust. It has been used and advocated by identity experts for years but was popularized in the DevOps and cloud native worlds by Google's BeyondCorp whitepaper (`https://cloud.google.com/beyondcorp`). The concept of zero trust should apply inside your clusters too!

Bugs in code can lead to access to underlying compute resources, which can then lead to breakouts from a container. Running as root in a privileged container when not needed can lead to a breakout if exploited via a code bug.

The Equifax breach in 2017 used a bug in the Apache Struts web application framework to run code on the server that was then used to infiltrate and extract data. Had this vulnerable web application been running on Kubernetes with a privileged container, the bug could have led to the attackers gaining access to the cluster.

When building containers, at a minimum, the following should be observed:

- **Run as a user other than root**: The vast majority of applications, especially micro services, don't need root. Don't run as root.

- **Only write to volumes**: If you don't write to a container, you don't need write access. Volumes can be controlled by Kubernetes. If you need to write temporary data, use an `emptyVolume` object instead of writing to the container's filesystem.

- **Minimize binaries in your container**: This can be tricky. There are those that advocate for "distro-less" containers that only contain the binary for the application, statically compiled. No shells, no tools. This can be problematic when trying to debug why an application isn't running as expected. It's a delicate balance.

- **Scan containers for known Common Vulnerability Exposures (CVEs); rebuild often**: One of the benefits of a container is that it can be easily scanned for known CVEs. There are several tools and registries that will do this for you. Once CVEs have been patched, rebuild. A container that hasn't been rebuilt in months, or years even, is every bit as dangerous as a server that hasn't been patched.

> **Important Note**
>
> Scanning for CVEs is a standard way to report security issues. Application and OS vendors will update CVEs with patches to their code that fix the issues. This information is then used by security scanning tools to act on when a container has a known issue that has been patched.

At the time of writing, the most restrictive defaults for any Kubernetes distribution on the market belong to Red Hat's OpenShift. In addition to sane default policies, OpenShift runs pods with a random user ID, unless the pod definition specifies an ID.

It's a good idea to test your containers on OpenShift, even if it's not your distribution for production use. If a container will run on OpenShift, it's likely to work with almost any security policy a cluster can throw at it. The easiest way to do this is with Red Hat's CodeReady Containers (`https://developers.redhat.com/products/codeready-containers`). This tool can run on your local laptop and launches a minimal OpenShift environment that can be used for testing containers.

> **Note**
>
> While OpenShift has very tight security controls out of the box, it doesn't use PSPs. It has its own policy system that pre-dates PSPs, called **Security Context Constraints (SCCs)**. SCCs are similar to PSPs but don't use RBAC for associating with pods.

PSP details

PSPs are tightly bound to how Linux processes run. The policy itself is a list of potential options any Linux process can have.

A PSP has several categories of privileges:

- **Privilege**: Does the pod need to run as a privileged pod? Does the pod need to do something that will change the underlying OS or environment?

- **Host interaction**: Does the pod need to interact with the host directly? For instance, does it need host filesystem access?

- **Volume types**: What kind of volumes can this pod mount? Do you want to limit it to specific volumes such as secrets but not disks?

- **User context**: What user will the process be allowed to run as? In addition to determining the allowed user ID and group ID ranges, SELinux and AppArmor contexts can be set as well.

A simple, unprivileged policy might look as follows:

```
apiVersion: policy/v1beta1
kind: PodSecurityPolicy
metadata:
  name: pod-security-policy-default
spec:
  fsGroup:
    rule: 'MustRunAs'
    ranges:
    # Forbid adding the root group.
    - min: 1
      max: 65535
  runAsUser:
    rule: 'MustRunAs'
    ranges:
    # Forbid adding the root group.
    - min: 1
      max: 65535
  seLinux:
    rule: RunAsAny
  supplementalGroups:
    rule: 'MustRunAs'
    ranges:
    # Forbid adding the root group.
    - min: 1
      max: 65535
  volumes:
```

```
      - emptyDir
      - secret
      - configMap
      - persistentVolumeClaim
```

The spec doesn't mention whether the containers can be privileged, nor does it mention any resources from the host that can be accessed. This means that if the pod definition attempts to mount the host's filesystem directly or to start as root, the pod will fail. Any permissions must be explicitly enabled in order for a pod to use them.

This policy limits which users a pod can run to anything except root by specifying the MustRunAs option, which is set to between 1 and 65535; it does not include user 0 (root).

Finally, the policy allows the mounting of standard volume types that most pods might need. Few, if any, pods need to be able to mount the node's filesystem.

Having this policy in place would have stopped the breakout we used earlier to get access to the node's filesystem. Here's a YAML of the pod we tried running earlier:

```
---
spec:
  hostPID: true
  containers:
  - name: '1'
    image: alpine
    command:
    - nsenter
    - "--mount=/proc/1/ns/mnt"
    - "--"
    - "/bin/bash"
    stdin: true
    tty: true
    imagePullPolicy: IfNotPresent
    securityContext:
      privileged: true
```

There are two highlighted settings. The first is hostPID, which lets the pod share the process ID space with the node. One of the technologies used by the Linux kernel to enable containers is cgroups, which isolate processes in containers. In Linux, cgroups will give processes in containers a different process ID than what it would be if simply run on the node. As shown, the processes for all containers can be viewed from the node. Running ps -A -elf | grep java from inside the pod will have a different ID than what's coming from the node. Since the hostPID option wasn't set to true on our policy, the PodSecurityPolicy enforcement webhook would reject this pod:

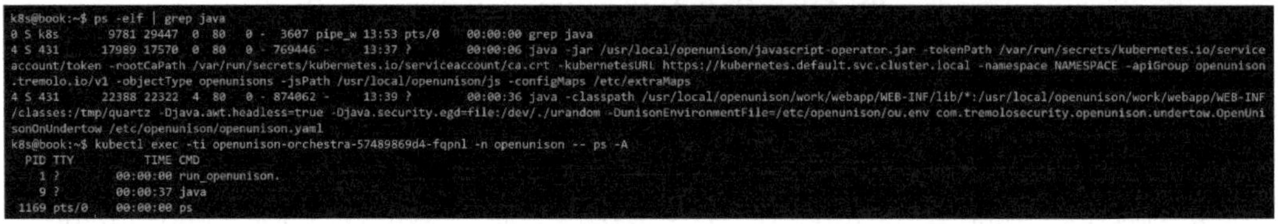

Figure 10.2 – Process ID from the host and from inside a container

The next highlighted portion is the security context setting privileged to true. These two settings will allow the container to run as if it's a root user logged into a node. Again, the default PSP would have stopped this because privilege wasn't enabled. The PSP controller would stop it.

Next, examine the NGINX Ingress controller's recommended PSP from https://raw.githubusercontent.com/kubernetes/ingress-nginx/master/docs/examples/psp/psp.yaml:

```
apiVersion: policy/v1beta1
kind: PodSecurityPolicy
metadata:
  .

  .

.spec:
  allowedCapabilities:
  - NET_BIND_SERVICE
  allowPrivilegeEscalation: true
  .

  .


  hostPID: false
```

```
hostPorts:
- min: 80
  max: 65535
```

In a typical web server running on a host, the process will start as root (or at least a privileged user), then downgrades itself to an unprivileged user so that it can open ports 80 and 443 for HTTP and HTTPS. These ports are under 1024 and so are reserved in Linux for root processes.

If you're wondering whether a web server needs to be able to run on ports 80 or 443 in Kubernetes, it doesn't. As discussed earlier in this book, the vast majority of deployments have a load balancer in front of them that can map 80 and 443 to any port. This should really be an exception, not the rule. The NGINX Ingress controller was released at a time when security wasn't as front and center in Kubernetes as it is today. Also, deployment models weren't quite as mature.

To allow similar behavior as an NGINX web server would have running directly on a host, NGINX wants to be able to open ports from 80 up and escalate to privileged, specifically using the NET_BIND_SERVICE privilege so that the web server can open ports 80 and 443 without running the entire process as root.

As discussed earlier, the vast majority of containers do not need special privileges. Instances of getting access to these special privileges should be few and far between and need to be reserved only for specific use cases. When evaluating systems that may run on a cluster, it's important to see whether the vendor or project provides a PSP that's been tested to work. If not, assume it is unprivileged and use the tools discussed later in this chapter to debug a specific policy.

Assigning a PSP

Once a policy is designed, it needs to be assigned. This is often the hardest part of deploying PSPs. The mechanism for determining whether a PSP is applied to a pod is the union of two sets of permissions:

- **The user that submitted the pod**: This can get tricky as users rarely submit pods directly. The best practice is to create a Deployment or a StatefulSet. Controllers then create Pods (though not directly). The user that "creates" the pod is the correct controller's service account, not the user that submitted the Deployment or StatefulSet. This can mean that usually only one or two service accounts ever actually create pods.

- **The service account the pod runs as**: Each pod can define a service account that the pod can run as. This service account is scoped at the pod level, not on individual containers.

By "union," Kubernetes will combine these permissions to determine which capabilities are to be allowed. For instance, if the controller's service account that submitted the pod has no privileges, but the service account for the pod can run as root, then the *best* policy will be chosen to apply to the pod that allows the pod to run as root. This process can be confusing and difficult to debug, and can often create unexpected results. A policy cannot be directly requested by a pod; it has to be assigned. It is important to keep policies constrained to make it more likely that the correct policy is applied.

Policies are evaluated and applied using special RBAC objects. Just as with the policy objects created to authorize access to APIs, both a `Role/ClusterRole` and a `RoleBinding/ClusterRoleBinding` need to be created. Instead of applying to specific APIs, RBAC objects that apply to `PodSecurityPolicy` objects use the `apiGroups` of `policy`, the resources of PSPs, and the `use` verb. The `use` verb doesn't have any corresponding HTTP action. The binding objects are generally the same as when authorizing API usage, but the subjects are generally service accounts, not users.

The first policy created previously is a good generic minimum access policy. To apply it across the cluster, first create a `ClusterRole`:

```yaml
apiVersion: rbac.authorization.k8s.io/v1
kind: ClusterRole
metadata:
  name: default-psp
rules:
- apiGroups:
  - policy
  resourceNames:
  - pod-security-policy-default
  resources:
  - podsecuritypolicies
  verbs:
  - use
```

The `resourceNames` section is the only part of the policy that is specific to the PSP being referenced. Everything else in the policy is boilerplate. The `ClusterRoleBinding` will apply this across the cluster:

```yaml
apiVersion: rbac.authorization.k8s.io/v1
kind: ClusterRoleBinding
metadata:
```

```
    name: default-psp
roleRef:
  apiGroup: rbac.authorization.k8s.io
  kind: ClusterRole
  name: default-psp
subjects:
- apiGroup: rbac.authorization.k8s.io
  kind: Group
  name: system:authenticated
```

When new pods are created, if no other policy applies, then the restricted policy will be used.

> **Note**
>
> If you're coming from the OpenShift ecosystem and are used to using SCCs, the authorization process is different. SCCs contain information on who is authorized directly on the object, whereas `PodSecurityPolicy` objects rely on RBAC.

Aren't they going away?

When Kubernetes 1.11 was released in 2018, it was revealed that PSPs will likely never go **General Availability (GA)**. This revelation was based on feedback that PSPs were difficult to use and the issues were systemic from their design. The discussion that came out of this revelation focused on three potential solutions:

- **Fix PSPs/reimplement a new standard**: These two options are bundled together because it's believed "fixing" PSPs will result in a standard that breaks backward-compatibility, resulting in a new policy system. Another option that's been floated is to port OpenShift's SCC implementation upstream.

- **Remove PSPs**: An argument has been made that this should be implementation-specific and so up to the implementer. Since PSPs are implemented using an admission controller, the argument is that this can be left to third parties.

- **Provide a "basic" implementation**: This is a hybrid approach where the upstream Kubernetes build supports a subset of PSPs and relies on custom admission controllers to support more advanced implementations.

There have not been any clear favorites as to which direction to go. What has been made clear is that PSPs will not be deprecated and removed until well after a replacement has become generally available. With Kubernetes 1.19, a new policy of not allowing APIs to remain in alpha or beta mode for more than three releases has forced the `PodSecurityPolicy` API to be deprecated. The API won't be removed until version 1.22, which isn't scheduled for release until January 2023 at the earliest (assuming at least 6 months between releases).

There are multiple approaches for protecting against an eventual deprecation of PSPs:

- **Don't use them at all**: This isn't a great approach. It leaves the nodes of a cluster open.

- **Avoid ad hoc policies**: Automating the policy application process will make it easier to move to whatever replaces PSPs.

- **Use another technology**: There are other options for PSP implementations that will be covered in the *Alternatives to PSPs* section.

Make a decision on PSPs based on your implementation needs. To stay updated on the progress of PSPs, watch the issue on GitHub: `https://github.com/kubernetes/enhancements/issues/5`.

Enabling PSPs

Enabling PSPs is very simple. Adding `PodSecurityPolicy` to the API server's list of admission controllers will send all newly created Pod objects through the `PodSecurityPolicy` admission controller. This controller does two things:

- **Identifies the best policy**: The best policy to use is identified by the capabilities requested by a pod's definition. A pod cannot explicitly state which policy it wants to enforce, only what capabilities it wants.

- **Determines whether the Pod's policy is authorized**: Once a policy is identified, the admission controller needs to determine whether the creator of the pod or the `serviceAccount` of the pod is authorized to use that policy.

The combination of these two criteria can lead to unexpected results. The creator of the pod isn't the user that submits the `Deployment` or `StatefulSet` definition. There's a controller that watches for `Deployment` updates and creates a `ReplicaSet`. There is a controller that watches for `ReplicaSet` objects and creates (`Pod`) objects. So, instead of the user who created the `Deployment` being the one that needs to be authorized, the `serviceAccount` for the `ReplicaSet` controller is. It's typical for blog posts and many default configurations to assign a privileged policy to all of the `ServiceAccount` objects in the `kube-system` namespace. This includes the `ServiceAccount` that the `ReplicaSet` controller runs as, which means it could create a pod with a privileged PSP without the creator of the `Deployment` or the `serviceAccount` of the pod being authorized to do so. It's important to press on your vendors to provide certified PSP definitions that have been tested.

Before enabling the admission controller, it's important to first create initial policies. The policy set from `https://raw.githubusercontent.com/PacktPublishing/Kubernetes-and-Docker-The-Complete-Guide/master/chapter10/podsecuritypolicies.yaml` has two policies and associated RBAC bindings. The first policy is the unprivileged policy that was described earlier in this chapter. The second policy is a privileged policy that is assigned to most of the `ServiceAccount` objects in the `kube-system` namespace. The `ReplicaSet` controller's `ServiceAccount` is not assigned access to the privileged policy. If a `Deployment` needs to create a privileged pod, the pod's `serviceAccount` will need to be authorized via RBAC to use the privileged policy. The first step is to apply these policies; the policy file is in the `chapter10` folder of your cloned repo:

1. Go into the `chapter10` folder and create the PSP object using `kubectl`:

    ```
    kubectl create -f podsecuritypolicies.yaml
    podsecuritypolicy.policy/pod-security-policy-default
    created
    clusterrole.rbac.authorization.k8s.io/default-psp created
    clusterrolebinding.rbac.authorization.k8s.io/default-psp
    created
    podsecuritypolicy.policy/privileged created
    clusterrole.rbac.authorization.k8s.io/privileged-psp
    created
    rolebinding.rbac.authorization.k8s.io/kube-system-psp
    created
    ```

2. Once the policies are created, `docker exec` into the control plain container and edit `/etc/kubernetes/manifests/kube-apiserver.yaml`. Look for `- --enable-admission-plugins=NodeRestriction` and change it to `- --enable-admission plugins=PodSecurityPolicy,NodeRestriction`. Once the API server pod is restarted, all new and updated pod objects will go through the `PodSecurityPolicy` admission controller.

> **Note**
>
> Managed Kubernetes offerings often pre-configure the `PodSecurityPolicy` admission controller. All pods are granted privileged access, so everything just "works." Enabling PSPs is a matter of creating the policies and the RBAC rules but not explicitly enabling them.

3. Since policies are enforced through an admission controller, any pods started that don't have access to a privileged policy will continue to run. For instance, the NGINX Ingress controller is still running. Checking the annotations of any pod using `kubectl describe` will show that there are no annotations for which policy is being used. In order to apply policies to all of the running pods, they must all be deleted:

```
kubectl delete pods --all-namespaces --all
 pod "nginx-ingress-controller-7d6bf88c86-q9f2j" deleted
 pod "calico-kube-controllers-5b644bc49c-8lkvs" deleted
 pod "calico-node-r6vwk" deleted
 pod "calico-node-r9ck9" deleted
 pod "coredns-6955765f44-9vw6t" deleted
 pod "coredns-6955765f44-qrcss" deleted
 pod "etcd-cluster01-control-plane" deleted
 pod "kube-apiserver-cluster01-control-plane" deleted
 pod "kube-controller-manager-cluster01-control-plane"
 deleted
 pod "kube-proxy-n2xf6" deleted
 pod "kube-proxy-tkxh6" deleted
 pod "kube-scheduler-cluster01-control-plane" deleted
 pod "dashboard-metrics-scraper-c79c65bb7-vd2k8" deleted
 pod "kubernetes-dashboard-6f89967466-p7rv5" deleted
```

```
pod "local-path-provisioner-7745554f7f-lklmf" deleted
pod "openunison-operator-858d496-zxnmj" deleted
pod "openunison-orchestra-57489869d4-btkvf" deleted
```

It will take a few minutes to run because the cluster needs to rebuild itself. Everything from etcd to the network is rebuilding its pods. After the command completes, watch all the pods to make sure they come back.

4. Once all the Pod objects are back, take a look at the OpenUnison pod's annotations:

```
kubectl describe pod -l application=openunison-orchestra
-n openunison
Name:          openunison-orchestra-57489869d4-jmbk2
Namespace:     openunison
Priority:      0
Node:          cluster01-worker/172.17.0.3
Start Time:    Thu, 11 Jun 2020 22:57:24 -0400
Labels:        application=openunison-orchestra
               operated-by=openunison-operator
               pod-template-hash=57489869d4
Annotations:   cni.projectcalico.org/podIP:
10.240.189.169/32
               cni.projectcalico.org/podIPs:
10.240.189.169/32
               kubernetes.io/psp: pod-security-policy-
default
```

The highlighted annotation shows that OpenUnison is running under the default restricted policy.

5. While OpenUnison is running, attempts to log in will fail. The NGINX Ingress pods aren't running. As we discussed earlier in the chapter, NGINX needs to be able to open ports 443 and 80, but using the default policy won't allow this to happen. Confirm why NGINX isn't running by inspecting the events in the ingress-nginx namespace:

```
$ kubectl get events -n ingress-nginx
2m4s        Warning    FailedCreate        replicaset/
nginx-ingress-controller-7d6bf88c86   Error creating:
pods "nginx-ingress-controller-7d6bf88c86-" is forbidden:
unable to validate against any pod security policy:
[spec.containers[0].securityContext.capabilities.add:
```

```
Invalid value: "NET_BIND_SERVICE": capability may not
be added spec.containers[0].hostPort: Invalid value: 80:
Host port 80 is not allowed to be used. Allowed ports:
[] spec.containers[0].hostPort: Invalid value: 443: Host
port 443 is not allowed to be used. Allowed ports: []]
```

6. Even though the NGINX Ingress project provides polices and RBAC bindings, let's debug this as if it doesn't. Inspecting the `Deployment` object, the key block in the spec is as follows:

```
ports:
- containerPort: 80
  hostPort: 80
  name: http
  protocol: TCP
- containerPort: 443
  hostPort: 443
  name: https
  protocol: TCP

    .

    .

    .

securityContext:
  allowPrivilegeEscalation: true
  capabilities:
    add:
    - NET_BIND_SERVICE
    drop:
    - ALL
  runAsUser: 101
```

First, the pod is declaring that it wants to open ports 80 and 443. Next, its `securityContext` declares that it wants a privilege escalation and it wants the `NET_BIND_SERVICE` capability to open those ports without being root.

7. Similar to the `audit2rbac` tool used when debugging RBAC policies, Sysdig
   has published a tool that will inspect the pods in a namespace and generate
   a recommended policy and RBAC set. Download the latest version from
   `https://github.com/sysdiglabs/kube-psp-advisor/releases`:

```
./kubectl-advise-psp inspect   --namespace=ingress-nginx
apiVersion: policy/v1beta1
kind: PodSecurityPolicy
metadata:
  creationTimestamp: null
  name: pod-security-policy-ingress-nginx-20200611232031
spec:
  defaultAddCapabilities:
  - NET_BIND_SERVICE
  fsGroup:
    rule: RunAsAny
  hostPorts:
  - max: 80
    min: 80
  - max: 443
    min: 443
  requiredDropCapabilities:
  - ALL
  runAsUser:
    ranges:
    - max: 101
      min: 101
    rule: MustRunAs
  seLinux:
    rule: RunAsAny
  supplementalGroups:
    rule: RunAsAny
  volumes:
  - secret
```

Compare this policy to the one provided by the NGINX Ingress project that was examined earlier in the chapter; you'll see that it's more restrictive on the ports and user, but less restrictive on the group. The `Deployment` declared the user but not the group, so `kube-psp-advisor` didn't know to restrict it. Unlike `audit2rbac`, `kube-psp-advisor` isn't scanning a log to see what is denied; it is proactively inspecting pod definitions to create policies. If a pod doesn't declare that it needs to run as root but just starts a container that runs as root, then `kube-psp-advisor` won't generate a proper policy.

8. Create a policy file from `kube-psp-advisor` called `psp-ingress.yaml`:

```
$ ./kubectl-advise-psp inspect   --namespace=ingress-nginx
> psp-ingress.yaml
```

9. Deploy the PSP using `kubectl`:

```
$ kubectl create -f ./psp-ingress.yaml -n ingress-nginx
```

10. Next, create RBAC bindings for the `nginx-ingress-serviceaccount` `ServiceAccount` (as referenced in the Deployment) to have access to this policy:

```
apiVersion: rbac.authorization.k8s.io/v1
kind: Role
metadata:
  name: nginx-ingress-psp
  namespace: ingress-nginx
rules:
- apiGroups:
  - policy
  resourceNames:
  - pod-security-policy-ingress-nginx-20200611232826
  resources:
  - podsecuritypolicies
  verbs:
  - use

---
apiVersion: rbac.authorization.k8s.io/v1
kind: RoleBinding
```

```
metadata:
  name: nginx-ingress-psp
  namespace: ingress-nginx
roleRef:
  apiGroup: rbac.authorization.k8s.io
  kind: Role
  name: nginx-ingress-psp
subjects:
- kind: ServiceAccount
  name: nginx-ingress-serviceaccount
  namespace: ingress-nginx
```

11. Once the RBAC objects are created, the Deployment needs to be updated to force Kubernetes to attempt to recreate the pods since the API server will stop trying after a certain point:

```
$ kubectl scale deployment.v1.apps/nginx-ingress-
controller --replicas=0 -n ingress-nginx
deployment.apps/nginx-ingress-controller scaled
$ kubectl scale deployment.v1.apps/nginx-ingress-
controller --replicas=1 -n ingress-nginx
deployment.apps/nginx-ingress-controller scaled
$ kubectl get pods -n ingress-nginx
NAME                                         READY
STATUS    RESTARTS    AGE
nginx-ingress-controller-7d6bf88c86-h4449    0/1
Running    0            21s
```

If you check the annotations on the pod, the `PodSecurityPolicy` annotation will be there and OpenUnison is accessible again.

> **Note**
> A side effect of using RBAC to control PSP authorization is that an admin in a namespace is able to create `ServiceAccount` objects that can run privileged containers. Stopping this capability while still allowing a namespace admin to create RBAC policies in their namespace will be discussed in the next chapter.

Congratulations, you have successfully implemented PSPs on your cluster! Try running the breakout code we ran earlier in this chapter and you'll see that it won't work. The Pod won't even start! Seeing that the NGINX Ingress controller wouldn't start and debugging it gave you the tools to understand how to work through issues after enabling policy enforcement.

Alternatives to PSPs

If not PSPs, then what? That really depends on a cluster's use case. There have been attempts to implement the full PodSecurityPolicy enforcement specification in OPA, which will be discussed in more detail in the next chapter. Several other projects have attempted to implement PSPs, if not the exact spec as the PodSecurityPolicy object. Given how fluid the space is, this chapter isn't going to enumerate all of the projects that are attempting to do this.

In May 2020, the authentication special interest group (sig-auth) published the *pod security standards* document to make it easier for different implementations of security policies to standardize on vocabulary and nomenclature. The standards were published on the Kubernetes website (https://kubernetes.io/docs/concepts/security/pod-security-standards/).

Be wary of implementing this logic on your own in your own admission controller as a validating webhook. Just as with any security implementation, great care needs to be taken to not only validate the expected outcome but also to make sure that unexpected scenarios are handled in an expected way. For instance, what happens if a Deployment is used to create a Pod versus creating a Pod directly? What happens when someone tries to inject invalid data into the definition? Or if someone tries to create a side car or an init container? When choosing an approach, it's important to ensure that any implementation has a thorough testing environment.

Summary

In this chapter, we began by exploring the importance of protecting nodes, the differences between containers and VMs from a security standpoint, and how easy it is to exploit a cluster when nodes aren't protected. We also looked at secure container design, and finally, we implemented and debugged a PSP implementation.

Locking down the nodes of your cluster provides one less vector for attackers. Encapsulating the policy makes it easier to explain to your developers how to design their containers and makes it easier to build secure solutions.

So far, all of our security has been built on Kubernetes' standard technologies and is nearly universal across Kubernetes distributions. In the next chapter, we'll work on applying policies that are beyond the scope of Kubernetes using dynamic admission controllers and the OPA.

Questions

1. True or false – containers are "lightweight VMs."

    A. True

    B. False

2. Can a container access resources from its host?

    A. No, it's isolated.

    B. If marked as privileged, yes.

    C. Only if explicitly granted by a policy.

    D. Sometimes.

3. How could an attacker gain access to a cluster through a container?

    A. A bug in the container's application can lead to a remote code execution, which can be used to break out of a vulnerable container and then used to get the kubelet's credentials.

    B. Compromised credentials with the ability to create a container in one namespace can be used to create a container that mounts the node's filesystem to get the kubelet's credentials.

    C. Both of the above.

4. How does the `PodSecurityPolicy` admission controller determine which policy to apply to a pod?

    A. By reading an annotation on the pod's definition

    B. By comparing the pod's requested capabilities and the policies authorized via the union of the pod's creator and its own `ServiceAccount`

    C. By comparing the Pod's requested capabilities and the policies authorized for its own `ServiceAccount`

    D. By comparing the pod's requested capabilities and the policies authorized for the pod's creator

5. What mechanism enforces PSPs?

    A. An admission controller that inspects all pods on creation and update

    B. The `PodSecurityPolicy` API

    C. The OPA

    D. Gatekeeper

6. True or false – the `PodSecurityPolicy` API will be removed quickly.

    A. True

    B. False

7. True or false – containers should generally run as root.

    A. True

    B. False

11
Extending Security Using Open Policy Agent

So far, we have covered Kubernetes' built in authentication and authorization capabilities, which help to secure a cluster. While this will cover most use cases, it doesn't cover all of them. Several security best practices that Kubernetes can't handle are pre-authorizing container registries and ensuring that resource requests are on all **Pod** objects.

These tasks are left to outside systems and are called dynamic admission controllers. The **Open Policy Agent** (**OPA**), and its Kubernetes native sub-project, GateKeeper, are one of the most popular ways to handle these use cases. This chapter will detail the deployment of OPA and GateKeeper, how it's architected, and how to develop policies.

In this chapter, we will cover the following topics:

- Introduction to validating webhooks
- What is OPA and how does it work?
- Using Rego to write policies

- Enforcing memory constraints
- Enforcing Pod security policies using OPA

Technical requirements

To complete the hands-on exercises in this chapter, you will require an Ubuntu 18.04 server, running a KinD cluster with the configuration from *Chapter 8*, *RBAC Policies and Auditing*.

You can access the code for this chapter at the following GitHub repository: `https://github.com/PacktPublishing/Kubernetes-and-Docker-The-Complete-Guide/tree/master/chapter11`.

Introduction to dynamic admission controllers

There are two ways to extend Kubernetes:

- Build a custom resource definition so that you can define your own objects and APIs.

- Implement a webhook that listens for requests from the API server and responds with the necessary information. You may recall that in *Chapter 7*, *Integrating Authentication into Your Cluster*, we explained that a custom webhook was used to validate tokens.

Starting in Kubernetes 1.9, a webhook can be defined as a dynamic admission controller, and in 1.16, the dynamic admission controller API became **Generally Available** (**GA**).

The protocol is very straightforward. Once a dynamic admission controller is registered for a specific object type, the webhook is called with an HTTP post every time an object of that type is created or edited. The webhook is then expected to return JSON that represents whether it is allowed or not.

> **Important note**
>
> As of 1.16, `admission.k8s.io/v1` is at GA. All examples will use the GA version of the API.

The request submitted to the webhook is made up of several sections:

- **Object Identifiers**: The `resource` and `subResource` attributes identify the object, API, and group. If the version of the object is being upgraded, then `requestKind`, `requestResource`, and `requestSubResource` are specified. Additionally, `namespace` and `operation` are provided to know where the object is and whether it is a `CREATE`, `UPDATE`, `DELETE`, or `CONNECT` operation.

- **Submitter Identifiers**: The `userInfo` object identifies the user and groups of the submitter. The submitter and the user who created the original request are not always the same. For instance, if a user creates a `Deployment`, then the `userInfo` object won't be for the user who created the original `Deployment`; it will be for the `ReplicaSet` controller's service account because the `Deployment` creates a `ReplicaSet` that creates the `Pod`.

- **Object**: `object` represents the JSON of the object being submitted, where `oldObject` represents what is being replaced if this is an update. Finally, `options` specifies additional options for the request.

The response from the webhook will simply have two attributes, the original `uid` from the request, and `allowed`, which can be **true** or **false**.

The `userInfo` object can create complications quickly. Since Kubernetes often uses multiple layers of controllers to create objects, it can be difficult to track usage creation based on a user who interacts with the API server. It's much better to authorize based on objects in Kubernetes, such as namespace labels or other objects.

A common use case is to allow developers to have a "sandbox" that they are administrators in, but that has very limited capacity. Instead of trying to validate the fact that a particular user doesn't try to request too much memory, annotate a personal namespace with a limit so that the admission controller has something concrete to reference regardless of whether the user submits a `Pod` or a `Deployment`. This way, the policy will check the `annotation` on the `namespace` instead of the individual user. To ensure that only the user who owns the namespace is able to create something in it, use RBAC to limit access.

One final point on generic validating webhooks: there is no way to specify a key or password. It's an anonymous request. While in theory, a validating webhook could be used to implement updates, it is not recommended.

Now that we've covered how Kubernetes implements dynamic access controllers, we'll look at one of the most popular options in OPA.

What is OPA and how does it work?

OPA is a lightweight authorization engine that fits well in Kubernetes. It didn't get its start in Kubernetes, but it's certainly found a home there. There's no requirement to build dynamic admission controllers in OPA, but it's very good at it and there are extensive resources and existing policies that can be used to start your policy library.

This section provides a high-level overview of OPA and its components with the rest of the chapter getting into the details of an OPA implementation in Kubernetes.

OPA architecture

OPA is comprised of three components – the HTTP listener, the policy engine, and the database:

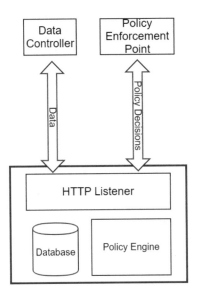

Figure 11.1 – OPA architecture

The database used by OPA is in memory and ephemeral. It doesn't persist information used to make policy decisions. On the one hand, this makes OPA very scalable since it is essentially an authorization microservice. On the other hand, this means that every instance of OPA must be maintained on its own and must be kept in sync with authoritative data:

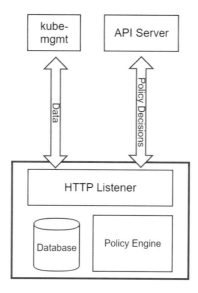

Figure 11.2 – OPA in Kubernetes

When used in Kubernetes, OPA populates its database using a side car, called *kube-mgmt*, which sets up watches on the objects you want to import into OPA. As objects are created, deleted, or changed, *kube-mgmt* updates the data in its OPA instance. This means that OPA is "eventually consistent" with the API server, but it won't necessarily be a real-time representation of the objects in the API server. Since the entire etcd database is essentially being replicated over and over again, great care needs to be taken in order to refrain from replicating sensitive data, such as `Secrets`, in the OPA database.

Rego, the OPA policy language

We'll cover the details of Rego in the next section in detail. The main point to mention here is that Rego is a policy evaluation language, not a generic programming language. This can be difficult for developers who are used to languages such as Golang, Java, or JavaScript, which support complex logic such as iterators and loops. Rego is designed to evaluate policy and is streamlined as such. For instance, if you wanted to write code in Java to check that all the container images in a `Pod` starting with one of a list of registries, it would look something like the following:

```java
public boolean validRegistries(List<Container>
containers,List<String> allowedRegistries) {
   for (Container c : containers) {
       boolean imagesFromApprovedRegistries = false;
      for (String allowedRegistry : allowedRegistries) {
```

```
        imagesFromApprovedRegistries =
imagesFromApprovedRegistries   || c.getImage().
startsWith(allowedRegistry);
    }
    if (! imagesFromApprovedRegistries) {
      return false;
    }
  }
  return true;
}
```

This code iterates over every container and every allowed registry to make sure that all of the images conform to the correct policy. The same code in Rego is much smaller:

```
invalidRegistry {
  ok_images = [image | startswith(input_images[j],input.
parameters.registries[_]) ; image = input_images[j] ]
  count(ok_images) != count(input_images)
}
```

The preceding rule will evaluate to `true` if any of the images on the containers come from unauthorized registries. We'll cover the details as to how this code works later in the chapter. The key to understanding why this code is so much more compact is that much of the boilerplate of loops and tests are inferred in Rego. The first line generates a list of conforming images, and the second line makes sure that the number of conforming images matches the number of total images. If they don't match, then one or more of the images must come from invalid registries. The ability to write compact policy code is what makes Rego so well suited for admission controllers.

GateKeeper

Thus far, everything discussed has been generic to OPA. It was mentioned in the beginning of the chapter that OPA didn't get its start in Kubernetes. Early implementations had a sidecar that kept the OPA database in sync with the API server, but you had to manually create policies as `ConfigMap` objects and manually generate responses for webhooks. In 2018, Microsoft debuted GateKeeper, `https://github.com/open-policy-agent/gatekeeper`, to provide a Kubernetes-native experience.

In addition to moving from `ConfigMap` objects to proper custom resources, GateKeeper adds an audit function that lets you test policies against existing objects. If an object violates a policy, then a violation entry is created to track it. This way, you can get a snapshot of the existing policy violations in your cluster or know whether something was missed during GateKeeper downtime due to an upgrade.

A major difference between GateKeeper and generic OPA is that in GateKeeper, OPA's functionality is not exposed via an API anyone can call. OPA is embedded, with GateKeeper calling OPA directly to execute policies and keep the database up to date. Decisions can only be made based on data in Kubernetes or by pulling data at evaluation time.

Deploying GateKeeper

The examples that will be used will assume the use of GateKeeper instead of a generic OPA deployment. Based on the directions from the GateKeeper project, use the following command:

```
$ kubectl apply -f https://raw.githubusercontent.com/open-
  policy-agent/gatekeeper/master/deploy/gatekeeper.yaml
```

This launches the GateKeeper namespace `Pods`, and creates the validating webhook. Once deployed, move on to the next section. We'll cover the details of using GateKeeper throughout the rest of this chapter.

Automated testing framework

OPA has a built-in automated testing framework for your policies. This is one of the most valuable aspects of OPA. Being able to test policies consistently before deployment can save you hours of debugging time. When writing policies, have a file with the same name as your policies file, but with `_test` in the name. For instance, to have test cases associated with `mypolicies.rego`, have the test cases in `mypolicies_test.rego` in the same directory. Running `opa test` will then run your test cases. We'll show how to use this to debug your code in the next section.

Having covered the basics of OPA and how it is constructed, the next step is to learn how to use Rego to write policies.

Using Rego to write policies

Rego is a language specifically designed for policy writing. It is different to most languages you have likely written code in. Typical authorization code will look something like the following:

```
//assume failure
boolean allowed = false;
//on certain conditions allow access
if (someCondition) {
  allowed = true;
}
//are we authorized?
if (allowed) {
  doSomething();
}
```

Authorization code will generally default to unauthorized, with a specific condition having to happen in order to allow the final action to be authorized. Rego takes a different approach. Rego is generally written to authorize everything unless a specific set of conditions happens.

Another major difference between Rego and more general programming languages is that there are no explicit "if/then/else" control statements. When a line of Rego is going to make a decision, the code is interpreted as "if this line is false, stop execution." For instance, the following code in Rego says "if the image starts with myregistry.lan/, then stop execution of the policy and pass this check, otherwise generate an error message":

```
not startsWith(image,"myregistry.lan/")
msg := sprintf("image '%v' comes from untrusted registry",
[image])
```

The same code in Java might look as follows:

```
if (! image.startsWith("myregistry.lan/")) {
    throw new Exception("image " + image + " comes from
untrusted registry");
}
```

This difference between inferred control statements and explicit control statements is often the steepest part of the learning curve when learning Rego. Where this can produce a steeper learning curve than other languages, Rego more than makes up for it by making it easy to test and build policies in an automated and manageable way.

OPA can be used to automate the testing of policies. This is incredibly important when writing code that the security of your cluster relies upon. Automating your testing will help speed your development and will increase your security by catching any bugs introduced into previously working code by means of new working code. Next, let's work through the life cycle of writing an OPA policy, testing it, and deploying it to our cluster.

Developing an OPA policy

A common example of using OPA is to limit which registries a Pod can come from. This is a common security measure in clusters to help restrict which Pods can run on a cluster. For instance, we've mentioned Bitcoin miners a few times. If the cluster won't accept Pods except from your own, internal registry, then that's one more step that needs to be taken for a bad actor to abuse your cluster. First, let's write our policy, taken from the OPA documentation website (https://www.openpolicyagent.org/docs/latest/kubernetes-introduction/):

```
package k8sallowedregistries
invalidRegistry {
  input_images[image]
  not startswith(image, "quay.io/")
}
input_images[image] {
  image := input.review.object.spec.containers[_].image
}
input_images[image] {
  image := input.review.object.spec.template.spec.
containers[_].image
}
```

The first line in this code declares the package our policy is in. Everything is stored in OPA in a package, both data and policies. Packages in OPA are like directories on a filesystem. When you place a policy in a package, everything is relative to that package. In this case, our policy is in the k8sallowedregistries package.

The next section defines a rule. This rule ultimately will be **undefined** if our Pod has an image that comes from quay.io. If the Pod doesn't have an image from quay.io, the rule will return true, signifying that the registry is invalid. GateKeeper will interpret this as a failure and return false to the API server when the Pod is evaluated during a dynamic admission review.

The next two rules look very similar. The first of the input_images rules says "evaluate the calling rule against every container in the object's spec.container", matching Pod objects directly submitted to the API server, and extract all the image values for each container. The second input_images rule states: "evaluate the calling rule against every container in the object's spec.template.spec.containers" to short circuit Deployment objects and StatefulSets.

Finally, we add the rule that GateKeeper requires to notify the API server of a failed evaluation:

```
violation[{"msg": msg, "details": {}}] {
  invalidRegistry
  msg := "Invalid registry"
}
```

This rule will return an empty msg if the registry is valid. It's a good idea to break up your code into code that makes policy decisions and code that responds with feedback. This makes it easier to test, which we'll do next.

Testing an OPA policy

Once we have written our policy, we want to set up an automated test. Just as with testing any other code, it's important that your test cases cover both expected and unexpected input. It's also important to test both positive and negative outcomes. It's not enough to corroborate that our policy allowed a correct registry; we also need to make sure it stops an invalid one. Here are eight test cases for our code:

```
package k8sallowedregistries
test_deployment_registry_allowed {
    not invalidRegistry with input as {"apiVersion"...
}
test_deployment_registry_not_allowed {
    invalidRegistry with input as {"apiVersion"...
}
test_pod_registry_allowed {
```

```
        not invalidRegistry with input as {"apiVersion"...
}
test_pod_registry_not_allowed {
        invalidRegistry with input as {"apiVersion"...
}
test_cronjob_registry_allowed {
        not invalidRegistry with input as {"apiVersion"...
}
test_cronjob_registry_not_allowed {
        invalidRegistry with input as {"apiVersion"...
}
test_error_message_not_allowed {
        control := {"msg":"Invalid registry","details":{}}
        result = violation with input as {"apiVersion":"admissi…
        result[_] == control
}
test_error_message_allowed {
        result = violation with input as {"apiVersion":"admissi…
        control := {"msg":"Invalid registry","details":{}}
}
```

There are eight tests in total; two tests to make sure that the proper error message is returned when there's an issue, and six tests covering two use cases for three input types. We're testing simple Pod definitions, Deployment, and CronJob. To validate success or failure as expected, we have included definitions that have image attributes that include docker.io and quay.io for each input type. The code is abbreviated for print, but can be downloaded from https://github.com/PacktPublishing/Kubernetes-and-Docker-The-Complete-Guide/tree/master/chapter11/simple-opa-policy/rego/.

To run the tests, first install the OPA command-line executable as per the OPA website – `https://www.openpolicyagent.org/docs/latest/#running-opa`. Once downloaded, go to the `simple-opa-policy/rego` directory and run the tests:

```
$ opa test .
data.kubernetes.admission.test_cronjob_registry_not_allowed:
FAIL (248ns)
--------------------------------------------------------------
PASS: 7/8
FAIL: 1/8
```

Seven of the tests passed, but `test_cronjob_registry_not_allowed` failed. The `CronJob` submitted as `input` should not be allowed because its `image` uses *docker.io*. The reason it snuck through was because `CronJob` objects follow a different pattern to `Pod` and `Deployment`, so our two `input_image` rules won't load any of the container objects from the `CronJob`. The good news is that when the `CronJob` ultimately submits the `Pod`, GateKeeper will not validate it, thereby preventing it from running. The bad news is that no one will know this until the `Pod` was supposed to be run. Making sure we pick up `CronJob` objects in addition to our other objects with containers in them will make it much easier to debug because the `CronJob` won't be accepted.

To get all tests passing, add a new `input_container` rule to the `limitregistries.rego` file in the Github repo that will match the container used by a `CronJob`:

```
input_images [image] {
   image := input.review.object.spec.jobTemplate.spec.template.
spec.containers[_].image
}
```

Now, running the tests will show that everything passes:

```
$ opa test .
PASS: 8/8
```

With a policy that has been tested, the next step is to integrate the policy into GateKeeper.

Deploying policies to GateKeeper

The policies we've created need to be deployed to GateKeeper, which provides Kubernetes custom resources that policies need to be loaded into. The first custom resource is `ConstraintTemplate`, which is where the Rego code for our policy is stored. This object lets us specify parameters in relation to our policy enforcement, and we'll cover this next. To keep things simple, create a template with no parameters:

```
apiVersion: templates.gatekeeper.sh/v1beta1
kind: ConstraintTemplate
metadata:
  name: k8sallowedregistries
spec:
  crd:
    spec:
      names:
        kind: K8sAllowedRegistries
        listKind: K8sAllowedRegistriesList
        plural: k8sallowedregistries
        singular: k8sallowedregistries
      validation: {}
  targets:
    - target: admission.k8s.gatekeeper.sh
      rego: |
        package k8sallowedregistries
          .
          .
          .
```

The entire source code for this template is available at `https://raw.githubusercontent.com/PacktPublishing/Kubernetes-and-Docker-The-Complete-Guide/master/chapter11/simple-opa-policy/yaml/gatekeeper-policy-template.yaml`.

Once created, the next step is to apply the policy by creating a constraint based on the template. Constraints are objects in Kubernetes based on the configuration of `ConstraintTemplate`. Notice that our template defines a custom resource definition. This gets added to the `constraints.gatekeeper.sh` API group. If you look at the list of CRDs on your cluster, you'll see `k8sallowedregistries` listed:

```
PS C:\Users\mlb> kubectl get crds
NAME                                                    CREATED AT
bgpconfigurations.crd.projectcalico.org                 2020-07-04T17:14:08Z
bgppeers.crd.projectcalico.org                          2020-07-04T17:14:08Z
blockaffinities.crd.projectcalico.org                   2020-07-04T17:14:06Z
clusterinformations.crd.projectcalico.org               2020-07-04T17:14:08Z
configs.config.gatekeeper.sh                            2020-07-04T17:45:26Z
constraintpodstatuses.status.gatekeeper.sh              2020-07-04T17:45:26Z
constrainttemplatepodstatuses.status.gatekeeper.sh      2020-07-04T17:45:26Z
constrainttemplates.templates.gatekeeper.sh             2020-07-04T17:45:26Z
felixconfigurations.crd.projectcalico.org               2020-07-04T17:14:06Z
globalnetworkpolicies.crd.projectcalico.org             2020-07-04T17:14:08Z
globalnetworksets.crd.projectcalico.org                 2020-07-04T17:14:08Z
hostendpoints.crd.projectcalico.org                     2020-07-04T17:14:08Z
ipamblocks.crd.projectcalico.org                        2020-07-04T17:14:06Z
ipamconfigs.crd.projectcalico.org                       2020-07-04T17:14:07Z
ipamhandles.crd.projectcalico.org                       2020-07-04T17:14:06Z
                                                        2020-07-04T17:14:08Z
k8sallowedregistries.constraints.gatekeeper.sh          2020-07-06T11:09:46Z
                                                        2020-07-04T17:14:08Z
networksets.crd.projectcalico.org                       2020-07-04T17:14:08Z
oidc-sessions.openunison.tremolo.io                     2020-07-04T17:20:20Z
openunisons.openunison.tremolo.io                       2020-07-04T17:20:20Z
users.openunison.tremolo.io                             2020-07-04T17:20:20Z
PS C:\Users\mlb>
```

Figure 11.3 – CRD created by ConstraintTemplate

Creating the constraint means creating an instance of the object defined in the template.

To keep from causing too much havoc in our cluster, we're going to restrict this policy to the `openunison` namespace:

```
apiVersion: constraints.gatekeeper.sh/v1beta1
kind: K8sAllowedRegistries
metadata:
  name: restrict-openunison-registries
spec:
  match:
    kinds:
      - apiGroups: [""]
```

```
        kinds: ["Pod"]
    - apiGroups: ["apps"]
      kinds:
      - StatefulSet
      - Deployment
    - apiGroups: ["batch"]
      kinds:
      - CronJob
  namespaces: ["openunison"]
parameters: {}
```

The constraint limits the policy we wrote to just Deployment, CronJob, and Pod objects in the OpenUnison namespace. Once created, if we try to kill the openunison-operator Pod, it will fail to successfully be recreated by the replica set controller because the image comes from dockerhub.io, not quay.io:

```
PS C:\Users\mlb> kubectl get pods -n openunison
NAME                                         READY   STATUS      RESTARTS   AGE
check-certs-orchestra-1593914400-pd5f5       0/1     Completed   0          40h
check-certs-orchestra-1594000800-zxjxr       0/1     Completed   0          16h
openunison-operator-858d496-5p4dm            1/1     Running     0          7h
openunison-orchestra-57489869d4-f46rm        1/1     Running     0          2d
PS C:\Users\mlb> kubectl delete pod -l app=openunison-operator -n openunison
pod "openunison-operator-858d496-5p4dm" deleted
PS C:\Users\mlb> kubectl get pods -n openunison
NAME                                         READY   STATUS      RESTARTS   AGE
check-certs-orchestra-1593914400-pd5f5       0/1     Completed   0          40h
check-certs-orchestra-1594000800-zxjxr       0/1     Completed   0          16h
openunison-orchestra-57489869d4-f46rm        1/1     Running     0          2d
PS C:\Users\mlb> kubectl get events -n openunison
LAST SEEN   TYPE      REASON         OBJECT                                       MESSAGE
26s         Normal    Killing        pod/openunison-operator-858d496-5p4dm        Stopping container openunison-operator
8s          Warning   FailedCreate   replicaset/openunison-operator-858d496       Error creating: admission webhook "validat
ion.gatekeeper.sh" denied the request: [denied by restrict-openunison-registries] Invalid registry
PS C:\Users\mlb>
```

Figure 11.4 – Pod fails to create because of GateKeeper policy

Next, look at the policy object. You will see that there are several violations in the `status` section of the object:

```
totalViolations: 6
violations:
- enforcementAction: deny
  kind: CronJob
  message: Invalid registry
  name: check-certs-orchestra
  namespace: openunison
- enforcementAction: deny
  kind: Deployment
  message: Invalid registry
  name: openunison-operator
  namespace: openunison
- enforcementAction: deny
  kind: Deployment
  message: Invalid registry
  name: openunison-orchestra
  namespace: openunison
- enforcementAction: deny
  kind: Pod
  message: Invalid registry
  name: check-certs-orchestra-1593914400-pd5f5
  namespace: openunison
- enforcementAction: deny
  kind: Pod
  message: Invalid registry
  name: check-certs-orchestra-1594000800-zxjxr
  namespace: openunison
- enforcementAction: deny
  kind: Pod
  message: Invalid registry
  name: openunison-orchestra-57489869d4-f46rm
  namespace: openunison
```

Figure 11.5 – List of objects that violate the image registry policy

Having deployed your first GateKeeper policy, you may quickly notice it has a few issues. The first is that the registry is hardcoded. This means that we'd need to replicate our code for every change of registry. It's also not flexible for the namespace. All of Tremolo Security's images are stored in `docker.io/tremolosecurity`, so instead of limiting a specific registry server, we may want flexibility for each namespace and to allow multiple registries. Next, we'll update our policies to provide this flexibility.

Building dynamic policies

Our current registry policy is limiting. It is static and only supports a single registry. Both Rego and GateKeeper provide functionality to build a dynamic policy that can be reused in our cluster and configured based on individual namespace requirements. This gives us one code base to work from and debug instead of having to maintain repetitive code. The code we're going to use is in `https://github.com/packtpublishing/Kubernetes-and-Docker-The-Complete-Guide/blob/master/chapter11/parameter-opa-policy/`.

When inspecting `rego/limitregistries.rego`, the main difference between the code in `parameter-opa-policy` and `simple-opa-policy` comes down to the `invalidRegistry` rule:

```
invalidRegistry {
  ok_images = [image | startswith(input_images[i],input.
parameters.registries[_]) ; image = input_images[i] ]
  count(ok_images) != count(input_images)
}
```

The goal of the first line of the rule is to determine which images come from approved registries using a comprehension. Comprehensions provide a way to build out sets, arrays, and objects based on some logic. In this case, we want to only add images to the `ok_images` array that start with any of the allowed registries from `input.parameters.registries`.

To read a comprehension, start with the type of brace. Ours starts with a square bracket, so the result will be an array. Objects and sets can also be generated. The word between the open bracket and the pipe character, (|), is called the head and this is the variable that will be added to our array if the right conditions are met. Everything to the right of the pipe character, (|), is a set of rules used to determine what `image` should be and if it should have a value at all. If any of the statements in the rule resolve to undefined or false, the execution exits for that iteration.

The first rule of our comprehension is where most of the work is done. The `startswith` function is used to determine whether each of our images starts with the correct registry name. Instead of passing two strings to the function, we instead pass arrays. The first array has a variable we haven't declared yet, `i`, and the other uses an underscore (`_`) where the index would usually be. The `i` is interpreted by Rego as "do this for each value in the array, incrementing by 1 and let it be referenced throughout the comprehension." The underscore is shorthand in Rego for "do this for all values." Since we specified two arrays, every combination of the two arrays will be used as input to the `startswith` function. That means that if there are two containers and three potential pre-approved registries, then `startswith` will be called six times. When any of the combinations return **true** from `startswith`, the next rule is executed. That sets the `image` variable to `input_image` with index i, which then means that image is added to `ok_images`. The same code in Java would look something like the following:

```java
ArrayList<String> okImages = new ArrayList<String>();
for (int i=0;i<inputImages.length;i++) {
  for (int j=0;j<registries.length;j++) {
    if (inputImages[i].startsWith(registries[j])) {
      okImages.add(inputImages[i]);
    }
  }
}
```

One line of Rego eliminated seven lines of mostly boilerplate code.

The second line of the rule compares the number of entries in the `ok_images` array with the number of known container images. If they are equal, we know that every container contains a valid image.

With our updated Rego rules for supporting multiple registries, the next step is to deploy a new policy template (if you haven't done so already, delete the old `k8sallowedregistries` `ConstraintTemplate` and `restrict-openunison-registries` `K8sAllowedRegistries`). Here's our updated `ConstraintTemplate`:

```yaml
apiVersion: templates.gatekeeper.sh/v1beta1
kind: ConstraintTemplate
metadata:
  name: k8sallowedregistries
spec:
  crd:
```

```
    spec:
      names:
        kind: K8sAllowedRegistries
        listKind: K8sAllowedRegistriesList
        plural: k8sallowedregistries
        singular: k8sallowedregistries
      validation:
        openAPIV3Schema:
          properties:
            registries:
              type: array
              items: string
    targets:
      - target: admission.k8s.gatekeeper.sh
        rego: |
          package k8sallowedregistries
          .
          .
          .
```

Beyond including our new rules, the highlighted section shows that we added a schema to our template. This will allow for the template to be reused with specific parameters. This schema goes into the `CustomResourceDefenition` that will be created and is used to validate input for the `K8sAllowedRegistries` objects we'll create in order to enforce our pre-authorized registry lists.

Finally, let's create our policy for the `openunison` namespace. Since the only containers that are running in this namespace should come from Tremolo Security's `dockerhub.io` registry, we'll limit all Pods to `docker.io/tremolosecurity/` using the following policy:

```
apiVersion: constraints.gatekeeper.sh/v1beta1
kind: K8sAllowedRegistries
metadata:
  name: restrict-openunison-registries
spec:
  match:
```

```
        kinds:
          - apiGroups: [""]
            kinds: ["Pod"]
          - apiGroups: ["apps"]
            kinds:
            - StatefulSet
            - Deployment
          - apiGroups: ["batch"]
            kinds:
            - CronJob
        namespaces: ["openunison"]
      parameters:
        registries: ["docker.io/tremolosecurity/"]
```

Unlike our previous version, this policy specifies which registries are valid instead of embedding the policy data directly into our Rego. With our policies in place, let's try to run the busybox container in the openunison namespace to get a shell:

```
Windows PowerShell                                              —    □    ×

yaml>kubectl run --generator=run-pod/v1 tmp-shell --rm -i --tty --image busybox -n openunison -- /bin/bash
Flag --generator has been deprecated, has no effect and will be removed in the future.
Error from server ([denied by restrict-openunison-registries] Invalid registry): admission webhook "validatio
n.gatekeeper.sh" denied the request: [denied by restrict-openunison-registries] Invalid registry
yaml>
```

Figure 11.6 – Failed busybox shell

Using this generic policy template, we can restrict which registries the namespaces are able to pull from. As an example, in a multi-tenant environment, you may want to restrict all Pods to the owner's own registry. If a namespace is being used for a commercial product, you can stipulate that only that vendor's containers can run in it. Before moving on to other use cases, it's important to understand how to debug your code and handle Rego's quirks.

Debugging Rego

Debugging Rego can be challenging. Unlike more generic programming languages such as Java or Go, there's no way to step through code in a debugger. Take the example of the generic policy we just wrote for checking registries. All the work was done in a single line of code. Stepping through it wouldn't do much good.

To make Rego easier to debug, the OPA project provides a trace of all failed tests when verbose output is set on the command line. This is another great reason to use OPA's built-in testing tools.

To make better use of this trace, Rego has a function called `trace` that accepts a string. Combining this function with `sprintf` lets you more easily track where your code is not working as expected. In the `chapter11/paramter-opa-policy-fail/rego` directory, there's a test that will fail. There is also an `invalidRegistry` rule with multiple trace options added:

```
invalidRegistry {
  trace(sprintf("input_images : %v", [input_images]))
  ok_images = [image |
    trace(sprintf("image %v", [input_images[j]]))
    startswith(input_images[j], input.parameters.registries[_])
;
    image = input_images[j]
  ]
  trace(sprintf("ok_images %v", [ok_images]))
  trace(sprintf("ok_images size %v / input_images size
%v", [count(ok_images), count(input_images)]))
  count(ok_images) != count(input_images)
}
```

When the test is run, OPA will output a detailed trace of every comparison and code path. Wherever it encounters the `trace` function, a "note" is added to the trace. This is the equivalent of adding print statements in your code to debug. The output of the OPA trace is very verbose, and far too much text to include in print. Running `opa test. -v` in this directory will give you the full trace you can use to debug your code.

Using existing policies

Before moving into more advanced use cases for OPA and GateKeeper, it's important to understand the implications of how OPA is built and used. If you inspect the code we worked through in the previous section, you might notice that we aren't checking for `initContainers`. We're only looking for the primary containers. `initContainers` are special containers that are run before the containers listed in a `Pod` are expected to end. They're often used to prepare the filesystem of a volume mount and for other "initial" tasks that should be performed before the containers of a `Pod` have run. If a bad actor tried to launch a `Pod` with an `initContainers` that pulls in a Bitcoin miner (or worse), our policy wouldn't stop it.

It's important to be very detailed in the design and implementation of policies. One of the ways to make sure you're not missing something when building policies is to use policies that already exist and have been tested. The GateKeeper project maintains several libraries of pre-tested policies and how to use them in its GitHub repo at `https://github.com/open-policy-agent/gatekeeper/tree/master/library`. Before attempting to build one of your own policies, see whether one already exists there first.

This section provided an overview of Rego and how it works in policy evaluation. It didn't cover everything, but should give you a good point of reference for working with Rego's documentation. Next, we'll learn how to build policies that rely on data from outside our request, such as other objects in our cluster.

Enforcing memory constraints

So far in this chapter, we've built policies that are self-contained. When checking whether an image is coming from a pre-authorized registry, the only data we needed was from the policy and the containers. This is often not enough information to make a policy decision. In this section, we'll work on building a policy that relies on other objects in your cluster to make policy decisions.

Before diving into the implementation, let's talk about the use case. It's a good idea to include at least memory requirements on any `Pod` submitted to the API server. There are certain namespaces though where this doesn't make as much sense. For instance, many of the containers in the `kube-system` namespace don't have CPU and memory resource requests.

There are multiple ways we could handle this. One way is to deploy a constraint template and apply it to every namespace we want to enforce memory resource requests on. This can lead to repetitive objects or require us to explicitly update policies to apply them to certain namespaces. Another method is to add a label to the namespace that lets OPA know it needs all `Pod` objects to have memory resource requests. Since Kubernetes already has `ResourceQuota` objects for managing memory, we can also establish whether a namespace has a `ResourceQuota` and, if it does, then we know there should be memory requests.

For our next example, we'll write a policy that says any `Pod` created in a namespace that has a `ResourceQuota` must have a memory resource request. The policy itself should be pretty simple. The pseudocode will look something like this:

```
if (hasResourceQuota(input.review.object.metdata.namespace) &&
containers.resource.requests.memory == null) {
  generate error;
}
```

The hard part here is understanding if the namespace has a `ResourceQuota`. Kubernetes has an API, which you could query, but that would mean either embedding a secret into the policy so it can talk to the API server or allowing anonymous access. Neither of those options are a good idea. Another issue with querying the API server is that it's difficult to automate testing since you are now reliant on an API server being available wherever you run your tests.

We discussed earlier that OPA can replicate data from the API server in its own database. GateKeeper uses this functionality to create a "cache" of objects that can be tested against. Once this cache is populated, we can replicate it locally to provide test data for our policy testing.

Enabling the GateKeeper cache

The GateKeeper cache is enabled by creating a `Config` object in the `gatekeeper-system` namespace. Add this configuration to your cluster:

```
apiVersion: config.gatekeeper.sh/v1alpha1
kind: Config
metadata:
  name: config
  namespace: "gatekeeper-system"
spec:
  sync:
    syncOnly:
      - group: ""
        version: "v1"
        kind: "Namespace"
      - group: ""
        version: "v1"
        kind: "ResourceQuota"
```

This will begin replicating `Namespace` and `ResourceQuota` objects in GateKeeper's internal OPA database. Let's create a `Namespace` with a `ResourceQuota` and one without a `ResourceQuota`:

```
apiVersion: v1
kind: Namespace
metadata:
  name: ns-with-no-quota
spec: {}
---
apiVersion: v1
kind: Namespace
metadata:
  name: ns-with-quota
spec: {}
---
kind: ResourceQuota
apiVersion: v1
metadata:
  name: memory-quota
  namespace: ns-with-quota
spec:
  hard:
    requests.memory: 1G
    limits.memory: 1G
```

After a moment, the data should be in the OPA database and ready to query.

> **Important note**
> The GateKeeper service account has read access to everything in your cluster with its default installation. This includes secret objects. Be careful what you replicate in GateKeeper's cache as there are no security controls from inside a Rego policy. Your policy could very easily log secret object data if you are not careful. Also, make sure to control who has access to the `gatekeeper-system` namespace. Anyone who gets hold of the service account's token can use it to read any data in your cluster.

Mocking up test data

In order to automate testing of our policy, we need to create test data. In the previous examples, we used data injected into the `input` variable. Cache data is stored in the `data` variable. Specifically, in order to access our resource quota, we need to access `data.inventory.namespace["ns-with-quota"]["v1"]["ResourceQuota"]["memory-quota"]`. This is the standard way for you to query data from Rego in GateKeeper. Just as we did with input, we can inject a mocked-up version of this data by creating a data object. Here's what our JSON will look like:

```
{
    "inventory": {
        "namespace":{
            "ns-with-no-quota" : {},
            "ns-with-quota":{
                "v1":{
                    "ResourceQuota": {
                        "memory-quota":{
                            "kind": "ResourceQuota",
                            "apiVersion": "v1",
                            "metadata": {
                                "name": "memory-quota",
                                "namespace": "ns-with-
quota"
                            },
                            "spec": {
                                "hard": {
                                    "requests.memory": "1G",
                                    "limits.memory": "1G"
}}}}}}}}
```

When you look at `chapter11/enforce-memory-request/rego/enforcememory_test.rego`, you'll see the tests have `with input as {...}` with `data as {...}` with the preceding document as our control data. This lets us test our policies with data that would exist in GateKeeper without having to deploy our code in a cluster.

Building and deploying our policy

Just as before, we've written test cases prior to writing our policy. Next, we'll
examine our policy:

```
package k8senforcememoryrequests
violation[{"msg": msg, "details": {}}] {
   invalidMemoryRequests
   msg := "No memory requests specified"
}
invalidMemoryRequests {
    data.
      inventory
      .namespace
      [input.review.object.metadata.namespace]
      ["v1"]
      ["ResourceQuota"]
    containers := input.review.object.spec.containers

    ok_containers = [ok_container |
      containers[j].resources.requests.memory ;
      ok_container = containers[j]   ]

    count(containers) != count(ok_containers)
}
```

This code should look familiar. It follows a similar pattern as our earlier policies. The first
rule, violation, is the standard reporting rule for GateKeeper. The second rule is where
we test our Pod. The first line will fail and exit out if the namespace for the specified
Pod doesn't contain a ResourceQuota object. The next line loads all of the containers
of the Pod. After this, a composition is used to construct a list of containers that has
memory requests specified. Finally, the rule will only succeed if the number of compliant
containers doesn't match the total number of containers. If invalidMemoryRequests
succeeds, this means that one or more containers does not have memory requests
specified. This will force msg to be set and violation to inform the user of the issue.

To deploy, add `chapter11/enforce-memory-request/yaml/gatekeeper-policy-template.yaml` and `chapter11/enforce-memory-request/yaml/gatekeeper-policy.yaml` to your cluster. To test this, create a Pod without memory requests in both our `ns-with-quota` and `ns-with-no-quota` namespaces:

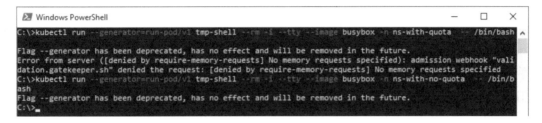

Figure 11.7 – Creating pods without memory requests

The first attempt to create a Pod in the `ns-with-quota` namespace fails because our `require-memory-requests` policy rejected it since `ns-with-quota` has a `ResourceQuota` in it. The second attempt succeeds because it is running in a namespace with no `ResourceQuota`.

Most of this chapter has been spent writing policies. The final use case for OPA will focus on using GateKeeper's prebuilt policies to replace Pod security policies.

Enforcing Pod Security Policies using OPA

In *Chapter 10, Creating Pod Security Policies*, we discussed the fact that the existing Pod security policy implementation for Kubernetes would never become "GA". One of the alternatives to using the Kubernetes implementation was to use OPA and GateKeeper to enforce the same policies, but in OPA instead of on the API server. This process works differently to the standard implemented by Kubernetes, but using it can keep your clusters more vendor-independent and less susceptible to the changes that will eventually arise with whatever comes next for Kubernetes' Pod security policies.

GateKeeper's policies are all published at `https://github.com/open-policy-agent/gatekeeper/tree/master/library/pod-security-policy`. They're built as a series of `ConstraintTemplate` objects and example constraints. This approach to Pod security policies makes for some specific differences in how policies are implemented.

The first major difference is that using GateKeeper, you have to declare everything in your Pod definition so that GateKeeper has something to audit against. This isn't necessary with Pod security policies because Kubernetes will mutate the Pod definition to conform to the policy. To illustrate this, look at the `openunison-operator`, `Deployment`, in the `openunison` namespace in our KinD cluster. No `runAsUser` is declared. Now look at the actual Pod definition and you'll see that `runAsUser` is set to `1`. GateKeeper version 3 isn't yet capable of supporting Pod mutation, so in order to ensure that `Deployment` or `Pod` has `runAsUser` set, a separate mutating webhook needs to set the `runAsUser` attribute accordingly.

The next major difference between the Kubernetes standard policy implementation and using GateKeeper is how a Pod is assigned a policy. The Kubernetes standard implementation uses a combination of RBAC, leveraging both the account information of the submitter and `serviceAccount` of the `Pod`, and the capabilities requested by the `Pod` to determine which policy to use. This can lead to some unexpected results when assigning policies. GateKeeper instead provides the same matching criteria as any other constraint implemented by GateKeeper, using namespaces and label selectors.

For example, to run a Pod using a privileged constraint, you may create the constraint with a specific `labelSelector`. Then, when the Pod is submitted, that label needs to be on the `Pod` so GateKeeper knows to apply it. This makes it much easier to explicitly apply policies to a `Pod`. It doesn't cover how to enforce the labeling of resources. You may not want someone to be able to label their own `Pod` as privileged.

Finally, GateKeeper's library of policies are broken up instead of being part of one object. In order to apply a policy that enforces an unprivileged container that runs in a certain user range, you need two separate policy constraint implementations and two separate constraints.

As of the time of writing, you couldn't replicate what we built in *Chapter 10*, *Creating Pod Security Policies*, without significant additional work. The goal of the GateKeeper project is to get to that point in the future. The more complete solution is still the standard implementation of Pod security policies in Kubernetes.

Summary

In this chapter, we explored how to use GateKeeper as a dynamic admission controller to provide additional authorization policies on top of Kubernetes' built-in RBAC capabilities. We looked at how GateKeeper and OPA are architected. Finally, we learned how to build, deploy, and test policies in Rego.

Extending Kubernetes' policies leads to a stronger security profile in your clusters and provides greater confidence in the integrity of the workloads running on your cluster. Using GateKeeper can also help catch previously missed policy violations through its application of continuous audits. Using these capabilities will provide a stronger foundation for your cluster.

This chapter focused on whether or not to launch a `Pod`. In the next chapter, we'll learn how to track what `Pods` are doing once active.

Questions

1. Are OPA and GateKeeper the same thing?

    A. Yes.

    B. NO.

2. How is Rego code stored in GateKeeper?

    A. It is stored as `ConfigMap` objects that are watched.

    B. Rego has to be mounted to the Pod.

    C. Rego needs to be stored as secret objects.

    D. Rego is saved as a `ConstraintTemplate`.

3. How do you test Rego policies?

    A. In production

    B. Using an automated framework built directly into OPA

    C. By first compiling to Web Assembly

4. In Rego, how do you write a `for` loop?

    A. You don't need to; Rego will identify iterative steps.

    B. By using the `for all` syntax.

    C. By initializing counters in a loop.

    D. There are no loops in Rego.

5. What is the best way to debug Rego policies?

   A. Use an IDE to attach to the GateKeeper container in a cluster.

   B. In production.

   C. Add trace functions to your code and run the `opa test` command with `-v` to see execution traces.

   D. Include `System.out` statements.

6. Constraints all need to be hardcoded.

   A. True.

   B. False.

7. GateKeeper can replace Pod security policies.

   A. True.

   B. False.

12
Auditing using Falco and EFK

Bad people do bad things.

Good people do bad things.

Accidents happen.

Each of the preceding statements has one thing in common: when any one of them occurs, you need to find out what happened.

Too often, auditing is considered only when we think of some form of attack. While we certainly require auditing to find "bad people", we also need to audit everyday standard system interactions.

Kubernetes includes logs for most of the important system events that you will need to audit, but it doesn't include everything. As we discussed in previous chapters, all API interactions will be logged by the system, which includes the majority of events you need to audit. However, there are tasks that users execute that will not go through the API server and may go undetected if you are relying on API logs for all of your auditing.

There are tools to address the gaps in the native logging functionality. Open source projects such as Falco will provide enhanced auditing for your pods, providing details for events that are logged by the API server.

Logs without a logging system are not very useful. Like many components in Kubernetes, there are many open source projects that provide a full logging system. One of the most popular systems is the EFK stack, which includes Elasticsearch, Fluentd, and Kibana.

All of these projects will be covered in detail throughout this chapter. You will deploy each of these components to gain hands-on experience and to reinforce the material covered in this chapter.

In this chapter, we will cover the following topics:

- Exploring auditing
- Introducing Falco
- Exploring Falco's configuration files
- Deploying Falco
- Falco kernel module

Technical requirements

To complete the exercises in this chapter, you will need to meet the following technical requirements:

- An Ubuntu 18.04 server with a minimum of 8 GB of RAM and at least 5 GB of free disk space for Docker volumes
- A KinD cluster installed using the instructions in *Chapter 4, Deploying Kubernetes using KinD*
- Helm3 binary (should also have been installed in *Chapter 4, Deploying Kubernetes using KinD*)

You can access the code for this chapter at the GitHub repository for the book, available at `https://github.com/PacktPublishing/Kubernetes-and-Docker-The-Complete-Guide`.

Exploring auditing

In most environments where you run Kubernetes clusters, you will need to have an auditing system in place. While Kubernetes has some auditing features, they are often too limited for an enterprise to rely on for a complete audit trail, and logs are often only stored on each host filesystem.

In order to correlate events, you are required to pull all the logs you want to search through on your local system, and manually look through logs or pull them into a spreadsheet and attempt to create some macros to search and tie information together.

Fortunately, there are many third-party logging systems available for Kubernetes. Optional pay systems such as Splunk and Datadog are popular solutions and open source systems including the EFK stack are commonly used and included with many Kubernetes distributions. All of these systems include some form of a log forwarder that allows you to centralize your Kubernetes logs so you can create alerts, custom queries, and dashboards.

Another limitation of native auditing is the limited scope of events, which are limited to API access. While this is important to audit, most enterprises will need to augment or customize the base set of auditing targets beyond simple API events. Extending the base auditing features can be a challenge and most companies will not have the expertise or time to create their own auditing add-ons.

One area of auditing that Kubernetes is missing concerns pod events. As we mentioned, the base auditing capabilities of Kubernetes focus on API access. Most tasks performed by users will trigger a call to the API server. Let's take an example of a user executing a shell on a pod to look at a file. The user would use `kubectl exec -it <pod name> bash` to spawn a bash shell on the pod in interactive mode. This actually sends a request to the API server, the main call of which to execute is as follows:

```
I0216 11:42:58.872949    13139 round_trippers.go:420] POST
https://0.0.0.0:32771/api/v1/namespaces/ingress-nginx/pods/
nginx-ingress-controller-7d6bf88c86-knbrx/exec?command=bash&con
tainer=nginx-ingress-controller&stdin=true&stdout=true&tty=true
```

Looking at the event, you can see that an `exec` command was sent to the `nginx-ingress-controller` pod to run the bash process.

There may be good reasons that someone is running a shell, for example, to look at an error log or to fix an issue quickly. But the issue here is that, once inside the running pod, any command that is executed does not access the Kubernetes API, and therefore, you will not receive any logged events for the actions executed in the pod. To most enterprises, this is a large hole in the auditing system since no end-to-end audit trail would exist if the action conducted in the container were malicious.

To audit all shell access to pods would lead to many false-positive leads, and in the event that a pod was restarted, you would lose any local audit files in the pod. Instead, you may ignore simple shell access, but you want to log an event if someone tries to execute certain tasks from the shell, such as modifying the `/etc/passwd` file.

So, you may ask, "*What is the solution?*" The answer is to use Falco.

Introducing Falco

Falco is an open source system from Sysdig that adds anomaly detection functionality for pods in Kubernetes clusters. Out of the box, Falco includes a base set of powerful, community-created rules that can monitor a number of potentially malicious events, including the following:

- When a user attempts to modify a file under `/etc`
- When a user spawns a shell on a pod
- When a user stores sensitive information in a secret
- When a pod attempts to make a call to the Kubernetes API server
- Any attempts to modify a system ClusterRole
- Or any other custom rule you create to meet your needs

When Falco is running on a Kubernetes cluster it watches events, and based on a set of rules, it logs events on the Falco pod that can be picked up by a system such as Fluentd, which would then forward the event to an external logging system.

In this chapter, we will explain the configuration of Falco using the technical requirements for our company scenario for FooWidgets. By the end of the chapter, you will know how to set up Falco on a Kubernetes cluster using custom configuration options. You will also understand the rules used by Falco and how to create rules when you need to audit an event that is not included in the base rules. Finally, you will forward events using Fluentd to Elasticsearch using Kibana to visualize the events generated by Falco.

Exploring Falco's configuration files

Before you install Falco, you need to understand the configuration options that are available, and that starts with the initial configuration file that will be used to configure how Falco creates events.

The Falco project includes a set of base configuration files that you can use for your initial auditing. It is highly likely that you will want to change the base configuration to fit your specific enterprise requirements. In this section, we will go over a Falco deployment and provide a basic understanding of the configuration files.

Falco is a powerful system that can be customized to fit almost any requirement you may have for security. Since it is so extensible, it's not possible to cover every detail of the configuration in a single chapter, but like many popular projects, there is an active GitHub community at `https://github.com/falcosecurity/falco` where you can post issues or join their Slack channel.

The Falco configuration files include a base configuration file and the rules files that contain the events that will be audited by the system. The base configuration file is a simple YAML file that contains `key:value` pairs for each configuration option, along with other YAML files that use `key:value` pairs, but they contain details and configurations for the audit events.

There are four base configuration files that you can use to configure your deployment, as follows:

- `falco.yaml`
- `falco_rules.yaml`
- `falco_rules.local.yaml`
- `k8s_audit_rules.yaml`

The included configuration files will work out of the box, but you may want to change some of the values to fit your logging requirements. In this section, we will explain the most important configuration options in detail. The first three configuration files are part of a base Falco deployment and will be explained in detail in this chapter. The last configuration file is not required for a base Falco installation. It is an add-on that can be enabled to add additional auditing functionalities to the API server.

The falco.yaml configuration file

The first file you will need to edit is the **base configuration file** to configure how Falco creates audit events. It allows you to customize the base settings of Falco including the event output format, timestamp configuration, and endpoint targets such as a Slack channel. Let's have a detailed walkthrough of this file and try to understand it bit by bit.

The first section in the configuration file is the `rules_files` section. This section takes the format of the key `rules_file`, and the values for the rule file(s) with a dash. (This can also be represented as `rules_file: [file1, file2, file3, etc...]`.)

We will explain the function of each rule file in this chapter. In this example configuration, we are telling Falco to use three files as rules, and each file is mounted from a ConfigMap during installation:

```
rules_file:
  - /etc/falco/falco_rules.yaml
  - /etc/falco/falco_rules.local.yaml
  - /etc/falco/k8s_audit_rules.yaml
```

The next set of values will configure how Falco outputs events, including the time format, and the option to output events as text or JSON.

By default, the `time_format_iso_8601` value is set to `false`, which tells Falco to use the local `/etc/localtime` format. Setting the value to `true` tells Falco to stamp each event using the date format of YYYY-MM-DD, a time format using a 24-hour clock, and a time zone of UTC.

Selecting the appropriate format is a decision for your organization. If you have a global organization it may beneficial to set all of your logging to use the ISO 8601 format. However, if you have a regional organization you may be more comfortable using your local date-and-time format since you may not need to worry about correlating events against logging systems in other time zones:

```
time_format_iso_8601: false
```

The next two lines allow you to configure the output of events as either text or JSON format. The default value is set to `false`, which tells Falco to output events in text format. If the first key is set to `false`, the second value will not be evaluated since JSON is not enabled:

```
json_output: false
json_include_output_property: true
```

You may need to output the events in JSON format, depending on the format that your logging system requires. As an example, if you were going to send Falco events to an Elasticsearch server, you might want to enable JSON to allow Elasticsearch to parse the alerts field. Elasticsearch does not require the events to be sent in JSON format and for the lab in this module, we will leave this set to the default value, `false`.

The following are some examples of the same type of event in both text format and JSON format:

- The Falco text log output looks as follows:

```
19:17:23.139089915: Notice A shell was spawned in
a container with an attached terminal (user=root
k8s.ns=default k8s.pod=falco-daemonset-9mrn4
container=0756e87d121d shell=bash parent=runc
cmdline=bash terminal=34816 container_id=0756e87d121d
image=<NA>) k8s.ns=default k8s.pod=falco-daemonset-9mrn4
container=0756e87d121d k8s.ns=default k8s.pod=falco-
daemonset-9mrn4 container=0756e87d121d
```

- The Falco JSON log output looks as follows:

```
{"output":"20:47:39.535071657: Notice A shell
was spawned in a container with an attached
terminal (user=root k8s.ns=default k8s.pod=falco-
daemonset-mjv2d container=daeaaf1c0551 shell=bash
parent=runc cmdline=bash terminal=34816 container_
id=daeaaf1c0551 image=<NA>) k8s.ns=default k8s.
pod=falco-daemonset-mjv2d container=daeaaf1c0551
k8s.ns=default k8s.pod=falco-daemonset-mjv2d
container=daeaaf1c0551","priority":"Notice","rule":
"Terminal shell in container","time":"2020-
02-13T20:47:39.535071657Z", "output_fields":
{"container.id":"daeaaf1c0551","container.image.
repository":null,"evt.time":1581626859535071657,"k8s.
ns.name":"default","k8s.pod.name":"falco-daemonset-
mjv2d","proc.cmdline":"bash","proc.name":"bash","proc.
pname":"runc","proc.tty":34816,"user.name":"root"}}
```

Continuing on, the next two options tell Falco to log **Falco-level** events to `stderr` and `syslog`:

```
log_stderr: true
log_syslog: true
```

This setting does not have any impact on the events that your rules file will be monitoring, but rather configures how **Falco system events** will be logged:

```
log_stderr: true
log_syslog: true
log_level: info
```

The default for both options is `true`, so all events will be logged to `stderr` and `syslog`.

Next is the logging level you want to capture, with accepted values including `emergency`, `alert`, `critical`, `error`, `warning`, `notice`, `info`, and `debug`.

Continuing on, the priority level specifies the rulesets that will be used by Falco. Any ruleset that has a rule priority equal to or higher than the configured value will be evaluated by Falco to generate alerts:

```
priority: debug
```

The default value is debug. Other values that can be set are emergency, alert, critical, error, warning, notice, and info.

Next up is the value to enable or disable buffered_output. By default, buffered_outputs is set to false:

```
buffered_outputs: false
```

To pass system calls, Falco uses a shared buffer that can fill up, and when the value is set to true, the buffer can be configured to tell Falco how to react. The default values are usually a good starting value for an initial configuration. The Falco team has a detailed explanation of dropped events on their main documentation page at https://falco.org/docs/event-sources/dropped-events/.

The syscall_events_drops setting can be set to ignore, log, alert, and exit. The rate configures how often Falco will execute the configured actions. The value is actions per second, so this example tells Falco to execute one action every 30 seconds:

```
syscall_event_drops:
  actions:
    - log
    - alert
  rate: .03333
  max_burst: 10
```

The outputs section allows you to throttle the notifications from Falco, containing two values, rate and max_burst:

```
outputs:
  rate: 1
  max_burst: 1000
```

The syslog_output section tells Falco to output events to syslog. By default, this value is set to true:

```
syslog_output:
  enabled: true
```

In certain use cases, you may want to configure Falco to output events to a file in addition to, or as a replacement to, stdout. By default, this is set to false, but you can enable it by setting it to true and providing a filename. The keep_alive value is set to false by default, which configures Falco to keep the file open and write data continuously without closing the file. If it is set to false, the file is opened for each event as they occur, and closed once the events have been written:

```
file_output:
  enabled: false
  keep_alive: false
  filename: ./events.txt
```

By default, Falco will output events to stdout, so it is set to true. If you have a requirement to disable logging events to stdout, you can change this value to false:

```
stdout_output:
  enabled: true
```

The webserver configuration is used to integrate Kubernetes audit events with Falco. By default, it is enabled to listen on port 8765 using HTTP.

You can enable secure communication by changing the ssl_enabled value to true, and supplying a certificate for the ssl_certificate value:

```
webserver:
  enabled: true
  listen_port: 8765
  k8s_audit_endpoint: /k8s_audit
  ssl_enabled: false
  ssl_certificate: /etc/falco/falco.pem
```

Falco can be configured to alerts to other systems. In our example configuration, they show an example using jq and curl to send an alert to a Slack channel. By default, this section is **disabled**, but if you want to call an external program when alerts are triggered, you can enable the option and provide the program to be executed. Similar to the file output described previously, the keep_alive option defaults to false, which tells Falco to run the program for each event:

```
program_output:
  enabled: false
```

```
  keep_alive: false
  program: "jq '{text: .output}' | curl -d @- -X POST https://
hooks.slack.com/services/XXX"
```

Falco can send alerts to an HTTP endpoint. We will be deploying an add-on for Falco called `falcosidekick`, which runs a web server to receive requests from the Falco pod. It is disabled by default, but we have enabled it and set it to the name of the service that will be created later in the chapter when we deploy `Falcosidekick`:

```
http_output:
  enabled: true
  url: http://falcosidekick:2801
```

The remaining sections of the file are used to enable and configure a gRPC server. This is not a common configuration when using Falco with Kubernetes, and is only provided here since it's in the base `falco.yaml` file:

```
grpc:
  enabled: false
  bind_address: "0.0.0.0:5060"
  threadiness: 8
  private_key: "/etc/falco/certs/server.key"
  cert_chain: "/etc/falco/certs/server.crt"
  root_certs: "/etc/falco/certs/ca.crt"
grpc_output:
  enabled: false
```

The base configuration is just the initial configuration file to a Falco deployment. It only sets the Falco system configuration; it doesn't create any rules, which are used to create alerts. In the next section, we will explain how to configure the files used to create Falco alerts.

Falco rules config files

Recall that in our configuration file, the first section had a key called `rules_files` and the key can have multiple values. The values that you provide will contain the filenames, which are mounted using a `configmap`, telling Falco what to audit and how to alert us about a given event.

Rules files can contain three types of elements:

- **Rules**: Configures Falco alerts
- **Macros**: Creates a function that can shorten definitions in a rule
- **Lists**: A collection of items that can be used in a rule

In the upcoming subsections, we'll go over each of these elements.

Understanding rules

Falco includes a set of example Kubernetes rules that you can use as-is, or you can modify the existing rules to fit your specialized requirements.

Falco is a powerful auditing system that enhances cluster security. Like any system that provides auditing, creating rules to monitor systems can become complex and Falco Kubernetes no exception. To use Falco effectively, you need to understand how it uses the rules files and how you can correctly customize the rules to fit your requirements.

A default Falco installation will include three rulesets:

Rules File	Overview
`falco_rules.yaml`	The base rules provided by Falco. This base ruleset should not be edited since the file may be replaced by future Falco deployments. Any changes or additional rules should be added to the `falco_rules.local.yaml` file.
`falco_rules.local.yaml`	This contains custom rules required by your organization. Also used to modify rules that are included in the base `falco_rules.yaml` file.
`k8s_audit_rules.yaml`	This contains rules that are used when Falco is integrated with Kubernetes audit events. The file is included and added to the `configmap`, but the integration is not configured by default.

Table 12.1 – Rules files overview

Each of the rules files have the same syntax, so before explaining each file in greater detail, let's explain how rules, macros, and lists work together to create rules.

Our first example will generate an alert when a pod that is not part of Kubernetes itself tries to contact the API server. This type of activity may signal that an attacker is looking to exploit the Kubernetes API server. To accomplish the most efficient alert, we don't want to generate alerts from pods that are part of the Kubernetes cluster that need to communicate with the API server.

The included rules list includes this event. In the `falco_rules.yaml` file, there is a rule for API server communication:

```
- rule: Contact K8S API Server From Container
  desc: Detect attempts to contact the K8S API Server from a
container
  condition: evt.type=connect and evt.dir=< and (fd.typechar=4
or fd.typechar=6) and container and not k8s_containers and k8s_
api_server
  output: Unexpected connection to K8s API Server
from container (command=%proc.cmdline %container.info
image=%container.image.repository:%container.image.tag
connection=%fd.name)
  priority: NOTICE
  tags: [network, k8s, container, mitre_discovery]
```

You can see that a rule may contain multiple conditions and values. Falco includes a large set of conditions that can be checked, so let's start by explaining this rule in detail.

To explain how this rule works, we break down each section in the following table:

Rule Option	Description
`rule`	Provides a name for our rule. In the example, the name is `Contact K8S API Server From Container`.
`desc`	Provides a description for our rule, which should be more descriptive than the rule option. In our example, the description is `Detect attempts to contact the K8S API Server from a container`.
`condition`	This contains the logic that will decide whether a rule is to be triggered. The example rule will be explained in detail in the next section.
`output`	This creates the output that will be sent to the log.

Table 12.2 – Parts of a Falco rule

Most of the table is fairly straightforward, but the condition section has some complex logic that may not make much sense to you. Like most logging systems, Falco uses its own syntax for creating rule conditions.

Since rules can be difficult to create, the Falco community has provided an extensive list of premade rules. Many people will find that the community rules will fully meet their needs, but there are scenarios where you might need to create custom rules, or need to change one of the existing rules to reduce alerts for events you may not be concerned about. Before you attempt to create or change an event, you need to understand the full logic of a condition.

Covering all of the logic and syntax that Falco offers is beyond the scope of this book, but understanding the example rule is the first step to creating or editing existing rules.

Understanding conditions (fields and values)

The example condition contains a few different conditions that we will break down here into three sections to describe each part of the condition in steps.

The first component of a condition is the `class fields`. A condition can contain multiple class fields and can be evaluated using standard `and`, `not`, or `equals` conditions. Breaking down the example condition, we are using the `event (evt)` and `file descriptor (fd)` class fields:

Figure 12.1 – Class field example

Each class may have a `field` value:

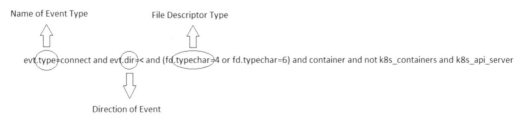

Figure 12.2 – Class Field Value

Finally, each field type will have a `value`:

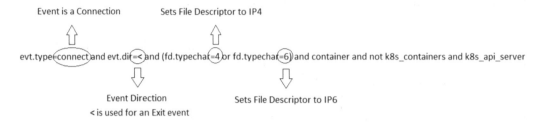

Figure 12.3 – Values in conditions

> **Important note**
>
> You can get a complete list of the available classes from Falco's website at `https://falco.org/docs/rules/supported-fields/`.

Falco has a number of class fields and values for rules. There are too many classes to explain in a single chapter, but to help with creating your own custom rules, we have provided an explanation using the original example condition:

```
condition: evt.type=connect and evt.dir=< and (fd.typechar=4 or
fd.typechar=6) and container and not k8s_containers and k8s_
api_server
```

The following table explains the event class and its values:

Event (EVT) Class	
Value	**Description**
`type`	The type of event. In our example, the type value is set to connect, since the event we want to watch for will use a network connection.
`dir`	The direction of the event. This sets the direction to either enter (>) or exit (<). In the example, it's watching for a connection that is exiting the pod.

Table 12.3 – Event class example

Along with using the event class, the rule also uses the file descriptor class, which is explained as follows:

File Descriptor (FD) Class	
Value	Description
typechar	Sets the type of class to watch for. The values can be (f) file, (4) IPv4, (6) IPv6, (u) unix, (p) pipe, (e) eventfd, (s) signalfd, (l) eventpoll, (i) notify, or (o) unknown. In the example, the value uses an or statement of 4 or 6. Setting it to both will trigger an alert based on either IPv4 or IPv6.

Table 12.4 – File descriptor example

The last part of the rule that starts with and container value will include any container. However, since we do not want to send alerts for valid communications from Kubernetes itself, the value and not k8s_containers and k8s_api_server tells the condition to omit the Kubernetes container and the api_server. The values in this example use macros that have been defined in the falco_rules.yaml file. We will discuss macros in the next section.

Using macros

Macros allow you to create a collection to make rule creation quicker and easier. In the previous example, the condition used two macros, k8s_containers and k8s_api_server.

The k8s_containers macro has been defined to contain the condition:

```
# In a local/user rules file, list the namespace or container
images that are
# allowed to contact the K8s API Server from within a
container. This
# might cover cases where the K8s infrastructure itself is
running
# within a container.
- macro: k8s_containers
  condition: >
    (container.image.repository in (gcr.io/google_containers/
hyperkube-amd64,
    gcr.io/google_containers/kube2sky, sysdig/agent, sysdig/
falco,
    sysdig/sysdig, falcosecurity/falco) or (k8s.ns.name =
"kube-system"))
```

Macros, like rules, use classes to create conditions. To evaluate `k8s_containers` condition, macros use two classes:

- The `container.image.repository` class field, which validates the repositories for the condition.

- The `k8s.ns.name` class field, which is used to include any containers running in the `kube-system` namespace.

The `k8s_api_server` has been defined to contain the condition:

```
- macro: k8s_api_server
  condition: (fd.sip.name="kubernetes.default.svc.cluster.
local")
```

For the `k8s_api_server` condition, macros use a single class field to evaluate the condition – the `fd.sip.name` class field – which checks the domain name of the **server IP (SIP)**. If it is equal to `kubernetes.default.svc.cluster.local` it is considered a match.

Using both of the preceding macros for the rules condition will stop any Kubernetes cluster pods from generating alerts when communicating with the API server.

Understanding lists

Lists allow you to group items into a single object that can be used in rules, macros, or nested in other lists.

A list only requires two keys in a rules file, `list` and `items`. For example, rather than listing a number of binaries on a condition, you could group the binaries into a `list`:

```
- list: editors
  items: [vi, nano, emacs]
```

Using lists allows you to use a single entry, rather than including multiple items in a condition.

Rules can be challenging, but as you read more of the included rules and start to create your own, it will become easier. So far, we have introduced the basics on how to create rules, macros, and lists. With a basic understanding of these objects under our belts, we will move on to the next configuration file where you will create and append Falco rules.

Creating and appending to custom rules

Falco comes with a number of base rules that are located in the `falco_rules.yaml` file. This file should never be edited – if you need to change or create a new rule, you should edit the `falco_rules.local.yaml` file.

Appending to an existing rule

> **Important note**
>
> You are not limited to only appending to rules. Falco allows you to append rules, macros, and lists.

The included `falco_rules.local.yaml` is empty by default. You only need to edit this file if an existing rule needs to be modified or removed or a new rule needs to be added. Since the file is used to change or add values to the base `falco_rules.yaml` file, the order in which the files are used by Falco is very important.

Falco will build rules based on the name from all rules files. The files are read and evaluated in the order that they are referenced in the base Falco configuration file. The base file that we used as an example at the beginning of this chapter has the following order for its rules files:

```
rules_file:
  - /etc/falco/falco_rules.yaml
  - /etc/falco/falco_rules.local.yaml
  - /etc/falco/k8s_audit_rules.yaml
```

Notice that the `falco.rules.local.yaml` file is after the base `falco_rules.yaml` file. Keeping control of the order of the files will help you to track any expected/unexpected behaviors of your rules.

Using an example from the Falco documentation, let's show how to append to a rule.

The original rule from `falco_rules.yaml` is shown in the following code block:

```
- rule: program_accesses_file
  desc: track whenever a set of programs opens a file
  condition: proc.name in (cat, ls) and evt.type=open
  output: a tracked program opened a file (user=%user.name
command=%proc.cmdline file=%fd.name)
  priority: INFO
```

As the description states, this rule will trigger whenever a set of programs opens a file. The condition will trigger when `cat` or `ls` is used to open a file.

The current rule does not omit the open operation from any users. You have decided that you do not need to know when the root user uses either `cat` or `ls` to open a file, and you want to stop Falco from generating alerts for root.

In the `falco_rules.local.yaml` file, you need to create an `append` for the existing rule. To append to a rule, you must use the same rule name, then add `append: true` and any changes you want to make to the rule. An example is shown in the following snippet:

```
- rule: program_accesses_file
  append: true
  condition: and not user.name=root
```

Creating a new rule is easier than appending to an existing rule. Let's see how it works.

Creating a new rule

Since you are creating a new rule, you only need to add a standard rule to the `falco_rules.local.yaml`. As it is a new rule, it will simply be added to the list of rules that Falco uses to create alerts.

> **Important note**
>
> Falco's configuration files are read from a ConfigMap, so you will need to restart the Falco pods if you change any values in the ConfigMap.

Congratulations! A lot of information has been presented to you here, and you probably want to see Falco in action to put your knowledge to work. In the next section, we explain how to deploy Falco, and you will finally get to see it in action.

Deploying Falco

We have included a script to deploy Falco, called `falco-install.sh`, in the GitHub repository in the `chapter12` folder.

The two most popular methods of deploying Falco to a Kubernetes cluster are using the official Helm chart or a DaemonSet manifest from the Falco repo. For the purposes of this module, we will deploy Falco using a modified DaemonSet installation from the book's GitHub repository.

To deploy Falco using the included script, execute the script from within the `chapter12` folder by executing `./install-falco.sh`. We have also included a script called `delete-falco.sh` in the same directory that will remove Falco from the cluster.

The steps that the script performs are detailed in the following list and will be explained in additional detail in this section.

The script executes the following tasks in two sections:

In **Section 1**, it creates a Falco probe and performs the following steps:

1. Installs Go using `apt`
2. Pulls Falco's `driverkit-builder` container
3. Pulls the driverkit source from Git and builds the executable
4. Creates an ubuntu-generic Falco probe using driverkit
5. Copies `falco.ko` to the `modules` folder
6. Adds a Falco probe using `modprobe`

In **Section 2**, it adds Falco to the cluster, performing the following steps:

1. Creates a Falco namespace
2. Creates a ConfigMap called `falco-config` from the files in `falco/falco-config`
3. Deploys the Falco DaemonSet

To better understand the installation scripts and why these steps are required, we will explain the installation details, starting with Falco probes.

Falco kernel module

Falco deploys a kernel module to monitor system calls on the host system. Since kernel modules must be compatible with the host kernel, you need to have a module that works with the worker node's host operating system.

Falco attempts to load or create a module in a few different ways:

*   If there is a pre-built module available for the hosts kernel, Falco will download and use the module automatically.
*   If no pre-built module exists for the worker node's kernel, Falco will attempt to build a module using any installed kernel-headers from the host.

At the time of writing, Falco offers an early-access alternative method for Falco probes, where they are created using a utility called **driverkit**. This new utility automates the creation of a new probe based on the kernel information of the host machine. The process of creating a probe using driverkit will be covered in detail since we will use it to create a Falco probe for our KinD cluster.

> **Important note**
>
> If your nodes do not have the correct kernel-headers installed, Falco pods will attempt to download a precompiled probe that matched the host's kernel version.
>
> You can find your kernel information by executing `uname -r` on your host, then check for support by searching the available probes at the following link:
>
> `https://s3.amazonaws.com/download.draios.com/stable/sysdig-probe-binaries/index.html`
>
> Since this requires internet connectivity, it may not be an option for you to use in an enterprise environment where many servers run in air-gapped environments. In this type of environment, it is more common to use the driverkit or kernel-headers creation methods.

Creating a kernel module using installed kernel headers

> **Important note**
>
> As I mentioned, we will not be using this method to create a kernel module. This section is only for your reference. We will instead be using driverkit, which is covered in the next section

On a standard Kubernetes node, you may or may not need to install the Linux headers. Depending on how you created your base worker nodes, the kernel-headers may already be included with your installation. If a module isn't available and you do not have the headers installed on the hosts, the Falco pods will fail to start and the pods will go into a `crashloopback` state. This means that before deploying Falco, you need to have your module creation process selected and configured.

The required packages, version, and repository are different for various Linux installations. If you intend to install the headers on your nodes, you will need to know what modules are required, along with any additional repos. Since we have been using Ubuntu as our distribution for the hands-on exercises, we will provide the steps to add the kernel-headers for Ubuntu systems.

Using headers to create the Falco module

Falco has introduced a utility called DriverKit that we will use to create the kernel module for our KinD Falco installation. We include the process to use kernel-headers as a backup procedure in cases where the Falco DriverKit may not support your Linux distribution.

If you plan to have Falco create a kernel module using headers, the first step is to download the kernel-headers for your Linux release.

To download the correct headers for Ubuntu, you can use the `uname -r` command along with `apt get` for `linux-headers`.

`sudo apt install linux-headers-$(uname -r)`

`uname -r` will append the kernel version that is running on the host, providing the `apt install` command with the running kernel. On our example host, the running kernel is `4.4.0-142-generic`, making our `apt install` command `sudo apt install linux-headers- linux-headers-4.4.0-142-generic`.

After installation, you can verify that the headers have been added by looking at the `/lib/modules/` directory, where you will see a directory named after the kernel version; in our example, this is `4.4.0-142-generic`.

> **Important note**
> The headers must be installed on every worker node that will be running Falco.

Now that the headers are installed, the Falco pods will build a kernel module when they start up using the installed headers on the worker node.

As discussed earlier, a newer method has come out from the team that uses a utility called driverkit. This process creates a kernel module that you can add to a host using modprobe. We have selected this as our probe creation process to make deploying Falco on a KinD cluster easier than using the header creation process.

Creating a kernel module using driverkit

There are specialized use cases where installing kernel-headers may be challenging or impossible. If you cannot use the headers to build your module, you can create a module using a Falco utility called driverkit.

Driverkit allows you to create a kernel module for a number of different Linux distributions. At the time of writing, this utility currently supports the following distributions:

- Ubuntu-generic
- Ubuntu-aws
- CentOS 8
- CentOS 7
- CentOS 6
- AmazonLinux
- AmazonLinux2
- Debian
- Vanilla Kernel

The team is actively looking for suggestions for other distributions, so we can be sure that additional distributions will be added as driverkit is developed.

We will go over the details to create a module for Ubuntu, using the Ubuntu-generic option.

Driverkit requirements

Before you can create a module using driverkit, you need to meet a few prerequisites:

- A running Docker daemon.
- Go should be installed (since we are using Ubuntu, we will use `longsleep/golang-backports`).
- Your target kernel version and kernel revision.

If you are going to use the installation script in the GitHub repository, all of the build and module installation steps are taken care of, but to better understand the process, we will explain it in full in the next section.

Installing Falco's driverkit

The first step to building a kernel module is to install the required dependencies for driverkit:

1. The first requirement is to install Go. Since we are using Ubuntu, we can install Go using `snap`:

    ```
    sudo snap install --classic go
    ```

    You should already have Go variables in your profile from the KinD installation in *Chapter 5, Kubernetes Bootcamp.* If you are using a machine that is different from your KinD host, add any required Go variables.

2. We have selected to build using the Docker build method. There are multiple methods documented on the driverkit project page with which you can build the module if you want to use a different build method. We will pull the Docker image so it's ready to execute when we run the build:

    ```
    docker pull falcosecurity/driverkit-builder
    ```

3. Once the container has been downloaded, we can build the driverkit executable. The build process will download the source from GitHub and then use Go to create the executable file. The complete process will take a few minutes to complete:

    ```
    GO111MODULE="on" go get github.com/falcosecurity/
    driverkit
    ```

4. The executable will be created in your Go path. To verify that the driverkit executable was created successfully, check the version by typing the following command:

    ```
    driverkit -v
    ```

5. This may return a version number, or in the current early release, it may just return the following:

    ```
    driverkit version -+
    ```

If the driverkit command returns `-+` or a version number, it was successfully created. However, if you received a `driverkit: command not found` error when you checked the version, the build may have failed or your Go path may not have been set correctly in your environment variable. If you cannot find the executable after running the build, verify that your Go environment variables are correct, and run the Go build step again.

Creating the module and adding it to the host

With driverkit built and verified, we can build our module and add it to the host.

Before building the module, we need to know the kernel version and release of our host. For our example, we will use the KinD cluster we have been using for the previous chapters in this book. Linux has some commands built in to get the two details we need:

1. To get the kernel version, execute uname -v, and for the release, uname -r:

```
surovich@bookvm:/$ uname -v
#100-Ubuntu SMP Wed Apr 22 20:32:56 UTC 2020
surovich@bookvm:/$ uname -r
4.15.0-99-generic
```

Figure 12.4 – Docker host Kernel version

The version is the number after the # symbol and before the dash. On our host, we have a version of 100. The release is the full name that was returned from the uname -r command. You will need provide both of these to the driverkit command to build the kernel module.

2. If you are using the installation script, we retrieve the options and supply them automatically. If you are doing this step manually, you can use the following two lines of code to store the information in variables to be passed to the build command:

```
kernelversion=$(uname -v | cut -f1 -d'-' | cut -f2 -d'#')
kernelrelease=$(uname -r)
```

We use the cut command to remove the unnecessary information from the uname -v command and store it in a variable called kernelversion. We also store the output from the uname -r command in a variable called kernelrelease.

3. Now, you can use the Docker image we pulled and the driverkit executable to create the module:

```
driverkit docker --output-module /tmp/
falco.ko --kernelversion=$kernelversion
--kernelrelease=$kernelrelease --driverversion=dev
--target=ubuntu-generic
```

4. The module build process will take a minute, and once the build completes, driverkit will show you the location of the new module:

```
INFO driver building, it will take a few seconds
processor=docker
INFO kernel module available
path=/tmp/falco.ko
```

5. For the last step to add the new module, we need to copy it to the correct location and load the module using modprobe:

```
sudo cp /tmp/falco.ko /lib/modules/$kernelrelease/falco.
ko
sudo depmod
sudo modprobe falco
```

6. You can verify that the module has been added by running lsmod:

```
lsmod | grep falco
```

If the load was successful, you will see an output similar to the following:

```
falco                    634880  4
```

That's it! You now have the Falco module on the host and it will be available to your KinD cluster.

Using the module on a cluster

On a standard Kubernetes cluster, a Falco deployment will map the /dev mount in the Falco container to the host's /dev mount. By mounting /dev, the Falco pod can use the kernel module that is running on the worker node's host operating system.

Using the module in KinD

You may be asking yourself how adding the Falco module to the host will make it available to a KinD cluster? We only added it to the host itself, and the KinD cluster is a container running in another Docker container. So, how can a KinD pod use a module from the Docker host?

Remember that KinD has a feature to mount extra volumes when it starts the KinD containers? In our installation, we added a mount point for /dev:/dev, which will create a mount inside our container that mounts to the host's /dev filesystem. If we look at the host's /dev filesystem, we will see Falco entries in the list, noted by the following:

```
cr-------- 1 root root     244,   0 May  4 00:58 falco0
```

This is what the Falco pod will use as its module when it starts up.

But wait! We just said that /dev is mounted in our KinD container, pointing to the host's /dev filesystem. So how does a container in the Kubernetes cluster have access to the /dev filesystem?

If we take a look at the Falco DaemonSet file we will use in the next section, we will see that the manifest creates a few mount points for the pod.

One of the volumeMount entries is as follows:

```
- mountPath: /host/dev
  name: dev-fs
  readOnly: true
```

The volumeMount entry is using a volume that is declared in the *volumes* section of the DaemonSet:

```
- name: dev-fs
  hostPath:
    path: /dev
```

When a Falco pod starts it will mount the pod's /dev mount to the KinD container's /dev mount. Finally, the KinD container's /dev mount is mounted to the Docker host's /dev where the Falco module is located. (Remember the metaphor of nesting dolls.)

With all of the prerequisites in place, we are ready to deploy Falco.

Deploying the Falco Daemonset

If you are going to run the install-falco.sh script from the GitHub repository, Falco will be installed using the same steps provided in this section. In the book's GitHub repo, all of the Falco files are located in the chapter12 directory.

Since this chapter has a few different pieces, a description of the `chapter12` directory's contents is provided in the following diagram:

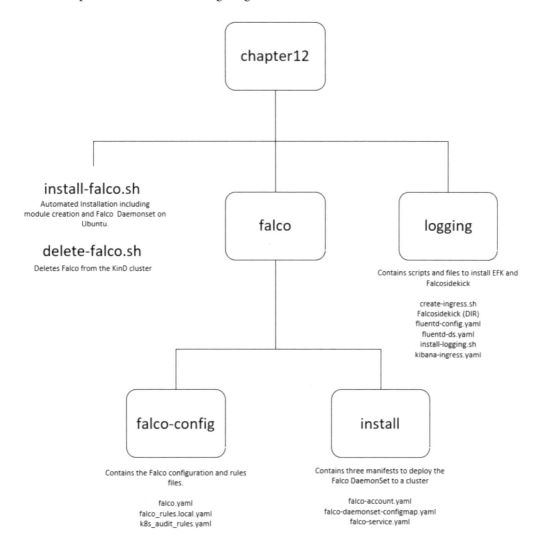

Figure 12.5 – Diagram of the chapter12 directory in the book's GitHub repository

Remember that Falco includes a set of standard rules that include standard auditing rules. We have put the rules files in the `falco/falco-config` directory. The only value we have changed from the default installation is the logging format, which we changed to JSON, and additionally set the values for `http_output` to use Falcosidekick.

To deploy the Falco DaemonSet manually, you need to deploy the three manifests in the `install` directory and create a secret using the `falco-config` directory contents.

Creating the Falco service account and service

Since we want to run Falco in a dedicated namespace, we need to create a namespace called `falco` on our cluster. Run the following command:

```
kubectl create ns falco
```

Like all Kubernetes applications, we need to create an account that has the correct RBAC permission for the application to perform the necessary tasks. Our first step is to create that service account, which will be used to assign RBAC permissions in the DaemonSet deployment:

1. Using `kubectl`, create the service account:

   ```
   kubectl apply -f falco/install/falco-account.yaml -n
   falco
   ```

2. Next, we need to create a service for Falco. The included `falco-service.yaml` file will create a new service on TCP port `8765`. Using kubectl, apply the manifest:

   ```
   kubectl apply -f falco/install/falco-service.yaml -n
   falco
   ```

3. Falco uses files for the base configuration and rules. Since we are running Falco in Kubernetes, we need to store the files in a Kubernetes object so they can be used by the Falco pods. To store the files in a ConfigMap, create a new ConfigMap called `falco-config` using all of the files in the `falco-config` directory:

   ```
   kubectl create configmap falco-config --from-file=falco/
   falco-config -n falco
   ```

> **Important note**
>
> If you need to modify any of the configuration files after you deploy Falco, you should delete the ConfigMap and recreate it using the newly updated files. After updating the ConfigMap, you will also need to restart each Falco pod to reload the updated files from the ConfigMap.

4. The last step is to deploy the DaemonSet:

```
kubectl apply -f falco/install/falco-daemonset-configmap.
yaml -n falco
```

Once the Falco pod(s) are running, you can verify the health by looking at the logs for the pod. The output will look similar to the following output (the errors are expected, Falco is trying to find the kernel module in all locations, some of which do not exist, causing the "errors"):

```
* Setting up /usr/src links from host
* Unloading falco-probe, if present
* Running dkms install for falco
Error! echo
Your kernel headers for kernel 4.15.0-99-generic cannot be found at
/lib/modules/4.15.0-99-generic/build or /lib/modules/4.15.0-99-generic/source.
* Running dkms build failed, couldn't find /var/lib/dkms/falco/a259b4bf49c3330d9ad6c3eed9eb1a31954259a6/build/make.log
* Trying to load a system falco-probe, if present
* Trying to find precompiled falco-probe for 4.15.0-99-generic
Cannot find kernel config
Tue May  5 19:07:46 2020: Falco initialized with configuration file /etc/falco/falco.yaml
Tue May  5 19:07:46 2020: Loading rules from file /etc/falco/falco_rules.yaml:
Tue May  5 19:07:46 2020: Loading rules from file /etc/falco/falco_rules.local.yaml:
Tue May  5 19:07:47 2020: Loading rules from file /etc/falco/k8s_audit_rules.yaml:
Tue May  5 19:07:47 2020: Starting internal webserver, listening on port 8765
```

Figure 12.6 – Successful Falco pod startup log

You now have a Falco DaemonSet set up that will audit events in your pods.

> **Important note**
>
> You may receive an error on the last line of the Falco pod logs, similar to the following example:
>
> **Tue May 5 20:38:14 2020: Runtime error: error opening device /host/dev/ falco0. Make sure you have root credentials and that the falco-probe module is loaded. Exiting.**
>
> In this case, your Falco module may not be loaded, so go back to the modprobe steps and execute them again. You should not need to restart the Falco pod as the change will be picked up and Falco will start logging once it can see the module in the /dev directory.

Of course, to be useful, we need the events to be forwarded to a central logging system. In a default deployment, Falco logs are only available on the pod running on each host. If you have 30 hosts, you will have 30 unique Falco logs, one on each host. Finding an event in a decentralized system, as the saying goes, is like looking for a needle in a haystack.

Falco logs use standard output, so we can easily forward the logs to any third-party logging system. While there are many options that we could select as our logging server, we have chosen to forward our logs using **Elasticsearch, Fluentd, and Kibana** (**EFK**) along with Falcosidekick.

Deploying EFK

Our first step will be to deploy **Elasticsearch** to receive event data. To install Elasticsearch, we require persistent storage for the data. Luckily, we are using a KinD cluster so we have persistent storage thanks to Rancher's local provisioner.

To make the deployment easy, we will deploy our stack using Bitnami's Helm charts for Elasticsearch and Kibana. You will need to have the Helm binary installed to deploy the charts to the cluster. If you are doing the exercises in the book, you should already have Helm3 installed from the KinD deployment in *Chapter 5, Kubernetes Bootcamp*.

Verify you have Helm installed and running by running the `helm version` command. If Helm is installed on your path, you should receive a reply with the version of Helm you are running:

```
version.BuildInfo{Version:"v3.2.0",
GitCommit:"e11b7ce3b12db2941e90399e874513fbd24bcb71",
GitTreeState:"clean", GoVersion:"go1.13.10"}
```

If you receive an error, you will need to reinstall Helm before continuing.

In the GitHub repository, we have included a script to deploy EFK. The script is called `install-logging.sh` and is located in the `chapter12/logging` directory. Like all of the previous scripts, we will go over the details of the script and the commands that are executed.

Creating a new namespace

Since we may want to delegate access to a centralized logging team, we will create a new namespace called `logging`:

```
kubectl create ns logging
```

Adding chart repos to Helm

Since we are going to use Helm to deploy charts from Bitnami, we need to add the Bitnami chart repository to Helm. You add chart repos using the `helm repo add <repo name> <repo url>` command:

```
helm repo add bitnami https://charts.bitnami.com/bitnami
```

You should receive a confirmation that Bitnami has been added:

```
"bitnami" has been added to your repositories
```

Once the Bitnami repository has been added, you can start to deploy charts from the Bitnami repo.

Deploying the Elasticsearch chart

The Elasticsearch deployment will store data on persistent disks. We want to control the size of the created disks, so we pass values in the `helm install` command to limit the size to 1 GB.

To deploy Bitnami's Elasticsearch with the options, use the following `helm install` command. We are only setting a few values for our installation, but like any Helm chart, there is a long list of options that allow us to customize the installation. For our example deployment, we are only setting the persistent volume size to 1 GB and the number of data replicas to 2. We also want the chart to be deployed in the `logging` namespace, so we also add the `--namespace logging` option:

```
helm install elasticsearch bitnami/elasticsearch --set master.
persistence.size=1Gi,data.persistence.size=1Gi,data.replicas=2
--namespace logging
```

Once you start to deploy the chart, you will receive a warning about the `vm.max_map_count` kernel setting. For our KinD clusters, the included `initContainer` will set this value on our worker node. In a production environment, you may not allow privileged pods to run, which will cause the initContainer to fail. If you do not allow privileged pods to run in your cluster (which is a **very** good idea), you will need to set this value manually on each host before deploying Elasticsearch.

You can check the status of the deployment by checking the pods in the `logging` namespace. Using `kubectl`, verify that all of the pods are in a running state before moving on to the next step:

```
kubectl get pods -n logging
```

You should receive the following output:

```
NAME                                                              READY   STATUS    RESTARTS   AGE
elasticsearch-elasticsearch-coordinating-only-569849ff87-5f87j    1/1     Running   1          10m
elasticsearch-elasticsearch-coordinating-only-569849ff87-7btph    1/1     Running   1          10m
elasticsearch-elasticsearch-data-0                                1/1     Running   1          10m
elasticsearch-elasticsearch-data-1                                1/1     Running   0          10m
elasticsearch-elasticsearch-master-0                              1/1     Running   1          10m
elasticsearch-elasticsearch-master-1                              1/1     Running   1          10m
```

Figure 12.7 – Elasticsearch pod list

As we can see, the Helm chart created a few Kubernetes objects. The main objects include the following:

- The Elasticsearch server pod (`elasticsearch-elasticsearch-coordinating-only`)

- The Elasticsearch Data StatefulSet (`elasticsearch-elasticsearch-data-x`)

- The Elasticsearch Master StatefulSet (`elasticsearch-elasticsearch-master-x`)

Each StatefulSet created a PersistentVolumeClaim of 1 GB for each pod that was created. We can view the PVCs using `kubectl get pvc -n logging`, producing the following output:

```
NAME                                         STATUS   VOLUME                                       CAPACITY
data-elasticsearch-elasticsearch-data-0      Bound    pvc-c6e73902-5b64-4fe2-9e6b-db3ce157942d     1Gi
data-elasticsearch-elasticsearch-data-1      Bound    pvc-901cc0c3-49e3-4125-b39f-98f35124fe7b     1Gi
data-elasticsearch-elasticsearch-master-0    Bound    pvc-c9009c3d-3ade-492f-8260-afc3881a3bb4     1Gi
data-elasticsearch-elasticsearch-master-1    Bound    pvc-624be8ff-bcc0-4498-97d4-43ccc151f727     1Gi
```

Figure 12.8 – PVC list used by Elasticsearch

Three ClusterIP services were created since Elasticsearch will only be used by other Kubernetes objects. We can view the services using `kubectl get services -n logging`, producing the following output:

```
NAME                                                       TYPE        CLUSTER-IP
service/elasticsearch-elasticsearch-coordinating-only      ClusterIP   10.107.207.18
service/elasticsearch-elasticsearch-data                   ClusterIP   10.109.103.120
service/elasticsearch-elasticsearch-master                 ClusterIP   10.110.38.222
```

Figure 12.9 – Elasticsearch services

By looking at the pods, services, and PVCs, we can confirm that the chart deployment was successful and we can move on to the next component, Fluentd.

Deploying Fluentd

We have included a Fluentd deployment located in the GitHub repo in the `chapter12/logging` directory.

Fluentd is a common log forwarder used with Kubernetes to forward logs to a central location. We are installing it to forward Kubernetes logs to Elasticsearch to provide a complete example of an EFK deployment. Our Falco events will be forwarded using Falcosidekick.

The first step to deploying Fluentd to a cluster is to apply a Fluentd configuration. The `fluentd-config.yaml` file will create a ConfigMap that contains the configuration options for the Fluentd deployment.

Configuring Fluentd is outside of the scope for this book. To forward logs using Fluentd, we do need to explain the `output.conf` section of the ConfigMap, which configures the host that Fluentd will send logs to.

In the `fluentd-config.yaml` file, at the bottom of the file, you will see a section titled `output.conf`:

```
output.conf: |-
  <match **>
    @id elasticsearch
    @type elasticsearch
    @log_level info
    type_name _doc
    include_tag_key true
    host elasticsearch-elasticsearch-coordinating-only.logging.svc
    port 9200
    logstash_format true
```

Figure 12.10 – Fluentd output configuration

You can see that we have options set for `id` and `type` of `elasticsearch`, and the host setting has been set to `elasticsearch-elasticsearch-coordinating-only.logging.svc`. If you go back a few pages and look at the output from the `kubectl get services -n logging` command, you will see a service with that name in the output. This is the service that must be targeted when interacting with the Elasticsearch deployment:

```
elasticsearch-elasticsearch-coordinating-only    ClusterIP
10.107.207.18
```

Notice that we also added the namespace and svc to the hostname. The Fluentd DaemonSet will install to the `kube-system` namespace, so to communicate with a service in another namespace, we need to supply the full name to the service. In our KinD cluster, we do not need to add the cluster name to the `hostname` value.

We can deploy the ConfigMap using `kubectl apply`:

```
kubectl apply -f fluentd-config.yaml
```

After the ConfigMap, we can deploy the DaemonSet with the following command:

```
kubectl apply -f fluentd-ds.yaml
```

Verify that the Fluentd pod(s) is running by checking the pods in the `kube-system` namespace:

```
kubectl get pods -n kube-system
```

Since we only have one node, we only see one Fluentd pod:

```
fluentd-es-v2.8.0-gxt8w                1/1      Running    0        79s
```

Figure 12.11 – Fluentd DaemonSet pod list

Fluentd will be used to forward **all** container logs to Elasticsearch.

To make it easier to use Kibana, which we will look at later in this chapter, we want to forward the Falco logs without any other container logs. The easiest way to do this is to use another project from the Falco team, called Falcosidekick.

Deploying Falcosidekick

Falco has a utility that can format and forward Falco events to different logging servers. The project is on GitHub at `https://github.com/falcosecurity/falcosidekick`. At the time of writing, it supports 15 different logging systems, including Slack, Teams, Datadog, Elasticsearch, AWS Lamda, SMTP, and Webhooks.

Since Falcosidekick opens up an easy forwarding method for various different backends, we are going to deploy it to forward the Falco events to Elasticsearch.

To deploy Falcosidekick, we will use Helm to deploy the chart using a local copy from our GitHub repository. The chart files are located in the `chapter12/logging/falcosidekick` directory:

1. Like all charts, we can use a `values.yaml` file to configure the chart options. We have provided a preconfigured file that has the required entries to send Falco events to our Elasticsearch deployment. The entries in the file that we have configured are shown in the following code block. We had to configure the host port to target our Elasticsearch service with HTTP and port `9200`:

    ```
    elasticsearch:
        host port: "http://elasticsearch-elasticsearch-
    coordinating-only.logging.svc:9200"
        index: "falco"
        type: "event"
        minimumpriority: ""
    ```

2. The easiest way to deploy the chart is to change your working directory to the `falcosidkick` directory. Once you are in the directory, run the following `helm install` command to deploy the chart:

```
helm install falcosidekick -f values.yaml . --namespace
falco
```

3. To verify the chart was deployed correctly, grab the logs from the Falcosidekick instance running in the `logging` namespace:

```
kubectl logs falcosidekick-7656785f89-q2z6q -n logging
2020/05/05 23:40:25 [INFO]  : Enabled Outputs :
Elasticsearch
2020/05/05 23:40:25 [INFO]  : Falco Sidekick is up and
listening on port 2801
```

4. Once the Falcosidekick pod starts to receive data from the Falco pods, the log files will have entries showing a successful Elasticsearch Post:

```
2020/05/05 23:42:40 [INFO]  : Elasticsearch - Post OK
(201)
2020/05/05 23:42:40 [INFO]  : Elasticsearch - Post OK
(201)
2020/05/05 23:42:40 [INFO]  : Elasticsearch - Post OK
(201)
2020/05/05 23:42:40 [INFO]  : Elasticsearch - Post OK
(201)
```

What does this give us so far? We have deployed Elasticsearch to store the information that the Fluentd agent will forward from our worker node. Right now, our worker node is sending all of its logs to the Elasticsearch instance using the Fluentd agent, and Falcosidekick is forwarding the Falco events.

Elasticsearch will have a lot of information to sort through to make the data useful. To parse the data and create useful information for the logs, we need to install a system that we can use to create custom dashboards and to search the collected data. This is where the **K** in the **EFK** stack comes in. The next step in our deployment is to install Kibana.

Deploying Kibana

The next chart will install the Kibana server. We chose to use a deployment that is only serving Kibana over HTTP with no authentication. In a production environment, you should enable both to increase your security. Of course, Kibana is not accessible outside of the cluster yet, so we need to create an ingress rule that will configure our NGINX Ingress to direct traffic to the pod:

1. To deploy Kibana to the cluster using the Bitnami chart, use the following commands:

   ```
   helm install kibana --set elasticsearch.
   hosts[0]=elasticsearch-elasticsearch-coordinating-only --
   elasticsearch.port=9200,persistence.size=1Gi --namespace
   logging bitnami/kibana
   ```

2. Once the deployment has started, you will see some output from Helm that tells you how to port-forward using kubectl to access Kibana:

   ```
   Get the application URL by running these commands:
     export POD_NAME=$(kubectl get pods --namespace logging
   -l "app.kubernetes.io/name=kibana,app.kubernetes.io/
   instance=kibana" -o jsonpath="{.items[0].metadata.name}")
     echo "Visit http://127.0.0.1:8080 to use your
   application"
     kubectl port-forward svc/kibana 8080:80
   ```

You can ignore these instructions since we going to expose Kibana using an ingress rule so it can be accessed on any workstation on your network.

Creating an ingress rule for Kibana

For the ingress rule, we will create a rule based on a nip.io domain:

1. To create the ingress rule with the correct nip.io name, we have provided a script in the chaper12/logging folder called create-ingress.sh:

   ```
   ingressip=$(hostname -I | cut -f1 -d' ')
   ingress=`cat "kibana-ingress.yaml" | sed "s/
   {hostip}/$ingressip/g"`
   echo "$ingress" | kubectl apply -f -
   ```

The script will find the IP address of the Docker host and patch the ingress manifest with a nip.io host using **kibana.w.x.y.z.nip.ip** (here, **w.x.y.z** will contain the host's IP address).

2. Once the ingress rule has been created, the details to access your Kibana dashboard will be displayed:

```
You can access your Kibana dashboard in any browser on
your local network using http://kibana.10.2.1.107.nip.io
```

Now that we have Kibana installed, we can open the Kibana dashboard to start our configuration.

Using the Kibana dashboard

To browse to the Kibana dashboard, follow these steps:

1. Open a browser from any machine on your local network.

2. Use the ingress name that was shown from the `install-ingress.sh` script. In our example, we would browse to `http://kibana.10.2.1.107.nip.io`.

3. The request will come back to your client with the IP address `10.2.1.107` and will be sent to your Docker host on port `80`.

> **Tip**
> Remember that we exposed the Docker container for the KinD worker node on ports `80` and `443`.

4. When your Docker host receives the request for the hostname on port `80`, it will be forwarded to the Docker container and ultimately it will then hit the NGINX Ingress controller.

5. NGINX will look for a rule that matches the hostname and will send the traffic to the Kibana pod. In your browser, you will be presented with the Kibana welcome screen:

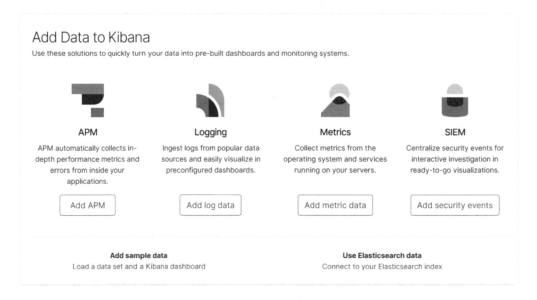

Figure 12.12 – Kibana welcome screen

While you now have a fully functioning audit logging system running, you still have one more step to use Kibana: you need to create a default index.

Creating a Kibana Index

To view logs or create visualizations and dashboards, you need to create an index. You can have multiple indexes on a single Kibana server, allowing you to view different logs from a single location. On our example server, we will have two different sets of incoming logs, one that starts with the name logstash and the other with the name falco.

The data in the logstash files container consists of the Kubernetes log files, which includes all logs that are being forwarded by the Fluentd forwarder. The Falco files are being forwarded by Falcosidekick and only contain the alerts from the Falco pods. For the purposes of this chapter, we will focus on the Falco files since they contain only Falco data:

1. In Kibana, click the setup tool ⊙ located on the left-hand side to open the Kibana management page.

2. To create an index and set it to default, click on index patterns link in the upper-left section of the browser.

3. Next, click on the upper-right button to create a new index pattern.

4. Since we only want to create an index that contains the Falco data, enter `falco*` in the box. This will create an index that contains all current and future Falco logs:

Figure 12.13 – Kibana index pattern definition

5. Click the **Next step** button to continue.

6. In the configuration settings, click the dropdown and select **time**, then click **Create index pattern** to create the pattern:

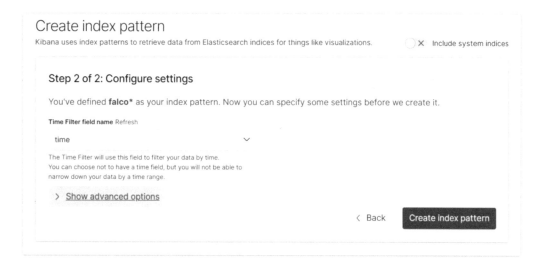

Figure 12.14 – Creating an index

7. Finally, set the index to the default index by clicking the star in the upper right of the final screen:

Figure 12.15 – Setting a default index

That's it, you now have a full Falco logging system running on your cluster.

To start viewing data, click the discover button ⊘ located in the upper left of the Kibana screen, which will take you to the main Kibana page where you will see events from your cluster:

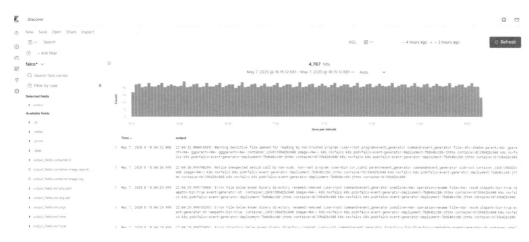

Figure 12.16 – Kibana homepage

You can search for events by typing keywords into the search field. This is helpful if you are looking for a single type of event, and know what value(s) to search for.

The real benefit of logging systems like Kibana is the ability to create custom dashboards that provide a view into multiple events that can be grouped by counts, averages, and more. In the next section, we will explain how to create a dashboard that provides a collection of Falco events.

Creating dashboards is a skill that you need to develop, and it will take time to understand how to group data and what values to use in a dashboard. This section is meant to provide you with the basic tools you need to start creating dashboards like the following:

Figure 12.17 – Example dashboard

People love dashboards, and Kibana provides tools to create dynamic and easily interpreted views of a system. Dashboards can be created using any data that Kibana has access to, including Falco events. Before we create a dashboard, let's understand what a *visualization* means.

Visualizations

A visualization is a graphical representation of a collection of data – in our context, from a Kibana index. Kibana includes a set of visualizations that allow you to group data into tables, gauges, horizontal bars, pie charts, vertical bars, and more.

To create a new visualization, click on the visualize icon 🏛 on the left-hand bar that looks like a small graph. This will bring up the new visualization selection screen. Then, follow these steps:

1. To select the visualization you want to create, select it from the list. Let's use a common one for this visualization, the pie chart:

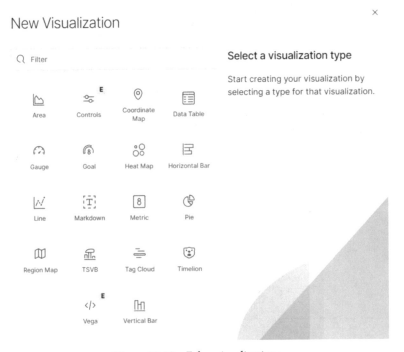

Figure 12.18 – Falco visualizations

2. Each visualization requires a source. For our example, we only have one index created called `falco*`, so select that as the source:

Figure 12.19 – Selecting a visualization source

3. The next step is to select a metric and a bucket. A metric defines how you want to aggregate the results from the bucket. The bucket is the value you want to visualize. For our example, we want our pie chart to display the total count of event priorities, ranging from **error**, **notice**, and **warning** to **debug**.

4. First, set the metric aggregation value to **Count**:

Figure 12.20 – Visualization metric options

5. Next, we need to select the field we want to aggregate. For **Aggregation**, select **Terms**, and for **Field**, select **priority.keyword**:

Figure 12.21 – Selecting bucket values

6. Before saving the visualization, you can preview the results by clicking the arrow button at the top of the metric box. A preview of the results will be shown in the right-hand pane:

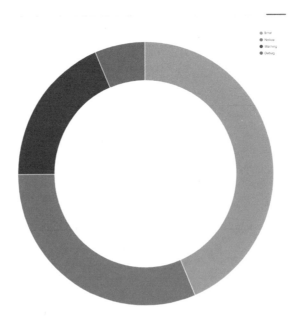

Figure 12.22 – Visualization preview

7. If the results are what you expected, you can save the visualization by clicking the **Save** link at the top of the main view. Enter a name for the visualization so you can find it later when you create a dashboard:

Figure 12.23 – Saving a new visualization

When you save the visualization, it will remain on screen, but you should see a confirmation in the lower-right corner that the save was successful.

To create additional visualizations, you only need to click on the visualization button again and select your desired type to create another one. Using what we went over for the first visualization, create two additional visualizations that use the following parameters:

- **Visualization Type**: Horizontal bar

  Source: `falco*`

  Metrics: Aggregation: Count

  Buckets: X-Axis, Aggregation: Terms, Field: `rule.keyword`

  Metrics: Count, Size: 5, Custom label: Top 5 Falco Rules

  Visualization Name: Top 5 Falco Rules

- **Visualization Type**: Data Table

  Source: `falco*`

  Metrics: Aggregation: Count

Buckets: Split rows, Aggregation: Terms, Field: `output_fields.fd.name.` `keyword`, Metric: Count, Size: 5, Custom label: Top 5 Modified Files

Visualization Name: Top 5 Falco Modified Files

In the next section, we will create a dashboard that displays the visualizations that you created.

Creating a dashboard

Dashboards allow you to display visualizations in a collection that is easy to read with information updated every minute:

1. To create a dashboard, click on the dashboard button 🔲 on the sidebar.

    The button looks like 4 stacked blocks.

2. This will bring up the **Create your first dashboard screen**. Click the **Create new dashboard** button to start creating your dashboard.

    You will be presented a blank dashboard with a single button on the screen:

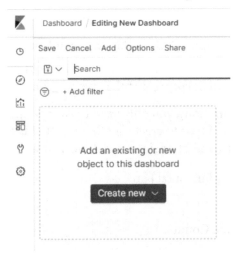

Figure 12.24 – Creating a new dashboard

3. This button provides you the option to use an existing visualization or to create a new one. Since we created three visualizations earlier, click the **Add an existing** link. Once selected, all existing visualizations will be presented on the right-hand side of the dashboard in the **Add panels** box:

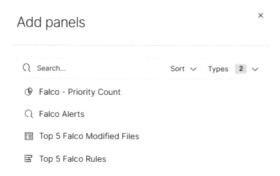

Figure 12.25 – Adding panels to a dashboard

4. We want to add the three visualizations that we created: **Falco - Priority Count**, **Top 5 Falco Modified Files**, and **Top 5 Falco Rules**. To add each one, click on each of them **once**.

5. Once you have added all of the visualizations to the dashboard, you can close the **Add panels** pane by clicking the **X** in the upper right-hand of that pane. Once it's closed, you should see your dashboard with the visualizations you selected:

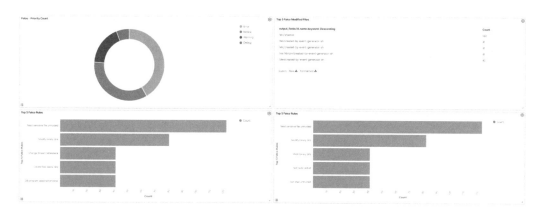

Figure 12.26 – Dashboard view after adding visualizations

Oops! It looks like we may have added the Top 5 Falco Rules visualization twice. When we went through the steps to add a visualization, we emphasized a key word in the step: "To add each one, click on each of them **once**." Visualizations are added each time you click on them. When we added the Falco rules to our dashboard, we double-clicked it.

If you did happen to double-click a visualization, it will be added to the dashboard twice. If you accidentally added a visualization twice, you can simply remove one of them by clicking the gear in the corner of the visualization and selecting **Delete from dashboard**:

Figure 12.27 – Deleting a panel from a dashboard

6. After deleting the duplicate visualization, you can save the dashboard by clicking the save link at the top of your browser window. This will prompt you to save your dashboard, so give it the name `Falco Dashboard` and click **Save**:

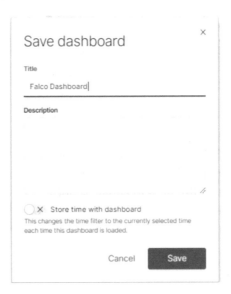

Figure 12.28 – Saving a dashboard

Once you save a dashboard, it will be available via the dashboards button on the left-hand side of the Kibana homepage. This is the same button you used earlier to create the first dashboard.

Summary

This chapter covered how to create an enhanced auditing system to your Kubernetes cluster. We started the chapter by introducing Falco, an auditing add-on that was donated to the CNCF by Sysdig. Falco adds a level of auditing that Kubernetes does not include, and combined with the including auditing functionality, provides an audit trail for everything from API access to actions in a pod.

Logs aren't beneficial if you can't store them in a logging system that allows you to store logs on persistent storage and usually offers a management interface to search logs and create dashboards. We installed the common EFK stack on our KinD cluster and created a custom dashboard to show Falco events in Kibana.

With the topics you learned in this chapter, you should have a strong foundational knowledge of how to add Falco to a cluster and use EFK to store logs and present data in visualizations and dashboards.

While logging and auditing are important, it is equally important to have a process to restore workloads in the event of a disaster. In the next chapter, we will introduce Velero, an open source backup utility from Heptio.

Questions

1. If you need to edit an included Falco rule, which file would you edit?

    A. `falco.yaml`

    B. `falco_rules.yaml`

    C. `falco_rules.changes.yaml`

    D. `falco_rules.local.yaml`

2. Which of the following is a common log forwarder used by Kubernetes?

    A. Kube-forwarder.

    B. Fluentd.

    C. Forwarder.

    D. Kubernetes doesn't use forwarders.

3. What is the product that provides a way to present logs using visualizations and dashboards when you deploy the EFK stack?

   A. Fluentd

   B. Elasticsearch

   C. Kibana

   D. Excel

4. Which of the following tools forwards only Falco logs to a central logging system?

   A. Falco.

   B. Falcosidekick.

   C. The Kubernetes API server.

   D. All products forward every log, not just the Falco logs.

5. What is the name of the object in Falco that allows you to create a collection of items?

   A. Lists

   B. Rules

   C. Arrays

   D. Collections

13
Backing Up Workloads

Accidents and disasters happen, and just like you may have insurance for these events in real life, you should have insurance for your cluster and the workloads.

Most Kubernetes distributions do not include any components to back up workloads, but there are a number of products available from both the open source community and vendor-supported solutions from companies such as Kasten.

In this chapter, you will be introduced to Velero, which can be used to back up workloads in the cluster. We will explain how to use Velero to back up namespaces and schedule backup jobs, as well as how to restore workloads.

In this chapter, we will cover the following topics:

- Understanding Kubernetes backups
- Performing an etcd backup
- Introducing and setting up Heptio's Velero
- Using Velero to back up workloads
- Managing Velero using the CLI
- Restoring from a backup

Technical requirements

To perform the hands-on experiments in this chapter, you will need the following:

- A KinD Kubernetes cluster
- A new Ubuntu 18.04 server with a minimum of 4 GB of RAM

You can access the code for this chapter at the following GitHub repository: `https://github.com/PacktPublishing/Kubernetes-and-Docker-The-Complete-Guide`.

Understanding Kubernetes backups

Backing up a Kubernetes cluster requires backing up not only the workloads running on the cluster but also the cluster itself. Remember that the cluster state is maintained in an etcd database, making it a very important component that you need to back up to recover from any disasters.

Creating a backup of the cluster and the running workloads allows you to do the following:

- Migrate clusters.
- Create a development cluster from a production cluster.
- Recover a cluster from a disaster.
- Recover data from persistent volumes.
- Namespace and deployment recovery.

In this chapter, we will provide the details and tools to back up your etcd database and every namespace and object in the cluster.

> **Important Note**
>
> Recovering a cluster from a complete disaster in an enterprise usually involves backing up custom SSL certificates for various components, such as Ingress controllers, load-balancers, and the API server.
>
> Since the process to back up all custom components is different for all environments, we will focus on the procedures that are common among most Kubernetes distributions.

As you know, the cluster state is maintained in etcd, and if you lose all of your etcd instances, you will lose your cluster. In a multi-node control plane, you would have a minimum of three etcd instances, providing redundancy for the cluster. If you lose a single instance, the cluster would remain running and you could build a new instance of etcd and add it to the cluster. Once the new instance has been added, it will receive a copy of the etcd database and your cluster will be back to full redundancy.

In the event that you lost all of your etcd servers without any backup of the database, you would lose the cluster, including the cluster state itself and all of the workloads. Since etcd is so important, the etcdctl utility includes a built-in backup function.

Performing an etcd backup

Since we are using KinD for our Kubernetes cluster, we can create a backup of the etcd database, but we will not be able to restore it.

Our etcd server is running in a pod on the cluster called etcd-cluster01-control-plane, located in the kube-system namespace. The running container includes the etcdctl utility, and we can execute a backup using kubectl commands.

Backing up the required certificates

Most Kubernetes installations store certificates in /etc/kuberetes/pki. In this respect, KinD is no different, so we can back up our certificates using the docker cp command. Let's see how to do this in two simple steps:

1. First, we will create a directory to store the certificates and the etcd database. Change your directory to the chapter13 folder where you cloned the book repository. Under the chapter13 folder, create a directory named backup and make it your current path:

    ```
    mkdir backup
    cd ./backup
    ```

2. To back up the certificates located on the API server, use the following docker cp command:

    ```
    docker cp cluster01-control-plane:/etc/kubernetes/pki ./
    ```

    This will copy the contents of the pki folder on the control plane node to your localhost in a new folder in the chapter13/backup/pki folder.

The next step is to create a backup of the etcd database.

Backing up the etcd database

To back up the etcd database on your KinD cluster, follow these steps:

> **Important Note**
>
> Older versions of `etcdctl` required you to set the API version to 3 using `ETCDCTL_API=3`, since they defaulted to the version 2 API. Etcd 3.4 changed the default API to 3, so we do not need to set that variable before using `etcdctl` commands.

1. Back up the database in the etcd pod and store it in the container's root folder. Using `kubectl exec`, run a shell on the etcd pod:

```
kubectl exec -it etcd-cluster01-control-plane /bin/sh -n
kube-system
```

2. In the etcd pod, back up the etcd database using `etcdctl`:

```
etcdctl snapshot save etcd-snapshot.db --endpoints=ht
tps://127.0.0.1:2379 --cacert=/etc/kubernetes/pki/etcd/
ca.crt --cert=/etc/kubernetes/pki/etcd/healthcheck-
client.crt --key=/etc/kubernetes/pki/etcd/healthcheck-
client.key
```

You will receive the following output:

```
{"level":"info","ts":1591637958.297016,"caller":"snapshot
/v3_snapshot.go:110","msg":"created temporary db
file","path":"etcd-snapshot.db.part"}
{"level":"warn","ts":"2020-06-08T17:39:18.323Z","caller":
"clientv3/retry_interceptor.go:116","msg":"retry stream
intercept"}
{"level":"info","ts":1591637958.3238735,"caller":
"snapshot/v3_snapshot.go:121","msg":"fetching snapshot",
"endpoint":"https://127.0.0.1:2379"}
{"level":"info","ts":1591637958.7283804,"caller":"
snapshot/v3_snapshot.go:134","msg":"fetched snapshot",
"endpoint":"https://127.0.0.1:2379","took":0.431136053}
Snapshot saved at etcd-snapshot.db
{"level":"info","ts":1591637958.732125,"caller":"snapshot
/v3_snapshot.go:143","msg":"saved","path":"etcd-
snapshot.db"}
```

3. Exit the etcd pod.

4. Copy the backup to your local machine:

```
kubectl cp kube-system/etcd-cluster01-control-plane:
etcd-snapshot.db ./etcd-snap-kind.db
```

5. Verify that the copy was successful by viewing the contents of the current folder:

```
ls -la
```

You should see the pki directory and the etcd backup, etcd-snap-kind.db. If you do not see your backup, repeat the steps again and watch for any errors in the output.

Of course, this process only backs up the etcd database once. In the real world, you should create a scheduled process that executes a snapshot of etcd at regular intervals and stores the backup file in a safe, secure location.

> **Note**
>
> Due to how KinD runs the control plane, we cannot use the restore procedures in this section. We are providing the steps in this section so that you know how to restore a corrupt etcd database or node in an enterprise environment.

Introducing and setting up Heptio's Velero

Velero is an open source backup solution for Kubernetes from Heptio. It offers many features that are only available in commercial products, including scheduling, backup hooks, and granular backup controls – all for no charge.

While Velero is free, it has a learning curve since it does not include an easy-to-use GUI like most commercial products. All operations in Velero are carried out using their command-line utility, an executable called velero. This single executable allows you to install the Velero server, create backups, check the status of backups, restore backups, and more. Since every operation for management can be done with one file, restoring a cluster's workloads becomes a very easy process. In this chapter, we will create a second KinD cluster and populate it with a backup from an existing cluster.

But before that, we need to take care of a few requirements.

Velero requirements

Velero consists of a few components to create a backup system:

- **The Velero CLI**: This provides the installation of Velero components. It is used for all backup and restore functions.

- **The Velero server**: Responsible for executing backing up and restore procedures.

- **Storage provider plug-ins**: Used for backup and restoring specific storage systems.

Outside of the base Velero components, you will also need to provide an object storage location that will be used to store your backups. If you do not have an object storage solution, you can deploy MinIO, which is an open source project that provides an S3-compatible object store. We will deploy MinIO in our KinD cluster to demonstrate the backup and restore features provided by Velero.

Installing the Velero CLI

The first step to deploy Velero is to download the latest Velero CLI binary. To install the CLI, follow these steps:

1. Download the release from Velero's GitHub repository:

    ```
    wget  https://github.com/vmware-tanzu/velero/releases/
    download/v1.4.0/velero-v1.4.0-linux-amd64.tar.gz
    ```

2. Extract the contents of the archive:

    ```
    tar xvf velero-v1.4.0-linux-amd64.tar.gz
    ```

3. Move the Velero binary to /usr/bin:

    ```
    sudo mv velero-v1.4.0-linux-amd64/velero  /usr/bin
    ```

4. Verify that you can run the Velero CLI by checking the version:

    ```
    velero version
    ```

You should see from the output from Velero that you are running version 1.4.0:

```
Client:
    Version: v1.4.0
    Git commit: 5963650c9d64643daaf510ef93ac4a36b6483392
<error getting server version: the server could not find the requested resource (post serverstatusrequests.velero.io)>
```

Figure 13.1 – Velero client version output

You can safely ignore the last line, which shows an error in finding the Velero server. Right now, all we have installed is the Velero executable, so we will install the server in the next step.

Installing Velero

Velero has minimal system requirements, most of which are easily met:

- A Kubernetes cluster running version 1.10 or higher
- The Velero executable
- Images for the system components
- A compatible storage location
- A volume snapshot plugin (optional)

Depending on your infrastructure, you may not have a compatible location for the backups or snapshotting volumes. Fortunately, if you do not have a compatible storage system, there are open source options that you can add to your cluster to meet the requirements.

In the next section, we will explain the natively supported storage options and since our example will use a KinD cluster, we will install open source options to add compatible storage to use as a backup location.

Backup storage location

Velero requires an S3-compatible bucket to store backups. There are a number of officially supported systems, including all object-store offerings from AWS, Azure, and Google.

Along with the officially supported providers, there are a number of community- and vendor-supported providers from companies such as DigitalOcean, Hewlett Packard, and Portworx. The following chart lists all of the current providers:

> **Important Note**
>
> In the following table, the **Backup Support** column means that the plugin provides a compatible location to store Velero backups. Volume Snapshot Support means that the plugin supports backing up persistent volumes.

Vendor	Backup Support	Volume Snapshot Support	Support
Amazon	AWS S3	AWS EBS	Official
Various	S3-compatible	AWS EBS	Official
Google	Google Cloud Storage	GCE disks	Official
Microsoft	Azure Blob Storage	Azure Managed Disks	Official
Vmware	Not supported	vSphere volumes	Official
Kubernetes CSI	Not supported	CSI volumes	Official
Alibaba Cloud	Alibaba Cloud OSS	Alibaba Cloud	Community
DigitalOcean	DigitalOcean object storage	DigitalOcean Volumes Block Storage	Community
HP	Not supported	HPE storage	Community
OpenEBS	Not supported	OpenEBS cStor volume	Community
Portworx	Not supported	Portworx volume	Community
restic (Beta)	Not supported	Kubernetes volumes	Community
Storj	Storj object storage	Not supported	Community

Table 13.1 – Velero storage options

> **Note**
>
> Velero's AWS S3 driver is compatible with many third-party storage systems, including EMC ECS, IBM Cloud, Oracle Cloud, and MinIO.

If you do not have an existing object storage solution, you can deploy the open source S3 provider, MinIO.

Now that we have the Velero executable installed, and our KinD cluster has persistent storage, thanks to the auto-provisioner from Rancher, we can move on to the first requirement – adding an S3-compatible backup location for Velero.

Deploying MinIO

MinIO is an open source object storage solution that is compatible with Amazon's S3 cloud services API. You can read more about MinIO on its GitHub repository at `https://github.com/minio/minio`.

If you install MinIO using a manifest from the internet, be sure to verify what volumes are declared in the deployment before trying to use it as a backup location. Many of the examples on the internet use `emptyDir: {}`, which is not persistent.

We have included a modified MinIO deployment from the Velero GitHub repository in the `chapter13` folder. Since we have persistent storage on our cluster, we edited the volumes in the deployment to use **PersistentVolumeClaims** (**PVCs**), which will use the auto-provisioner for Velero's data and configuration.

To deploy the MinIO server, change directories to `chapter13` and execute `kubectl create`. The deployment will create a Velero namespace, PVCs, and MinIO on your KinD cluster:

```
kubectl create -f minio-deployment.yaml
```

This will deploy the MinIO server and expose it as `minio` on port `9000/TCP`, as follows:

Figure 13.2 – Minio service creation

The MinIO server can be targeted by any pod in the cluster, with correct access keys, using `minio.velero.svc` on port `9000`.

Exposing the MinIO dashboard

MinIO includes a dashboard that allows you to browse the contents of the S3 buckets on the server. To allow access to the dashboard, you can deploy an Ingress rule that exposes the MinIO service. We have included an example Ingress manifest in the `chapter13` folder. You can create it using the included file, or from the following manifest:

1. Remember to change the host to include the host's IP address in the `nip.io` URL:

```
apiVersion: networking.k8s.io/v1beta1
kind: Ingress
metadata:
  name: minio-ingress
```

```
    namespace: velero
  spec:
    rules:
    - host: minio.[hostip].nip.io
      http:
        paths:
        - path: /
          backend:
            serviceName: minio
            servicePort: 9000
```

2. Once deployed, you can use a browser on any machine and open the URL you used for the Ingress rule. On our cluster, the host IP is `10.2.1.121`, so our URL is `minio.10.2.1.121.nip.io`:

Figure 13.3 – MinIO dashboard

3. To access the dashboard, supply the access key and secret key from the MinIO deployment. If you used the MinIO installer from the GitHub repository, the access key and secret key are `packt/packt`.

4. Once logged in, you will see a list of buckets and any items that are stored in them. Right now, it will be fairly empty since we haven't created a backup yet. We will revisit the dashboard after we execute a backup of our KinD cluster:

Figure 13.4 – MinIO Browser

> **Important Note**
>
> If you are new to object storage, it is important to note that while this deploys a storage solution in your cluster, it **will not** create a StorageClass or integrate with Kubernetes in any way. All pod access to the S3 bucket is done using the URL that we will provide in the next section.

Now that you have an S3-compatible object store running, you need to create a configuration file that Velero will use to target your MinIO server.

Creating the S3 target configuration

First, we need to create a file with credentials to the S3 bucket. When we deployed the MinIO manifest from the `chapter13` folder, it created an initial key ID and access key, `packt/packt`:

1. Create a new credential file in the `chapter13` folder called `credentials-velero`:

    ```
    vi credentials-velero
    ```

2. Add the following lines to the credentials file and save the file:

    ```
    [default]
    aws_access_key_id = packt
    aws_secret_access_key = packt
    ```

    Now, we can deploy Velero using the Velero executable and the `install` option.

3. Execute the Velero installation using the following command from inside the chapter13 folder to deploy Velero:

```
velero install \
    --provider aws \
    --plugins velero/velero-plugin-for-aws:v1.1.0 \
    --bucket velero \
    --secret-file ./credentials-velero \
    --use-volume-snapshots=false \
    --backup-location-config
region=minio,s3ForcePathStyle="true",s3Url=http://minio.
velero.svc:9000
```

Let's explain the installation options and what the values mean:

Option	Description
--provider	Configures Velero to use a storage provider. Since we are using MinIO, which is S3-compatible, we are passing aws as our provider.
--plugins	Tells Velero the backup plugin to use. For our cluster, since we are using MinIO for object storage, we selected the AWS plugin.
--bucket	The name of the S3 bucket that you want to target.
--secret-file	Points to the file that contains the credentials to authenticate with the S3 bucket.
--use-volume-snapshots	Will enable or disable volume snapshots. Since we do not want to back up persistent disks, we set this value to false.
--backup-location-config	The S3 target location where Velero will store backups. Since MinIO is running in the same cluster as Velero, we can target S3 using the name minio.velero.svc:9000. We will also create an Ingress rule to the MinIO service that will allow access to the MinIO dashboard and allow S3 requests externally via the Ingress URL.
--use-restic	If you want to back up persistent volumes but you don't have a compatible volume snapshot provider, you can enable the restic plugin using this option. For additional details on restic and its features and limitations, see the restic section on the Velero GitHub page at https://velero.io/docs/v1.4/restic/.

Table 13.2 – Velero Install Options

When you execute the install, you will see a number of objects being created, including a number of **CustomResourceDefinitions (CRDs)** and secrets that Velero uses to handle backup and restore operations. If you run into issues with your Velero server starting up correctly, there are a few CRDs and secrets that you can look at that may have incorrect information. In the following table, we explain some of the common objects that you may need to interact with when using Velero:

CustomResourceDefinition	Name	Description
backups.velero.io	Backup	Each backup that is created will create an object called backup, which includes the settings for each backup job.
backupstoragelocations. velero.io	BackupStorageLocation	Each backup storage location creates a BackupStorageLocation object that contains the configuration to connect to the storage provider.
schedules.velero.io	Schedule	Each scheduled backup creates a Schedule object that contains the schedule for a backup.
volumesnapshotlocations. velero.io	VolumeSnapshotLocation	If enabled, the VolumeSnapshotLocation object contains the information on the storage used for volume snapshots.

Secret Name	Description
cloud-credentials	Contains the credentials to connect to the storage provider in Base64 format. If your Velero pod fails to start up, you may have an incorrect value in the data.cloud spec.
velero-restic-credentials	If you are using the restic plugin, this will contain your repository password. Similar to cloud-credentials. If you experience issues connecting to the volume snapshot provider, verify that the repository password is correct.

Table 13.3 – Velero's CRDs and Secrets

While most of your interaction with these objects will be through the Velero executable, it is always a good practice to understand how utilities interact with the API server. Understanding the objects and what their functions are is helpful if you do not have access to the Velero executable but you need to view, or potentially change, an object value to address an issue quickly.

Now that we have Velero installed, and a high-level understanding of Velero objects, we can move on to creating different backup jobs for a cluster.

Using Velero to back up workloads

Velero supports running a "one-time" backup with a single command or on a recurring schedule. Whether you chose to run a single backup or a recurring backup, you can back up all objects or only certain objects using `include` and `exclude` flags.

Running a one-time cluster backup

To create an initial backup, you can run a single Velero command that will back up all of the namespaces in the cluster.

Executing a backup without any flags to include or exclude any cluster objects will back up every namespace and all of the objects in the namespace.

To create a one-time backup, execute the `velero` command with the `backup create <backup name>` option. In our example, we have named the backup `initial-backup`:

```
velero backup create initial-backup
```

The only confirmation you will receive from this is that the backup request was submitted:

```
Backup request "initial-backup" submitted successfully.
Run `velero backup describe initial-backup` or `velero backup
logs initial-backup` for more details.
```

Fortunately, Velero also tells you the command to check the backup status and logs. The last line of the output tells us that we can use the `velero` command with the `backup` option and either `describe` or `logs` to check the status of the backup operation.

The `describe` option will show all of the details of the job:

```
Name:             initial-backup
Namespace:        velero
Labels:           velero.io/storage-location=default
Annotations:      velero.io/source-cluster-k8s-gitversion=v1.18.2
                  velero.io/source-cluster-k8s-major-version=1
                  velero.io/source-cluster-k8s-minor-version=18

Phase:  Completed

Namespaces:
  Included:  *
  Excluded:  <none>

Resources:
  Included:        *
  Excluded:        <none>
  Cluster-scoped:  auto

Label selector:  <none>

Storage Location:  default

Velero-Native Snapshot PVs:  auto

TTL:  720h0m0s

Hooks:  <none>

Backup Format Version:  1

Started:    2020-06-27 16:49:54 +0000 UTC
Completed:  2020-06-27 16:50:01 +0000 UTC

Expiration:  2020-07-27 16:49:54 +0000 UTC

Total items to be backed up:  384
Items backed up:              384

Velero-Native Snapshots: <none included>
```

Figure 13.5 – The Velero describe output

> **Note**
>
> To reinforce the previous section, where we mentioned some of the CRDs that Velero uses, we also want to explain where the Velero utility retrieves this information from.
>
> Each backup that is created will create a backup object in the Velero namespace. For our initial backup, a new backup object named `initial-backup` was created. Using `kubectl`, we can describe the object to see similar information that the Velero executable will provide.

As shown in *Figure 13.5*, the describe option shows you all of the settings for the backup job. Since we didn't pass any options to the backup request, the job contains all the namespaces and objects. Some of the most important details to verify are the phase, total items to be backed up, and the items backed up.

If the status of the phase is anything other than success, you may not have all the items that you want in your backup. It's also a good idea to check the backed-up items; if the number of items backed up is less than the items to be backed up, our backup did not back up all of the items.

You may need to check the status of a backup, but you may not have the Velero executable installed. Since this information is in a CR, we can describe the CR to retrieve the backup details. Running kubectl describe on the backup object will show the status of the backup:

```
kubectl describe backups initial-backup -n velero
```

If we jump to the bottom of the output from the describe command, you will see the following:

```
Spec:
  Hooks:
  Included Namespaces:
    *
  Storage Location:  default
  Ttl:               720h0m0s
Status:
  Completion Timestamp:  2020-06-27T16:50:01Z
  Expiration:            2020-07-27T16:49:54Z
  Format Version:        1.1.0
  Phase:                 Completed
  Progress:
    Items Backed Up:  384
    Total Items:      384
  Start Timestamp:  2020-06-27T16:49:54Z
  Version:          1
```

Figure 13.6 – The kubectl describe output on the backup resource

In the output, you can see that the phase is completed, the start and completion times, and the number of objects that were backed up and included in the backup.

It's good practice to use a cluster add-on that can generate alerts based on information in log files or the status of an object, such as AlertManager. You always want a successful backup, and if a backup fails, you should look into the failure immediately.

Scheduling a cluster backup

Creating a one-time backup is useful if you have a cluster operation scheduled or if there is a major software upgrade in a namespace. Since these events will be rare, you will want to schedule a backup that will back up the cluster at regular intervals, rather than random one-time backups.

To create a scheduled backup, you use the `schedule` option and create a tag with the Velero executable. Along with the schedule and create, you need to provide a name for the job and the `schedule` flag, which accepts *cron*-based expressions. The following schedule tells Velero to back up at 1 AM every day:

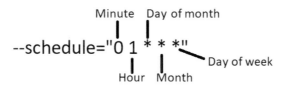

Figure 13.7 – Cron scheduling expression

Using the information in *Figure 13.7*, we can create a backup that will create a backup at 1 a.m., using the following `velero schedule create` command:

```
velero schedule create cluster-daily --schedule="0 1 * * *"
```

Velero will reply that a schedule has been successfully created:

```
Schedule "cluster-daily" created successfully.
```

If you are not familiar with cron and the options that are available, you should read the cron package documentation at `https://godoc.org/github.com/robfig/cron`.

cron will also accept some shorthand expressions, which may be easier than using the standard cron expressions. The following table contains the shorthand for predefined schedules:

Shorthand Value	Description
`@yearly`	Executes once a year at midnight on January 1st
`@monthly`	Executes once a month, on the first day of the month, at midnight
`@weekly`	Executes once a week, on Sunday morning at midnight
`@daily`	Executes daily at midnight
`@hourly`	Executes at the beginning of each hour

Table 13.4 – cron shorthand scheduling

Using the values from the shorthand table to schedule a backup job that executes daily at midnight, we use the following Velero command:

```
velero schedule create cluster-daily --schedule="@daily"
```

Scheduled jobs will create a backup object when the job is executed. The backup name will contain the name of the schedule, with a dash and the date and time of the backup. Using the name from the preceding example, our initial backup was created with the name `cluster-daily-20200627174947`. Here, `20200627` is the date the backup ran, and `174947` is the time the backup ran in UTC time. This is the equivalent of **2020-06-27 17:49:47 +0000 UTC**.

All of our examples so far have been configured to back up all of the namespaces and objects in the cluster. You may need to create different schedules or exclude/include certain objects based on your specific clusters.

In the next section, we will explain how to create a custom backup that will allow you to use specific tags to include and exclude namespaces and objects.

Creating a custom backup

When you create any backup job, you can provide flags to customize what objects will be included in or excluded from the backup job. Some of the most common flags are detailed here:

Flag	Description
`--exclude-namespaces`	Comma-separated list of namespaces to exclude from the backup job.
	Example: `--exclude-namespaces web-dev1,web-dev2`
`--exclude-resources`	Comma-separated list of resources to exclude, formatted as `resource.group`.
	Example: `--exclude-resources storageclasses.storage.k8s.io`
`--include-namespaces`	Comma-separated list of namespaces to include in the backup job.
	Example: `--include-namespaces web-dev1,web-dev2`

Flag	Description
`--selector`	Configures the backup to include only objects that match a label selector. Accepts a single value only. Example: `--selector app.kubernetes.io/name=ingress-nginx`
`--ttl`	Configures how long to keep the backup in hours, minutes, and seconds. By default, the value is set for 30 days, or `720h0m0s`. Example: `--ttl 24h0m0s` This will delete the backup after 24 hours.

Table 13.5 – Velero backup flags

To create a scheduled backup that will run daily and include only Kubernetes system namespaces, we would create a scheduled job using the `--include-namespaces` flag:

```
velero schedule create cluster-ns-daily --schedule="@daily"
--include-namespaces ingress-nginx,kube-node-lease,kube-
public,kube-system,local-path-storage,velero
```

Since Velero commands use a CLI for all operations, we should start by explaining the common commands you will use to manage backup and restore operations.

Managing Velero using the CLI

Right now, all Velero operations must be done using the Velero executable. Managing a backup system without a GUI can be a challenge at first, but once you get comfortable with the Velero management commands, it becomes easy to perform operations.

The Velero executable accepts two options:

- Commands
- Flags

A command is an operation such as `backup`, `restore`, `install`, and `get`. Most initial commands require a second command to make a complete operation. For example, a `backup` command requires another command, such as `create` or `delete`, to form a complete operation.

There are two types of flags – command flags and global flags. Global flags are flags that can be set for any command, while command flags are specific to the command being executed.

Like many CLI tools, Velero includes built-in help for every command. If you forget some syntax or want to know what flags can be used with a command, you can use the -h flag to get help:

```
velero backup create -h
```

The following is the abbreviated help output for the backup create command:

```
Create a backup

Usage:
  velero backup create NAME [flags]

Examples:
        # create a backup containing all resources
        velero backup create backup1

        # create a backup including only the nginx namespace
        velero backup create nginx-backup --include-namespaces nginx

        # create a backup excluding the velero and default namespaces
        velero backup create backup2 --exclude-namespaces velero,default

        # view the YAML for a backup that doesn't snapshot volumes, without sending it to the
  server
        velero backup create backup3 --snapshot-volumes=false -o yaml

        # wait for a backup to complete before returning from the command
        velero backup create backup4 --wait

Flags:
      --exclude-namespaces stringArray                    namespaces to exclude from the backup
      --exclude-resources stringArray                     resources to exclude from the backup,
```

Figure 13.8 – Velero help output

We find Velero's help system to be very helpful; once you get comfortable with the Velero basics, you will find that the built-in help provides enough information for most commands.

Using common Velero commands

Since many of you may be new to Velero, we wanted to provide a quick overview of the most commonly used commands to get you comfortable with operating Velero.

Listing Velero objects

As we have mentioned, Velero management is driven by using the CLI. You can imagine that as you create additional backup jobs, it may become difficult to remember what has been created. This is where the get command comes in handy.

The CLI can retrieve, or get, a list of the following Velero objects:

- Backup-locations
- Backups
- Plugins
- Restores
- Schedules
- Snapshot locations

As you may expect, executing `velero get <object>` will return a list of the objects managed by Velero:

```
velero get backups
```

Here is the output:

```
NAME                                STATUS       CREATED
backup-initial                      Completed    2020-06-27 04:24:38 +0000 UTC
cluster-daily-20200627175009        Completed    2020-06-27 17:50:09 +0000 UTC
cluster-daily-20200627174947        Completed    2020-06-27 17:49:47 +0000 UTC
cluster-ns-daily-20200627180800     Completed    2020-06-27 18:08:00 +0000 UTC
day2                                Completed    2020-06-27 04:25:59 +0000 UTC
initial-backup                      Completed    2020-06-27 16:49:54 +0000 UTC
selector-example                    Completed    2020-06-27 18:00:03 +0000 UTC
selector-example2                   Completed    2020-06-27 18:00:54 +0000 UTC
```

Figure 13.9 – The velero get output

All the `get` commands will produce a similar output, which contains the names of each object and any unique values for the objects.

The `get` command is useful for a quick look at what objects exists, but it's usually used as the first step toward executing the next command, `describe`.

Retrieving details for a Velero object

After you get the name of the object that you want the details for, you can use the `describe` command to get the details of the object. Using the output from the `get` command in the previous section, we want to view the details for the `cluster-daily-20200627175009` backup job:

```
velero describe backup cluster-daily-20200627175009
```

The output of the command provides all the details for the requested object. You will find yourself using the `describe` command to troubleshoot issues such as backup failures.

Creating and deleting objects

Since we have already used the `create` command a few times, we will focus on the `delete` command in this section.

To recap, the `create` command allows you to create objects that will be managed by Velero, including backups, schedules, restores, and locations for backups and snapshots. We have created a backup and a schedule, and in the next section, we will create a restore.

Once an object is created, you may discover that you need to delete it. To delete objects in Velero, you use the `delete` command, along with the object and name you want to delete.

In our `get backups` output example, we had a backup called `day2`. To delete that backup, we would execute the following `delete` command:

```
velero delete backup day2
```

Since a delete is a one-way operation, you will need to confirm that you want to delete the object. Once confirmed, it may take a few minutes for the object to be removed from Velero since it waits until all associated data is removed:

```
Are you sure you want to continue (Y/N)? y
Request to delete backup "day2" submitted successfully.
The backup will be fully deleted after all associated data (disk snapshots, backup files, restores) are removed.
```

Figure 13.10 – Velero delete output

As you can see in the output, when we delete a backup, Velero will delete all of the objects for the backup, including the snapshot's backup files and restores.

There are additional commands that you can use, but the commands covered in this section are the main commands you need to get comfortable with Velero.

Now that you can create and schedule backups, and know how to use the help system in Velero, we can move on to using a backup to restore objects.

Restoring from a backup

With any luck, you will rarely need to execute a restore of any Kubernetes object. Even if you haven't been in the IT field long, you have likely experienced a personal situation where you had a drive failure, or accidentally deleted an important file. If you don't have a backup of the data that was lost, it is a very frustrating situation. In the enterprise world, missing data or not having a backup can lead to huge revenue losses, or in some scenarios, large fines in regulated industries.

To run a restore from a backup, you use the `create restore` command with the `--from-backup <backup name>` tag.

Earlier in the chapter, we created a single, one-time backup, called `initial-backup`, which includes every namespace and object in the cluster. If we decided that we needed to restore that backup, we would execute a restore using the Velero CLI:

```
velero restore create --from-backup initial-backup
```

The output from the `restore` command may seem odd:

```
Restore request "initial-backup-20200627194118" submitted
successfully.
```

At a quick glance, it may seem like a backup request was made since Velero replies with `"initial-backup-20200627194118" submitted successfully`. Velero uses the backup name to create a restore request, and since we named our backup `initial-backup`, the restore job name will use that name and append the date and time of the restore request.

You can view the status of the restore using the `describe` command:

```
velero restore describe initial-backup-20200627194118
```

Depending on the size of the restore, it may take some time to restore the entire backup. During the restore phase, the status of the backup will be `InProgress`. Once completed, the status will change to `Completed`.

Restoring in action

With all of the theory behind us, let's use two examples to see Velero in action. For the examples, we will start with a simple deployment that will delete and restore on the same cluster. The next example will be more complex; we will use the backup for our main KinD cluster and restore the cluster objects to a new KinD cluster.

Restoring a deployment from a backup

For the first example, we will create a simple deployment using an NGINX web server. We will deploy the application, verify that it works as expected, and then delete the deployment. Using the backup, we will restore the deployment and test that the restore worked by browsing to the web server's home page.

We have included a deployment in the chapter13 folder of your cloned repository. This deployment will create a new namespace, the NGINX deployment, a service, and an Ingress rule for our exercise. The deployment manifest has also been included.

As with any Ingress rule we have created throughout the book, you will need to edit its URL to reflect your host's IP address for nip.io to work correctly. Our lab server has an IP address of 10.2.1.121 – change this IP to your host's IP:

1. Edit the manifest from the GitHub repository under the chapter13 folder called nginx-deployment.yaml to include your niop.io URL. The section you need to change is shown here:

```
spec:
  rules:
  - host: nginx-lab.10.2.1.121.nip.io
```

2. Deploy the manifest using kubectl:

```
kubectl apply -f nginx-deployment.yaml
```

This will create the objects we need for the deployment:

```
namespace/nginx-lab created
pod/nginx-deployment created
ingress.networking.k8s.io/nginx-ingress created
service/nginx-lab created
```

3. Finally, test the deployment using any browser and open the URL from the Ingress rule:

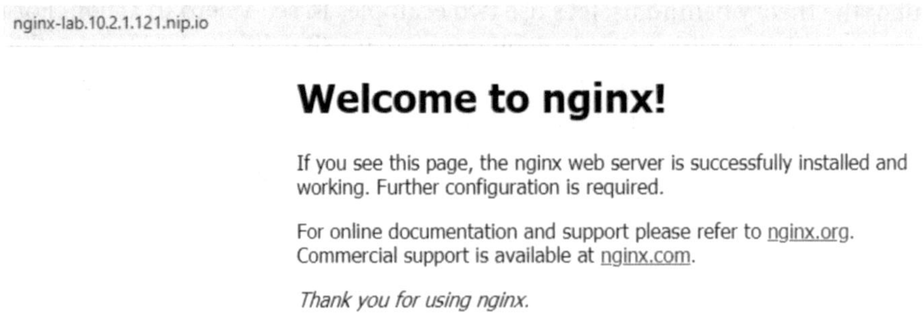

nginx-lab.10.2.1.121.nip.io

Welcome to nginx!

If you see this page, the nginx web server is successfully installed and working. Further configuration is required.

For online documentation and support please refer to nginx.org. Commercial support is available at nginx.com.

Thank you for using nginx.

Figure 13.11 – Verify that NGINX is running

Now that you have verified that the deployment works, we need to create a backup using Velero.

Backing up the namespace

Create a one-time backup of the new namespace using the Velero `create backup` command. Assign the backup job the name `nginx-lab`:

```
velero create backup nginx-lab --include-namespaces=nginx-lab
```

Since the namespace only contains a small deployment, the backup should complete quickly. Verify that the backup has completed successfully by using the `describe` command:

```
velero backup describe nginx-lab
```

Verify that the phase status is complete. If you have an error in the phase status, you may have entered the namespace name incorrectly in the `create backup` command.

After you verify that the backup has been successful, you can move on to the next step.

Simulating a failure

To simulate an event that would require a backup of our namespace, we will delete the entire namespace using `kubectl`:

```
kubectl delete ns nginx-lab
```

It may take a minute to delete the objects in the namespace. Once you have returned to a prompt, the deletion should have completed.

Verify that the NGINX server does not reply by opening the URL in a browser; if you are using the same browser from the initial test, refresh the page. You should receive an error when refreshing or opening the URL:

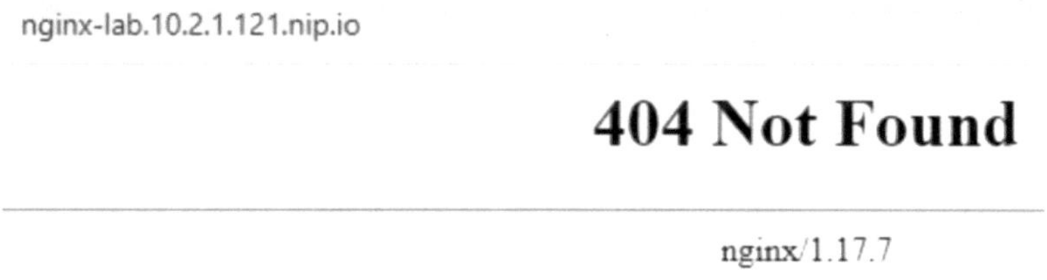

nginx-lab.10.2.1.121.nip.io

404 Not Found

nginx/1.17.7

Figure 13.12 – Verify whether NGINX is running

With the confirmation that the NGINX deployment has been deleted, we will restore the entire namespace and objects from the backup.

Restoring a namespace

Imagine this is a "real-world" scenario. You receive a phone call that a developer has accidentally deleted every object in their namespace and they do not have the source files.

Of course, you are prepared for this type of event. You have several backup jobs running in your cluster and you tell the developer that you can restore it to the state it was in last night from a backup:

1. We know that the backup's name is `nginx-lab`, so using Velero, we can execute a `restore create` command with the `--from-backup` option:

    ```
    velero create restore --from-backup nginx-lab
    ```

2. Velero will return that a restore job has been submitted:

    ```
    Restore request "nginx-lab-20200627203049" submitted
    successfully.
    Run `velero restore describe nginx-lab-20200627203049` or
    `velero restore logs nginx-lab-20200627203049` for more
    details.
    ```

3. You can check the status using the `velero restore describe` command:

    ```
    velero restore describe nginx-lab-20200627203049
    ```

4. Verify that the phase status shows `completed`, and verify that the deployment has been restored by browsing to the URL or refreshing the page if you already have it open:

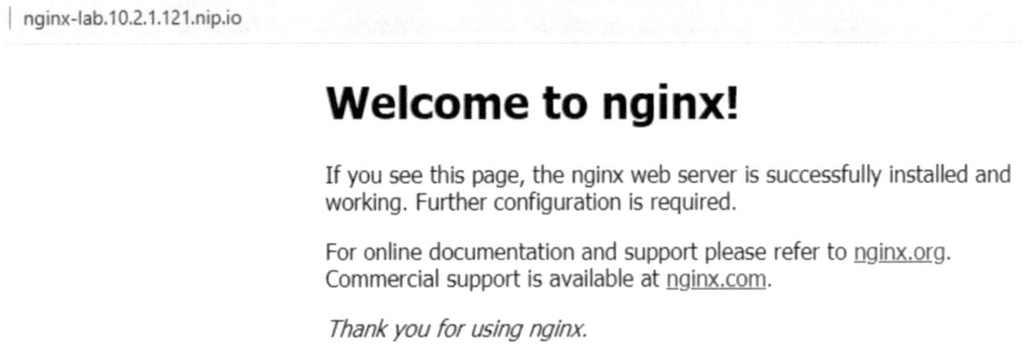

nginx-lab.10.2.1.121.nip.io

Welcome to nginx!

If you see this page, the nginx web server is successfully installed and working. Further configuration is required.

For online documentation and support please refer to nginx.org. Commercial support is available at nginx.com.

Thank you for using nginx.

Figure 13.13 – Verify that NGINX has been restored

Congratulations, you just saved the developer a lot of work because you had a backup of the namespace!

Velero is a powerful product that you should consider using in every cluster to protect the workloads from disasters.

Using a backup to create workloads in a new cluster

Restoring objects in a cluster is just one use case for Velero. While it is the main use case for most users, you can also use your backup files to restore a workload or all workloads on another cluster. This is a useful option if you need to create a new development or disaster recovery cluster.

> **Important Note**
>
> Remember that Velero backup jobs are only the namespaces and objects in the namespaces. To restore a backup to a new cluster, you must have a running cluster running Velero before you can restore any workloads.

Backing up the cluster

By this point in the chapter, we assume that you have seen this process a few times and that you know how to use the Velero CLI. If you need a refresher, you can go back a few pages in the chapter for reference, or use the CLI help function.

First, we should create a few namespaces and add some deployments to each one to make it more interesting:

1. Let's create a few demo namespaces:

    ```
    kubectl create ns demo1
    kubectl create ns demo2
    kubectl create ns demo3
    kubectl create ns demo4
    ```

2. We can add a quick deployment to a namespace using the `kubectl run` command:

    ```
    kubectl run nginx --image=bitnami/nginx -n demo1
    kubectl run nginx --image=bitnami/nginx -n demo2
    kubectl run nginx --image=bitnami/nginx -n demo3
    kubectl run nginx --image=bitnami/nginx -n demo4
    ```

    Now that we have some additional workloads, we need to create a backup of the cluster.

3. Back up the new namespaces using a backup name of `namespace-demo`:

    ```
    velero backup create namespace-demo --include-namespaces=
    demo1,demo2,demo3,demo4
    ```

Before moving on, verify that the backup has been completed successfully.

Building a new cluster

Since we are only demonstrating how Velero can be used to create workloads on a new cluster from a backup, we will create a simple single-node KinD cluster as our restore point:

> **Note**
>
> This section gets a little complex since you will have two clusters in your `kubeconfig` file. Follow the steps carefully if you're new to switching config contexts.
>
> Once we have completed this exercise, we will delete the second cluster since we will not need to have two clusters.

1. Create a new KinD cluster with the name `velero-restore`:

    ```
    kind create cluster --name velero-restore
    ```

    This will create a new single-node cluster that contains both the control plane and worker node, and it will set your cluster context to the new cluster.

2. Once the cluster has deployed, verify that your context has been switched to the `velero-restore` cluster:

    ```
    kubectl config get-contexts
    ```

    The output is as follows:

    ```
    CURRENT   NAME                  CLUSTER               AUTHINFO              NAMESPACE
              kind-cluster01        kind-cluster01        kind-cluster01
    *         kind-velero-restore   kind-velero-restore   kind-velero-restore
    ```

    Figure 13.14 – Verifying your current context

3. Verify that the current context is set to the `kind-velero-restore` cluster. You will see an * in the current field of the cluster that is being used.

4. Finally, verify the namespaces in the cluster using `kubectl`. You should only see the default namespaces that are included with a new cluster:

```
NAME                 STATUS    AGE
default              Active    5m42s
kube-node-lease      Active    5m44s
kube-public          Active    5m44s
kube-system          Active    5m44s
local-path-storage   Active    5m36s
```

Figure 13.15 – New cluster namespaces

Now that we have a new cluster created, we can start the process to restore the workloads. The first step is to install Velero on the new cluster, pointing to the existing S3 bucket as the backup location.

Restoring a backup to the new cluster

With our new KinD cluster up and running, we need to install Velero to restore our backup. We can use most of the same manifests and settings that we used in the original cluster, but since we are in a different cluster, we need to change the S3 target to the external URL we used to expose the MinIO dashboard.

Installing Velero in the new cluster

We already have the `credentials-velero` file in the `chapter13` folder, so we can jump right in to installing Velero using the `velero install` command:

1. Be sure to change the IP address in `s3Url target` to your host's IP address:

```
velero install \
    --provider aws \
    --plugins velero/velero-plugin-for-aws:v1.1.0 \
    --bucket velero \
    --secret-file ./credentials-velero \
    --use-volume-snapshots=false \
    --backup-location-config
region=minio,s3ForcePathStyle="true",s3Url=http://
minio.10.2.1.121.nip.io
```

2. The install will take a few minutes, but once the pod is up and running, view the log files to verify that the Velero server is up and running and connected to the S3 target:

```
kubectl logs deployment/velero -n velero
```

3. If all of your settings were correct, the Velero log will have an entry saying that it has found backups in the backup location that need to be synced with the new Velero server (The number of backups may be different for your KinD cluster):

```
time="2020-06-27T22:14:02Z" level=info msg="Found 9
backups in the backup location that do not exist in the
cluster and need to be synced" backupLocation=default
controller=backup-sync logSource="pkg/controller/backup_
sync_controller.go:196"
```

4. After confirming the installation, verify that Velero can see the existing backup files using `velero get backups`:

```
NAME                             STATUS      CREATED                          EXPIRES
backup-initial                   Completed   2020-06-27 04:24:38 +0000 UTC    29d
cluster-daily-20200627175009     Completed   2020-06-27 17:50:09 +0000 UTC    29d
cluster-daily-20200627174947     Completed   2020-06-27 17:49:47 +0000 UTC    29d
cluster-full-demo                Completed   2020-06-27 21:53:24 +0000 UTC    29d
```

Figure 13.16 – Viewing backups on the new cluster

Your backup list will differ from ours, but you should see the same list that you had in the original cluster.

At this point, we can use any of the backup files to create a restore job in the new cluster.

Restoring a backup in a new cluster

In this section, we will use the backup that was created in the previous section and restore the workloads to a brand new KinD cluster to simulate a workload migration.

The backup that was created of the original cluster, after we added the namespaces and deployment, was called `namespace-demo`:

1. Using that backup name, we can restore the namespaces and objects by running the `velero restore create` command:

```
velero create restore --from-backup=namespace-demo
```

2. Wait for the restore to complete before moving on to the next step. To verify that the restore was successful, use the `velero describe restore` command with the name of the restore job that was created when you executed the `create restore` command. In our cluster, the restore job was assigned the name `namespace-demo-20200627223622`:

```
velero restore describe namespace-demo-20200627223622
```

3. Once the phase has changed from `InProgress` to `Completed`, verify that your new cluster has the additional demo namespaces using `kubectl get ns`:

```
NAME                  STATUS   AGE
default               Active   38m
demo1                 Active   119s
demo2                 Active   119s
demo3                 Active   118s
demo4                 Active   118s
ingress-nginx         Active   11m
kube-node-lease       Active   38m
kube-public           Active   38m
kube-system           Active   38m
local-path-storage    Active   38m
nginx-lab             Active   11m
velero                Active   24m
```

Figure 13.17 – Viewing backups on the new cluster

4. You will see that the new namespaces were created, and if you look at the pods in each namespace, you will see that each has a pod called `nginx`. You can verify that the pods were created using kubectl get pods. For example, to verify the pods in the demo1 namespace: **kubectl get pods -n demo1**

The output is as follows:

```
NAME    READY   STATUS    RESTARTS   AGE
nginx   1/1     Running   0          2m13s
```

Figure 13.18 – Verifying pods in restored namespaces

Congratulations! You have successfully restored objects from one cluster into a new cluster.

Deleting the new cluster

Since we do not need two clusters, let's delete the new KinD cluster that we restored the backup to:

1. To delete the cluster, execute the `kind delete cluster` command:

   ```
   kind delete cluster --name velero-restore
   ```

2. Set your current context to the original KinD cluster, `kind-cluster01`:

   ```
   kubectl config use-context kind-cluster01
   ```

You are now ready to continue to the final chapter of the book, *Chapter 14*, *Provisioning a Platform*.

Summary

Backing up clusters and workloads is a requirement for any enterprise cluster. In this chapter, we reviewed how to back up the etcd cluster database using `etcdctl` and the snapshot feature. We also went into detail on how to install Heptio's Velero in a cluster to back up and restore workloads. We closed out the chapter by copying workloads from an existing backup by restoring an existing backup on a new cluster.

Having a backup solution allows you to recover from a disaster or human error. A typical backup solution allows you to restore any Kubernetes object, including namespaces, persistent volumes, RBAC, services, and service accounts. You can also take all of the workloads from one cluster and restore them on a completely different cluster for testing or troubleshooting.

Coming up next, in our final chapter, we will pull together many of the previous lessons in this book to build a platform for both your developers and your admins. We will add source control and pipelines to build a platform, allowing a developer to build a "project," checking in source code to create a running application.

Questions

1. True or false – Velero can only use an S3 target to store backup jobs.

    A. True

    B. False

2. If you do not have an object storage solution, how can you provide an S3 target using a backend storage solution such as NFS?

    A. You can't – there is no way to add anything in front of NFS to present S3.

    B. Kubernetes can do this using native CSI features.

    C. Install MinIO and use the NFS volumes as persistent disks in the deployment.

    D. You don't need to use an object store; you can use NFS directly with Velero.

3. True or false – Velero backups can only be restored on the same cluster where the backup was originally created.

    A. True

    B. False

4. What utility can you use to create an etcd backup?

    A. Velero.

    B. MinIO.

    C. There is no reason to back up the etcd database.

    D. `etcdctl`.

5. Which command will create a scheduled backup that runs every day at 3 a.m.?

    A. `velero create backup daily-backup`

    B. `velero create @daily backup daily-backup`

    C. `velero create backup daily-backup -schedule="@daily3am"`

    D. `velero create schedule daily-backup --schedule="0 3 * * *"`

14
Provisioning a Platform

Every chapter in this book, up until this point, has focused on the infrastructure of your cluster. We have explored how to deploy Kubernetes, how to secure it, and how to monitor it. What we haven't talked about is how to deploy applications.

In this, our final chapter, we're going to work on building an application deployment platform using what we've learned about Kubernetes. We're going to build our platform based on some common enterprise requirements. Where we can't directly implement a requirement, because building a platform on Kubernetes can fill its own book, we'll call it out and provide some insights.

In this chapter, we will cover the following topics:

- Designing a pipeline
- Preparing our cluster
- Deploying GitLab
- Deploying Tekton
- Deploying ArgoCD
- Automating project onboarding using OpenUnison

Technical requirements

To perform the exercises in this chapter, you will need a clean KinD cluster with a minimum of 8 GB of memory, 75 GB storage, and 4 CPUs. The system we will build is minimalist but still requires considerable horsepower to run.

You can access the code for this chapter at the following GitHub repository: `https://github.com/PacktPublishing/Kubernetes-and-Docker-The-Complete-Guide`.

Designing a pipeline

The term "pipeline" is used extensively in the Kubernetes and DevOps world. Very simply, a pipeline is a process, usually automated, that takes code and gets it running. This usually involves the following:

Figure 14.1 – A simple pipeline

Let's quickly run through the steps involved in this process:

1. Storing the source code in a central repository, usually Git

2. When code is committed, building it and generating artifacts, usually a container

3. Telling the platform – in this case, Kubernetes – to roll out the new containers and shut down the old ones

This is about as basic as a pipeline can get and isn't of much use in most deployments. In addition to building our code and deploying it, we want to make sure we scan containers for known vulnerabilities. We may also want to run our containers through some automated testing before going into production. In enterprise deployments, there's often a compliance requirement where someone takes responsibility for the move to production as well. Taking this into account, the pipeline starts to get more complex:

Figure 14.2 – Pipeline with common enterprise requirements

The pipeline has added some extra steps, but it's still linear with one starting point, a commit. This is also very simplistic and unrealistic. The base containers and libraries your applications are built on are constantly being updated as new **Common Vulnerabilities and Exposures** (**CVEs**), a common way to catalog and identify security vulnerabilities, are discovered and patched. In addition to having developers that are updating application code for new requirements, you will want to have a system in place that scans both the code and the base containers for available updates. These scanners watch your base containers and can do something to trigger a build once a new base container is ready. While the scanners could call an API to trigger a pipeline, your pipeline is already waiting on your Git repository to do something, so it would be better to simply add a commit or a pull request to your Git repository to trigger the pipeline:

Figure 14.3 – Pipeline with scanners integrated

This means your application code is tracked and your operational updates are tracked in Git. Git is now the source of truth for not only what your application code is but also operations updates. When it's time to go through your audits, you have a ready-made change log! If your policies require you to enter changes into a change management system, simply export the changes from Git.

So far, we have focused on our application code and just put **Rollout** at the end of our pipeline. The final rollout step usually means patching a `Deployment` or `StatefulSet` with our newly built container, letting Kubernetes do the work of spinning up new `Pods` and scaling down the old ones. This could be done with a simple API call, but how are we tracking and auditing that change? What's the source of truth?

Our application in Kubernetes is defined as a series of objects stored in etcd that are generally represented as code using YAML files. Why not store those files in a Git repository too? This gives us the same benefits as storing our application code in Git. We have a single source of truth for both the application source and the operations of our application! Now, our pipeline involves some more steps:

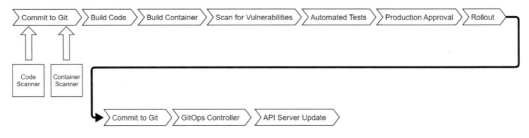

Figure 14.4 – GitOps pipeline

In this diagram, our rollout updates a Git repository with our application's Kubernetes YAML. A controller inside our cluster watches for updates to Git and when it sees them, gets the cluster in sync with what's in Git. It can also detect drift in our cluster and bring it back to alignment with our source of truth.

This focus on Git is called **GitOps**. The idea is that all of the work of an application is done via code, not directly via APIs. How strict you are with this idea can dictate what your platform looks like. Next, we'll explore how opinions can shape your platform.

Opinionated platforms

Kelsey Hightower, a developer advocate for Google and leader in the Kubernetes world, once said: "Kubernetes is a platform for building platforms. It's a better place to start; not the endgame." When you look at the landscape of vendors and projects building Kubernetes-based products, they all have their own opinions of how systems should be built. As an example, Red Hat's **OpenShift Container Platform** (**OCP**) wants to be a one-stop-shop for multi-tenant enterprise deployment. It builds in a great deal of the pipeline we discussed. You define a pipeline that is triggered by a commit, which builds a container and pushes it into its own internal registry that then triggers a rollout of the new container. Namespaces are the boundaries of tenants. Canonical is a minimalist distribution that doesn't include any pipeline components. Managed vendors such as Amazon, Azure, and Google provide the building blocks of a cluster and the hosted build tools of a pipeline but leave it to you to build out your platform.

There is no correct answer as to which platform to use. Each is opinionated and the right one for your deployment will depend on your own requirements. Depending on the size of your enterprise, it wouldn't be surprising to see more than one platform deployed!

Having looked at the idea of opinionated platforms, let's explore the security impacts of building a pipeline.

Securing your pipeline

Depending on your starting point, this can get complex quickly. How much of your pipeline is one integrated system, or could it be described using a colorful American colloquialism involving duct tape? Even in platforms where all the components are there, tying them together can often mean building a complex system. Most of the systems that are part of your pipeline will have a visual component. Usually, the visual component is a dashboard. Users and developers may need access to that dashboard. You don't want to maintain separate accounts for all those systems, do you? You'll want to have one login point and portal for all the components of your pipeline.

After determining how to authenticate the users who use these systems, the next question is how to automate the rollout. Each component of your pipeline requires configuration. It can be as simple as an object that gets created via an API call or as complex as tying together a Git repo and build process with SSH keys to automate security. In such a complex environment, manually creating pipeline infrastructure will lead to security gaps. It will also lead to impossible-to-manage systems. Automating the process and providing consistency will help you both secure your infrastructure and keep it maintainable.

Finally, it's important to understand the implications of GitOps on our cluster from a security standpoint. We discussed authenticating administrators and developers to use the Kubernetes API and authorizing access to different APIs in *Chapter 7, Integrating Authentication into Your Cluster*, and *Chapter 8, RBAC Policies Using Active Directory Users*. What is the impact if someone can check in a `RoleBinding` that assigns them the `admin ClusterRole` for a namespace and a GitOps controller automatically pushes it through to the cluster? As you design your platform, consider how developers and administrators will want to interact with it. It's tempting to say "Let everyone interact with their application's Git registry," but that means putting the burden on you as the cluster owner for many requests. As we discussed in *Chapter 8, RBAC Policies Using Active Directory*, this could make your team the bottleneck in an enterprise. Understanding your customers, in this case, is important in knowing how they want to interact with their operations even if it's not how you intended.

Having touched on some of the security aspects of GitOps and a pipeline, let's explore the requirements for a typical pipeline and how we will build it.

Building our platform's requirements

Kubernetes deployments, especially in enterprise settings, will often have the following basic requirements:

- **Development and test environments**: At least two clusters to test the impacts of changes on the cluster level to applications

- **Developer sandbox**: A place where developers can build containers and test them without worrying about impacts on shared namespaces

- **Source control and issue tracking**: A place to store code and track open tasks

In addition to these basic requirements, enterprises will often have additional requirements, such as regular access reviews, limiting access based on policy, and workflows that assign responsibility for actions that could impact a shared environment.

For our platform, we want to encompass as many of these requirements as possible. To better automate deployments onto our platform, we're going to define each application as having the following:

- **A development namespace**: Developers are administrators.

- **A production namespace**: Developers are viewers.

- **A source control project**: Developers can fork.

- **A build process**: Triggered by updates to Git.

- **A deploy process**: Triggered by updates to Git.

In addition, we want our developers to have their own sandbox so that each user will get their own namespace for development.

> **Important Note**
> In a real deployment, you will want to separate your development and production environments into separate clusters. This makes it much easier to test cluster-wide operations, such as upgrades, without impacting running applications. We're doing everything in one cluster to make it easier for you to set up on your own.

To provide access to each application, we will define three roles:

- **Owners**: Users that are application owners can approve access for other roles inside their application. This role is assigned to the application requestor and can be assigned by application owners. Owners are also responsible for pushing changes into development and production.

- **Developers**: These are users that will have access to an application's source control and can administer the application's development namespace. They can view objects in the production namespace but can't edit anything. This role can be requested by any users and is approved by an application owner.

- **Operations**: These users have the capabilities as developers, but can also make changes to the production namespace as needed. This role can be requested by any user and is approved by the application owner.

We will also create some environment-wide roles:

- **System approvers**: Users with this role can approve access to any system-wide roles.

- **Cluster administrators**: This role is specifically for managing our cluster and the applications that comprise our pipeline. It can be requested by anyone and must be approved by a member of the system approvers role.

- **Developers**: Anyone who logs in gets their own namespace for development. These namespaces cannot be requested for access by other users. These namespaces are not directly connected to any CI/CD infrastructure or Git repositories.

Even with our very simple platform, we have six roles that need to be mapped to the applications that make up our pipeline. Each application has its own authentication and authorization processes that these roles will need to be mapped to. This is just one example of why automation is so important to the security of your clusters. Provisioning this access manually based on email requests can become unmanageable quickly.

The workflow that developers are expected to go through with an application will line up with the GitOps flow we designed previously:

- Application owners will request an application be created. Once approved, a Git repository will be created for application code, pipeline build manifests, and Kubernetes manifests. Development and production namespaces will be created as well with appropriate `RoleBinding` objects. Groups will be created that reflect the roles for each application, with approval for access to those groups delegated to the application owner.

- Developers and operations staff are granted access to the application by either requesting it or having it provided directly by an application owner. Once granted access, updates are expected in both the developer's sandbox and the development namespace. Updates are made in a user's fork for the Git repository, with pull requests used to merge code into the main repositories that drive automation.

- All builds are controlled via "scripts" in the application's source control.

- All artifacts are published to a centralized container registry.

- All production updates must be approved by application owners.

This basic workflow doesn't include typical components of a workflow, such as code and container scans, periodic access recertifications, or requirements for privileged access. The topic of this chapter can easily be a complete book on its own. The goal isn't to build a complete enterprise platform but to give you a starting point for building and designing your own system.

Choosing our technology stack

In the previous parts of this section, we talked about pipelines in a generic way. Now, let's get into the specifics of what technology is needed in our pipeline. We identified earlier that every application has application source code and Kubernetes manifest definitions. It also has to build containers. There needs to be a way to watch for changes to Git and update our cluster. Finally, we need an automation platform so that all these components work together.

Based on our requirements for our platform, we want technology that has the following features:

- **Open source**: We don't want you to buy anything just for this book!

- **API-driven**: We need to be able to provision components and access in an automated way.

- **Has a visual component that supports external authentication**: This book focuses on enterprise, and everyone in the enterprise loves their GUIs. Just not having different credentials for each application.

- **Supported on Kubernetes**: This is a book on Kubernetes.

To meet these requirements, we're going to deploy the following components to our cluster:

- **Git Registry – GitLab**: GitLab is a powerful system that provides a great UI and experience for working with Git that supports external authentication (that is, **Single Sign-On (SSO)**). It has integrated issue management and an extensive API. It also has a Helm chart that we have tailored for the book to run a minimal install.

- **Automated Builds – Tekton**: Originally the build portion of the Knative project for Kubernetes function-as-a-service deployments, Tekton was spun off into its own project to provide build services for generic applications. It runs in Kubernetes with all interactions being via the Kubernetes API. There's an early stage dashboard too!

- **Container Registry – simple Docker registry**: There are many very capable open source registries. Since this deployment will get complex quickly, we decided just to use the registry provided by Docker. There won't be any security on it, so don't use it in production!

- **GitOps – ArgoCD**: ArgoCD is a collaboration between Intuit and Weaveworks to build a feature-rich GitOps platform. It's Kubernetes native, has its own API, and stores its objects as Kubernetes custom resources, making it easier to automate. Its UI and CLI tools both integrate with SSO using OpenID Connect.

- **Access, authentication, and automation – OpenUnison**: We'll continue to use OpenUnison for authentication into our cluster. We're also going to integrate the UI components of our technology stack as well to provide a single portal for our platform. Finally, we'll use OpenUnison's workflows to manage access to each system based on our role structure and provision the objects needed for everything to work together. Access will be provided via OpenUnison's self-service portal.

Reading through this technology stack, you might ask "Why didn't you choose *XYZ*?" The Kubernetes ecosystem is diverse with no shortage of great projects and products for your cluster. This is by no means a definitive stack, nor is it even a "recommended" stack. It's a collection of applications that meets our requirements and lets us focus on the processes being implemented, rather than learning a specific technology.

You might also find that there's quite a bit of overlap between even the tools in this stack. For instance, GitLab has GitOps capabilities and its own build system, but we chose not to use them for this chapter. We did that so that you can see how to tie different systems together to build a platform. Your platform may use GitHub's SaaS solution for source control but run builds internally and combine with Amazon's container registry. We wanted you to see how these systems can be connected to build a platform instead of focusing on specific tools.

This section was a very deep exploration of the theory behind pipeline design and looking at common requirements for building a Kubernetes-based platform. We identified technology components that can implement those requirements and why we chose them. With this knowledge in hand, it's time to build!

Preparing our cluster

Before we begin deploying our technology stack, we need to do a couple of things. I recommend starting with a fresh cluster. If you're using the KinD cluster from this book, start with a new cluster. We're deploying several components that need to be integrated and it will be simpler and easier to start fresh rather than potential struggling with previous configurations. Before we start deploying the applications that will make up our stack, we're going to deploy JetStack's cert-manager to automate certificate issuing, a simple container registry, and OpenUnison for authentication and automation.

Deploying cert-manager

JetStack, a Kubernetes-focused consulting company, created a project called `cert-manager` to make it easier to automate the creation and renewal of certificates. This project works by letting you define issuers using Kubernetes custom resources and then using annotations on `Ingress` objects to generate certificates using those issuers. The end result is a cluster running with properly managed and rotated certificates without generating a single **certificate signing request** (**CSR**) or worrying about expiration!

The `cert-manager` project is most often mentioned with *Let's Encrypt* (`https://letsencrypt.org/`) to automate the publishing of certificates that have been signed by a commercially recognized certificate authority for free (as in beer). This is possible because *Let's Encrypt* automates the process. The certificates are only good for 90 days and the entire process is API-driven. In order to drive this automation, you must have some way of letting *Let's Encrypt* verify ownership of the domain you are trying to get a certificate for. Throughout this book, we have used `nip.io` to simulate DNS. If you have a DNS service that you can use and is supported by `cert-manager`, such as Amazon's Route 53, then this is a great solution.

Since we're using `nip.io`, we will deploy `cert-manager` with a self-signed certificate authority. This gives us the benefit of having a certificate authority that can quickly generate certificates without having to worry about domain validation. We will then instruct our workstation to trust this certificate as well as the applications we deploy so that everything is secured using properly built certificates.

> **Important Note**
>
> Using a self-signed certificate authority is a common practice for most enterprises for internal deployments. This avoids having to deal with potential validation issues where a commercially signed certificate won't provide much value. Most enterprises are able to distribute an internal certificate authority's certificates via their Active Directory infrastructure. Chances are your enterprise has a way to request either an internal certificate or a wildcard that could be used too.

The steps to deploy `cert-manager` are as follows:

1. From your cluster, deploy the `cert-manager` manifests:

    ```
    $ kubectl apply --validate=false -f https://github.com/
    jetstack/cert-manager/releases/download/v0.16.1/cert-
    manager.yaml
    ```

2. Once the Pods are running in the `cert-manager` namespace, create a self-signed certificate that we'll use as our certificate authority. In the `chapter14/shell` directory of the Git repository for this book is a script called `makeca.sh` that will generate this certificate for you:

    ```
    $ cd Kubernetes-and-Docker-The-Complete-Guide/chapter14/
    shell/
    $ sh ./makeca.sh
    Generating RSA private key, 2048 bit long modulus (2
    primes)
    ...........................................................
    ...........................................................
    ...........................+++++
    ...................+++++
    e is 65537 (0x010001)
    ```

3. There is now an SSL directory with a certificate and a key. The next step is to create a secret from these files that will become our certificate authority:

    ```
    $ cd ssl/
    $ kubectl create secret tls ca-key-pair --key=./tls.key
    --cert=./tls.crt -n cert-manager
    secret/ca-key-pair created
    ```

4. Next, create the `ClusterIssuer` object so that all of our `Ingress` objects can have properly minted certificates:

```
$ cd ../../yaml/
$ kubectl create -f ./certmanager-ca.yaml
clusterissuer.cert-manager.io/ca-issuer created
```

5. With `ClusterIssuer` created, any `Ingress` object with the `cert-manager.io/cluster-issuer: "ca-issuer"` annotation will have a certificate signed by our authority created for them. One of the components we will be using for this is our container registry. Kubernetes uses Docker's underlying mechanisms for pulling containers, and KinD will not pull images from registries running without TLS or using an untrusted certificate. To get around this issue, we need to import our certificate into both our worker and nodes:

```
$ cd ~/
$ kubectl get secret ca-key-pair -n cert-manager -o json
| jq -r '.data["tls.crt"]' | base64 -d > internal-ca.crt
$ docker cp internal-ca.crt cluster01-worker:/usr/local/
share/ca-certificates/internal-ca.crt
$ docker exec -ti cluster01-worker update-ca-certificates
Updating certificates in /etc/ssl/certs...
1 added, 0 removed; done.
Running hooks in /etc/ca-certificates/update.d...
done.
$ docker restart cluster01-worker
$ docker cp internal-ca.crt cluster01-control-plane:/usr/
local/share/ca-certificates/internal-ca.crt
$ docker exec -ti cluster01-control-plane update-ca-
certificates
Updating certificates in /etc/ssl/certs...
1 added, 0 removed; done.
Running hooks in /etc/ca-certificates/update.d...
done.
$ docker restart cluster01-control-plane
```

The first command extracts the certificate from the secret we created to host the certificate. The next set of commands copies the certificate to each container, instructs the container to trust it, and finally, restarts the container. Once your containers are restarted, wait for all the Pods to come back; it could take a few minutes.

> **Important Note**
>
> Now would be a good time to download `internal-ca.crt`; install it onto your local workstation and potentially into your browser of choice. Different operating systems and browsers do this differently, so check the appropriate documentation on how to do this. Trusting this certificate will make things much easier when interacting with applications, pushing containers, and using command-line tools.

With `cert-manager` ready to issue certificates and both your cluster and your workstation trusting those certificates, the next step is to deploy a container registry.

Deploying the Docker container registry

Docker, Inc. provides a simple registry. There is no security on this registry, so it is most certainly not a good option for production use. The `chapter14/yaml/docker-registry.yaml` file will deploy the registry for us and create an `Ingress` object. Before deploying, edit this file, changing all instances of `192-168-2-140` to a dash representation of your cluster's IP address. For instance, my cluster is running on `192.168.2.114`, so I will replace `192-168-2-140` with `192-168-2-114`. Then, run `kubectl create` on the manifest to create the registry:

```
$ kubectl create -f ./docker-registry.yaml
namespace/docker-registry created
statefulset.apps/docker-registry created
service/docker-registry created
ingress.extensions/docker-registry created
```

Once the registry is running, you can try accessing it from your browser:

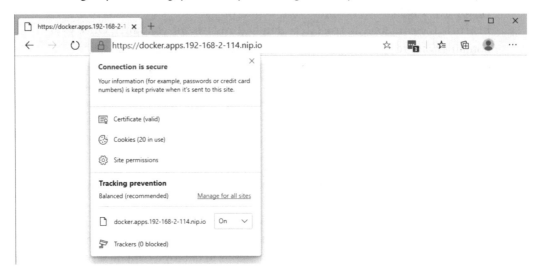

Figure 14.5 – Accessing the container registry in a browser

You won't see much since the registry has no web UI, but you also shouldn't get a certificate error. That's because we deployed `cert-manager` and are issuing signed certificates! With our registry running, the last component to deploy is OpenUnison.

Deploying OpenUnison

In *Chapter 7, Integrating Authentication into Your Cluster*, we introduced OpenUnison to authenticate access to our KinD deployment. OpenUnison comes in two flavors. The first, which we have already deployed, is a login portal that lets us authenticate using a central source and pass group information to our RBAC policies. The second is an automation portal that we'll use as the basis for integrating the systems that will manage our pipeline. This portal will also give us a central UI for requesting projects to be created and managing access to our project's systems.

We defined that each project we deploy will have three "roles" that will span several systems. Will your enterprise let you create and manage groups for every project we create? Some might, but Active Directory is a critical component in most enterprises, and write access can be difficult to get. It's unlikely that the people who run your Active Directory are the same people who you report to when managing your cluster, complicating your ability to get an area of Active Directory that you have administrative rights in. The OpenUnison automation portal lets you manage access with local groups that can be easily queried, just like with Active Directory, but you have control to manage them. We'll still authenticate against our central SAML provider, though.

To facilitate OpenUnison's automation capabilities, we need to deploy a database to store persistent data and an SMTP server to notify users when they have open requests or when requests have been completed. For the database, we'll deploy the open source MariaDB. For an **Simple Mail Transfer Protocol (SMTP)** (email) server, most enterprises have very strict rules about sending emails. We don't want to have to worry about getting email set up for notifications, so we'll run a "black hole" email service that just disregards all SMTP requests:

1. First, run the `chapter14/yaml/mariadb.yaml` manifest from the book's GitHub repository. No changes need to be made.

2. Next, deploy the SMTP black hole:

    ```
    $ kubectl create ns blackhole
    namespace/blackhole created
    $ kubectl create deployment blackhole
    --image=tremolosecurity/smtp-blackhole -n blackhole
    deployment.apps/blackhole created
    $ kubectl expose deployment/blackhole --type=ClusterIP
    --port 1025 --target-port=1025 -n blackhole
    service/blackhole exposed
    ```

3. With MariaDB and our SMTP service deployed, we're able to deploy OpenUnison. Follow *steps 1–5* in the *Deploying OpenUnison* section of *Chapter 7, Integrating Authentication into Your Cluster*, to deploy the OpenUnison operator and Kubernetes dashboard.

4. Next, create a `Secret` to store credentials for accessing MariaDB and the SMTP service. We hardcoded passwords into our deployment for MariaDB for simplicity's sake, so make sure to generate long, random passwords for your production database account! Create the following `Secret` in your cluster:

    ```
    apiVersion: v1
    type: Opaque
    metadata:
      name: orchestra-secrets-source
      namespace: openunison
    data:
      K8S_DB_SECRET: aW0gYSBzZWNyZXQ=
      SMTP_PASSWORD: ""
    ```

```
  OU_JDBC_PASSWORD: c3RhcnR0MTIz
  unisonKeystorePassword: aW0gYSBzZWNyZXQ=
kind: Secret
```

5. We're going to reuse the Helm values we used in *step 2* in the *Configuring your cluster for impersonation* section of *Chapter 7, Integrating Authentication into Your Cluster*, with three changes.

6. First, change the image from `docker.io/tremolosecurity/openunison-k8s-login-saml2:latest` to `docker.io/tremolosecurity/openunison-k8s-saml2:latest`.

7. Next, Base64-encode your `internal-ca.crt` file into a single line and add it to the `trusted_certs` section of `values.yaml`:

```
$ base64 -w 0 < internal-ca.crt
LS0tLS1CRUdJTiBDRVJUSUZJQ0FURS0tLS0
tCk1JSUREVENDQWZXZ0F3SUJ...
```

8. Add SMTP and database sections. The updates to `values.yaml` will look as follows. I removed most of the unchanged portions to save space:

```
trusted_certs:
  - name: internal-ca
    pem_b64: LS0tLS1CRUdJTiB...
saml:
  idp_url: https://portal.apps.tremolo.io/idp-test/
metadata/dfbe4040-cd32-470e-a9b6-809c8f857c40
  metadata_xml_b64: ""

database:
  hibernate_dialect: org.hibernate.dialect.
MySQL5InnoDBDialect
  quartz_dialect: org.quartz.impl.jdbcjobstore.
StdJDBCDelegate
  driver: com.mysql.jdbc.Driver
  url: jdbc:mysql://mariadb.mariadb.svc.cluster.
local:3306/unison
  user: unison
  validation: SELECT 1
```

```
smtp:
  host: blackhole.blackhole.svc.cluster.local
  port: 1025
  user: none
  from: donotreply@domain.com
  tls: false
```

9. Deploy OpenUnison using the Helm chart:

    ```
    $ helm install orchestra tremolo/openunison-k8s-saml2
    --namespace openunison -f ./openunison-values.yaml
    ```

10. Once OpenUnison is deployed, edit the `orchestra` OpenUnison object to remove
    the `unison-ca` key. Remove the block that looks like this:

    ```
    - create_data:
        ca_cert: true
        key_size: 2048
        server_name: k8sou.apps.192-168-2-114.nip.io
        sign_by_k8s_ca: false
        subject_alternative_names:
        - k8sdb.apps.192-168-2-114.nip.io
        - k8sapi.apps.192-168-2-114.nip.io
      import_into_ks: certificate
      name: unison-ca
      tls_secret_name: ou-tls-certificate
    ```

11. Delete the `ou-tls-certificate` Secret:

    ```
    $ kubectl delete secret ou-tls-certificate -n openunison
    secret "ou-tls-certificate" deleted
    ```

12. Edit the `openunison` Ingress object, adding `cert-manager.io/cluster-
    issuer: ca-issuer` to the list of `annotations`.

13. Complete the SSO integration with the testing identity provider using *steps 4–6*
    from the *Configuring your cluster for impersonation* section of *Chapter 7, Integrating
    Authentication into Your Cluster*.

14. Log in to OpenUnison, then log out.

15. The OpenUnison automation portal doesn't do anything with the groups from the testing identity provider. In order to become a cluster administrator, you must be "bootstrapped" into the environment's groups:

```
$ kubectl exec -ti mariadb-0 -n mariadb -- mysql -u \
  unison --password='startt123' \
  -e "insert into userGroups (userId,groupId) values
(2,1);" \
  unison
$ kubectl exec -ti mariadb-0 -n mariadb -- mysql -u \
  unison --password='startt123' \
  -e "insert into userGroups (userId,groupId) values
(2,2);" \   unison
```

16. Finally, log back in. You will be a global administrator and a cluster administrator for your cluster.

With OpenUnison deployed, you can now remotely administer your cluster. Depending on how you are accessing your cluster, it may be easier to use your workstation to directly manage your cluster for the rest of the steps in this chapter.

You'll notice that there are different "badges" in OpenUnison now. In addition to getting a token or accessing the dashboard, you can request a new namespace to be created or access the ActiveMQ dashboard. You'll also see that the title bar has additional options, such as **Request Access**. OpenUnison will become our self-service portal for deploying our pipelines without having to manually create objects in our applications or cluster. We're not going to go into these in detail until we talk about using OpenUnison to automate the deployment of our pipelines.

With your cluster prepared, the next step is to deploy the components for our pipeline.

Deploying GitLab

When building a GitOps pipeline, one of the most important components is a Git repository. GitLab has many components besides just Git, including a UI for navigating code, a web-based **integrated development environment** (**IDE**) for editing code, and a robust identity implementation to manage access to projects in a multi-tenant environment. This makes it a great solution for our platform since we can map our "roles" to GitLab groups.

In this section, we're going to deploy GitLab into our cluster and create two simple repositories that we'll use later when we deploy Tekton and ArgoCD. We'll focus on the automation steps when we revisit OpenUnison to automate our pipeline deployments.

GitLab deploys with a Helm chart. For this book, we built a custom `values` file to run a minimal install. While GitLab comes with features that are similar to ArgoCD and Tekton, we won't be using them. We also didn't want to worry about high availability. Let's begin:

1. Create a new namespace called `gitlab`:

    ```
    $ kubectl create ns gitlab
    namespace/gitlab created
    ```

2. We need to add our certificate authority as a secret for GitLab to trust talking to OpenUnison and the webhooks we will eventually create for Tekton:

    ```
    $ kubectl get secret ca-key-pair \
      -n cert-manager -o json | jq -r '.data["tls.crt"]' \
      | base64 -d > tls.crt
    $ kubectl create secret generic \
      internal-ca --from-file=. -n gitlab
    ```

3. Open `chapter14/gitlab/secret/provider` in your favorite text editor. Replace `local.tremolo.dev` with the full domain suffix for your cluster. For instance, my cluster is running on `192.168.2.114`, so I'm using the `apps.192-168-2-114.nip.io` suffix. Here's my updated `Secret`:

    ```
    name: openid_connect
    label: OpenUnison
    args:
      name: openid_connect
      scope:
        - openid
        - profile
      response_type: code
      issuer: https://k8sou.apps.192-168-2-114.nip.io/auth/
    idp/k8sIdp
      discovery: true
      client_auth_method: query
    ```

```
    uid_field: sub
    send_scope_to_token_endpoint: false
    client_options:
      identifier: gitlab
      secret: secret
      redirect_uri: https://gitlab.apps.192-168-2-114.nip.
  io/users/auth/openid_connect/callback
```

> **Important Note**
>
> We're using a client secret of `secret`. This should not be done for a production cluster. If you're deploying GitLab into production using our templates as a starting point, make sure to change this.

4. Create the `secret` for GitLab to integrate with OpenUnison for SSO. We'll finish the process when we revisit OpenUnison:

```
$ kubectl create secret generic gitlab-oidc --from-file=.
-n gitlab
secret/gitlab-oidc created
```

5. Edit `chapter14/yaml/gitlab-values.yaml`. Just as in *step 3*, replace `local.tremolo.dev` with the full domain suffix for your cluster. For instance, my cluster is running on `192.168.2.114`, so I'm using the `apps.192-168-2-114.nip.io` suffix.

6. If your cluster is running on a single virtual machine, now would be a good time to create a snapshot. If something goes wrong during the GitLab deployment, it's easier to revert back to a snapshot since the Helm chart doesn't do a great job of cleaning up after itself on a delete.

7. Add the chart to your local repository and deploy GitLab:

```
$ helm repo add gitlab https://charts.gitlab.io
$ "gitlab" has been added to your repositories
$ helm install gitlab gitlab/gitlab -n gitlab -f
chapter14/yaml/gitlab-values.yaml
NAME: gitlab
LAST DEPLOYED: Sat Aug  8 14:50:13 2020
NAMESPACE: gitlab
STATUS: deployed
```

```
REVISION: 1
WARNING: Automatic TLS certificate generation with
cert-manager is disabled and no TLS certificates were
provided. Self-signed certificates were generated.
```

8. It will take a few minutes to run. Even once the Helm chart has been installed, it can take 15–20 minutes for all the Pods to finish deploying. While GitLab is initializing, we need to update the web frontend's `Ingress` object to use a certificate signed by our certificate authority. Edit the `gitlab-webservice Ingress` object in the `gitlab` namespace. Change the `kubernetes.io/ingress.class: gitlab-nginx` annotation to `kubernetes.io/ingress.class: nginx`. Also, change `secretName` from `gitlab-wildcard-tls` to `gitlab-web-tls`:

```
apiVersion: extensions/v1beta1
kind: Ingress
metadata:
  annotations:
    cert-manager.io/cluster-issuer: ca-issuer
    kubernetes.io/ingress.class: nginx
    kubernetes.io/ingress.provider: nginx
    .

    .

    .


  tls:
  - hosts:
    - gitlab.apps.192-168-2-114.nip.io
    secretName: gitlab-web-tls
status:
  loadBalancer: {}
```

9. We next need to update our GitLab shell to accept SSH connections on port 2222. This way, we can commit code without having to worry about blocking SSH access to your KinD server. Edit the `gitlab-gitlab-shell Deployment` in the `gitlab` namespace. Find `containerPort: 2222` and insert `hostPort: 2222` underneath, making sure to maintain the spacing. Once the Pod relaunches, you'll be able to SSH to your GitLab hostname on port 2222.

10. To get your root password to log in to GitLab, get it from the secret that was generated:

```
$ kubectl get secret gitlab-gitlab-initial-root-password
-o json -n gitlab | jq -r '.data.password' | base64 -d
10xtSWXfbvH5umAbCk9NoN0wAeYsUo9jRVbXrfLn
KbzBoPLrCGZ6kYRe8wdREcDl
```

You now can log in to your GitLab instance by going to https://gitlab.apps.x-x-x-x.nip.io, where x-x-x-x is the IP of your server. Since my server is running on 192.168.2.114, my GitLab instance is running on https://gitlab.apps.192-168-2-114.nip.io/.

Creating example projects

To explore Tekton and ArgoCD, we will create two projects. One will be for storing a simple Python web service, while the other will store the manifests for running the service. Let's begin:

1. The top of the GitLab screen will ask you to add an SSH key. Do that now so that we can commit code. Since we're going to be centralizing authentication via SAML, GitLab won't have a password for authentication.

2. Create a project and call it hello-python. Keep the visibility **private**.

3. Clone the project using SSH. Because we're running on port 2222, we need to change the URL provided by GitLab to be a proper SSH URL. For instance, my GitLab instance gives me the URL git@gitlab.apps.192-168-2-114.nip.io:root/hello-python.git. This needs to be changed to ssh://git@gitlab.apps.192-168-2-114.nip.io:2222/root/hello-python.git.

4. Once cloned, copy the contents of chapter14/python-hello into your repository and push to GitLab:

```
$ cd chapter14/python-hello
$ git archive --format=tar HEAD > /path/to/hello-python/
data.tar
$ cd /path/to/hello-python
$ tar -xvf data.tar
README.md
source/
```

```
source/Dockerfile
source/helloworld.py
source/requirements.txt
$ git add *
$ git commit -m 'initial commit'
$ git push
```

5. In GitLab, create another project called `hello-python-operations` with visibility set to private. Clone this project and copy the contents of `chapter14/python-hello-operations` into the repository, and then push it.

Now that GitLab is deployed with some example code, we are able to move on to the next step, building an actual pipeline!

Deploying Tekton

Tekton is the pipeline system we're using for our platform. Originally part of the Knative project for building function-as-a-service on Kubernetes, Tekton was broken out into its own project. The biggest difference between Tekton and other pipeline technologies you may have run is that Tekton is Kubernetes-native. Everything from its execution system, definition, and webhooks for automation are able to run on just about any Kubernetes distribution you can find. For example, we'll be running it in KinD and Red Hat has moved to Tekton as the main pipeline technology used for OpenShift starting in 4.1.

The process of deploying Tekton is pretty straightforward. Tekton is a series of operators that look for the creation of custom resources that define a build pipeline. The deployment itself only takes a couple of `kubectl` commands:

```
$ kubectl apply --filename \  https://storage.googleapis.com/
tekton-releases/pipeline/latest/release.yaml
$ kubectl apply --filename \ https://storage.googleapis.com/
tekton-releases/triggers/latest/release.yaml
```

The first command deploys the base system needed to run Tekton pipelines. The second command deploys the components needed to build webhooks so that pipelines can be launched as soon as code is pushed. Once both commands are done and the Pods in the `tekton-pipelines` namespace are running, you're ready to start building a pipeline! We'll use our Python Hello World web service as an example.

Building Hello World

Our Hello World application is really straightforward. It's a simple service that echoes back the obligatory "hello" and the host the service is running on just so we feel like our service is doing something interesting. Since the service is written in Python, we don't need to "build" a binary, but we do want to build a container. Once the container is built, we want to update the Git repository for our running namespace and let our GitOps system reconcile the change to redeploy our application. The steps for our build will be as follows:

1. Check out our latest code.

2. Create a tag based on a timestamp.

3. Build our image.

4. Push to our registry.

5. Patch a Deployment YAML file in the `operations` namespace.

We'll build our pipeline one object at a time. The first set of tasks is to create an SSH key that Tekton will use to pull our source code:

1. Create an SSH key pair that we'll use for our pipeline to check out our code. When prompted for a passphrase, just hit *Enter* to skip adding a passphrase:

    ```
    $ ssh-keygen -f ./gitlab-hello-python
    ```

2. Log in to GitLab and navigate to the `hello-python` project we created. Click on **Settings** | **Repository** | **Deploy Keys**, and click **Expand**. Use `tekton` as the title and paste the contents of the `github-hello-python.pub` file you just created into the **Key** section. Keep **Write access allowed** *unchecked* and click **Add Key**.

3. Next, create the `python-hello-build` namespace and the following secret. Replace the `ssh-privatekey` attribute with the Base64-encoded content of the `gitlab-hello-python` file we created in *step 1*. The annotation is what tells Tekton which server to use this key with. The server name is the `Service` in the GitLab namespace:

    ```
    apiVersion: v1
    data:
      ssh-privatekey: ...
    kind: Secret
    ```

```
metadata:
  annotations:
    tekton.dev/git-0: gitlab-gitlab-shell.gitlab.svc.
cluster.local
  name: git-pull
  namespace: python-hello-build
type: kubernetes.io/ssh-auth
```

4. Create an SSH key pair that we'll use for our pipeline to push to the `operations` repository. When prompted for a passphrase, just hit *Enter* to skip adding a passphrase:

    ```
    $ ssh-keygen -f ./gitlab-hello-python-operations
    ```

5. Log in to GitLab and navigate to the `hello-python-operations` project we created. Click on **Settings** | **Repository** | **Deploy Keys**, and click **Expand**. Use `tekton` as the title and paste the contents of the `github-hello-python-operations.pub` file you just created into the **Key** section. Make sure **Write access allowed** is *checked* and click **Add Key**.

6. Next, create the following secret. Replace the `ssh-privatekey` attribute with the Base64-encoded content of the `gitlab-hello-python-operations` file we created in *step 4*. The annotation is what tells Tekton which server to use this key with. The server name is the `Service` we created in *step 6* in the GitLab namespace:

    ```
    apiVersion: v1
    data:
      ssh-privatekey: ...
    kind: Secret
    metadata:
      name: git-write
      namespace: python-hello-build
    type: kubernetes.io/ssh-auth
    ```

7. Create a service account for tasks to run, as with our secret:

    ```
    $ kubectl create -f chapter14/tekton-serviceaccount.yaml
    ```

8. We need a container that contains both `git` and `kubectl` in it. We'll build `chapter14/docker/PatchRepoDockerfile` and push it to our internal registry. Make sure to replace `192-168-2-114` with the hostname for your server's IP address:

```
$ docker build -f ./PatchRepoDockerfile -t \
  docker.apps.192-168-2-114.nip.io/gitcommit/gitcommit .
$ docker push \
  docker.apps.192-168-2-114.nip.io/gitcommit/gitcommit
```

Every `Task` object can take inputs and produce results that can be shared with other `Task` objects. Tekton can provide runs (whether it's `TaskRun` or `PipelineRun`) with a workspace where the state can be stored and retrieved from. Writing to workspaces allows us to share data between `Task` objects.

Before deploying our task and pipeline, let's step through the work done by each task. The first task generates an image tag and gets the SHA hash of the latest commit. The full source is in `chapter14/yaml/tekton-task1.yaml`:

```
- name: create-image-tag
  image: docker.apps.192-168-2-114.nip.io/gitcommit/gitcommit
  script: |-
    #!/usr/bin/env bash
    export IMAGE_TAG=$(date +"%m%d%Y%H%M%S")
    echo -n "$(resources.outputs.result-image.url):$IMAGE_TAG"
> /tekton/results/image-url
    echo "'$(cat /tekton/results/image-url)'"

    cd $(resources.inputs.git-resource.path)
    RESULT_SHA="$(git rev-parse HEAD | tr -d '\n')"
    echo "Last commit : $RESULT_SHA"
    echo -n "$RESULT_SHA" > /tekton/results/commit-tag
```

Each step in a task is a container. In this case, we're using the container we built previously that has `kubectl` and `git` in it. We don't need `kubectl` for this task but we do need `git`. The first block of code generates an image name from the `result-image` URL and a timestamp. We could use the latest commit, but I like having a timestamp so that I can quickly tell how old a container is. We save the full image URL to `/text/results/image-url`, which corresponds to a result we defined in our task called `image-url`. This can be referenced by our pipeline or other tasks by referencing `$(tasks.generate-image-tag.results.image-url)`, where `generate-image-tag` is the name of our `Task`, and `image-url` is the name of our result.

Our next task, in `chapter14/yaml/tekton-task2.yaml`, generates a container from our application's source using Google's Kaniko project (`https://github.com/GoogleContainerTools/kaniko`). Kaniko lets you generate a container without needing access to a Docker daemon. This is great because you don't need a privileged container to build your image:

```
steps:
- args:
  - --dockerfile=$(params.pathToDockerFile)
  - --destination=$(params.imageURL)
  - --context=$(params.pathToContext)
  - --verbosity=debug
  - --skip-tls-verify
  command:
  - /kaniko/executor
  env:
  - name: DOCKER_CONFIG
    value: /tekton/home/.docker/
  image: gcr.io/kaniko-project/executor:v0.16.0
  name: build-and-push
  resources: {}
```

The Kaniko container is what's called a "distro-less" container. It's not built with an underlying shell, nor does it have many of the command-line tools you may be used to. It's just a single binary. This means that any variable manipulation, such as generating a tag for the image, needs to be done before this step. Notice that the image being created doesn't reference the result we created in the first task. It instead references a parameter called imageURL. While we could have referenced the result directly, it would make it harder to test this task because it is now tightly bound to the first task. By using a parameter that is set by our pipeline, we can test this task on its own. Once run, this task will generate and push our container.

Our last task, in chapter14/yaml/tekton-task-3.yaml, does the work to trigger ArgoCD to roll out a new container:

```
- image: docker.apps.192-168-2-114.nip.io/gitcommit/gitcommit
  name: patch-and-push
  resources: {}
  script: |-
    #!/bin/bash

    export GIT_URL="$(params.gitURL)"
    export GIT_HOST=$(sed 's/.*[@]\(.*\)[:].*/\1/' <<< "$GIT_URL")

    mkdir /usr/local/gituser/.ssh
    cp /pushsecret/ssh-privatekey /usr/local/gituser/.ssh/id_rsa
    chmod go-rwx /usr/local/gituser/.ssh/id_rsa
    ssh-keyscan -H $GIT_HOST > /usr/local/gituser/.ssh/known_hosts

    cd $(workspaces.output.path)
    git clone $(params.gitURL) .

    kubectl patch --local -f src/deployments/hello-python.yaml -p '{"spec":{"template":{"spec":{"containers":[{"name":"python-hello","image":"$(params.imageURL)"}]}}}}' -o yaml > /tmp/hello-python.yaml
    cp /tmp/hello-python.yaml src/deployments/hello-python.yaml
    git add src/deployments/hello-python.yaml
```

```
git commit -m 'commit $(params.sourceGitHash)'
git push
```

The first block of code copies the SSH keys into our home directory, generates known_hosts, and clones our repository into a workspace we defined in the Task. We don't rely on Tekton to pull the code from our operations repository because Tekton assumes we won't be pushing code, so it disconnects the source code from our repository. If we try to run a commit, it will fail. Since the step is a container, we don't want to try to write to it, so we create a workspace with emptyDir, just like emptyDir in a Pod we might run. We could also define workspaces based on persistent volumes. This could come in handy to speed up builds where dependencies get downloaded.

We're copying the SSH key from /pushsecret, which is defined as a volume on the task. Our container runs as user 431, but the SSH keys are mounted as root by Tekton. We don't want to run a privileged container just to copy the keys from a Secret, so instead, we mount it as if it were just a regular Pod.

Once we have our repository cloned, we patch our deployment with the latest image and finally, commit the change using the hash of the source commit in our application repository. Now we can track an image back to the commit that generated it! Just as with our second task, we don't reference the results of tasks directly to make it easier to test.

We pull these tasks together in a pipeline – specifically, chapter14/yaml/tekton-pipeline.yaml. This YAML file is several pages long, but the key piece defines our tasks and links them together. You should never hardcode values into your pipeline. Take a look at our third task's definition in the pipeline:

```
- name: update-operations-git
  taskRef:
    name: patch-deployment
  params:
    - name: imageURL
      value: $(tasks.generate-image-tag.results.image-url)
    - name: gitURL
      value: $(params.gitPushUrl)
    - name: sourceGitHash
      value: $(tasks.generate-image-tag.results.commit-tag)
  workspaces:
  - name: output
    workspace: output
```

We reference parameters and task results, but nothing is hardcoded. This makes our Pipeline reusable. We also include the runAfter directive in our second and third task to make sure that our tasks are run in order. Otherwise, tasks will be run in parallel. Given each task has dependencies on the task before it, we don't want to run them at the same time. Next, let's deploy our pipeline and run it:

1. Add the chapter14/yaml/tekton-source-git.yaml file to your cluster; this tells Tekton where to pull your application code from.

2. Edit chapter14/yaml/tekton-image-result.yaml, replacing 192-168-2-114 with the hash representation of your server's IP address, and add it to your cluster.

3. Edit chapter14/yaml/tekton-task1.yaml, replacing the image host with the host for your Docker registry, and add the file to your cluster.

4. Add chapter14/yaml/tekton-task2.yaml to your cluster.

5. Edit chapter14/yaml/tekton-task3.yaml, replacing the image host with the host for your Docker registry, and add the file to your cluster.

6. Add chapter14/yaml/tekton-pipeline.yaml to your cluster.

7. Add chapter14/yaml/tekton-pipeline-run.yaml to your cluster.

You can check on the progress of your pipeline using kubectl, or you can use Tekton's CLI tool called tkn (https://github.com/tektoncd/cli). Running tkn pipelinerun describe build-hello-pipeline-run -n python-hello-build will list out the progress of your build. You can rerun the build by recreating your run object, but that's not very efficient. Besides, what we really want is for our pipeline to run on a commit!

Building automatically

We don't want to manually run builds. We want builds to be automated. Tekton provides the trigger project to provide webhooks so whenever GitLab receives a commit, it can tell Tekton to build a PipelineRun object for us. Setting up a trigger involves creating a Pod, with its own service account that can create PipelineRun objects, a Service for that Pod, and an Ingress object to host HTTPS access to the Pod. You also want to protect the webhook with a secret so that it isn't triggered inadvertently. Let's deploy these objects to our cluster:

1. Add chapter14/yaml/tekton-webhook-cr.yaml to your cluster. This ClusterRole will be used by any namespace that wants to provision webhooks for builds.

2. Edit `chapter14/yaml/tekton-webhook.yaml`. At the bottom of the file is an `Ingress` object. Change `192-168-2-114` to represent the IP of your cluster, with dashes instead of dots. Then, add the file to your cluster:

```
apiVersion: extensions/v1beta1
kind: Ingress
metadata:
  name: gitlab-webhook
  namespace: python-hello-build
  annotations:
    cert-manager.io/cluster-issuer: ca-issuer
spec:
  rules:
  - host: "python-hello-application.build.192-168-2-114.
nip.io"
    http:
      paths:
      - backend:
          serviceName: el-gitlab-listener
          servicePort: 8080
        pathType: ImplementationSpecific
  tls:
  - hosts:
    - "python-hello-application.build.192-168-2-114.nip.
io"
    secretName: ingresssecret
```

3. Log in to GitLab. Go to the **Admin Area | Network**. Click on **Expand** next to **Outbound Requests**. Check **Allow requests to the local network from web hooks and services** and click **Save changes**.

4. Go to the `hello-python` project we created and click on **Settings | Webhooks**. For the URL, use your `Ingress` host with HTTPS – for instance, `https://python-hello-application.build.192-168-2-114.nip.io/`. For **Secret Token**, use `notagoodsecret`, and for **Push events**, set the branch name to **master**. Finally, click on **Add webhook**.

5. Once added, click on **Test**, choosing **Push Events**. If everything is configured correctly, a new `PipelineRun` object should have been created. You can run `tkn pipelinerun list -n python-hello-build` to see the list of runs; there should be a new one running. After a few minutes, you'll have a new container and a patched Deployment in the `python-hello-operations` project!

We covered quite a bit in this section to build our application and deploy it using GitOps. The good news is that everything is automated; a push will create a new instance of our application! The bad news is that we had to create over a dozen Kubernetes objects and manually make updates to our projects in GitLab. In the last section, we'll automate this process. First, let's deploy ArgoCD so that we can get our application running!

Deploying ArgoCD

So far, we have a way to get into our cluster, a way to store code, and a system for building our code and generating images. The last component of our platform is our GitOps controller. This is the piece that lets us commit manifests to our Git repository and make changes to our cluster. ArgoCD is a collaboration between Intuit and Weaveworks. It provides a great UI and is driven by a combination of custom resources and Kubernetes-native `ConfigMap` and `Secret` objects. It has a CLI tool, and both the web and CLI tools are integrated with OpenID Connect, so it will be easy to add SSO with our OpenUnison. Let's deploy ArgoCD and use it to launch our `hello-python` web service:

1. Deploy using the standard YAML from `https://argoproj.github.io/argo-cd/getting_started/`:

```
$ kubectl create namespace argocd
$ kubectl apply -n argocd -f https://raw.githubusercontent.com/argoproj/argo-cd/stable/manifests/install.yaml
```

2. Create the `Ingress` object for ArgoCD by editing `chapter14/yaml/argocd-ingress.yaml`. Replace all instances of `192-168-2-140` with your IP address, replacing the dots with dashes. My server's IP is `192.168.2.114`, so I'm using `192-168-2-114`. Once done, add the file to your cluster.

3. Get the root password by running `kubectl get pods -n argocd -l app.kubernetes.io/name=argocd-server -o name | cut -d'/' -f 2`. Save this password.

4. Edit the `argocd-server Deployment` in the `argocd` namespace. Add `--insecure` to the command:

```
spec:
  containers:
  - command:
    - argocd-server
    - --staticassets
    - /shared/app
    - --repo-server
    - argocd-repo-server:8081
    - --insecure
```

5. You can now log in to ArgoCD by going to the `Ingress` host you defined in *step 2*. You will need to download the ArgoCD CLI utility as well from `https://github.com/argoproj/argo-cd/releases/latest`. Once downloaded, log in by running `./argocd login grpc-argocd.apps.192-168-2-114.nip.io`, replacing `192-168-2-114` with the IP of your server, with dashes instead of dots.

6. Create the `python-hello` namespace.

7. Before we can add our GitLab repository, we need to tell ArgoCD to trust our
    GitLab instance's SSH host. Since we will have ArgoCD talk directly to the GitLab
    shell service, we'll need to generate known_host for that Service. To make this
    easier, we included a script that will run known_host from outside the cluster
    but rewrite the content as if it were from inside the cluster. Run the chapter14/
    shell/getSshKnownHosts.sh script and pipe the output into the argocd
    command to import known_host. Remember to change the hostname to reflect
    your own cluster's IP address:

    ```
    $ ./chapter14/shell/getSshKnownHosts.sh gitlab.apps.192-
    168-2-114.nip.io | argocd cert add-ssh --batch
    Enter SSH known hosts entries, one per line. Press CTRL-D
    when finished.
    Successfully created 3 SSH known host entries
    ```

8. Next, we need to generate an SSH key to access the python-hello-operations
    repository:

    ```
    $ ssh-keygen -f ./argocd-python-hello
    ```

9. Add the public key to the python-hello-operations repository by going
    to the project and clicking on **Settings | Repository**. Next to **Deploy Keys**, click
    Expand. For **Title**, use argocd. Use the contents of argocd-python-hello.
    pub and click **Add key**. Then, add the key to ArgoCD using the CLI and replace the
    public GitLab host with the gitlab-gitlab-shell Service hostname:

    ```
    $ argocd repo add git@gitlab-gitlab-shell.gitlab.
    svc.cluster.local:root/hello-python-operations.git
    --ssh-private-key-path ./argocd-python-hello
    repository 'git@gitlab-gitlab-shell.gitlab.svc.cluster.
    local:root/hello-python-operations.git' added
    ```

10. Our last step is to create an `Application` object. You can create it through the web UI or the CLI. You can also create it by creating an `Application` object in the `argocd` namespace, which is what we'll do. Create the following object in your cluster (`chapter14/yaml/argocd-python-hello.yaml`):

```
apiVersion: argoproj.io/v1alpha1
kind: Application
metadata:
  name: python-hello
  namespace: argocd
spec:
  destination:
    namespace: python-hello
    server: https://kubernetes.default.svc
  project: default
  source:
    directory:
      jsonnet: {}
      recurse: true
    path: src
    repoURL: git@gitlab-gitlab-shell.gitlab.svc.cluster.
local:root/hello-python-operations.git
    targetRevision: HEAD
  syncPolicy:
    automated: {}
```

This is about as basic of a configuration as possible. We're working off of simple manifests. ArgoCD can work off of jsonet and Helm too. After this application is created, look at the Pods in the `python-hello` namespace. You should have one running! Making updates to your code will result in updates to the namespace.

We now have a code base that can be deployed automatically with a commit. We spent a couple dozen pages, ran dozens of commands, and created more than 20 objects to get there. Instead of manually creating these objects, it would be best to automate the process. Now that we have the objects that need to be created, we can automate the onboarding. In the next section, we will take the manual process of building the links between GitLab, Tekton, and ArgoCD to line up with our business processes.

Automating project onboarding using OpenUnison

Earlier in this chapter, we deployed the OpenUnison automation portal. This portal lets users request new namspaces to be created and allows developers to request access to these namespaces via a self-service interface. The workflows built into this portal are very basic but create the namespace and appropriate `RoleBinding` objects. What we want to do is build a workflow that integrates our platform and creates all of the objects we created manually earlier in this chapter. The goal is that we're able to deploy a new application into our environment without having to run the `kubectl` command (or at least minimize its use). This will require careful planning. Here's how our developer workflow will run:

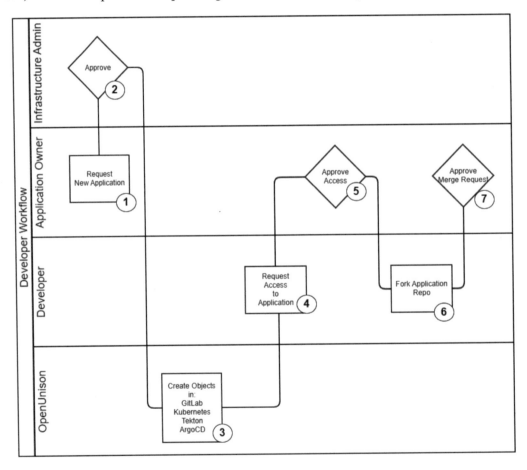

Figure 14.6 – Platform developer workflow

Let's quickly run through the workflow that we see in the preceding figure:

1. An application owner will request an application be created.

2. The infrastructure admin approves the creation.

3. At this point, OpenUnison will deploy the objects we manually created. We'll detail those objects shortly.

4. Once created, a developer is able to request access to the application

5. The application owner(s) approve access to the application.

6. Once approved, the developer will fork the application source base and do their work. They can launch the application in their developer workspace. They can also fork the build project to create a pipeline and the development environment operations project to create manifests for the application. Once the work is done and tested locally, the developer will push the code into their own fork, then request a merge request.

7. The application owner will approve the request and merge the code from GitLab.

Once the code is merged, ArgoCD will synchronize the build and operations projects. The webhook in the application project will kick off a Tekton pipeline that will build our container and update the development operations project with the tag for the latest container. ArgoCD will synchronize the updated manifest into our application's development namespace. Once testing is completed, the application owner submits a merge request from the development operations workspace to the production operations workspace, triggering ArgoCD to launch into production.

Nowhere in this flow is there a step called "operations staff uses `kubectl` to create a namespace." This is a simple flow and won't totally avoid your operations staff from using `kubectl`, but it should be a good starting point. All this automation requires an extensive set of objects to be created:

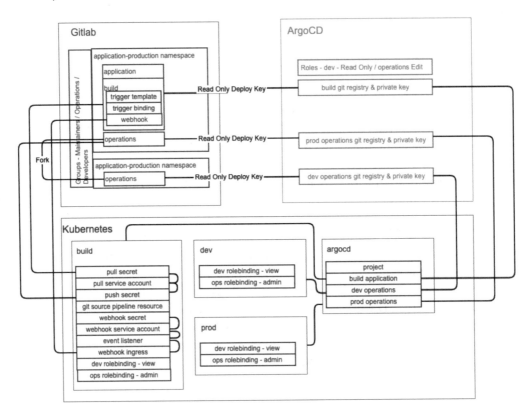

Figure 14.7 – Application onboarding object map

In GitLab, we create a project for our application code, operations, and build pipeline. We also fork the operations project as a development operations project. For each project, we generate deploy keys and register webhooks. We also create groups to match the roles we defined earlier in this chapter.

For Kubernetes, we create namespaces for the development and production environments. We also create a namespace for the Tekton pipeline. We add the keys as needed to `Secrets`. In the build namespace, we create all the scaffolding to support the webhook that will trigger automatic builds. That way, our developers only need to worry about creating their pipeline objects.

In our last application, ArgoCD, we will create an `AppProject` that hosts our build and both operations namespaces. We will also add the SSH keys we generated when creating our GitLab projects. Each project also gets an `Application` object in our `AppProject` that instructs ArgoCD how to synchronize from GitLab. Finally, we add RBAC rules to ArgoCD so that our developers can view their application synchronization status but owners and operations can make updates and changes.

You don't need to build this out yourself! `chapter14/openunison` is the source for OpenUnison that implements this flow. If you want to see every object we create, refer to `chapter14/openunison/src/main/webapp/WEB-INF/workflows/30-NewK8sNamespace.xml`. This workflow does everything we just described. We also included `chapter14/python-hello` as our example application, `chapter14/python-hello-operations` for our manifests, and `chapter14/python-hello-build` as our pipeline. You'll need to tweak some of the objects in these three folders to match your environment, mostly updating the hostnames.

With our developer workflow designed and example projects ready to go, next we'll update OpenUnison, GitLab, and ArgoCD to get all this automation to work!

Integrating GitLab

We configured GitLab for SSO when we first deployed the Helm chart. The `gitlab-oidc` Secret we deployed has all the information GitLab needs to access SSO from OpenUnison. We still need to configure OpenUnison though. We could hardcode the SSO configuration into our OpenUnison source base or we could dynamically add it as a custom resource. In this instance, we'll add the SSO connection via a custom resource:

1. Edit `chapter14/yaml/gitlab-trust.yaml`, replacing `192-168-2-140` with the server IP your cluster is running on. My cluster is on `192.168.2.114`, so I'll replace it with `192-168-2-114`. Add `chapter14/yaml/gitlab-trust.yaml` to your cluster. This file tells OpenUnison to establish a trust with GitLab for SSO.

2. Edit `chapter14/yaml/gitlab-url.yaml`, replacing `192-168-2-140` with the server IP your cluster is running on. My cluster is on `192.168.2.114`, so I'll replace it with `192-168-2-114`. Add `chapter14/yaml/gitlab-url.yaml` to your cluster. This file tells OpenUnison to add a badge to the portal for GitLab.

3. Log in to GitLab as root. Go to your user's profile area and click on **Access Tokens**. For **Name**, use `openunison`. Leave **Expires** blank and check the API scope. Click **Create personal access token**. Copy and paste the token into a notepad or some other place. Once you leave this screen, you can't retrieve this token again.

4. Edit the `orchestra-secrets-source` Secret in the `openunison` namespace. Add two keys:

```
apiVersion: v1
data:
  K8S_DB_SECRET: aW0gYSBzZWNyZXQ=
  OU_JDBC_PASSWORD: c3RhcnR0MTIz
  SMTP_PASSWORD: ""
  unisonKeystorePassword: aW0gYSBzZWNyZXQ=
  gitlab: c2VjcmV0   GITLAB_TOKEN: S7CCuqHfpw3a6GmAqEYg
kind: Secret
```

Remember to Base64-encode the values. The `gitlab` key matches the secret in our `oidc-provider` Secret. `GITLAB_TOKEN` is going to be used by OpenUnison to interact with GitLab to provision the projects and groups we defined in our onboarding workflow. With GitLab configured, next is ArgoCD.

Integrating ArgoCD

ArgoCD has built-in support for OpenID Connect. It wasn't configured for us in the deployment, though:

1. Edit the `argocd-cm` ConfigMap in the `argocd` namespace, adding the `url` and `oidc.config` keys, as shown in the following cde block. Make sure to update `192-168-2-140` to match your cluster's IP address. Mine is `192.168.2.114`, so I'll be using `192-168-2-114`:

```
apiVersion: v1
data:
  url: https://argocd.apps.192-168-2-140.nip.io
  oidc.config: |-
    name: OpenUnison
    issuer: https://k8sou.apps.192-168-2-140.nip.io/auth/
idp/k8sIdp
    clientID: argocd
    requestedScopes: ["openid", "profile", "email",
"groups"]
```

> **Important Note**
>
> We don't specify a client secret with ArgoCD because it has both a CLI and a web component. Just like with the API server, it makes no sense to worry about a client secret that will need to reside on every single workstation that will be known to the user. It doesn't add any security in this case, so we will skip it.

2. Edit `chapter14/yaml/argocd-trust.yaml`, replacing `192-168-2-140` with the server IP your cluster is running on. My cluster is on `192.168.2.114`, so I'll replace it with `192-168-2-114`. Add `chapter14/yaml/argocd-trust.yaml` to your cluster. This file tells OpenUnison to establish a trust with ArgoCD for SSO.

3. Edit `chapter14/yaml/argocd-url.yaml`, replacing `192-168-2-140` with the server IP your cluster is running on. My cluster is on `192.168.2.114`, so I'll replace it with `192-168-2-114`. Add `chapter14/yaml/argocd-url.yaml` to your cluster. This file tells OpenUnison to add a badge to the portal for ArgoCD.

4. While most of ArgoCD is controlled with Kubernetes custom resources, there are some ArgoCD-specific APIs. To work with these APIs, we need to create a service account. We'll need to create this account and generate a key for it:

```
$ kubectl patch configmap argocd-cm -n argocd -p
'{"data":{"accounts.openunison":"apiKey","accounts.
openunison.enabled":"true"}}'
$ argocd account generate-token --account openunison
```

5. Take the output of the `generate-token` command and add it as the `ARGOCD_TOKEN` key to the `orchestra-secrets-source` Secret in the `openunison` namespace. Don't forget to Base64-encode it.

6. Finally, we want to create ArgoCD RBAC rules so that we can control who can access the web UI and the CLI. Edit the `argocd-rbac-cm` ConfigMap and add the following keys. The first key will let our systems administrators and our API key do anything in ArgoCD. The second key maps all users that aren't mapped by `policy.csv` into a role into a nonexistent role so that they won't have access to anything:

```
data:
  policy.csv: |-
    g, k8s-cluster-administrators,role:admin
    g, openunison,role:admin
  policy.default: role:none
```

With ArgoCD integrated, the last step to world automation is updating our OpenUnison custom resource!

Updating OpenUnison

OpenUnison is already deployed. The last step to launching an automation portal with our developer workflows built in is to update the orchestra OpenUnison custom resource. Update the image as in the following code block. Add non_secret_data, replacing hosts to match with your cluster's IP. Finally, add the new secrets we created to the list of secrets the operator needs to import:

```
image: docker.io/tremolosecurity/openunison-k8s-definitive-
guide:latest



non_secret_data:


  - name: GITLAB_URL
    value: https://gitlab.apps.192-168-2-140.nip.io
  - name: GITLAB_SSH_HOST
    value: gitlab-gitlab-shell.gitlab.svc.cluster.local
  - name: GITLAB_WEBHOOK_SUFFIX
    value: gitlab.192-168-2-140.nip.io
  - name: ARGOCD_URL
    value: https://argocd.apps.192-168-2-140.nip.io
  - name: GITLAB_WRITE_SSH_HOST
    value: gitlab-write-shell.gitlab.svc.cluster.local


secret_data:
```

```
- K8S_DB_SECRET
- unisonKeystorePassword
- SMTP_PASSWORD
- OU_JDBC_PASSWORD
- GITLAB_TOKEN
- ARGOCD_TOKEN
```

In just a few minutes, the automation portal will be running. When you log in, you'll see badges for GitLab and ArgoCD. You'll also be able to click on **New Application** to begin deploying applications according to our workflow! You can use this as a starting point for designing your own automation platform or use it as a map for creating the various objects needed to integrate the tools on your platform.

Summary

Coming into this chapter, we hadn't spent much time on deploying applications. We wanted to close things out with a brief introduction to application deployment and automation. We learned about pipelines, how they are built, and how they run on a Kubernetes cluster. We explored the process of building a platform by deploying GitLab for source control, built out a Tekton pipeline to work in a GitOps model, and used ArgoCD to make the GitOps model a reality. Finally, we automated the entire process with OpenUnison.

Using the information in this chapter should give you direction as to how you want to build your own platform. Using the practical examples in this chapter will help you map the requirements in your organization to the technology needed to automate your infrastructure. The platform we built in this chapter is far from complete. It should give you a map for planning your own platform that matches your needs.

Finally, thank you. Thank you for joining us on this adventure of building out a Kubernetes cluster. We hope you have as much fun reading this book and building out the examples as we did creating it!

Questions

1. True or false: A pipeline must be implemented to make Kubernetes work.

    A. True

    B. False

2.   What are the minimum steps of a pipeline?

   A. Build, scan, test, and deploy

   B. Build and deploy

   C. Scan, test, deploy, and build

   D. None of the above

3.   What is GitOps?

   A. Running GitLab on Kubernetes

   B. Using Git as an authoritative source for operations configuration

   C. A silly marketing term

   D. A product from a new start-up

4.   What is the standard for writing pipelines?

   A. All pipelines should be written in YAML.

   B. There are no standards; every project and vendor has its own implementation.

   C. JSON combined with Go.

   D. Rust.

5.   How do you deploy a new instance of a container in a GitOps model?

   A. Use kubectl to update the Deployment or StatefulSet in the namespace.

   B. Update the Deployment or StatefulSet manifest in Git, letting the GitOps controller update the objects in Kubernetes.

   C. Submit a ticket that someone in operations needs to act on.

   D. None of the above.

6.   True or false: All objects in GitOps needs to be stored in your Git repository.

   A. True

   B. False

7.   True or false: Your way is the right way to automate your processes.

   A. True

   B. False

Assessments

Chapter 1

1. Correct answer: (B) False. A container that is based on one architecture cannot be run on a different architecture. For example, an image created using the x86 architecture will not run on an ARM-based architecture.

2. Correct answer: (D) Union filesystem. Docker uses the Union filesystem to manage multiple image layers. The layers are read from top to bottom to provide the appearance of a single filesystem.

3. Correct answer: (D) Overlay2. A system running a kernel that's version 4.0 or above will use the Overlay2 storage driver.

4. Correct answer: (C) Container layer. Any changes that are made to a running container's filesystem are stored in the topmost layer, called the container layer.

5. Correct answer: (C) `docker exec -it <container> /bin/bash`. The `docker exec` command is used to execute a process in a container. Using the `-it` option tells the exec command to use an interactive terminal for its execution. The process you want to execute is the last parameter, and since we want to gain access to the container's Bash shell, we are executing `/bin/bash`.

6. Correct answer: (B) False. When you stop a running container, the daemon will only stop the running image. The container layer will remain on the host's filesystem. If you want to delete the container, you must remove the container from the daemon using the `docker rm` command.

7. Correct answer: (B) `docker ps -a`. To view a list of all containers that are running and have been stopped, use the `docker ps -a` command. If you use `-all` or `-list`, the daemon will interpret the option as `-l`, which will only list the latest containers. Listing the latest containers will exclude containers that have been stopped for a longer period of time.

Chapter 2

1. Correct answers: (B) Bind mounts and (C) Volumes. Only a Docker volume and bind mount provide persistency to a container. tmpfs volumes are stored in RAM and are not written to disk.

2. Correct answer: (A) True. A volume must be created before it can be used in a container. If a volume is not created before running a container, Docker will create the volume before mounting it to the container.

3. Correct answer: (D) 32 GB. If a tmpfs size is not specified, Docker will create a volume that is equal to half of the host's RAM.

4. Correct answer: (B) False. Stopping or removing an image will not remove a persistent volume by default. To delete a volume, you can add the -v option to the docker rm command, or you can use the docker volume rm command to remove the volume manually.

5. Correct answer: (B) Named volumes. Only anonymous and named volumes are managed by the Docker daemon.

6. Correct answer: (D) You must manually delete the Bind folder. Since Bind mounts are not managed by Docker, the daemon cannot delete unused volumes. To remove a Bind mount, you need to manually delete the directory that the Bind mount used.

Chapter 3

1. Correct answer: (B) False. The default bridge assigned by Docker has limitations. It is considered a best practice to create a custom bridge network if you plan to run multiple containers on your host.

2. Correct answer: (C) 192.168.100.10:80. A socket is a combination of an IP address and a port. 192.168.100.10:80 is a socket for a server running a service on port 80 with an IP address of 192.168.100.10.

3. Correct answer: (C) docker run -p 8081:8080 -d nginx-web bitnami/nginx. Since the host has already bound port 8080 to another service, we cannot start the new container using 8080:8080. Since each Docker container has its own IP address, we can still use port 8080 for the container, but the incoming host port assignment must use an unused port. The only correct answer is C, since it binds the host's port, 8081, to the container port running on port 8080.

4. Correct answer: (D) `docker run --network=none -it badimage bash`. If you start a container without supplying any network options, the container will attempt to run on the default Docker bridge network. To start a container without a network you can set the network to none by running the image with the `-network=none` option.

5. Correct answer: (B) False. Being able to change the connected network on the fly is a feature of custom bridge networks.

6. Correct answer: (B) `65535`. The valid port range for IP ports is `1-65535`.

Chapter 4

1. Correct answer: (C) PersistentVolume. PersistentVolumes are claimed using PersistentVolumeClaims – PersistentVolume must exist before you can create a PersistentVolumeClaim.

2. Correct answer: (D) Rancher. KinD includes the local-path-provisioner, which was created by Rancher.

3. Correct answer: (A) Load balancer. When a cluster has multiple worker nodes, you need to install a load balancer in front of the cluster to direct traffic to the backend worker nodes.

4. Correct answer: (B) False. As shown in *Figure 5.9*, a Kubernetes cluster can have multiple CSIDrivers. This allows a cluster to connect to multiple backend storage systems.

Chapter 5

1. Correct answer: (D) Ingress controller. An Ingress controller is an add-on component used to expose services – it is not part of the control plane.

2. **Correct answer: (D) ETCD. ETCD is the database that Kubernetes uses to store all objects and their state.**

3. **Correct answer: (C) `kube-scheduler`. `kube-scheduler` uses various criteria from `kubelet` on each worker node to schedule a workload.**

4. **Correct answer: (B) `-v`. The `-v` option enables verbose output from a `kubectl` command.**

5. **Correct answer: (D)** NodePort. **When you create a** NodePort **service, it will be assigned a port between** 30000-32767. Each node will be updated with the service and the port to access it. Since each node knows the service, any node can service the incoming request.

6. **Correct answer: (A)** StatefulSet. **A** StatefulSet **will create each pod with a known name, based on the name assigned in the manifest. Each pod will receive the name with a number appended to it. To provide creation controls, as a pod is created, it must completely deploy before the next pod is created.**

Chapter 6

1. Correct answer: (D) By the selector label. When you create a service object, you include a selector that includes the label to match for the service endpoints. Any matching pods will be added as an endpoint.

2. Correct answer: (B) kubectl get ep <service name>. Services use endpoints to select the pods that receive requests to the service. One of the first steps when it comes to troubleshooting a service is to verify that endpoints have been assigned.

3. Correct answer: (B) False. Some distributions do include support for LoadBalancer services out of the box, but most still do not include support without the need to add a component such as MetalLB.

4. Correct answer: (D) Layer 4. The two load balancers used in Kubernetes are Layer 7 and Layer 4. Layer 7 load balancers run in Layer 7 of the OSI model and can only accept application-level traffic such as HTTP and HTTPS. Since Layer 4 load balancers run at a lower layer of the OSI model, they have access to lower level packets such as direct TCP and UDP.

5. Correct answer: (A) NodePort and ClusterIP. A base Kubernetes cluster does not allow the LoadBalancer type to use multiple protocols. Only ClusterIP and NodePort can create a single service that has both UDP and TCP protocols defined.

Chapter 7

1. Correct answer: (A) True. OpenID Connect is a standard published by IETF: `https://openid.net/specs/openid-connect-core-1_0.html`.

2. Correct answer: (B) `id_token`. `id_token` contains claims about the user's identity. `refresh_token` is used to get a new `id_token`. `access_token` is used to interact with the identity provider. `certificate_token` doesn't exist.

3. Correct answer: (C) Break-glass-in-case-of-emergency when all other authentication solutions are unavailable. Remember to keep this certificate and key pair under strict controls.

4. Correct answer: (D) An immutable ID not based on a user's name. This way, if a user's name ever changes, which happens more often than may be expected, their access isn't changed.

5. Correct answer: (D) Set as flags on the Kubernetes API server executable. How you set the flags will depend on your distribution, but ultimately, every distribution sets these flags on the API server's command.

6. Correct answer: (B) False. Impersonated users are not granted the default group; that is, `system:authenticated`. The reverse proxy needs to add this group.

7. Correct answer: (B) False. The Dashboard should never have its own privileges. Otherwise, anyone who can connect to it can use it.

Chapter 8

1. Correct answer: (A) False. RBAC is the preferred method for authorizing resources.

2. Correct answer: (C) apiGroups, resources, verbs.

3. Correct answer: (A) Kubernetes API reference. This is an invaluable tool that will list every URL for an API. This can be used to determine the resource.

4. Correct answer: (B) Define a ClusterRole and reference it in each namespace as a RoleBinding. This way, changes to the ClusterRole are reflected whenever it is referenced.

5. Correct answer: (D) Whenever possible, RoleBindings and ClusterRoleBindings should reference groups. Referencing users directly is an anti-pattern that is difficult to maintain, audit, and debug.

6. Correct answer: (B) False. RBAC requires all rights to be enumerated.

7. Correct answer: (B) False. Custom authorization webhooks are also available.

Chapter 9

1. Correct answer: (A) False. The Dashboard and make consistent throughout chapter is not inherently insecure; how it's deployed matters.

2. Correct answer: (A) No authentication, a token, injected from a reverse proxy. The dashboard has no way of collecting a username, password, or second factor.

3. Correct answer: (D) If a token is uploaded, it's encrypted and stored in the browser as a cookie. The dashboard doesn't persist the session in any backend.

4. Correct answer: (D) None of the above. The dashboard doesn't know how to refresh a token.

5. Correct answer: (D) Behind a reverse proxy. Use a reverse proxy to manage the login process, control sessions, and add multi-factor authentication.

6. Correct answer: (B) False. The 2.0+ versions of the dashboard support impersonation.

7. Correct answer: (B) False. Any reverse proxy can, if configured properly.

Chapter 10

1. Correct answer: (A) False. A container is a process, not a VM.

2. Correct answer: (B) If marked as privileged, yes. A privileged container can access a host's resources just like a privileged process can.

3. Correct answer: (C) Both. Attackers will string together multiple vulnerabilities to gain access to their target.

4. Correct answer: (B) By comparing the Pod's requested capabilities and the policies authorized via the union of the Pod's creator and its own `ServiceAccount`. Policies can't be explicitly set.

5. Correct answer: (A) An admission controller that inspects all Pods on creation and when they're updated. Policy enforcement is not handled by the `PodSecurityPolicy` API, only the definition of policies.

6. Correct answer: (B) False. It will take multiple years between determining a replacement, implementing it, and then the deprecation process.

7. Correct answer: (B) False. You wouldn't run a process as root on your server, so don't do it in a container.

Chapter 11

1. Correct answer: (B) False. GateKeeper is a tool originally built by Microsoft on top of OPA, but they are not the same thing.

2. Correct answer: (D) Rego is saved as a `ConstraintTemplate`, which is a `CustomResourceDefenition` defined by the `GateKeeper` project.

3. Correct answer: (B) Using an automated framework built directly into OPA. OPA's automated testing framework provides a powerful way to pre-validate Rego before deploying to GateKeeper.

4. Correct answer: (A) You don't need to as Rego will identify iterative steps. When using loops in Rego, use either the underscore to resolve all values or a placeholder (such as I or j) for array indexes. Rego will fill the counter by iterating over the array.

5. Correct answer: (C) Add trace functions to your code and run the `opa test` command with `-v` to see execution traces. `opa` will tell you where the problem is. Use its built-in tools.

6. Correct answer: (B) False. Constraint templates can include parameters that are defined using the same schema as any other CRD.

7. Correct answer: (B) False. Not at the time of writing, at least. GateKeeper can't mutate yet, so additional webhooks would need to be built to fill the gap.

Chapter 12

1. Correct answer: (D) `falco_rules.local.yaml`. Any changes to rules that have been customized to your installation should go in your `falco_rules.changes.yaml` file. You should not edit the include set of rules, which are part of `falco_rules.yaml`. The `falco.yaml` file is the base Falco configuration file and does not contain any rules.

2. Correct answer: (B) FluentD. There are many forwarders that are compatible with Kubernetes, but one of the most commonly used forwarders is FluentD.

3. Correct answer: (C) Kibana. The EFK stack includes ElasticSearch, FluentD, and Kibana. Kibana is the component that provides visualizations and dashboards for your logs.

4. Correct answer: (B) Falcosidekick. The Falcosidekick utility only forwards Falco logs to a central logging server.

5. Correct answer: (A) Lists. You can group a collection of items in Falco using Lists.

Chapter 13

1. Correct answer: (A) True. Velero backups can only use an S3 target to store backups.

2. Correct answer: (C) Install MinIO and use the NFS volumes as persistent disks in the deployment phase. You can install MinIO and use any persistent volumes with the deployment. MinIO will present the allocated storage as a S3 bucket, which are compatible with MinIO.

3. Correct answer: (B) False. One of Velero's features is the ability to use a backup from one cluster to restore namespaces and objects in a different cluster.

4. Correct answer: (D) etcdctl. etcdctl has an option to create a snapshot of the ETCD database.

5. Correct answer: (D) `Velero create schedule daily-backup --schedule="0 3 * * *"`. This command will create a scheduled backup job that runs at 3 a.m. every day. The schedule command accepts a tag called `-schedule` that uses cron expressions. `0 3 * * *` is a cron expression for 3 A.M. every day.

Chapter 14

1. Correct answer: (A) False. It's not a requirement, but it certainly makes life easier!

2. Correct answer: (D) None of the above. There is no minimum number of steps. How you implement your pipelines will depend on your own requirements.

3. Correct answer: (C) Using Git as an authoritative source for operations configuration. Instead of interacting directly with the Kubernetes API, you store your objects in a Git repository, letting a controller keep them in sync.

4. Correct answer: (B) There are no standards; every project and vendor has their own implementation. For this chapter, we used Tekton, which is a combination of YAML, containers, and shell scripts. Amazon, Azure, and GitHub all store their pipeline scripts in the application source. There is no requirement for what you write it in.

5. Correct answer: (B) Update the `Deployment` or `StatefulSet` manifest in Git, letting the GitOps controller update the objects in Kubernetes. The goal is to minimize the use of kubectl and maintain a log of changes in Git.

6. Correct answer: (B) False. This is nearly impossible. The operators model, where custom controllers create objects based on custom resources, would almost never work with this assumption. At least not yet. Once you've deployed the examples, you'll see Tekton creates objects that aren't in Git. Secrets are other objects that probably shouldn't be in Git either.

7. Correct answer: (A) True. Kubernetes is a platform for building platforms. While there are certainly common patterns and best practices, when all is said and done, the power of Kubernetes is that it gives you the flexibility to automate your systems in a way that best suits you.

Other Books You May Enjoy

If you enjoyed this book, you may be interested in these other books by Packt:

Learn Kubernetes Security

Kaizhe Huang, Pranjal Jumde

ISBN: 978-1-83921-650-3

- Understand the basics of Kubernetes architecture and networking

- Gain insights into different security integrations provided by the Kubernetes platform

- Delve into Kubernetes' threat modeling and security domains

- Explore different security configurations from a variety of practical examples

- Get to grips with using and deploying open source tools to protect your deployments

- Discover techniques to mitigate or prevent known Kubernetes hacks

Hands-On Kubernetes on Windows

Piotr Tylenda

ISBN: 978-1-83882-156-2

- Understand containerization as a packaging format for applications
- Create a development environment for Kubernetes on Windows
- Grasp the key architectural concepts in Kubernetes
- Discover the current limitations of Kubernetes on the Windows platform
- Provision and interact with a Kubernetes cluster from a Windows machine
- Create hybrid Windows Kubernetes clusters in on-premises and cloud environments

Leave a review - let other readers know what you think

Please share your thoughts on this book with others by leaving a review on the site that you bought it from. If you purchased the book from Amazon, please leave us an honest review on this book's Amazon page. This is vital so that other potential readers can see and use your unbiased opinion to make purchasing decisions, we can understand what our customers think about our products, and our authors can see your feedback on the title that they have worked with Packt to create. It will only take a few minutes of your time, but is valuable to other potential customers, our authors, and Packt. Thank you!

Index

Made in the USA
Thornton, CO
01/14/25 02:10:33